SCOTTISH LITERATURE INTERNATIONAL

Christianity in Scottish Literature

Edited by
JOHN PATRICK PAZDZIORA

Occasional Papers: Number 25
Association for Scottish Literature

Published by
Scottish Literature International
Scottish Literature
7 University Gardens
University of Glasgow
Glasgow G12 8QH

Scottish Literature International is an imprint of
the Association for Scottish Literature

www.asls.org.uk

ASL is a registered charity no. SC006535

First published 2023

© ASL and the individual contributors

'Scotland' by Alastair McIntosh (p. xxxii) is
reprinted by kind permission of the author.

All rights reserved. No part of this book may be
reproduced, stored in a retrieval system, or
transmitted in any form or means, electronic,
mechanical, photocopying, recording or otherwise,
without the prior permission of the
Association for Scottish Literature.

A CIP catalogue for this title
is available from the British Library

ISBN 978-1-908980-37-3

Contents

Acknowledgements   vii

Introduction: The Wrong End of a Telescope   ix
   John Patrick Pazdziora

One   Relic, Text, and Practice in Adomnán of Iona's
       Vita Sancti Columbae   1
       Duncan Sneddon

Two   'Mater Sanctissima': Sanctity and Motherhood in the
       Miracula of St Margaret of Scotland   16
       Claire Harrill

Three   Liturgy and Literature in Late Medieval Scotland:
       Continuity and Discontinuity   35
       David Jasper

Four   Post-Reformation Developments in Kirk Attitudes to
       Scottish Theatre   53
       Ian Brown

Five   Eccentrics as Spokespersons for Tobias Smollett
       on Religion   70
       J. Walter McGinty

Six   A Working-Class Poet from the Eastern Border:
       Robert Davidson (1778–1855)   85
       Barbara Bell

Seven   Walter Scott's *Religious Discourses*   106
       J. H. Alexander

| Eight | 'The Sermon Pump': Failed Preachers in George MacDonald's Fiction
John Patrick Pazdziora | 123 |

| Nine | Margaret Oliphant in a Land of Death: Representations of Other-Worlds in Nineteenth-Century Scottish Writing
Rebecca McLean | 147 |

| Ten | 'If Heaven is a' that man can dream': Religion and Scottish Poetry of the First World War
Silvia Mergenthal | 165 |

| Eleven | Approaching God in Scottish Renaissance Poetry
Dominique Delmaire | 179 |

| Twelve | George Mackay Brown and the Disenchantment of Orkney
Linden Bicket | 202 |

| Thirteen | A Post-Religious Incarnation in Alan Warner's *Morvern Callar*
Mike Kugler | 225 |

| Fourteen | Edwin Morgan's Last Things: Eschatology and his Post-Millennial Poetry
James McGonigal | 245 |

| Fifteen | God, War, and the Faeries: Mentoring and Carrying Stream in Writing *Poacher's Pilgrimage*
Alastair McIntosh | 269 |

Notes on contributors — 295

Index — 299

Biblical References — 306

Dedication

A book such as this, assembled over a course of years, must grow less quickly than the lives and families of its contributors. But I was still surprised at the number of children born to this volume's contributors between its inception and completion – the collection's own production babies, as it were. They form a loud and lively chorus, offering uncompromising commentary on their parents' academic preoccupations, jolting us away from academic texts to help them toddle out towards the uncertainties, fears, and wonders of the world as they may someday see it: Amy, Edmund, Joshua, Marcie, Rosa, and Rose. This book is for them.

John Patrick Pazdziora
Feast of Frederick Denison Maurice, Priest
Tokyo 2022

Acknowledgements

This anthology has its origin in the 2016 Association for Scottish Literature conference on religion and literature in Scotland, hosted by the University of Glasgow. Gerard Carruthers and Scott Spurlock, the conference organisers, suggested the initial concept for this volume to me and put me in contact with the conference presenters, some of whose papers appear reworked as chapters here. Without their encouragement, this book would not exist.

I am grateful to the College of Arts and Sciences of The University of Tokyo for generous financial and logistical support while the collection was being completed. The project was also supported by the Japan Society for the Promotion of Science (KAKENHI Grant number JP20K12957). At the Association for Scottish Literature, Ian Brown has been unwavering in his belief in this collection, while the indefatigable Duncan Jones and Pip Osmond-Williams have navigated it expertly through the labyrinths of production. Jamie Reid-Baxter generously gave me a sympathetic ear and sagacious advice at a crucial stage of the project's growth, while Benjamine Toussaint remained steadfast in her confidence that I could successfully complete such a project. Sho Kuno provided vital editorial assistance; Justin Stanislawski proofread the collection in manuscript. Each contributor has blessed this book not only with their fine chapters but with good humour, hard work, and boundless patience through the pandemic-laden editing process. All virtue found here is theirs; lingering vice belongs to the editor.

Introduction: The Wrong End of a Telescope

JOHN PATRICK PAZDZIORA

Robert Burns once imagined Scotland inhabited by a 'virtuous Populace', whose honest Christian piety and heartfelt prayers would 'stand a wall of fire around their much-lov'd ISLE'.[1] This idea that Christianity forms a vital aspect of the better part of Scotland's nature has long been engrained in the Scottish cultural mind. But it does not need a cynic to suspect that today Burns would find this prayerful firewall in tatters. A quarter-century ago, historian Callum Brown diagnosed the death of religion in Scotland.[2] There has been 'a crisis of religious practice', Brown wrote, noting that '[i]n extremely large numbers, [Scottish] people have stopped going to church, stopped becoming church members, and no longer recognise a substantial religious influence on their social lives.'[3] More recent evidence seems to sustain this 'haemorrhage of faith', as Brown eloquently terms it. In Scotland's 2011 census, fifty-four per cent of Scots identified as being some form of Christian, an eleven-point drop from sixty-five per cent in 2001.[4] Fewer people said they belonged to the Church of Scotland (32.4%) than to no religion (36.7%).[5] It appears Brown was right to declare that religion, and Protestant Christianity in particular, was being 'lifted like a shroud from rapidly liberalising Scottish society.'[6]

Despite the swift collapse of Christianity's influence on society, the thocht o Christ and Calvary (to plunder MacDiarmid's phrase) is aye liddenin in the Scots cultural heid.[7] On the one hand, it is perhaps impossible to fully understand the nature of the secularised world without understanding the religious world out of which it came. On the other, as the language and cadences of what Edwin Muir called the 'iron text' that crushed the poets – the Christian Bible and liturgies, creeds and catechisms – recede from general knowledge, the significance and complexities of the literature beaten into form against those texts become increasingly opaque.[8] The chapters of this volume, then, critically engage in a reflexive backward gaze to understand a literature infused with the language and beliefs of Christianity.

David Fergusson and Mark W. Elliott are probably right to suggest there is no 'distinctively Scottish theology'; they note that there is 'little evidence of a single, distinctive tradition with leading authorities and methods of study', and that while 'Scottish theology has been marked by recurrent themes, influences, and orientation, it does not constitute a single tradition of enquiry'.[9] In much the same way, Robert Crawford has written with admiration of 'the sheer plenitudinous multiplicity of imaginative writing by all the stay-at-homes, incomers and outgoers, all the royals, rebels and radicals who have through their artistry in several languages contributed over so many centuries to the literary history of Scotland'.[10] Combining two such multiplicities hardly creates a unified whole: there may be more ways of writing imaginatively about Scottish Christianity than there have been writers. I do not intend this introduction to engineer a single voice from this glorious polyphony. Rather, I wish to make a whistle-stop tour back through Scottish literary history to examine how Christianity has given different authors a scaffolding on which to build their manifold literary selves.

Let me pause first for a personal comment. In the early stages of preparing this volume, I would speak with a pitchman's enthusiasm about my marvellous editorial plans for its scope, its innovations, and – most grandly of all – its incisive explications into the Scottish national consciousness. I might have continued in that vein but for the thoughtful intervention of an astute older colleague. They endured my spiel patiently, then asked how my vaunted collection on Christianity would speak to their students – eager and intelligent Scottish young people from many different religious backgrounds or no religion at all. Would, for instance, Muslim or Sikh students be able to recognise their experiences of being Scottish amid my assemblage of Christian-inflected literary discourse?

It was a perceptive question, thoughtfully asked; it gave me pause. The study of literature, after all, is meant to reveal the complexities of how authors throughout history have created imagined selves – in the lives of characters of a novel or drama, in an ordering of word and image in poetry, or in the confessional performance of a sermon. For me to adopt an exclusionary critical framework, isolating the literature of 'our multiform, our infinite Scotland' within the contours of a single faith tradition, would very much be to defeat the point. I thought, too, of my own students in China and Japan, keen in their study of language and literature but with very little knowledge of Scotland, let alone Christianity, and some of whom are deeply committed to various forms of Buddhist practice. How could my vaunting collection speak to them?

I would discover my answer only gradually through the slow editing process. As I read and reread the compelling and thoughtful chapters gathered here, kindly contributed by scholars who wrote with broad humanism and nuanced criticism, I began to recognise the subtle ways Christianity and Scottish literature have spoken to one another. Despite stereotypes of theologically cantankerous Scots, Scottish literature has taken surprisingly little interest in Christian doctrine as such. Its emphasis has not been on adjudicating what or whether Christians should believe or on catwalking theological notions in literary gowns. Rather, Scottish literature has been concerned with the experience of being Christian, asking what it is like to go through life amid a culture shaped by various iterations of Christianity. The question is as much phenomenological as theological. By asking how to be Christian, Scottish writers found a cultural and ethical background for struggling with the most fundamental of human questions: *how to be*.

'Other people's Edinburghs'

A penetrating expression of this question, framed explicitly in relation to Scottish and Christian identities, appears in *The Prime of Miss Jean Brodie* (1961), the best-known novel by Muriel Spark (1918–2006). Miss Brodie takes her clique of favourite students on a historical tour of the Old Town in Edinburgh,

> which none of the girls had seen properly before, because none of their parents was so historically minded as to be moved to conduct

their young into the reeking network of slums which the Old Town constituted in those years.[11]

While Miss Brodie brusquely points out sites of interest and provides commentary on John Knox ('an embittered man'), the girls are bewildered and frightened by their first glimpse of actual poverty. The narration settles into the point of view of sardonic and vulnerable Sandy:

> At many times throughout her life Sandy knew with a shock, when speaking to people whose childhood had been in Edinburgh, that there were other people's Edinburghs quite different than hers, and with which she held only the names of districts and streets and monuments in common. Similarly, there were other people's nineteen-thirties.[12]

This passage is typical of the laconic, understated aggression of Spark's narrator. While the depths of Sandy's own awareness of 'other people's nineteen-thirties' is not clarified, the reader is given opportunity for unpleasant recognition; the statement follows closely on Sandy's thought that Miss Brodie's students are her personal *fascisti*.[13] Spark was sharply aware Miss Brodie's prime was contemporaneous with the rise of Hitler and the beginning of the Holocaust. Spark attended the Eichmann trial in Jerusalem the year *The Prime of Miss Jean Brodie* was published, fictionalising her experience in her 1965 novel *The Mandelbaum Gate*.[14] The almost viciously barbed reference here is aligned with 'other people's Edinburghs'. Read socio-politically, this suggests a disruption of Miss Brodie's influence on Sandy with her awareness that other, less privileged children, running about the slums and boarding in the 'cold and grey' schools, had perhaps a deeper connection to the city. Read historically, however, is the lesson Miss Brodie was attempting to teach: the depth of human experience is layered into the places of the city, and the immediacy of past experiences shape the self in the present.

Miss Brodie does not take the girls into St Giles' Cathedral, partly for logistical reasons and partly because of its overfamiliarity: 'They had nearly all been in St Giles's with its tattered blood-stained banners of the past.'[15] It is a deliberately odd omission for a history tour of the Old Town, as this monumental building ostensibly represents the spiritual union of Scotland with the Scottish Kirk, a meaning that Spark's narration implies, noting that Sandy is afraid of 'the outside of old Edinburgh churches' because they are 'of such dark stone, like presences almost the colour of the Castle rock'.[16] Kirk and castle, with their 'blood-stained banners' and 'dark stone', are the foundation of a national consciousness, a political unity imposed over Scotland. Here again, Miss Brodie's lesson is surprisingly nuanced: her decisive turning away from the nationalised symbol of a monolithic Scottish Christianity allows her pupils to form their own understanding both of Scottish religion and of their relation to it. Yet it is, of course, an understanding that Miss Brodie expects to be moulded by her own towering personality.

Miss Brodie has been 'attending evening classes in comparative religion at the University', and thus the girls learn 'that some honest people did not believe in God, not even Allah'.[17] She even seems to fold these ideas into her own teaching, asking two new girls, 'What religions are you?'[18] Yet Miss Brodie herself continues 'adhering to the strict Church of Scotland habits of her youth, and keeping the Sabbath', faithful to the way in which a narrow church upbringing has helped define her sense of self.[19] The girls only understand the idea imperfectly, consulting among themselves about their own religious differences – some are 'believing though not church-going', others 'Presbyterians and went to Sunday School', while one girl is 'Episcopalian and claimed that she did not believe in Jesus, but in the father, son, and holy ghost'.[20] There are, of course, real differences between these three traditions of Christianity, with real political conflicts between them throughout Scottish history. But the girls' similarity in class and their narrow experience mean they are more akin to each other than not; whatever doctrinal differences exist are more of degree than kind.

Indeed, Miss Brodie's nascent pluralism occupies a place curiously similar to her relatively liberated sexuality. It forms part of her private interests and leisure, gently influencing but not permeating her teaching, and offers a source of confused fascination for the girls. Miss Brodie, though curious about the ontological openness offered by the comparative religion class, remains in the politically dominant and socially acceptable Scottish Kirk, as she maintains a sexual relationship with the diffident but well-to-do Mr Lowther rather than pursing entanglement with the passionate but maimed Teddy Lloyd. In a way, too, Sandy's later conversion to Catholicism and her recreation as Sister Helena of the Transfiguration react both against Miss Brodie's sexual liberalism by taking a vow of celibacy and against her interest in pluralism through entire devotion to the Church. Miss Brodie is, in one sense, keeping her difficult balance between competing versions of herself – the poet with the pedagogue, the libertine with the tyrant, the young romantic with the old cynic. She attempts to seize her prime as a moment when all competing versions of herself coexist. Sandy observes that when Miss Brodie shows rare glimpses of her underlying emotional uncertainties, she 'looked beautiful and fragile, just as dark heavy Edinburgh itself could suddenly be changed into a floating city when the light was a special pearly white and fell upon one of the gracefully fashioned streets'.[21] Miss Brodie's strict adherence to Kirk and sabbath, folding it into the foundations of her life as the dark stone of the Edinburgh church undergirds the Castle rock, arguably helps maintain that primal unity and keep undesired versions of herself in check.

The good Dr Jekyll, too, is a churchgoer. The narrator of his strange history asserts that the doctor has 'always been known for charities' and eventually becomes 'no less distinguished for religion'.[22] Apparently Dr Jekyll, as a wealthy and respected man, consistently gives his money to help the less deserving. After the shocking and brutal murder of Sir Danvers Carew, however, Dr Jekyll begins giving his time as well: no longer finding it sufficient to write cheques from afar, he becomes 'distinguished' for his active piety. The narrator suggests there has been a kind of religious conversion experience, declaring that 'a new life began for Dr Jekyll'.[23] The phrase has a ring of the revival hall to it, an echo of tearful repentance and a whiff of the sawdust trail. For instance, in an early 1874 article trenchantly titled 'What Good Have Messrs. Moody and Sankey Done in Edinburgh?', an anonymous columnist wrote that D. L. Moody's tubthumping evangelistic sermons in the city

> made it as clear as noonday that salvation is not the mere setting right of man's existing faculties, but the impartation of new life in Christ, a new nature, a new creation, so that there exists two utterly opposed natures in the one responsible Christian man, and that 'these are contrary the one to the other;' and the knowledge of this gives young Christians immense relief, and a solid foundation for holiness at the very commencement of their Christian course.[24]

A 'new life' certainly gave relief to Dr Jekyll: 'his face seemed to open and brighten, as if with an inward consciousness of service; and for more than two months, the doctor was at peace.'[25]

Of course, it was not to last. Within a matter of months after his new life begins, Jekyll transforms once again into the malevolent, irredeemable Hyde. As Jekyll writes in his 'Full Statement of the Case':

> I was still cursed with my duality of purpose; and as the first edge of my penitence wore off, the lower side of me, so long indulged, so recently chained down, began to growl for licence. […] I was once more tempted to trifle with my conscience; and it was as an ordinary secret sinner, that I at last fell before the assaults of temptation.[26]

While it is unlikely that Robert Louis Stevenson (1850–1894) ever heard D. L. Moody preach, much of the subtle power of *Strange Case of Dr Jekyll and Mr Hyde* (1883) lies in its understanding of 'two utterly opposed natures in one Christian man', distinct yet brutally entwined in each other, the nobly elect and the horribly damned bound in an intractable interdependence. Thus, Jekyll laments, 'I chose the better part and was found wanting the strength to keep it'.[27] This extraordinary statement is an almost blasphemous juxtaposition of allusions to Luke 10. 42 and Daniel 5. 27. Crucially, Jekyll's claim both to have chosen and been found wanting are ambiguous as to where the fault lies – in himself, and his enjoyment of temptation, or in the inexplicable fiat of an unnamed god. In other words, was he divinely chosen to be damned, or has he damned himself?

Christian conversion, belief, and practice can hardly be said to form the main preoccupations of *Strange Case of Dr Jekyll and Mr Hyde*. Yet they unambiguously provide not only the broad socio-cultural context for the narrative but the intellectual soil from which the story grew. Jekyll undergoes his temptations and transformations as a committed Christian; he and his friends understand his experience in expressly Christian terms. Even his agonised dying cry – 'for God's sake, have mercy!' – echoes one of the ancient scriptural prayers of the Church. The literary world in which Jekyll and Hyde exist is distinctly Christian in its nature, its delineation of character, its codification of virtue, and its conception of evil.

'I canna change right into wrang'

Central to this literary world are what Glasgow-based theologian David Jasper has described as 'the biblical foundations of Western liturgical "being".[28] The Eucharistic liturgy, Jasper argues, 'is at its heart, and most deeply, a commitment to "doing" in remembrance lest we forget ourselves and each other'.[29] This implicitly allows the possibility that neglect of 'doing' – ritually, gratefully, verbally – off-balances the self to a state of forgetfulness, of isolation and ungratefulness rather than community and grace. The apposition of liturgical 'being' could thus be termed liturgical 'nonbeing', which is also 'nondoing'. Thus, when Jekyll laments that he is 'found wanting' in the strength to do good, he acknowledges the diminishment and depraved individuation of his self. Hyde, as an expression of self, selfish, is shunned irrevocably from the broader community. The self as constructed through liturgical 'being' is acknowledged as manifold, existing within shared community of faith gathered to 'do' the act of remembrance. Jasper eloquently describes this self as 'a strange and mixed community presented through the hermeneutical screen that is "me"'.

> For I am not simply body (material) but a larger self, a body and soul, an 'I' that talks to itself (foolishly and possibly idiotically at times), a tiny community of thought and being unto itself that ever

anxiously seeks communion with others through all the complexities of speech, writing, and text – or perhaps even just the Other – in a condition that we ought properly to call the liturgical.[30]

The question posed by the complex speech of these literary texts is: what happens when the manifold self turns against itself, when it rejects communion for the solipsism of a fanatically unified ego? What becomes of the self when this tiny, textual community is unable to maintain its 'difficult balance'?

> My love of low society, as such propensities as I was cursed with are usually termed, was, I think, of an uncommon kind, and indicated a nature, which, if not depraved by early debauchery, would have been fit for better things. I did not so much delight in the wild revel, the low humour, the unconfined liberty of those with whom I associated, as in the spirit of adventure, presence of mind in peril, and sharpness of intellect which they displayed in prosecuting their marauding upon the revenue, or similar adventures.[31]

The speaker is George Staunton, the Byronic villain of Walter Scott's *The Heart of Mid-Lothian* (1818). Notionally upright and respectable, of good Christian family, Staunton finds himself burdened with an inability to control – or perhaps to correctly channel – his mercurial appetites. A broodingly erotic rogue whose obsessive influence dominates the course of the narrative, Staunton's literary progeny arguably includes not only Jekyll/Hyde, but Gil-Martin in James Hogg's *Memoirs and Confessions of a Justified Sinner* (1824) and Heathcliff in Emily Brontë's *Wuthering Heights* (1847). Scott's characterisation is, however, arguably more nuanced than his imitators. Throughout the novel, Scott indicates that Staunton's hubris, more than carnal desire or intrinsic damnation, wreaks his undoing. Staunton understands his appetites through a rarefied Christian lens, exaggerating their force and their transgression to himself and thereby enacting worse folly than he would as an ordinary rascal. He declares that his 'propensities' are of 'an uncommon kind' owing to the inherent nobility of his nature. On the one hand, the narrative suggests this to be simply the arrogance of a young man mistaking youthful energy for ontological singularity: his proclivities seem no more unusual than overindulgence in alcohol, fondness for physical exertion, and enjoyment of sex. On the other hand, Staunton's religious conscience, exacerbated by his sensitive and cosseted personality, drives him into hysterical self-loathing. He names himself the devil – 'call me Apollyon, Abaddon, whatever name you shall chuse' – and declares himself 'a wretch, predestined to evil here and hereafter'.[32] He deserves, he says, to be counted among worst of the damned,

> if you call it sinful to have been the destruction of the mother that bore me – of the friend that loved me – of the woman that trusted me – of the innocent child that was born to me. If to have done all this is to be a sinner, and to survive it is to be miserable, then I am most guilty and most miserable indeed.[33]

Staunton's love of low company leads him from the comforts of his father's rectory in England to Scotland, where he fraternises with smugglers and leads 'a life of strange adventure' – many of the adventures, apparently, sexual. The first young woman he impregnates, Madge Wildfire, loses both the baby and her mind, becoming a petty criminal and vagrant. The next, Effie Deans, is condemned to death on the charge of murdering her infant. Staunton's predations destroy his victims both in mind and in body. By centring his relationships with women in his own narcissistic sense of depravity, he disrupts their own manifold selves, pinning their experiences to a fixed point – the loss of their children – which serves to feed his own superior damnation.

Against Staunton's egotistical depravity, Scott sets Effie's sister Jeanie Deans, who ranks among the most compelling characters in fiction. Where Staunton and his victims depict the lopsided stasis of presumed damnation, Jeanie embodies the liturgical doing and being posited by Jasper. A devout young woman from a Covenanting family, Jeanie's simplicity of nature and constancy of love are both rooted within her textual community, in which the language of the Christian scriptures permeates discussion and determines actions. Scott makes clear throughout the narrative, however, that it is not simply this text-based faith-community which gives Jeanie strength, but that she possesses a deep strength of will which she nurtures and buttresses with biblical terms. In one of the novel's great set-pieces, Staunton and Jeanie confront each other by night at Muschat's Cairn. Staunton attempts to frighten Jeanie into agreeing to perjure herself at Effie's murder trial to save her sister's life. His threats are abusive and charged with sexual menace; he 'offered a pistol at the unfortunate young woman', demanding, 'Will you destroy your sister, and compel me to shed more blood?'[34] Jeanie is terrified but insists 'I canna change right into wrang, or make that true which is false'.[35] Deeper than her fear of Staunton and the devil he may incarnate is Jeanie's trust in God. She declares, '[God] has given us a law […] for the lamp of our path; if we stray from it, we err against knowledge – I may not do evil, even that good may come out of it'.[36]

Crucially, Jeanie bases her resoluteness on her understanding of the scriptural text: as well as the ninth of the Ten Commandments – the prohibition against bearing false witness – she invokes Psalm 119, a prolonged hymn celebrating the Law and Commandments as beacons of wisdom, specifically verse 105: 'Thy word is a lamp unto my feet and a light unto my path.' The other half of the allusion is to Romans 3. 8. Scott's breadth of knowledge of the biblical text, and the ease with which he riffs it into dialogue, is formidable. Yet, while Jeanie believes her courage comes from the God of the Bible, Scott's narration adopts a degree of scepticism, suggesting that Jeanie is unaware of her own moral strength. Before her dangerous rendezvous with Staunton, Jeanie kneels to pray

> with fervent sincerity, that God would please to direct her what course to follow in her arduous and distressing situation. It was the belief of the time and sect to which she belonged, that special answers to prayer, differing little in their character from divine inspiration, were, as they expressed it, 'borne in upon their minds' in answer to

> their earnest petitions in a crisis of difficulty. Without entering into an abstruse point of divinity, one thing is plain; namely, that the person who lays open his doubts and distresses in prayer, with feeling and sincerity, must necessarily, in the act of doing so, purify his mind from the dross of worldly passions and interests, and bring it into that state, when the resolutions adopted are likely to be selected rather from a sense of duty, than from any inferior motive.[37]

Jeanie understands her Christianity 'through all the complexities of speech, writing, and text'.[38] Possessing knowledge of the divine Other through the written text of scripture, she attempts to communicate with the divine through direct speech – a textual practice which her faith community encourages and has to some extent codified. Scott, however, describes this intensely religious experience in non-religious terms, sidestepping prayer as 'an abstruse point' of theology to describe an experience which today might be called meditation or mindfulness. Even more intriguing, rather than an act of faith it is described as laying open doubt. Prayer, in this understanding, begins from uncertainty and unknowing. Its benefit is not that God responds, verbally or otherwise, but that the urges of the intercessor are stilled, allowing for mental clarity and an understanding of the self in relation to the community. The narrator concludes: 'Jeanie arose from her devotions, with her heart fortified to endure affliction, and encouraged to face difficulties.'[39] Her act of liturgical being and doing has reinforced the self she has created through her devotion to text and the God in the text; she finds the courage both to confront Staunton and to speak truth despite its bitter cost and the convenience of falsehood. Jeanie understands this strength to come through the different texts she reveres. The narrator, however, later implies a different source, remarking: 'Jeanie Deans possessed, with her excellently clear understanding, the concomitant advantage of promptitude of spirit, even in the extremity of distress.'[40]

'Contrair winds'

It is intriguing that Scott created Jeanie Deans and her family to be more intensely Christian, not only in beliefs and behaviour but also in the textual webs they use to create their individual and communal selves, than the majority of his readers. For present-day readers, this distancing from and contextualising of Jeanie's beliefs help make her more understandable. Jeanie Deans, at any rate, in spite or perhaps because of her piety, seems like a Scottish heroine who would readily find a new generation of admirers among today's secular and religiously diverse students, offering a compelling portrait of how to be deeply oneself in an unselfish, even sacrificial, way.

From the standpoint of Jeanie's own literary lineage, however, Scott was drawing on a deep tradition of textual devotion to the God offered for parsing in the biblical text. Spontaneous prayer as a form of words for doubt, faith mediated through ancient scriptures, and the grounding of one's manifold being through liturgical doing in remembrance all find precedent in the devotional poetry which thrived in Scotland throughout the Middle Ages and into the Reformation.[41] A helpful example is found in the work of Elizabeth Melville, Lady Culross (c. 1578–c. 1640), the first Scottish woman to publish work in print and a highly regarded poet during the reign of James VI and I.[42] Some of Melville's finest poems survive in manuscript, written at the end of a hand-copied volume of sermons on Hebrews 11 by the radical Presbyterian minister of Edinburgh, Robert Bruce (1554–1631), whom James VI and I exiled to Inverness.[43] The series of poems concludes with a seven-part sequence of Scottish sonnets, apparently undertaking the penitential work of soul-searching and self-condemnation which Melville's faith tradition expected. Sonnet IV uses sailing as its conceit:

> In brittil bark of fraill fant feble flesch
> my sillie saul with contrair winds is tost
> calms me corrupt, in storms I frett and fasch
> in rest I roust, in trubell all seims lost[44]

This kind of rhetoric takes inspiration from St Paul's lamentation of the divided self in Romans 7: 'for what I would, that do I not; but what I hate, that do I.' Perhaps drawing from St James's description of a person of weak faith as 'a wave of the sea driven with the wind and tossed', Melville ingeniously sets this against the tableau of a 'brittil bark' on the ocean, artfully describing it simultaneously in nautical and emotional terms: 'in storms I frett and fasch'.[45] The trouble here is not the voyage but the 'contrair' nature both of the wind and the voyager herself, unable to find ease even in rest. The second quatrain shifts the image from the tempestuousness of the water to the lack of safe harbour:

> no hold I have nor beild quhairof to bost
> my skill is small the schalds and rocks ar ryfe
> the storme of sin still drives on liward cost
> no anker serves but hope to save my lyve
> (ll. 5–8)

Throughout the sonnet, Melville elides the physical and natural with the internal and spiritual. The need for safe anchorage amid rocks and shoals invokes both the actual coast of Melville's native Fife and, once again, the Christian scriptures, specifically Hebrews 6. 18–19, in which hope in God is described as 'an anchor of the soul'. Sinfulness and inconstancy are as overwhelming as wind and storm, while the cry that 'my skill is small' suggests the inadequacy of the poet's own self to resist heaves of emotion and urges to self-indulge; in Sonnet III, the poet describes herself bitterly as a 'sensuall sow in filth'. It is perhaps not possible to know whether Melville is writing autobiographically or simply as a literary exercise in penitence. Certainly, this degree of self-loathing would be expected of a dutiful penitent, whether heartily felt or merely well intended. Yet the frustrations of physical overindulgence, emotional upset, and persistent anxiety will seem familiar enough to any present-day reader.

The sonnet begins to tonally shift in the final quatrain:

> alace my sins have raisd this storme and stryfe
> quhilk none can swage bot Jesus Chryst alone
> he can and will at neid these storms reprove
> thocht he delay till the thrid watche be gone
> (ll. 9–12)

The reference here is to Jesus's miraculous calming of a storm on the Sea of Galilee, scolding the wind as if it were a fractious child.[46] The poet declares herself helpless amid her own emotional upheaval and physical desires. There is something of both Jekyll and Staunton in this declaration: the poet is at war with herself and losing. Unlike both later characters, the poet here maintains Jesus's miraculous and life-affirming power over her own self. This sentiment seems akin to the experience of Jeanie Deans laying her heart open in prayer. Jesus, the poet says, 'can and will' bring calm and rest to her restless self.

Both the sophistication of Melville's theological mind and her mastery of the sonnet form appear in the closing couplet. The poet turns from describing her agitation to speaking a prayer: 'cum Jesus say take courage it is I / tho first I fear yit will I death defy' (ll. 13–14). This is another allusion to the Gospels, but to a different miracle: Jesus's walking on the water.[47] When Jesus calmed the storm, the narrative goes, he was actually in the boat with his students. In this miracle, however, his students are in the boat without him when a storm strikes and Jesus approaches the boat 'walking upon the sea'. The students' terror arises not only from the intensity of the waves but their inability to recognise Jesus, thinking him to be a ghost or evil spirit. Thus, in the final couplet, the poet shifts the nature of her distress and emotional upheaval: it is not that her attitude and impulses have control over her, but that she has not recognised Jesus's spiritual presence with her.

The final line deepens and changes the meaning of the sonnet. Hearing Jesus's voice – perhaps having his words 'borne in' upon her mind – will enable her to defy death. The poet's anxieties described in the quatrains have not merely been vicissitudes of mood or appetite, but incapacitating fear of her own mortality. The 'fant feble flesch' can be thus read literally: the poet is grappling with the knowledge of how temporary physical life is and how suddenly it can end. The literary movement in the sonnet, from remorse over sin to recognising Jesus in the face of death, is distinctly liturgical, moving from confession to sacramental participation in Christ's own death. The sonnet can be described as Eucharistic, an act of remembrance that Christ has died and has risen and is present with even the most cowering, timorous believer. Through this textual remembrance, the poet defines herself as she aspires to be, calming her own emotional and spiritual distress.

Melville expresses this act of remembrance in 'resolutely Calvinist' terms.[48] The Eucharistic impulse, however, is as old as Christianity itself and has existed in Scottish literature since its beginnings. In the ninth-century Old English poem 'The Dream of the Rood', written in the Northumbrian dialect 'from which the Scots language is derived',[49] the cross on which Jesus was crucified speaks to the poet in a vision, describing in anguished detail its experience of suffering together with Christ and holding him as he died.

> Rod wæs ic aræred: ahof ic ricne cynig,
> heofona hlaford; hyldan me ne dorste.
> þurhdrifan hi me mid deorcan næglum, on me syndon þa dolg gesiene,
> opene inwidhlemmas: ne dorste ic hira nænigum sceððan.
> (ll. 44–47)[50]

> (I was reared a cross: I raised the king aloft,
> heaven's liege-lord; I dared not bend.
> They scored me through with dark nails, on me still the scars remain,
> gaping cruel gashes: and I dared not stop anyone.)

The horror of the loyal tree, brutalised into a cross by faceless enemies, made to hold up its liege-lord, the young hero and gift-giver, to torment and ridicule, still echoes a thousand years later. Crucially, the tree's fear of intervening – 'ne dorste' – comes from its loyalty to Christ. It speaks contemptuously of its enemies – 'ealle ic mihte / feondas gyfellan' ('I could have taken all those fiends') (ll. 37–38) – but it understands that its king has chosen to suffer. The cross's own agony and dark trial lies in suffering with Christ in nonviolence rather than fighting to defend his life with its own. At the nadir of the vision, the natural world falls silent in agony as the tree cradles the dead body of the young king:

> sceadu forð eode
> wann under wolcnum. Weop eal gesceaft
> cwiðdon cyninges fyll: Crist wæs on rode.
> (ll. 54–56)

> (shadow loured round,
> wan under sky. All creation wept,
> keening the king's fall: Christ was on the cross.)

In the poem itself, this moment is a twofold act of remembrance. The tree is recalling both its own desolation and the world's lament; the poet is remembering the words the tree spoke in the dream. The death of Christ – the moment when shadows close over the corpse hung on the cross – is experienced through words for remembering. It is also a cry of pain. The memory bears bewildered immediacy, an agonising appeal which is both invocation and witness: 'Weop eall gesceaft'. After waking, the poet will ponder the beauty of the vision and take comfort in it, even while admitting loneliness, ageing, and approaching death (ll. 131ff). In the actual moment of Christ's death, however, and in the moment of textual remembrance layered over it, it is harsh and bitter emptiness, a suffering without intelligible meaning, shadows in the sky concealing a dying brightness.

Perhaps it is this difficult balance of brightness and death, of consolation and doubt, more than the vicissitudes of theological disputation, which winds a delicate thread through Scottish literature's interplay with Christianity. Asking how to be – whether being a Scot or a Christian, or both or neither – is asking what it is like to experience the extremities of life without shattering. For the Scottish authors discussed here, and for many others like them, Christianity has not necessarily offered a straightforward answer for their overwhelming questions, but it has provided a context for the ways that many different expressions of being and doing, of doing to be, of being in spite of nonbeing, could be expressed.

In his poem lamenting the death of John Davidson (1857–1909), Hugh MacDiarmid creates an image which hauntingly evokes this context.

MacDiarmid recalls that when, as a teenager, he heard 'the news of [Davidson's] suicide by walking into the sea', he 'felt as if the bottom had fallen out of my world'.[51] His later poem addresses Davidson directly, explaining:

> [...] something in me has always stood
> Since then looking down the sandslope
> On your small black shape by the edge of the sea,
> —A bullet-hole through a great scene's beauty,
> God through the wrong end of a telescope.[52]

This startling description presents the plain 'small black shape' and resolves into the implied violence of a 'bullet-hole' before shifting to the barely imaginable: God, made little and rendered artificially distant 'through the wrong end of a telescope'. These distorting optics will be familiar to most readers, but what God looks like remains an open question – perhaps simply a blot or tear, a violent gash in a seascape.

Crucially, the poet suggests that 'something in me' is always confronting this image, witnessing the suicide and experiencing its brutal destruction. The echo here of the cross crying that 'opene inwidhlemmas' from cruel nails still remain in its wood is surely coincidence, but it is a deeply telling one. The theologian Paul Tillich has written that the people 'in every civilization [are] anxiously aware of the threat of nonbeing' and struggle to find the courage to affirm life in spite of this anxiety.[53] Tillich argues that this anxiety and the sense of the meaninglessness is intrinsic to the experience of being:

> If one is asked how nonbeing is related to being-itself, one can only answer metaphorically: being 'embraces' itself and nonbeing. Being has nonbeing 'within' itself as that which is eternally present and that which is eternally overcome in the process of divine life.[54]

This may be what MacDiarmid suggests by enwrapping the act of suicide, the bullet-hole blot of a tiny God, in 'a great scene's beauty' – at once blaspheming the scene and deepening it, the inevitable and necessary flaw or breakage. The anxious tension of nonbeing, of silence where there should be words and emptiness where there should be presence, is a human condition. It is by no means the special province of Christianity or of Scotland. Tillich goes on to suggest – perhaps rightly – that 'living creativity' in this tension offers 'the pattern of the self-affirmation of every finite-being'.[55] Faced with 'the anxiety of nonbeing, the awareness of one's finitude as finitude', he says, the individual struggles with wondering: 'Is there a courage to be, a courage to affirm oneself in spite of the threat against [one's] ontic self-affirmation?'[56] It is beyond the scope of a literary study to answer that question. But literature itself, especially a literature which engages deeply with the faith tradition in which it has grown, may help provide clearer, more resonant forms of the question, to give reader, audience, and hearer courage – if not to answer, then to ask.

Chapter summaries and unanswered questions

This book, then, takes up some of these questions by asking what different Scottish writers have observed while peering through 'the wrong end of a telescope'. It is not a full historical survey of Scottish letters or the Scottish Kirk, nor it is meant to be. Key historical moments in Scotland's church history are thus treated only glancingly or not at all. Rather, it offers contrasting, sometimes disharmonious readings of what it means to be Christian and Scottish and how those two intertwined identities focus the individual self.

Fergusson and Elliott have posited a useful if 'somewhat arbitrary' three-fold chronological division for the history of Scottish theology: '(i) from the middle ages to the early Enlightenment; (ii) from the Enlightenment to the mid-nineteenth century; (iii) from the late nineteenth to until the very early twenty-first century.'[57] A similar chronology may be detected here, with the same qualifiers that it is 'largely presentational' and 'intended to be porous'.[58] If this schema places too great an emphasis on more recent writers, the imbalance is, I suggest, countered by the growing weight of anxiety both about Scottishness and Christianity apparent since at least the final decades of the nineteenth century. Similarly, practical considerations for confining this collection to a single volume have meant that many Scottish authors well suited for such study have simply been not addressed. An entire second volume could be prepared discussing just the texts quoted in this introduction. While the reader may feel some disappointment that a favourite book or author does not receive the top billing they deserve, the critical concepts and approaches present here will, I hope, suggest a variety of ways for looking at the engagement with Christianity in many other texts.

The book begins as Scottish Christianity did – on Iona: Duncan Sneddon looks at how the text of the *Vita Sancti Columbae* shaped the daily lives of the monks who lived there. Claire Harrill then discusses a later Scottish saint's cult, examining how the *Miracula* of St Margaret not only imagined a monastic community gathered around Margaret as their spiritual mother, but also reveals complex understandings of gender and maternity in medieval Scotland. From the monasteries the book turns to the Kirk, with David Jasper delineating the growth and development of the language of the *Scottish Prayer Book* (1637) through the tradition of vernacular devotional poetry of the sixteenth-century 'makars'. This sacred liturgical performance of devotion juxtaposes with the secular performance of the play as Ian Brown discusses the fraught coexistence of kirk and theatre, arguing for less acrimonious relations than are popularly assumed.

Around this point, the Enlightenment and the 1707 Union occur; literary texts become more inwardly focused, pondering how Christianity helps an individual self find their place in a rapidly shifting society. J. Walter McGinty looks at eccentric characters in the novels of Tobias Smollett (1721–1771), considering how their fantastic and often ridiculous opinions about religion may have helped Smollett slyly express his own unorthodox views. Barbara Bell examines the poetic career of Robert Davidson (1778–1855), whose Christian piety found expression in solidarity with the farmworkers and manual labourers of the Borders. J. H. Alexander then addresses the composition history and literary style of Walter Scott's *Religious Discourses* (1828), pondering to what extent they were meant as genuine expressions of belief or as a literary game. The editor of the volume adds a chapter about even more abysmal sermons, this time from the lips of stickit ministers in the novels of George MacDonald (1824–1905). Rebecca McLean writes about how Margaret Oliphant (1828–1897) turned towards the fantastic mode in her fiction to reconcile her many bereavements with Church teaching about death and the afterlife.

Bereavement emerges as a recurring motif in the long twentieth century. Silvia Mergenthal looks at how the Christian idea of the afterlife haunted Scottish poets during the First World War and how their verses draw from the imagery of crucifixion to make sense of their own trauma. While the War poets still maintained a strong if complicated sense of piety, the Scottish Renaissance poets generally rejected Christianity. But, as Dominique Delmaire shows, their writings nonetheless evince a sense of the divine, expressed in form closer to the Hegelian concept of being. George Mackay Brown (1921–1996) went even further, converting to Catholicism and attempting in his work to resacralise his beloved Orkney, as Linden Bicket's chapter demonstrates. Even when belief seems wholly absent, the symbols and metanarrative of Christianity still retain a formative power, as Michael Kugler shows in his reading of Alan Warner's *Morvern Callar* (1995) and its representation of suicide and ennui in the post-Thatcher Highlands. James McGonigal offers a reading of the final poetry collections of Edwin Morgan (1920–2010) through the eschatological framework of the Four Last Things: death, judgement, hell, and heaven. The collection concludes in the post-Christian present, with Alastair McIntosh's evocative autoethnographic account of inheriting the burdens of a believing, doubting, imperfect past and speaking it forward into an unknown but hopeful future.

Individually and collectively, these chapters address key aspects of the interpenetration of Christianity and Scottish literature. They also suggest a series of further questions, both from what has been discussed here and, crucially, what has not. To some extent, the questions are indicative of lacunae in this collection; these arise not from any incompletion in the essay individually, but through editorial choices I have made in gathering together the volume as a whole. More critically, such questions indicate areas where further research could be undertaken to illumine Scotland's symbiosis of sacred and literary text.

The first and most obvious question is about language. To what extent does Scottish Gaelic literature interact with Christianity differently than literature in Scots and English? That there is a difference seems inevitable: the historical and societal experience of the Gàidhealtachd has been different than that of the Scots- and English-speaking communities, including in the reception and practice of Christianity. The Christian texts, too, have been translated in Gaelic since 1767, and Gaelic liturgies and hymns find echoes and allusions in Gaelic-language literature. In a sense, this question has already been poignantly asked by Sorley MacLean, in his poem 'Ban-Ghàidheal':

> Am faca Tu i, Iùdhaich mhòir,
> rin abrar Aon Mhac Dhè?
> Am fac' thu 'coltas air Do thriall
> ri strì an fhìon-lios chèin?

> (Hast Thou seen her, great Jew,
> who art called the One Son of God?
> Hast Thou seen on Thy way the like of her
> labouring in the distant vineyard?)[59]

Obviously, the interaction of Christianity and Scottish Gaelic literature is intricate and multivalent, well beyond what one or two additional chapters tacked on to the present volume could even hope to introduce. This, combined with the editor's regrettably limited Gaelic, has resulted in the choice to focus this volume on Scots and English writers. Hopefully, a future volume dedicated wholly to Gaelic writers will restore balance and allow for fuller understanding both of literature and of Christianity itself.

The second question is also raised in MacLean's poem. The poet addresses Christ as 'Iùdhaich mhòir', identifying him through his Jewish ethnicity and religious tradition. Perhaps the emphasis here is that Jesus was himself a manual labourer from a small village, oppressed by an imperial power, and deeply familiar with 'fallas searbh air mala is gruaidh' ('a bitter sweat on brow and cheek').[60] Or perhaps it emphasises the intrinsic foreignness of Christianity to Scotland and the moral and physical weight which its 'iron text' bore down upon Scottish people. Perhaps it does both. Whatever the case, 'Jew' makes an uncomfortable metonymy for 'foreigner', and an inaccurate one. David Daiches, in his profound and moving memoir about growing up in Edinburgh's Jewish community, remarks, 'the whole point of my story is that I was not *between* two worlds but equally home in both'.[61] In this context, Daiches's own prodigious influence on the development of Scottish literary studies as a discipline does not seem insignificant. Nor does it seem trivial that on the 2011 census 1.7% of Scots reported 'some Gaelic language skills' while 2.2% identified as Muslim, Hindu, Sikh, Buddhist, or Jewish.[62] The second question, then, inquires how other religions have mingled with Scottish literature and envisioned Scottish identity. How has literature arising from these faith communities engaged with Scottishness, whether through Christianity or wholly through their own traditions?

The third question grows from the second, with the grim admission that minority peoples and religions have not invariably found welcome in Scotland, as recent reckonings with Scotland's all-too-willing participation in the transatlantic slave trade have painfully shown. And yet, in staggering contradiction, enslaved peoples found within Christianity a religious system which gave voice to the oppressed, speaking both of welcome to the stranger and liberty for the captive.[63] What, then, does literature by Scottish writers of colour have to say to this mercurial faith, both the tool of the oppressor and the weapon of the oppressed? How does humbly welcoming minority voices and experiences alter our understanding both of Scottish Christianity and the literatures which interact with it?

Each of these questions could sustain an entire volume such as this one. Certainly, they present what could pompously be called opportunities for further research but is also a chance to do more reading and deep reflection. It is, indeed, precisely to prompt such thoughtful reading this collection has been gathered. Robert Crawford, writing in his introduction to *Scotland's Books*, has declared, 'Scottish literature should never be confined to Scotland'.[64] In corollary, Scottish Christianity should never be confined to the merely Christian. Both Scotland's books and Scotland's churches contain a record of a people – virtuous or otherwise – struggling with the question of how to be, in their own place and their own way. The example of the questions they asked and the reasons they asked them, their grand covenants of faith and tiny communities of self, their anxieties and their failed attempts at doing, offer a place where any honest reader, of any nation or religion, can pause and ponder the divine riddle of their own humanity. As bard and tradition-bearer Alastair McIntosh writes in his poem 'Scotland':

> A person belongs
> inasmuch as they are willing
> to cherish and be cherished
> by this place
> and its peoples

Endnotes

1. Robert Burns, 'The Cotter's Saturday Night', in *Selected Poems and Songs*, ed. Robert P. Irvine (Oxford: Oxford University Press, 2012), p. 65, ll. 179–80.
2. Callum Brown, *Religion and Society in Scotland since 1707* (Edinburgh: Edinburgh University Press, 1997), p. 2: 'By the time Glasgow was "European City of Culture" in 1990, and the pubs stayed open until three o'clock in the morning all year long, nobody really doubted that religious Scotland was dead.' Cf. Callum Brown, *The Death of Christian Britain: Understanding Secularisation 1800–2000* (London and New York: Routledge, 2001).
3. Brown, *Religion and Society*, p. 158.
4. Scottish Public Health Observatory, 'Religion, spirituality and belief: demographics', *ScotPHO: Public Health Information for Scotland*, 18 September 2020. www.scotpho.org.uk/population-groups/religion-spirituality-and-belief/data/demographics/ [accessed 28 March 2022].
5. *Analysis of Equality Results from the 2011 Census – part 2* (Edinburgh: The Scottish Government, 2015), p. 51: www.gov.scot/publications/analysis-equality-results-2011-census-part-2/documents/. Curious readers may wish to compare these statistics with the forthcoming results of the 2022 census to see if the trend continues.
6. Brown, *Religion and Society*, p. ix.
7. Cp. Hugh MacDiarmid, *A Drunk Man Looks at the Thistle*, ed. Kenneth Buthlay (Edinburgh: Polygon, 2008), p. 145, ll. 1221–24.
8. Edwin Muir, 'Scotland 1941', in *Collected Poems*, 2nd edn (London: Faber and Faber, 1984), p. 97, l. 20.

9 David Fergusson and Mark W. Elliott, 'Scottish Theology: Contexts and Traditions', in *The History of Scottish Theology. Volume 1: Celtic Origins to Reformed Orthodoxy* (Oxford: Oxford University Press, 2019), pp. 1–11 (pp. 4, 5).
10 Robert Crawford, *Scotland's Books: A History of Scottish Literature* (Oxford: Oxford University Press, 2009), p. 17.
11 Muriel Spark, *The Prime of Miss Jean Brodie; The Girls of Slender Means; The Driver's Seat; The Only Problem*, Everyman's Library (London and New York: Alfred A. Knopf, 2004), p. 30.
12 Spark, pp. 31–32.
13 Ibid., p. 30.
14 For which see James Bailey, '"Repetition, boredom, despair": Muriel Spark and the Eichmann Trial', *Holocaust Studies* 17.2–3 (2011), pp. 185–206: doi.org/10.1080/17504902.2011.11087286.
15 Spark, p. 33.
16 Ibid.
17 Ibid., p. 34.
18 Ibid., p. 45.
19 Ibid.
20 Ibid., p. 34.
21 Ibid., p. 109.
22 Robert Louis Stevenson, *Strange Case of Dr Jekyll and Mr Hyde and Other Tales*, ed. Roger Luckhurst (Oxford: Oxford University Press, 2006), p. 28.
23 Ibid.
24 'What Good Have Moody and Sankey Done in Edinburgh?', in *Narrative of Messrs. Moody and Sankey's Labors in Scotland and Ireland, also in Anchester, Sheffield, and Birmingham, England* (New York: Anson D. F. Randolph and Company, 1875), pp. 29–21 (p. 29). This unabashedly partisan volume republishes edited selections from favourable newspaper coverage of Moody and Sankey's 1873–74 tour. The idea of 'new life' is a not infrequent Christian description of conversion, which seems to have gained widespread traction after the mid-nineteenth century revivalist movements. The ultimate source seems to be Romans 6. 4.
25 Stevenson, p. 28.
26 Ibid., p. 62.
27 Ibid., p. 60.
28 David Jasper, *The Sacred Community: Art, Sacrament, and the People of God* (Waco: Baylor University Press, 2012), p. 9.
29 Ibid., p. 11.
30 Ibid., p. 10.
31 Walter Scott, *The Heart of Mid-Lothian*, ed. David Hewitt and Alison Lumsden (Edinburgh: Edinburgh University Press, 2004), p. 299.
32 Ibid., pp. 98, 138.
33 Ibid., p. 138.
34 Ibid., p. 139.
35 Ibid., p. 141.
36 Ibid., p. 142.
37 Ibid., p. 131.

38 Jasper, p. 10.
39 Scott, p. 131.
40 Ibid., p. 188.
41 For a much fuller presentation of this poetic tradition, see Kenneth Steven (ed.), *Scottish Religious Poetry: From the Sixth Century to the Present* (Edinburgh: Saint Andrews Press, 2017), an update of the 2000 anthology ed. Meg Bateman, Robert Crawford, and James McGonigal.
42 Jamie Reid-Baxter, 'Afterword', in *Poems of Elizabeth Melville, Lady Culross*, ed. Jamie Reid-Baxter (Edinburgh: Solsequium, 2010), p. 98.
43 Ibid., p. 109.
44 '[A Sonnet Sequence]', in *Poems of Elizabeth Melville* (see Reid-Baxter above), ll. 1–4.
45 Romans 7. 15; James 1. 6.
46 Matthew 8. 23–27; Mark 4. 35–41; Luke 8. 22–25.
47 Matthew 14. 22–34; Mark 6. 45–53; John 6. 15–21.
48 Reid-Baxter, p. 128.
49 Robert Crawford and Mick Imlah (eds), *The Penguin Book of Scottish Verse* (London: Penguin, 2000), p. xvii.
50 'The Dream of the Rood', in *The Penguin Book of Scottish Verse* (see Crawford and Imlah above), my translation.
51 Hugh MacDiarmid, 'John Davidson: Influences and Influence', in *Selected Essays of Hugh MacDiarmid*, ed. Duncan Glen (Berkeley and Los Angeles: University of California Press, 1970), p. 197.
52 Ibid, ll. 4–8.
53 Paul Tillich, *The Courage to Be*, 3rd edn (New Haven and London: Yale University Press, 2014), p. 41.
54 Tillich, p. 33.
55 Ibid.
56 Ibid., pp. 34, 49.
57 Fergusson and Elliott, p. 6.
58 Ibid.
59 Somhairle MacGill-Eain / Sorley MacLean, 'Ban-Ghàidheal / A Highland Woman', in *The Penguin Book of Scottish Verse*, pp. 442–43, ll. 1–4. The translation is MacLean's.
60 Ibid., l. 6.
61 David Daiches, *Two Worlds: An Edinburgh Jewish Childhood* (Edinburgh and London: Canongate, 1997), p. 3.
62 *Scotland's Census 2011: Gaelic report (part 1)* (Edinburgh: National Records of Scotland, 2015), p. 4; *Analysis of Equality*, op. cit.
63 For a discussion of Scottish Kirk's role both in the slave trade and its abolition, see Iain Whyte, *Scotland and the Abolition of Black Slavery, 1756–1838* (Edinburgh: Edinburgh University Press, 2006).
64 Crawford, p. 6.

1. Relic, Text, and Practice in Adomnán of Iona's *Vita Sancti Columbae*

DUNCAN SNEDDON

Vita Sancti Columbae (*VSC*), or 'The Life of Saint Columba' was written by Adomnán, ninth abbot of Iona, in about the year 700.[1] Drawing on oral tradition, written accounts, Adomnán's own experiences, and established hagiographical models, it gives a non-linear, thematically arranged account of the works of Saint Columba – Iona's founder and first abbot, and a kinsman of Adomnán's – who had died about a century before.

This chapter investigates the use of *VSC* in the life of the Columban *familia*, the communities of the monastic network of which Iona was the head. While this subject could be approached from a number of different angles, this discussion considers the use of relics in the text, and argues that *VSC* might function as a kind of instruction manual for Columban cult practice.[2] This has been a relatively understudied aspect of both *VSC* and of the Columban cult. Gilbert Márkus has investigated the evidence in *VSC* III.23 for the presence of a hand relic within the Columban *familia*, and Thomas Owen Clancy argued that the 'crowd control barrier' in I.3 refers to a shrine for Columba's relics, but both of those are oblique references to what appear to be relics.[3] A fuller study of the objects explicitly identified within the text itself as having been blessed by Columba, or in some way being imbued with his power to effect miracles, offers greater insight into how Adomnán, one of the most powerful and influential shapers of the Columban cult, viewed the practice of that cult and mediated it textually.

Saints and relics

Saints' cults often involve the veneration or use of corporeal relics such as the bones and hair of the holy dead, a practice which has biblical precedent in the miraculous properties of Elisha's bones, contact with which revived a dead man in II Kings 13. 20–21. Márkus has argued, very plausibly, that the use of corporeal relics of Columba (in the form of hand bones), can be traced in *VSC* III.23.[4] Many saints' cults, however, also involved associative or contact relics, the veneration or use of things which a saint had used or touched, or which had been in contact with their tomb. Such associative relics included clothing, bells, and staffs which the saint in question had used during their life on earth.[5] This, too, had a biblical precedent, in the aprons and handkerchiefs touched by St Paul which cured the sick and drove evil spirits away from them in Acts 19. 11–12, as well as in the account in the Gospels of Matthew and Luke of the sick woman who was cured after, in faith, touching the hem of Christ's robe.[6]

Detailed accounts of how relics were actually used in cult practice usually come from much later sources than *VSC*, and we should be wary of reading such practices back into the early medieval period. Even so, we may get a useful insight into how Columban relics might have been used by considering accounts such as those of the hand relic of the Apostle St James in twelfth-century Reading, particularly when we bear in mind the possible hand relic of Columba mentioned in *VSC* III.23, and the repeated use of water in Adomnán's healing narratives, as shall be seen below. Simon Yarrow notes that 'the chief medium for bestowing the saint's favours on pilgrims' was placing the hand relic in water, and then pouring the water on those who sought the saint's blessing, and that the hand would also be used to make the sign of the cross over a sick person in order to heal them.[7]

The *petra salis* and manuscripts copied by Columba (II.7–9)

VSC contains accounts of several kinds of associative relics. In II.7, Columba blesses a *petra salis* and gives it to a certain Colcu, son of Cellach.[8] First it is used to effect cures for severe inflammations of the eyes, and later it and the pegs and the section of wall from which it was suspended are miraculously preserved during a fire which destroyed the rest of the village.

> Alio itidem in tempore Colgu filius Cellachi postulatam a sancto petram salis benedictam accipit sorori et suae nutrici profuturam; quae ofthalmiae laborabat ualde graui langore. Talem eulogiam

eadem soror et nutricia de manu fratris accipiens in pariete super lectum suspendit; cassuque post aliquantos contegit dies ut idem uiculus cum supradictae domucula feminae flamma uastante totus concremaretur. Mirum dictu illius parietis particula, ne beati uiri in ea deperiret suspensa benedictio, post totam ambustam domum stans inlessa permansit, nec ignis ausus es attingere binales in quibus talis pendebat salis petra sudes.

(So at another time, Colcu, Cellach's son, requested and received from the saint a piece of rock-salt, blessed for the benefit of his sister and foster-mother, who was suffering from a very severe inflammation of the eyes. That sister and foster-mother also received this blessing from her brother's hand, and hung it on the wall above her bed. It happened by a mischance, after some days, that the village was entirely burned down with devastating flame, including that woman's cottage. Strange to say, a small part of that wall remained, standing undamaged, after the whole house had been burned about it, so that the blessed man's blessing, hung up on it, should not perish. And the fire did not dare to touch the two pegs on which this rock-salt hung.)[9]

Similarly, the following two chapters, II.8–9, concern books which were copied out by Columba and which prove invulnerable to water damage, even after being submerged in rivers for extended periods. At the end of II.9, Adomnán writes that he has heard many similar stories about other manuscripts copied out by Columba, which must indicate that there were several churches which owned books copied out, or at least reputed to have been copied out, by the saint, and that these were accorded a high degree of status within these communities. He concludes:

> Haec duo quamlibet in rebus paruís peracta et per contraria ostensa elimenta, ignem scilicet et aquam, beati testantur honorem uiri et quanti et qualis meriti apud habeatur deum.

(These two things, although performed in small matters, and shown in contrary elements, namely fire and water, bear witness to the honour of the blessed man, and prove how greatly and how highly he is esteemed by God.)[10]

The existence of these associative relics, then, and Adomnán's documenting of them, are presented as demonstrations of Columba's sanctity. What Adomnán does not tell us is whether or not these relics had any continuing role in Columban cult practice. Likewise, he does not say what the churches which held the miraculously preserved manuscripts did with them. In II.8, the text copied out by the saint is not identified; it is simply described as being a single page written by Columba's hand ('librario folio sancti manu discriptio'). In II.9, the text is described as 'ymnorum liber septimaniorum' ('a book of hymns for the week'), and so had an obvious practical function in the liturgical routine of the church which held it, but there is no way of knowing if its use was in any way connected with specifically Columban devotion.

Since their miraculous preservation demonstrated Columba's sanctity, however, it is likely that they acquired a function as objects of Columban cult devotion, perhaps especially after being described in a text of such central importance to that cult as *VSC*, written by such a renowned author as Adomnán, if not before. There are other uses for relics which are well attested in other cults, such as being carried in procession on the saint's feast day or used in the swearing of oaths.[11] None of these are mentioned in connection with the objects Adomnán writes about in II.7–9, but a detailed description of the use of Columban associative relics in II.44 might help us to understand more about the use of such objects in the Columban church.

Columban relics and the end of a drought (II.44)

Valerie Flint notes that 'supplications for rain or against damaging storms throughout the [early medieval] period quite often involve the clothing of the saintly supplicants'.[12] She cites the examples of the tunics of Deodatus of Nevers and his friend Hildulph, used in times of drought, flood, and plague, and an account in Gregory the Great's *Dialogues* in which the tunic of the dead Abbot Eutichius was carried around fields after a long drought, after which the rains returned. These all, and especially the example given by Gregory, suggest that the actions of the *familia* in *VSC* II.44, with the added use of books written by Columba as well as his clothing, were in line with widely spread ideas in Western Christendom about how to deal with drought.

The miracle in II.44, of which Adomnán claims to have been an eyewitness, is set during a severe drought which afflicted Iona and the surrounding area. The situation was so severe that that the monastic community, reminded of the curse of the drought in Leviticus 26. 19–20, decided to take action:

> Nos itaque haec legentes, et inminentem plagam pertimescentes, hoc inito consilio fieri consiliati sumus, ut aliqui ex nostrís senioribus nuper aratum et seminatum campum cum sancti Columbae candida circumirent tunica, et librís stilo ipsius discriptís, leuarentque in aere et excuterent eandem per ter tunicam qua etiam hora exitus eius de carne indutus erat, et eius aperirent libros et legerent in colliculo angelorum, ubi aliquando caelestis patriae ciues ad beati uiri condictum uisi sunt discendere.

> (Reading this, and in dread of the impending stroke, we formed a plan, and decided upon this course: that some of our elders should go round the plain that had lately been ploughed and sown, taking with them the white tunic of Saint Columba, and books in his own handwriting; and should three times raise and shake in the air that tunic, which he wore in the hour of his departure from the flesh; and should open his books and read from them, on the hill of the angels, where at one time the citizens of the heavenly country were seen descending to confer with the holy man.)[13]

The rains indeed returned later on that same day. Adomnán concludes:

> Vnius itaque beati commemoratio nominis uiri, in tunica et librís commemorata, multís regionibus eadem uice et populís salubri subuenit oportunitate.

(Thus the commemoration of the name of one blessed man, made with his tunic and books, on that occasion brought saving and timely help to many districts and peoples.)[14]

Unfortunately, Adomnán does not tell us what the books were. There is no reason to believe that they were the books Columba is said to have copied out in II.8–9. Adomnán nowhere claims to have seen those books himself, and both of those miracles are said to have taken place in Ireland (at the River Boyne and in Leinster, respectively). The book in II.9 is said to belong to a certain Iógenán, a Pictish priest in Leinster.[15] While none of these observations rule out those books being the ones used by the monastic community here, there is no evidence in *VSC* to support the identification. There are, however, several other instances in *VSC* in which the saint is depicted engaged in scribal activity while at Iona itself.[16]

Neither does Adomnán tell us what parts of them were read out, but we have here an important and rare detailed account of how associative relics were actually used within the Columban *familia*. Whether or not the miraculous manuscripts described in II.8–9 were used in similar ways cannot now be known, but it would be surprising indeed if books which were written out by a major saint, and which were believed to have already demonstrated that they were invested with his sanctity, were not reverenced as relics in some way. It should be noted that another garment of Columba's is accorded miraculous properties in II.24, in which one of his monks, Findlugán, is protected from a spear thrust when wearing Columba's cowl. There is no indication that the cowl was later venerated or used as a relic, but the idea is clearly established that items of Columba's clothing are invested with something of his power.

Maugin and the *benedictio* (II.5)

Several healing miracles in *VSC* involve physical objects being blessed by Columba and then taken to afflicted individuals and used to heal them. We have already encountered one such object, the *petra salis* of II.7. Another is the consecrated bread that the saint instructs Silnán to take to Ireland, telling him to dip it in water and to sprinkle the water on people and animals afflicted by a plague.[17] There is also the story of Maugin, a holy woman living in Ireland, whom Columba prophetically knows has broken her hip in a fall. The way in which she is cured is again rather involved. Columba instructs another monk, this time Lugaid Lathir, to journey to see her:

> Quid plura? Lugaido obsecundanti et consequenter emigranti sanctus pineam tradit cum benedictione capsellam, dicens: 'Benedictio quae in hac capsellula contenetur quando ad Mauginam peruenies uisitandam in aquae uasculum intinguatur; eademquae benedictionis aqua super eius infundatur coxam. Et statim inuocato dei nomine coxale coniungetur os et densebitur; et sancta uirgo plenam recuperabit salutem.' Et hoc sanctus addit: 'En ego coram in huius capsae operculo numerum xxiii. annorum describo, quibus sacra uirgo in hac presenti post eandem salutem uictura est uita.'

> (Why say more? Lugaid obeyed, and was presently setting out, when the saint handed to him a little box of pine-wood with a blessing, saying: 'When you arrive to visit Maugin, let the blessing that is contained in this little box be dipped into a vessel of water, and let the same water of the blessing be poured over her hip; and as soon as the name of God has been invoked, the hip-bone will join and be knit together, and the virgin will regain complete health.' And the saint added this: 'See, in your presence I write on the lid of this box the number of the years, twenty-three, that the holy virgin will live in this present life, after this cure.')[18]

Again, the use of an object blessed by the saint, in conjunction with water, is used to work a cure. Once again, we might wish that Adomnán had provided us with more detail, in that he does not give us a clear description of the *benedictio* that was put in the box and to be dipped in water. Alan Orr Anderson and Marjorie Ogilvie Anderson suggest in a footnote that the object in question may have been a written prayer. While this is entirely plausible, it could equally have been just about any kind of small object.[19]

After all, in the course of Book II, bread and a stone (discussed below) are similarly used in conjunction with water, and in II.7 cures are effected with the *petra salis* (though not using water). These demonstrate that a quite wide range of objects could be considered valid media for carrying the miraculous power of the saint from one place to another. What was important was the fact of their being blessed by him to achieve a particular aim, not their particular forms or physical properties.

We also do not know whether the box, the *benedictio*, or both were still extant in Adomnán's time. If so, might Adomnán's description of the healing process reflect contemporary cult practice? Again, we cannot know for certain, but another chapter, II.33, provides a more detailed example.

Broichan and the white stone (II.33)

De Broichano mago ob ancellae retentionem infirmato, et pro eius liberatione sanato ('Concerning the magician Broichan, who was smitten with illness because he retained a female slave; and was cured, when he released her') is a complex chapter.[20] The saint demands that Broichan, a Pictish *magus* and the *nutricius* ('foster-father') of the king, Brude, release a Gaelic slave-woman as an act of *miseratione humanitatis* ('compassion of humanity'). When Broichan refuses to do so, Columba tells him that if he does not relent, he will die before Columba leaves the province. Leaving the king's household, he then comes to the River Ness:

> De quo uidelicet fluio lapidem attollens candidum, ad comites: 'Signate', ait, 'hunc candidum lapidem, per quem dominus in hoc gentili populo multas egrotorum perficiet santitates.'
>
> (From that river he took a white stone, and said to his companions: 'Mark this white stone. Through it the Lord will work many cures of the sick among this heathen people.')[21]

He then tells his companions that Broichan has been struck by an angel and is near death, struggling to breathe. He also tells them to await the arrival of two emissaries, sent to obtain healing for Broichan, who is now willing to release the girl. The emissaries duly arrive and relay the king's message to Columba:

> Quibus auditís legatorum uerbís sanctus binos de comitum numero ad regem cum lapide a sé benedicto mittit, dicens: 'Si in primís promiserit sé Broichanus famulam liberaturam, tum deinde hic lapillus intinguatur in aqua et síc eo bibat, et continuo salutem recuperabit. Si uero renuerit refragans absolui seruam, statim morietur.'
>
> Duo misi uerbo sancti obsequentes ad aulam deueniunt regiam, uerba uiri uenerabilis regi enarrantes. Quibus intimatis regi et nutricio eius Broichano ualde expauerunt. Eademque hora liberata famula santi legatis uiri adsignatur; lapis in aqua intingitur, mirumque in modum contra naturam lithus in aquís supernat quasi pomum uel nux, nec potuit sancti benedictio uiri submergi. De quo Broichanus natante bibens lapide statim a uicina rediit morte, intigramque carnis recuperauit salutem.

> (When he heard these words of the envoys, the saint sent two out of the number of his companions to the king, with the stone he had blessed, and said: 'If first Broichan promises that he will release the slave-girl, then let this small stone be dipped in water, and let him drink thereof, and he will at once recover health. But if he refuses, and opposes the slave-girl's release, he will immediately die.'
>
> The two emissaries went to the royal dwelling, in obedience to the saint's instructions, and repeated to the king the words of the venerable man. When these things had been made known to the king and to Broichan his foster-father, they were very much afraid. And in the same hour the slave-girl, set free, was handed over to the envoys of the holy man. The stone was dipped in water; and, in a marvellous manner, contrary to nature the stone floated in the water, as though it had been an apple or a nut. And the blessing of the holy man could not be submerged. After he had drunk of the floating stone, Broichan immediately returned from the brink of death, and recovered full bodily health.)[22]

Again, we can see the use of a blessed object along with water to effect a cure. Here the water must be drunk, a practice which we can also see in the much later book of the miracles of Dunstan of Canterbury by Eadmer of Canterbury (c. 1060–c. 1126). In that case Dunstan's staff, into which Dunstan had embedded a tooth of the Apostle Andrew, would be dipped into water. When sick people then drank the water, they would be cured of their illness.[23]

According to Adomnán the blessed object is described as having the additional miraculous property of floating in water despite being a stone. Aside from its being white, we have no further information available to identify what kind of stone it was. While we could posit a naturalistic interpretation and suggest that it was some kind of pumice, this does not seem likely as its floating would then not be at all miraculous. This is the only healing object in *VSC* which has a proviso attached: Broichan must release the woman or there will be no cure, no matter that Columba has somehow imbued the stone with miraculous power. The stone may carry within it the potential to effect a great miracle, but that potential is subordinate to the will of the saint. He must be obeyed or the stone's miraculous powers will not be of any use to Broichan. It may be that this points to a condition of cult practice: the favour of the saint is not available to all and sundry; there may be conditions attached. In II.46, for example, the Picts and the Irish in Britain are the only peoples spared from two outbreaks of plague that ravaged Britain and Europe as far south as Italy. Their preservation is explicitly stated to be a favour conferred by God because those peoples duly honour Columba's monasteries within their kingdoms. A second significant difference between this stone and the other blessed objects which effect cures is that we are told that it continued to be used to work more cures than the one for which it was originally sent. None of the other healing objects are explicitly said to be used for cures after their initial, immediate purpose is served.

> Talis uero lapis postea in thesauris regis reconditus multas in populo egritudinum sanitates, similiter in aqua natans intinctus, domino miserante efficit. Mirum dictu, ab his egrotis quorum uitae terminus superuenerat requisitus idem lapis nullo modo reperiri poterat. Sic

et in die obitus Brudei regis quaerebatur, nec tamen in eodem loco ubi fuerat prius reconditus inueniebatur.

(This stone was afterwards kept among the king's treasures. When it was dipped thus in water, and floated, it effected by the Lord's mercy many cures of diseases among the people. Strange to say, when it was sought by sick people whose time had come, the stone could by no means be found. So also it was looked for on the day of King Brude's death, and it was not found in the place where it had formerly been kept.)[24]

Here, we see a blessed healing object being kept and used in a context that was not only secular but pagan, with God mercifully allowing the pagan people to use the stone to cure their diseases, thus demonstrating his own power as manifested through his holy servant. Again, this raises a number of questions. Did the stone finally go missing permanently with Brude's death? If not, was it still used in Adomnán's day, a Columban relic among the Picts, who were Christians by then? Neither of these questions can be answered with any certainty. However, the fact that Adomnán does not claim to have seen the stone himself, when his high political position and diplomatic journeys would have given him the opportunity to do so if it was still extant, may suggest that it was no longer kept and used.

We can see, then, that different kinds of associative relics are used in *VSC*, for different ends and in different ways. The use of water in several of the healing miracles is notable, and though it is by no means unique to *VSC*, it is uncommonly prominent. By comparison, of the other three texts in the early group of Irish hagiographies (*Vita Sanctae Brigitae* by Cogitosus and the Patrician *vitae* by Muirchú and Tírechán), only the *Vita Sancti Patricii* by Muirchú has anything analogous, a miracle in which Patrick blesses some water to be sprinkled on a horse in order to cure its illness.[25] There is also an account of a proposed test of the Christian faith, with Patrick being told to throw his books into water, and that King Loíguire would adopt the Christian faith if the books were unharmed. The trial does not actually take place, however, as his druid objects on the basis that water

11

was one of Patrick's gods, and that the saint would thus have an unfair advantage in a water-based contest (Muirchú suggests that confusion arose because the druid had heard of Patrick baptising with water).[26] Similarly, the anonymous *Vita Sancti Cuthberti*, roughly contemporaneous with *VSC*, recounts a healing miracle in which Cuthbert provides blessed water for a sick nobleman, who is healed upon drinking it.[27] Robert Bartlett mentions several saints who blessed or touched water which was believed to have healing properties, but gives no instances at all of other objects being used in conjunction with water.[28] Flint notes that dust from a saint's tomb was sometimes mixed into water and drunk in order to effect cures, but of course this can only take place after the saint has died, and does not involve objects the saints themselves blessed or used when alive.[29] Since Adomnán can hardly be said to have been drawing on a hagiographical commonplace with his accounts of blessed objects being used in conjunction with water, then it seems highly likely that these stories represent genuine cult practice.

I suggest therefore that in these detailed descriptions of the use of associative relics, Adomnán may have been providing a sort of instruction manual for how to use relics to effect certain intended outcomes. If so, it is surely significant that these associative relics and blessed objects are all used in the text in instances in which the saint is not physically present. He blesses the objects and gives instructions for their use, but they are intended to be used by others. They retain the miraculous power with which he imbued them and are intended to function in his physical absence. It may be that Adomnán was recording not only the wonders worked by the saint or through his intercession in the past, but also suggesting how those who held Columban relics could use them in the future. What, for instance, would the monks at Iona do in the event of any drought in the future? They would still have had Columba's books and robe, and they also now had an account of how their predecessors, in the time of Adomnán the Illustrious, had used them when they needed their patron's aid. Would they not use the text in *VSC* as the basis for doing the same thing?

While there is a lack of direct evidence about the workings of many aspects of cult practice, I believe that it is useful to look at the text in this way attempted here to try to identify how certain narratives within the text might relate to such cult practices as the use of Columban relics. This approach opens up possibilities for thinking about what it was the *familia* actually did with this text, and what roles it had within the life of the community in which and for which it was produced.

Endnotes

This paper is based on work from my Ph.D. thesis (University of Edinburgh, 2018). I would like to thank my supervisors, Bill Aird, Abigail Burnyeat, and James E. Fraser, for their guidance and support, and also my viva examiners, Richard Sowerby and Alex Woolf, for their comments and advice. My research was funded by the Wolfson Foundation, with a Wolfson Postgraduate Scholarship in the Humanities, and I am grateful for their support.

1   Alan Orr Anderson and Marjorie Ogilvie Anderson (ed. and trans.), *Adomnán's Life of St Columba* (Oxford: Oxford University Press, 1991). All quotations of *VSC*, text and translation, are from this edition.
2   A fuller discussion is in Duncan Sneddon, 'Adomnán of Iona's *Vita Sancti Columbae*: a literary analysis' (unpublished doctoral thesis, University of Edinburgh, 2018), chapter 6.
3   Gilbert Márkus, 'Diormit: Columba's Right-Hand Man', *Innes Review* 60.2 (2009), pp. 164–69; Thomas Owen Clancy, 'Personal, Political, Pastoral: The Multiple Agenda of Adomnán's *Life of St Columba*', in Edward J. Cowan and Douglas Gifford (eds), *The Polar Twins* (Edinburgh: John Donald Press, 1999), pp. 39–60, at p. 47. There have also been studies of the Columban cult that focus on relics and 'cult accessories' as Ó Flionn calls them, such as bells and croziers and which have used *VSC* for references to the use of cult objects: Raghnall Ó Floinn, 'Insignia Columbae I', and Cormac Bourke, 'Insignia Columbae II': in Bourke (ed.), *Studies in the Cult of Saint Columba* (Dublin: Four Courts Press, 1997), pp. 136–61 and 162–83.
4   *VSC*, III.23, pp. 224–27; cf. Márkus.

5   Robert Bartlett, *Why Can the Dead Do Such Great Things?* (Princeton: Princeton University Press, 2013), pp. 244–50; Carmen Garcia Rodriguez, *El Culto De Los Santos En La España Romana Y Visigoda* (Madrid: Consejo Superior De Investigaciones Cientificas, Instituto Enrique Florez, 1966), p. 366.
6   Matthew 9. 20–22; Luke 8. 42b–48. More general statements of healings effected by sick people touching Christ's robe are also found in Matthew 14. 34–36 and Mark 6. 53–56.
7   Simon Yarrow, *Saints and their Communities: Miracle Stories in Twelfth-Century England* (Oxford: Oxford University Press, 2006), p. 199. Markús notes that Adomnán often describes Columba making the sign of the cross or some other such gesture when performing miracles.
8   *VSC*, II.7, pp. 104–05. The Andersons translate *petra salis* as 'rock-salt'. Sharpe prefers 'a block of salt', arguing that 'it is unlikely that rock-salt was mined in Ireland before the 19th century', and suggests rather the production of salt from sea water (Sharpe, *Life*, II.7, pp. 159–60, pp. 321–22, n. 228). While it should be noted that nothing in the story identifies its setting (or the provenance of the *petra salis*) as Irish, his translation seems to me to be more likely to be correct.
9   *VSC*, II.7.
10 *VSC*, II.9.
11 Bartlett, pp. 296–97, gives examples of relic processions; see also Rodriguez, pp. 368–69. Adomnán's own relics were taken to Ireland when his law was renewed in 727, and they were returned to Iona in 730. *AU, sub anno* 727.5; *sub anno* 730.3. For the use of relics in the swearing of oaths, see Julia M. H. Smith, 'Rulers and Relics, c. 750–c. 950. Treasure on Earth, Treasure in Heaven', *Past & Present*, Supplement 5 (2010), pp. 73–96, esp. pp. 79, 95. I am grateful to Rick Sowerby for the observation that it is seldom clear in early medieval sources whether the relics used in the swearing of oaths were corporeal or associative relics, as accounts usually say simply that oaths were sworn on the relics of a certain saint without elaboration on the nature of the relics themselves. However, since there were probably more associative than corporeal relics, it is likely that associative relics were used for this purpose (personal communication, 7 September 2016). Overbey notes that in early medieval Ireland, veneration of associative relics was apparently more common than veneration of corporeal relics: Karen Eileen Overbey, *Sacral Geographies: Saints, Shrines and Territory in Medieval Ireland* (Turnhout: Brepols, 2012), p. 5.
12 Valerie Flint, *The Rise of Magic in Early Medieval Europe* (Princeton: Princeton University Press, 1991), p. 187. Yarrow, p. 24, notes that a procession of the relics of Edmund the Martyr at his cult centre of Bury on 29 April 1095 was followed by rains that ended a drought and brought a good harvest later that year.
13 *VSC*, II.44.
14 *VSC*, II.44. Bartlett uses this miracle as his primary example of the use of clothing as an associative relic, and also cites examples from the cults of Martin of Tours and the Virgin Mary. He also notes that the veneration of books as associative relics was particularly prominent in Ireland: Bartlett, pp. 245–46, and 248.
15 *VSC*, II.8–9.
16 *VSC*, I.25; II.29; III.23. Only in the third of these is the text which Columba is writing identified: Psalm 34 (33 in the Vulgate).
17 *VSC*, II.4.

18 *VSC*, II.5.
19 Anderson and Anderson, *Life*, p. 103, n. 134: '*benedictio*: an object that has been blessed; but here possibly a written prayer. Cf. II.7.' Written blessings were sometimes worn as amulets, though there is no indication of that being the case here: Jacqueline Borsje, 'Celtic Spells and Counterspells', in Katja Ritari and Alexandra Bergholm (eds) *Understanding Celtic Religion: Revisiting the Pagan Past* (Cardiff: University of Wales Press, 2015), pp. 20–21. There is no mention in II.5 of Maugin or anybody else ever wearing the *benedictio*. However, Tuomi notes that, '[i]t is clear from studies done on textual amulets that they were not just worn physically without ever being read, seen, or otherwise used'. Ilona Tuomi, 'Parchment, Praxis and Performance of Charms in Early Medieval Ireland', *Incantatio* 3 (2013), p. 74. Don C. Skemer, although focusing mostly on later medieval material, writes, 'textual amulets could also be read, performed, displayed, visualized, and used interactively': *Binding Words: Textual Amulets in the Middle Ages* (University Park: Pennsylvania State University Press, 2006), p. 127. If we consider this *benedictio* to be an amulet, then the cure recorded here would certainly be an example of an amulet being 'used interactively'.
20 *VSC*, II.33. I am grateful to John Patrick Pazdziora for the suggestion that the white stone may be a reference to Revelation 2. 17. An important difference, of course, is that the white stone in *VSC* is a medium for conveying the saint's healing power, not a token of salvation.
21 Ibid.
22 Ibid.
23 Bernard J. Muir and Andrew J. Turner (ed. and trans.), 'Miracula S. Dunstani', in *Eadmer of Canterbury: Lives and Miracles of Saints Oda, Dunstan and Oswald* (Oxford: Oxford University Press, 2006), pp. 160–211, (pp. 208–11), § 29.
24 *VSC*, II.33.
25 Muirchú, *Vita Sancti Patricii*, I.24, pp. 108–11.
26 Muirchú, *Vita Sancti Patricii*, I.20, pp. 94–95.
27 Colgrave, *Anon. VSC*, IV.8, pp. 120–23.
28 Bartlett, p. 248.
29 Flint, p. 308.

2. 'Mater Sanctissima': Sanctity and Motherhood in the *Miracula* of St Margaret of Scotland

CLAIRE HARRILL

In the thirteenth-century *Miracula* of St Margaret of Scotland, which survives in a fifteenth-century manuscript of Dunfermline origin (Madrid, Biblioteca Real II 2097; henceforth in this article the Dunfermline Manuscript), Margaret engages in two specific and notable behaviours that are, at first glance, not typical of a female saint. She beats the sick and the demonic alike with a stick, and she leads an army into battle. Her *Life*, the *Vita Sanctæ Margaretæ Scotorum Reginæ* – which describes her marriage to Malcolm III, her pious acts in her lifetime, and her saintly death – forms something of a companion-piece to the *Miracula* as it appears in the Dunfermline Manuscript. Likewise in this *Vita*, as mother to eight children and active reformer of the Scottish Church, Margaret cannot be made to fit with Caroline Walker Bynum's long-established definition of a 'feminine sanctity' characterised primarily by mysticism, contemplation, and/or virgin martyrdom.[1] While Margaret's *Miracula* makes only brief explicit references to her earthly life, it does consistently frame her as a mother: mother to the nation of Scotland, mother to her monks at Dunfermline, and mother to her royal children. It is in this role of mother, furthermore, that Margaret leads her sons into battle, disciplines the wicked with beatings, and leads her community of monks – activities not heretofore associated with ideal medieval femininity by scholars.

But is the solution to conclude that Margaret is somehow 'masculine'? No, not least because the construction of gender along such prescriptive and binary lines is problematic regardless of whether we approach concepts of gender through a modern or medieval lens. In this chapter, I instead argue that Margaret embodies a specific kind of female sanctity: that of a '[m]ater sanctissima', a 'holy mother' in the mould of the Virgin Mary.[2] It is as a stern but loving parent that she appears with her corrective rod, and in a role like fellow mother-saints the Virgin and St Helena when she leads men into battle. The female models that shape Margaret's representation here speak to a more complex understanding of female saintly behaviour and identity, one that can indeed encompass power – including physical strength and military action – and authority, as long as this is under the aegis of motherhood.

Much has been said previously about the complex position of the queen, whose power and influence were poised between the public and the private.[3] This is especially intertwined in the business of producing royal heirs. However, little has yet been said about the representation of this power in literature, especially where motherhood extends beyond simply producing children to inherit the throne. In this chapter, I will demonstrate that, through motherhood, being female is not just compatible with the idea of leadership – and, specifically, leadership of men – but, in this instance, essential to it. It is Margaret's role as mother that makes her leadership on the battlefield and over a community of monks possible.

This is all the more striking given that Margaret's life was dominated by her roles as sister, wife, and mother, and the fact that she was held up after her death as a model to other women for being the perfect mother and queen.[4] St Margaret of Scotland (d. 1093) was many things during her lifetime: an Anglo-Saxon princess in exile, the sister of a failed rebel, a queen of the Scots, a pious ascetic, a stern but loving mother, a charitable patroness, and a church reformer.[5] Although many biographies of Margaret have been written, spanning from the years directly following her death to the present day, very little is known for sure about Margaret the woman herself, as distinct from the cult of Saint Margaret. What we do know about Margaret is that she was born sometime after 1045 and before 1050, either in Hungary or (possibly, but less likely) Kievan Rus'.[6] Her father, the aptly named Edward the Exile (d. 1057), was a son of Edmund Ironside (d. 1016), exiled by Cnut (d. 1035) on his assumption of the throne. All that is known of Margaret's mother's identity is her name – Agatha.

Margaret appears to have been raised in the Hungarian court until, in 1057, Edward the Exile was called back to England as a potential successor to the childless Edward the Confessor. Before long, either Edgar the Ætheling or the whole family became involved with an anti-Norman plot originating in the north of England and were forced to flee.⁷ Upon their arrival in Scotland, the family found refuge at the court of Malcolm III (d. 1093). Three years later, in 1070, Margaret married Malcolm, and though her *Vita* claims that Margaret married Malcolm only at the urging of her friends, the marriage was a successful one, producing eight children, six of whom were sons, and only ending when Malcolm and Margaret died within days of one another. Malcolm was killed in battle along with their eldest son, and Margaret died days afterwards, reportedly from a combination of the shock of this loss and the ravages of years of fasting and childbearing on her body.

He that spareth the rod hateth his son

In the *Vita Sanctæ Margaretæ Scotorum Reginæ*, ostensibly originally written by Margaret's own confessor, Turgot, prior of Durham, Margaret is held up as an ideal parent. But Margaret's model motherhood is somewhat different from what we consider to be good parenting now. In fact, the only aspect of her parental care that Turgot dwells on at any length is Margaret's loving strictness, specifically the fact that she beat her children so thoroughly that they became perfect examples of obedience and piety.

Turgot's *Vita* survives in two versions known after its manuscript witnesses as the 'Cotton' *Vita* and 'Dunfermline' *Vita*. The latter is an interpolated version of Turgot's original text, surviving alongside the *Miracula* in Madrid, Biblioteca Real II 2097. Both the 'Cotton' and 'Dunfermline' versions of Margaret's *Vitae* preserve the detail that Margaret raised her children according to the slightly modified scriptural message of Proverbs 13. 24. Turgot's twelfth-century *Vita* gives the original, '[qui] parcit virgæ odit filium', ('he who spares the rod hates the child'), but the 'Dunfermline' version adapts it slightly in order to emphasise the effect of parenting on the character of the child.⁸ The result of Margaret's parenting was that '[q]uo religioso matris studio, multos qui provectiores etate fuerant, morum honestate infants transcendebant' ('Through this religious zeal of the mother, the children transcended by their worthy character many who were more advanced in age').⁹ The 'evidence' for the success of this method of parenting is borne out in the pious successes of Margaret's two most powerful children, Matilda of Scotland (d. 1118), wife of Henry I, and David I (d. 1153) of Scotland, both of whom were briefly venerated as saints themselves. Matilda's own account of her childhood offers a different narrative: she complains not of her mother's violence, but of that of her aunt Christina, in whose care she was placed when she was sent to Wilton Abbey, where her aunt was a nun, to be educated. She complains of being forced to wear the veil, being slapped and insulted by Christina, and of tearing off her veil in rebellion and trampling it. This style of parenting that features strictness and corporal punishment seems to have played less well with its apparent recipients than with hagiographers.[10]

This parenting method is strongly evident too in Margaret's *Miracula*, in which she turns the rod as both corrective and cure on her spiritual children – her monks and those who come to Dunfermline looking for healing and guidance. We should, however, not understand this corporal punishment as a sign of Margaret's violence or aggression, but rather as a sign of her as dutiful and loving mother, and in particular a good parent to royal children. For example, in Miracle 2, Margaret cures a girl who cannot walk by threatening her, and the cure is explicitly formulated in terms of a fear of physical threat:

> Adueniens in hunc modum, regina uenerabilis oculos suos omni gemma splendidiores aduersum contractam erexit et baculum quem baiulabat in manu uelud minando subleuauit et adiungens dixit, 'Surge citissime, tibi dico, surge,' et admouens baculum uelud percussura tetigit eius latus sinistrum. Puella uero facta nimis de percussione eius timida et de comminacione ne amplius lederetur magis sollicita, quod per nouem annos in usu non habuit contra spem procedure temptauit.
>
> (The venerable queen, appearing in this way, lifted her eyes, more splendid than any jewel, towards the crippled girl and raised the staff she was carrying in her hand as if in threat. Then she said, 'Get up at once, I tell you, get up!', and, advancing the staff as if about to hit

her, she touched her left side. The girl was very frightened by the
blow and worried because of the threats that she might be harmed
more, so she attempted, without much hope, to walk, a thing she
had not been able to do for nine years.)[11]

Margaret appears 'minando' ('threatening') with her staff, which she wields 'uelud percussura' ('as if about to hit') the girl. However, she is not here to dispense violence, only healing. Instead of a blow comes a healing touch. Margaret may well be a healing mother, but she is also a frightening and authoritative mother, giving the order '[s]urge citissime' ('get up at once') and seeming to speak without sympathy which is, of course, by the logic of the miracle, proven to be the most effective form of healing. Margaret's stern words enable the girl to stand and walk, and the threat of the stick parallels the description of Margaret's treatment of her children in both versions of the *Vita* that we can identify with scripturally sanctioned parental discipline as a spur to good self-governance.

While this appears to be common practice for Margaret, this is, in fact, a very rare method of saintly healing and seems to be particular to Margaret herself.[12] There is scriptural precedent: this particular miracle is analogous to the account at John 5. 8–9 where Christ commands a paralysed man to pick up his bed and walk. The *baculum* or staff that Margaret bears in her hands furthermore recalls the comforting, and also potentially corrective, rod associated with God's role in the Bible as shepherd, as in Psalm 22. 4:

> Nam, etsi ambulavero in medio umbrae mortis, non timebo mala, quoniam tu mecum es. Virga tua, et baculus tuus, ipsa me consolata sunt.
>
> (For though I should walk in the midst of the shadow of death, I will fear no evils, for thou art with me. Thy rod and thy staff, they have comforted me.)[13]

In its function, the shepherd's rod represents both care and discipline; it is the tool which is – sometimes with force – used to control the sheep, while also acting as a symbol of the shepherd's guiding and protective role. This also implicitly positions Margaret as a leader of and carer for her people, and perhaps even in a role analogous to that of a priest, to her monks at Dunfermline.

Margaret's harsh words recall Christ's healing in the Bible, and her staff recalls the comforting and corrective role of God the shepherd, but she is nonetheless emphatically feminine in this passage, and specifically beautiful and queenly. Her eyes are like 'gemma' ('jewel[s]') and the awe and terror inspired by her simultaneously beautiful and frightening appearance in this miracle both stands as an outward sign of her formerly regal status, and recalls the terrifying beauty of the spouse in the Song of Songs:

> SPONSUS. Pulchra es, amica mea; suavis, et decora sicut Jerusalem; terribilis ut castrorum acies ordinata.
>
> (Thou art beautiful, O my love, sweet and comely as Jerusalem; terrible as an army set in array.) [14]

As with Margaret's violence here, the spouse's feminine beauty is juxtaposed with a simile whose referent is the masculine world of the battlefield – the 'castrorum acies ordinata' ('an army set in array'). As is also the case for Margaret, the spouse can be feminine *while* inspiring fear and being associated with violence. Respectively, sanctity and allegory make Margaret and the spouse more than simply naturalistic representations of motherhood; nor are we meant to understand either of them as masculine. We must thus nuance our idea of what could be contained within the medieval idea of the feminine. Furthermore, Margaret's likeness to the spouse offers a potential link with that most famous of holy mothers, the Virgin Mary. Bernard of Clairvaux (d. 1153), who post-dates Margaret but pre-dates her *Miracula*, saw the spouse in the Song of Songs as a figure for Mary, insofar as she combines both 'carnal and spiritual, the amalgam that was also Mary's special privilege' and that we might also see as the preserve of Margaret as mother, queen, and saint.[15]

Beating here manifests as a punishment and a spur to repentance rather than as an act of healing in a miracle that makes somewhat uncomfortable reading for the modern reader. In Miracle 33, a servant woman is forced to seek healing from Margaret after she engages in an affair with a man whose father has compelled him to marry a woman of his own social class. In this miracle, the woman remains passive throughout and yet is the single object of blame despite the fact that the man is an equal partner in the affair. The man 'ancillam domus paterne quamplurimum diligebat' ('was deeply in love with a servant from his father's house') and even though his father compels him to marry someone else, after his father dies, 'iuuenis ille, despecta propria uxore, predicte ancille furtiue adherebat' ('disdaining his own wife, became involved with the servant in secret').[16] It is nonetheless to the servant, not to the son, that the ghost of the father appears and 'manu sinistra iniecta per guttur arcius stringendo cepit, dexteraque caput ipsius circumquaque durissime uerberauit' ('grabbed her around the throat with his left hand, squeezing it tightly, while he beat her fiercely about the head with his right hand').[17] The dead father appears in a role analogous to Margaret herself, as a parent administering a corrective beating. However, instead of his son, the victim of this beating is the servant woman. Furthermore, this assault is not healing. It causes the woman to grow hideous tumours that make her deaf, mute, and blind until Margaret hears the prayers in her heart and comes to heal her with the words: 'O misera, peccatis tuis exigentibus talia pateris infortunia' ('Wretched woman, you are suffering this misfortune on account of your sins').[18] The sin belongs to the woman alone; her sins are inscribed on her sinful female body and Margaret's aid must be sought to remove them. The association here is clearly with parental discipline which is performed and endorsed by Margaret.

What is evident here, also, is that Margaret's beatings are performed in the service of healing, and her discipline is corrective rather than punitive. In this way, the beating administered by the non-saintly father of the man is only partially effective, acting as the spur that sends the woman in search of Margaret's healing, while Margaret's threats of violence are enough to heal. As a mother-figure, Margaret is able to embody both punishment and comfort, both threat and healing, whereas the father's role is partial: he can dispense violence, but he cannot mend it.

Margaret, mother to monks

Margaret acts also as spiritual mother, dispensing loving discipline to her monks. In Miracle 28, a doubting monk is violently beaten, which ultimately restores his faith:

> Monachus quidam, nomine Adam, diabolo instigante propriaque deuictus fragilitate, habebat in mente ad seculum redire. Quadam uero nocte, illo in stratu suo quiescente aduenit, ut sibi uidebatur, pater suus qui fuerat mortuus, illumque uerberauit tam acerrime quod fere exanimus factus, pre maxima sanguinis effusione uix ualebat flatum emitter, dicens illi, 'Cogitasti, miserrime, despecta tua professione quam Deo fecisti et famule sue sancta Margarite regine, ad seculum quasi canis ad uomitum redire, meque et omnes amicos tuos super hoc confundere? Ecce missus sum a ipsa domina tea a proposito tuo pessimo reuocare. Siquidem pro certo noueris quod si non uolueris resipiscere, multo grauiori te affligam flagellacione.'

> (A monk named Adam, at the instigation of the devil and conquered by his own weakness, had in mind to return to the secular world. One night while he lay in his bed, it seemed to him that his father, who was dead, came to him, and beat him so violently that he was almost unconscious and, because of the great loss of blood, scarcely able to breathe out. His father said to him, 'You wretch, are you thinking of disregarding the profession you made to God and his handmaid, St Margaret the queen, returning to the world like a dog to his vomit and bringing disgrace on me and all your kin because of it? Behold, I have been sent by that lady to call you back from your wicked resolve, for you should know for certain that, if you are not willing to come to your senses, I will beat you much more severely.')[19]

Although it is not Margaret herself administering the beating here, Margaret is once again associated with parental discipline. The father has been sent to his son *by* Margaret specifically to beat the fear of God (or, perhaps, the fear of Margaret) into his sinful child. Once again, the miracle dwells on physical threat, and parental corporal punishment is held up as an ideal corrective. It is also worth noting here that Margaret is referred to as 'Deo [...] famule', which Bartlett translates as 'handmaid' of God. This would suggest another link with the Virgin Mary, only the Magnificat Mary refers to herself as 'ancilla domini', not 'famule'. The choice of the word 'famule' – which is, in fact, the masculine form – for 'handmaid' rather than the more usual 'ancilla' is particularly striking here, given that Margaret's parallelism with the Virgin Mary is highlighted elsewhere in the *Miracula*. This may be simply a scribal variant; but while Bartlett translates it as 'handmaid', the *Dictionary of Medieval Latin from British Sources* lists only the feminine form 'famula' and gives as a possible definition '(w. *Christi* or similar) woman devoted to religion, usu. nun'. Margaret thus appears here as one professed to her own religious house. The choice in this instance of the unusual masculine form 'famule' may here serve not to alter in any way Margaret's gender, or her role as strict but loving mother, but rather link her more closely with her own foundation of monks.

In Miracle 36, Margaret uses her physical strength to defend rather than discipline a second doubting monk. In a vision, one of the monks sees Margaret beating back a pair of devilish-looking dogs:

> Erat quidam monachus in lecto suo nocte quadam quiescens, cui talis apparuit uisio. Vidit ipse duos canes, ingentes, horridos et hispidos, dormitorium intrare, quorum unus erat ruffus, alter uero nigerrimus. Ruffus autem, exiliens ipsumque strangulare cupiens, per guttur cepit et, ecce, adiutrix suorum propicia, sancta Margarita, uirgam manu tenens, ambos canes eadem uirga uerberando a dormitorio fugauit. Qua recendente, intrauerunt secundo predicti canes. Quibus iterum a sancta regina fugatis, recessit ipsa. Tertio sisquidem eisdem canibus dormitorum intrantibus, sanctissima Margarita, ut sibi uidebatur irata, minata est ut, si aliqui alicui suorum monachorum

inquietudinem aliquam inferre presumerent, sic illos uinculis strictos castigaret, ne alicui nocere ualerent de cetero. Monachus uero euigilans, que uiderat fratribus enarrauit.

(There was a monk, resting one night in his bed, who witnessed the following vision. He saw two huge wild and shaggy dogs enter the dormitory, one red, the other jet-black. The red one sprang up and seized him by the throat, desiring to strangle him, and behold, the gracious helper of her own, saint Margaret, carrying a staff in her hands, drove both dogs from the dormitory by beating them with that staff. When she went away, the dogs entered for a second time. They were again driven off by the holy queen, who then departed. When those dogs entered the dormitory for a third time, the most holy Margaret, who seemed to be angry, threatened that if anyone dared to cause any distress to any of her monks, she would punish them with such tight bonds that they would not be able to harm anyone ever again. The monk woke up and told the brethren what he had seen.)[20]

The violence and the colours of black and red are suggestive of the threats of hell for those who lose their faith, and the dogs serve to emblematise the threat of the outside world. Throughout the Bible, dogs embody the danger of worldliness and mistaken worship – as, for example, in the Book of Revelation, where they are identified with those who worship wrongly or who undertake mistaken devotion to worldly forces.[21] Just as with the monk in Miracle 28, part of the prescribed cure is a beating: 'uirgam manu tenens, ambos canes eadem uirga uerberando a dormitorio fugauit' ('carrying a staff in her hands, [St Margaret] drove both dogs from the dormitory by beating them with that staff').[22] As we have seen, this staff features frequently in Margaret's healing miracles, but here it is used defensively to fight off the dogs of worldliness and protect the spiritual resolve of the monk professed to her house. Just like the staff of the shepherd in the Bible, the staff is a tool of both protection and discipline, and that combination recalls the role of the parent – a role in which both mother and father have the same scope to enact both comfort and correction.

The question then arises of why the monks of Dunfermline would want to represent themselves as children, constantly subject to the protection and correction of a stern yet loving mother. In fact, the presence of Margaret as religious mother to her monks serves to construct them as religiously unassailable. They are protected by a saint who is herself constructed as analogous to the Virgin Mary – and in her staff-wielding moments, God himself. Her sometimes hands-on intervention in the spiritual lives of her monks acts as a guarantee of their correct religious practice. Furthermore, it suggests their own effective self-governance, since her discipline and regulation are internal and centre on her tomb in the abbey itself, forming an argument against outside interference in their practices.

Mothers on the battlefield

In defending the faithful from devilish animals, Margaret's behaviour seems to reflect that of the Virgin Mary. Wynkyn de Worde's *Myracles of Oure Lady*, in which the Virgin Mary protects a lay brother at a Carthusian house by threatening to beat the devil into submission, offers a fifteenth-century analogue for this episode:

> Sothely anone as this wycked spirite had straughte forth his honde to take hym, and with the hoke of yron al to tere hym as it is sayd above. Anone the gloryous moder of god, and truly the moder of mercy, in whome next after god he put all his hope vysybly came to hym and with a lyght yerd that she helde in her honde sayd to the wicked spyrytes, How durste ye wycked spyrytes come hether.[23]

This is not the only episode in which Margaret's motherly sainthood appears to be modelled on the Virgin Mary and another well-known mother-saint, St Helena. In Miracle 7, Margaret appears in what may initially appear to be a masculine role, protecting the Scots and Scotland from a Norwegian invasion and leading her sons into battle. However, close attention to both Margaret's representation as particular kind of mother-saint and analogy with the Virgin Mary and St Helena reveals that here, again, Margaret is inhabiting and exemplifying the role of an ideal mother.

In this miracle, a knight named John of Wemyss has a vision of Margaret in which she appears with her husband and sons dressed for battle and tells him she is leading them out to protect Scotland.[24] At this point, Wemyss asks the beautiful woman in the vision to identify herself and the armoured knights that accompany her, and she replies:

> Ego sum Margarita, Scotorum regina. Miles uero iste quem in manu duco meus erat maritus, nomine rex Malcolmus. Tres uero sequentes tres filii mei sunt et reges mecum in hac ecclesia iacentes.
>
> (I am Margaret, Queen of Scots. This knight I am leading by the hand was my husband, King Malcolm by name. The three following are my three sons, kings who lie with me in this church.)[25]

Margaret identifies herself by name, establishing the authenticity of the vision. Catherine Keene suggests that the author of the *Miracula* was aware of the Macrobian hierarchy of dreams and was careful to show Margaret authenticating dreams as distinct from waking visions, which were considered more reliable and authoritative than dreams.[26] She also identifies herself as queen of Scots with the present 'sum' whereas she designates Malcolm a past king of Scots with the past form 'erat'. As mother, Margaret appears here at the head of the family and as saint continues to act as queen of Scotland, while the husband and sons whose power was temporal are now part of Scotland's past. Speaking for both husband and sons, Margaret leads them by the hand. It is at this point that Margaret speaks to confirm the hereditary rights of her family, situating them within both royal responsibility and her own sanctity:

> Cui sancta regina: 'Cum istis ad Largys regnum defensura propero, victoriam actura de tiranno qui regnum meum suo nititur subiugare dominio. Nam michi hoc regnum a Deo accepi commendatum et heredibus meis inperpetuum.'

('I am hurrying with them to Largs', said the holy queen, 'to bring victory over that tyrant who is attempting to subject my kingdom to his power. For I have accepted this kingdom from God, and it is entrusted to me and my heirs forever.')[27]

Here, Margaret, as mother of both a dynasty of kings and the nation of Scots, articulates jointly her own and God's will that she act as national defender. It is not uncommon for male saints to act as defenders on the battlefield. Scottish saints Andrew and Columba are frequently invoked as battlefield saints, but the representation of female saints in this role is more unusual. Margaret would, however, be adopted as a national defender, one appropriate for the battlefield and inspiring to victory. She appeared on the banners carried into the Battle of Flodden in 1513, alongside St Andrew, who was heavily associated with defending in battle Scotland's right to independence.[28] Clearly, this idea of Margaret as defending mother had remained part of the national saintly iconography of Scotland.

Margaret is, furthermore, not the only defending mother-saint. Reading Margaret's *Vita* and *Miracula* alongside each other reveals that actions of reform and military leadership are options open to female saints who are mothers and queens, and Margaret is not here acting outside of accepted models for female saints. There are two existing mother-saints – the Virgin Mary and St Helena – who offer analogues for Margaret's behaviour. Margaret is explicitly compared to St Helena in her *Vita* in the description of her presence at the church reform councils:

> Quorum Conciliorum illud ceteris principalius fuisse constat, in quo sola cum paucissimis suorum contra perverse consuetudinis assertores, gladio spiritus, quod est verbum dei quando(que) biduo, queque triduo dimicabat.
>
> Crederes alteram ibi helenam residere, quia sicut illa quondam sentenciis scripturarum iudeos convicerat similiter nunc et hec regina illius gentis erroneos.

(Of these councils, the most important was one in which she alone with very few of her own contended for two and even three days against the proponents of perverse custom, with the sword of the spirit, which is the word of God.

You would have believed another Helen resided there, since just as she once had overcome the Jews with passage of Scripture, now similarly this queen overcame the errors of this people.)[29]

Furthermore, this is not the only parallel between Margaret and Helena. As well as having an association with church reform and a reputation for overcoming those in error through God's guidance, St Helena, the mother of the Emperor Constantine, was credited with bringing Christianity to the Jews in Jerusalem, and was associated with the True Cross, which, in Cynewulf's poem *Elene*, she finds along with the nails of the crucifixion in Jerusalem.[30] Margaret herself famously owned a piece of the true cross known as the 'Black Rood', which she brought with her to Scotland in a richly decorated reliquary. In Cynewulf's poem, St Helena is referred to as a 'guðcwene' ('battle-queen'), leading the army of her son the emperor Constantine to a secular and spiritual victory.[31] All three holy mothers – Margaret, Helena, and the Virgin Mary – take on a martial role and subdue their enemies by force. They lead men and protect the righteous, taking on a kind of divinely sanctioned militarised motherhood. Thus, when we see Margaret's actions here at Largs in their wider context, it is clear that she is part of a tradition of mother-saints militant.

Likewise, continental representations of the Virgin Mary show her as a military defender. For example, in Spain in the eleventh and twelfth centuries, the Virgin Mary came to be seen as a kind of patron of the Christian reconquest of the Iberian Peninsula, and her cult came to be associated with victory over one's enemies, particularly those who were non-Christian.[32] This may have stemmed from the account of the siege of Constantinople in 626. The patriarch of the city, Sergios I, placed an image of the Virgin Mary over the city's Golden Gate, and reportedly warned the besiegers that the Virgin would defeat them.[33] The evidence here is more limited than in the case of St Helena, but is nonetheless suggestive, once again, of the established role of the mother-defender on the battlefield. When in the Battle of Largs Miracle Margaret operates as a kind of peculiarly Scottish Virgin Mary, she is expressing both God's divine protection of Scottish sovereignty and the religious orthodoxy of the Scottish people: if Mary defends only good Christians, the implication is that if Margaret appears here in a similar role, then the Scots must be good Christians.

In the popular imagination, medieval gender roles manifest as a dichotomy that splits down the line of who fought: men could fight, and women were mothers. Margaret – and her analogues St Helena and the Virgin Mary – stand as evidence that the medieval conception of gender roles was much more complex and nuanced than this, and in fact it was *as* mothers that these women could appear on the battlefield as leaders in these texts. We have no record of Margaret appearing on the battlefield when she lived, but after her death as a saint she does important ideological work to defend Scotland in these texts; they form an argument for Scotland's divinely sanctioned independence, which is inextricably tied to the physical site of her tomb at Dunfermline, and the royal mausoleum there.[34]

Conclusion

Margaret, then, appears throughout her *Vita* and *Miracula* as an ideal mother: she shows loving discipline to her children, she protects her monks and her nation as their allegorical mother, and she provides the pious example and spiritual guidance expected of a mother. This prompts the question of why this is significant. In her *Vita*, Margaret is a model medieval mother, even if those ideals have evolved so far as to be entirely opposite in the present day, especially as regards corporal punishment. The idea that Margaret and her behaviour might be venerated comes as no surprise: she was a queen and a mother of kings. But exactly which behaviours are venerated in one whose saintliness rests so heavily on their femaleness – their motherhood – is instructive as to the complex relationship between gender, motherhood, and power in the Middle Ages. Specifically, it stands as proof that, in the role of mother, there was a distinct space in the medieval imagination for a woman acting as a leader of men – even on the battlefield and in an abbey of monks, spaces often considered the sole preserve of male leaders.

These two important strands of Margaret's saintliness appear to have endured. The 1661 printed adaptation of Turgot's *Vita* of Margaret presents itself as a kind of parenting manual and Margaret as an ideal mother and educator of children. Margaret also seems to have continued to be associated with a hope for Scottish victory in battle into the sixteenth century, when she appeared on banners carried into the battle by the Scottish army at the Battle of Flodden in 1513. As mother of kings and saintly protector, this Anglo-Saxon queen became cemented in the Scottish literary imagination as a kind of particularly Scottish Virgin Mary, as a mother-saint fiercely protecting her children, both subjects and descendants.

There is not necessarily so hard a line between 'masculine' and 'feminine' sanctity as has been heretofore argued. Apart from fasting to death, Margaret does not fit at all with ideas of 'feminine' sanctity, and yet she is, throughout her *Vita* and *Miracula*, a perfect mother and therefore – by extension – a perfect woman. Part of this is indeed to do with her role as queen, and the need to represent her as a perfect teacher of perfect children. These children who had to fight to take or keep their thrones then found hagiographies that underlined their own pious upbringing quite useful. It also speaks to the difficulty of combining the humbleness and self-denial required of a saint with the need to articulate the dignity and power of a royal line.

The Virgin Mary offers the perfect vehicle for this, being a self-sacrificing Queen of Heaven who nonetheless has a power second only to God himself. To be a Holy Mother, as Margaret is here, is to approach as nearly as possible the authority of God and is the one role in which a woman can surpass even her husband – a king – in authority, though this is, of course, only permissible after death and in the role of a saint. This chapter has, therefore, offered a new framework for understanding the nuanced ways in which saints, especially royal saints, negotiate between the gender inferiority of women and the unassailability of royal and religious power. I have dispelled the idea that motherhood is necessarily domestic and self-sacrificing in the medieval imagination, even for a saint whose denial of her physical body led to her death. Motherhood is not only compatible with power; it can be a route to it, and we can view with scepticism any claim that figures such as Margaret were only significant as queens and mothers insofar as they raised men who would go on to become kings.[35] Medieval femininity does not necessitate passivity or abjuration of the world, so long as one is also a mother.

Endnotes

1 Caroline Walker Bynum, *Holy Feast and Holy Fast: The Religious Significance of Food to Medieval Women* (Berkeley: University of California Press, 1987), p. 26.
2 Quotation from Miracle 13 of the *Miracula* of St Margaret of Scotland, in *The Miracles of St Æbbe of Coldingham and St Margaret of Scotland*, ed. and trans. Robert Bartlett (Oxford: Clarendon Press, 2003), pp. 104–05. All subsequent references to the *Miracula* are to this edition.
3 See in particular Theresa Earenfight, *Queenship in Medieval Europe* (New York: Palgrave Macmillan, 2013), John Carmi Parsons, *Medieval Queenship* (Stroud: Sutton, 1994), Pauline Stafford, *Queen Emma and Queen Edith: Queenship and Women's Power in Eleventh-Century England* (Oxford: Blackwell, 1997; paperback 2001), Fiona Downie, *She is But a Woman: Queenship in Scotland, 1424–1463* (Edinburgh: John Donald Publishers, 2006) and Lois L. Huneycutt, *Matilda of Scotland: A Study in Medieval Queenship* (Woodbridge: The Boydell Press, 2003).
4 Cf. Lois L. Huneycutt, 'The Idea of the Perfect Princess: The Life of St Margaret in the Reign of Matilda II (1100–1118)', *Anglo-Norman Studies* 12 (1989), pp. 81–97.
5 Biographical information on St Margaret's life is taken from Catherine Keene's 2013 biography of Margaret, *Saint Margaret, Queen of the Scots: A Life in Perspective* (New York: Palgrave Macmillan, 2013), and Margaret's entry in the *ODNB*, G. W. S. Barrow, 'Margaret [St Margaret] (d. 1093)' (accessed 25 October 2020). There are also several popular biographies of Margaret, which include: Samuel Cowan, *Life of the Princess Margaret, Queen of Scotland, 1070–1093* (Newcastle-on-Tyne: Mawson, Swan & Morgan Limited, 1911); T. Ratcliffe Barnett, *Margaret of Scotland: Queen and Saint; Her Influence on the Early Church in Scotland* (Edinburgh: Oliver and Boyd, 1926); A. M. D. Henderson-Howat, *Royal Pearl: The Life and Times of Margaret Queen of Scotland* (London: SPCK, 1948); Alan J. Wilson, *St Margaret: Queen of Scotland* (Edinburgh: John Donald, 1993, repr. 2001).

6   Kievan Rus' covered an area of land surrounding Kyiv that is now split between Russia, Ukraine, and Belarus.
7   Cf. Nicholas Hooper, 'Edgar the Ætheling: Anglo-Saxon Prince, Rebel and Crusader', *Anglo-Saxon England* 14 (1985), pp. 197–214; Donald Henson, *The English Elite in 1066: Gone but not forgotten* (Hockwood-cum-Wilton: Anglo-Saxon Books, 2001); Pauline Stafford, 'Chronicle D, 1067 and Women: Gendering Conquest in Eleventh-century England', in *Anglo-Saxons: Studies Presented to Cyril Roy Hart*, ed. Simon Keynes and Alfred P. Smyth (Dublin: Four Courts Press, 2006), pp. 208–23.
8   The 'Cotton' *Vita* gives '[qui] parcit virgæ odit filium' ('[he who] spares the rod hates the child'), p. 240.
9   The Dunfermline *Vita*, in *Saint Margaret, Queen of the Scots: A Life in Perspective*, ed. and trans. Catherine Keene (New York: Palgrave Macmillan, 2013), pp. 135–221 (p. 182).
10 For Matilda's account see Lois Huneycutt, 'Intercession and the High-Medieval Queen: The Esther Topos', in *The Power of the Weak: Studies on Medieval Women*, ed. Jennifer Carpenter and Sally-Beth MacLean (Urbana and Chicago: University of Illinois Press, 1995), pp. 126–46 (p. 135).
11 *Miracula*, pp. 76–77.
12 I am grateful to Ruth Salter at the University of Reading for discussing this with me.
13 Also known as Psalm 23. The numbering here is following the Douay-Rheims and Latin Vulgate Bible.
14 Canticles 6. 3 (Douay-Rheims–Latin Vulgate). All subsequent references are to this version.
15 Miri Rubin, *Mother of God: A History of the Virgin Mary* (London: Penguin, 2010), p. 151.
16 *Miracula*, pp. 128–29.
17 Ibid.
18 Ibid., pp. 130–31.
19 Ibid., pp. 122–25.
20 Ibid., pp. 132–35.
21 'Foris canes, et venefici, et impudici, et homicidae, et idolis servientes, et omnis qui amat et facit mendacium' ('Without are dogs, and sorcerers, and unchaste, and murderers, and servers of idols, and every one that loveth and maketh a lie'), Revelation 22. 15, DR–LV Bible.
22 *Miracula*, pp. 132–33.
23 The full account of this episode can be found in Wynkyn de Worde, *The Myracles of Oure Lady*, ed. Peter Whiteford (Heidelberg: Carl Winter, 1990), pp. 60–62.
24 This provides yet another link to the specific place and foundation over which Margaret was patron and in which this collection seems to have been compiled. Bartlett notes that Wemyss is in Fife and the church was appropriated to Dunfermline Abbey (p. 87, note 16). There is further evidence of a family connection that continued over time. In the early fourteenth century (c. 1319), Sir Michael Wemyss was named as one of the arbiters on the side of Dunfermline Abbey in a dispute between the monks of Dunfermline and the tenants of Leslie as to their respective borders. However, when the arbiters met in 1319–20 at Newbattle, Michael Wemyss was not among them, perhaps because he had died by that date. Sir James Balfour Paul, *The Scots Peerage*, 9 vols (Edinburgh: David Douglas, 1911), VIII, p. 478.

25 *Miracula*, pp. 88–89.
26 Keene, 'Envisioning a Saint', p. 69.
27 *Miracula*, pp. 88–89.
28 Tom Turpie, *Kind Neighbours: Scottish Saints and Society in the Later Middle Ages* (Leiden: Brill, 2015), p. 34.
29 Dunfermline *Vita*, p. 189.
30 Cynewulf, 'Elene', in *The Old English Elene, Phoenix and Physiologus*, ed. Albert Stanburrough Cook (New Haven: Yale University Press, 1919), pp. 3–46.
31 'Elene', in *The Old English Elene* above, line 331 (translation my own).
32 Linda B. Hall, *Mary, Mother and Warrior: The Virgin in Spain and the Americas* (Austin: University of Texas Press, 2004), pp. 18–20.
33 Hall, *Mother and Warrior*, p. 20.
34 I discuss this in more detail in: Claire Harrill, 'The Proper Place for a Queen? St Margaret of Scotland at Dunfermline Abbey' in *Gender and Mobility in Scotland and Abroad*, ed. S. Dye, E. Ewan and A. Glaze (Guelph: Guelph Series in Scottish Studies, 2018), pp. 169–82.
35 A claim about Margaret made by both J. H. S. Burleigh in *A Church History of Scotland* (London: Oxford University Press, 1960), p. 43–44, and David Baker in '"A Nursery of Saints": St Margaret of Scotland Reconsidered', in *Medieval Women*, ed. Derek Baker (Oxford: Blackwell, 1978), pp. 119–41.

3. Liturgy and Literature in Late Medieval Scotland: Continuity and Discontinuity

DAVID JASPER

The radical division between academic studies in literature and liturgical scholarship has to a large extent served to conceal a significant element in the life of the Church in Scotland in the later Middle Ages, and the making of the *Scottish Prayer Book* of 1637 that was to become so important, not so much in its own time, but in the Scottish Episcopal Church of the eighteenth and nineteenth centuries. What C. S. Lewis called the 'sudden extinction of a poetical literature which […] seemed "so fair, so fresshe, so liklie to endure"'[1] after John Knox and the Reformation in Scotland does nothing to obscure the brilliance of Middle Scots poetry that reached its height at the court of James IV (1473–1513) in the writings of such poets as the priest William Dunbar (c. 1460–1513/30) and Walter Kennedy (c. 1455–c. 1508), a king's clerk and probably therefore also in holy orders. Long before its last days at the beginning of the sixteenth century, Middle Scots literature had been, to a large extent, the work of churchmen,[2] to a great extent vanishing and then almost eradicated by puritan iconoclasm after the formal beginning of the Scottish Reformation on 17 August 1560. Then, the Scots Parliament confirmed the 'Confession of Faith professed and believed by the Protestants within the realm of Scotland'.[3] On the whole, literary studies in the past have very rarely mentioned the profoundly liturgical and ecclesial context within which such literature is written.[4] Liturgists, on the other hand, virtually ignore the context of sophisticated vernacular poetry in the prayer and devotional life of late medieval Scotland (as in England) and its importance within the Latin liturgy of the later Middle Ages before the Reformation of the early sixteenth century.[5] In Scotland, as in England, as I have argued in an earlier book:

> [T]here is an extraordinary continuity in liturgical vernacularity between the Middle Ages and its literature, and the English *Books*

of Common Prayer of the sixteenth century. English prayer books had long been part of lay devotion as well as that of many of the clergy who were not necessarily well-educated in Latin, and the liturgical language that came to fruition in the Renaissance genius of Thomas Cranmer and others [...] was deeply embedded in a vibrant literary tradition that was inextricably linked to the Latin liturgy of the Church.[6]

Certainly, the Scottish Reformation took a very different and more radical course from the Reformation in England as it gave birth to the national Church of England. But if there was deep discontinuity both in literature and liturgy after 1560, there was also a profound continuity that is sustained above all in the *Scottish Prayer Book* of 1637 (with its high degree of dependence upon Cranmer's *Prayer Book* of 1549, though in a particularly Scottish manner, as we shall see). This book, short-lived in its own time, was of enormous importance not only for the survival of the Scottish Episcopal Church in the eighteenth and nineteenth centuries, but more broadly in High Church Anglican liturgical practice and debates in the late nineteenth and early twentieth centuries.[7]

Scots in the fifteenth century tended to believe that the form of worship used in secular cathedrals and parish churches in Scotland had been forcibly imposed on them by the English King Edward I when he overran Scotland in 1296. It was not so much the form of worship that they objected to, but the manner of its imposition from a foreign power. Of King Edward, the Scottish poet 'Blind' Harry (c. 1440–c. 1492) wrote:

> The Roman bukis at than was in Scotland
> He gart be brocht to scham quhar thai thaim fand
> And but radem thai brynt thaim thar ilkan
> Salysbery oys our clerkis than has tan.[8]

The few surviving liturgical books from late medieval Scotland indicate the general and broad Scottish use of the English Sarum Rite, based upon 'Salisbury use', with some evidence of broader Continental elements imported from such dioceses as Cologne and Rouen, revisions and elements that were indicative of continuing Anglophobia in Scotland. Among Scottish clergy in the fifteenth century nationalism was, on the one hand, culturally constructive in as much as it helped to promote the founding of Scotland's first three universities at St Andrews, Glasgow, and Aberdeen, but it also resulted in a liturgical calendar that was over-cluttered with feasts of Scottish saints. By the beginning of the sixteenth century, liturgical practice in Scotland, though still ultimately rooted in the Sarum rite, added to the calendar some ninety feasts, many reflective of Celtic origins, and which, with Continental contributions, comprised the particular 'use of Scotland'.[9] In addition, early sixteenth-century 'makars' such as Dunbar and Kennedy are clearly indicative of a tradition of vernacular piety that was also matched in England and found in such poets as William Langland and the prolific monk John Lydgate, the writings of the latter certainly having a considerable influence on the Scottish poets.

The 'Scottish use' is well illustrated in the early sixteenth century by such liturgical texts as the Aberdeen Breviary. These were innovative in their time, not least as liturgical expressions, distinct from the more ancient English Sarum use, of a Scottish nationalism by the inclusion of such Scottish saints as Kentigern, Machar, and Margaret of Scotland. Jane Geddes, indeed, describes the Aberdeen Breviary as nothing short of an expression of 'religious patriotism' in Scotland.[10] But by the 1540s, in the final waning of the Middle Ages, some reformers in Scotland were prepared to welcome the vernacular English *Prayer Book* of 1549, a masterpiece of Cranmerian liturgical composition in English rooted in the Sarum rite and ancient liturgies as well as traditions of vernacular piety. But within less than twenty years, this English Book was supplanted by the Scottish *Book of Common Order*, or 'Knox's Liturgy', which drew upon the experience of John Knox's earlier ministry in Geneva and was prescribed for use by the Scottish General Assembly in 1562. It was while he was in Geneva that Knox published a number of tracts on Scotland and against England, notably *The First Blast of the Trumpet against the Monstrous Regiment of Women* (1558), a diatribe against Mary Tudor and government by women, which earned him the hostility of Queen Elizabeth who consequently refused him passage through

England on his return to Scotland in 1559. Nevertheless, it is important to recognise that this Scottish Book did contain a substantial amount of material drawn verbatim from Cranmer's first *Prayer Book*.[11] This included borrowings from Cranmer's own Prayer of Humble Access, provision for the use of the Lord's Prayer, the Apostle's Creed, and the Doxology, as well as metrical versions of the *Veni Creator*, the Evensong canticles of the *Nunc Dimittis* and the *Magnificat* and a rubric that acknowledged kneeling as the proper position for prayer. It was a book that, in many ways, looked backwards as much as it looked forwards.

It is important to remember that the approval of the *Westminster Directory for Public Worship* (February 1645) was still, at this time, almost a hundred years away. The Scottish reformers of the mid-sixteenth century met strong resistance from a profoundly conservative populace whose ancient devotion to the rhythm of the Christian liturgical year was both culturally deep and connected to the provision of holidays through the observance of its numerous religious festivals. This pattern of the liturgical year is reflected in secular poetry which, in turn, as we shall see in the poems of William Dunbar, reflects back upon the liturgical language of the Church. Indeed, throughout the course of the radical Reformation in Scotland, dictated in very large part by political events and energy of Scottish nationalism, there yet remained an older, deep religious traditionalism within literature and liturgy. This was still felt much later in the making of the 1637 *Scottish Prayer Book*, a work that is often wrongly credited with too much of the influence of the much later English Archbishop of Canterbury, William Laud (1573-1645). It was, in fact, a thoroughly Scottish book and with more ancient cultural and religious roots. On the matter of the supposedly English and Laudian nature of 1637, Gordon Donaldson, author of the still standard work *The Making of the Scottish Prayer of 1637* (1954), is quite clear:

> If the book be examined in the light of English and Scottish criticism of the English Book of Common Prayer, it will appear that the compilers of the Scottish book took great pains to meet some of the objections and that a serious attempt was made to incorporate

existing Scottish usages or preferences and to conciliate Scottish prejudices.[12]

The substance of this claim will be given greater attention later in this chapter, but first we must turn in more detail to the 'makars' of the reign of James IV of Scotland and their effect upon the later vernacular liturgy of Scotland that stand apart from the traditions of Presbyterian worship. In England in the late medieval tradition of vernacular worship in *Primers* (primers were prayer books, usually in English, for lay people based on the much more elaborate monastic 'hours')[13] and other books of lay devotion, popular religious verse in English and the vernacular writings of church poets like John Lydgate (who was, in fact, far better known in Scotland than Geoffrey Chaucer, c. 1340–1400) in works like the *Merita Missae* (a layperson's guide to the Mass dating from about 1470)[14] had a profound and largely unacknowledged effect on Archbishop Cranmer's 1549 *Prayer Book*. Both before and after the English Reformation, the distinction between liturgical, religious, and secular verse was much more fluid than is generally acknowledged.

So too in Scotland the Latin Mass and its usage not only affected secular devotion and verse, but the opposite was also the case. As the vernacular replaced, or more often stood alongside, Latin in late medieval worship as that stood on the hinge of the Reformation, so the court poets of James IV influenced the tradition of vernacular worship in Scotland that found its final and in some ways greatest formal expression in the *Prayer Book* of 1637. This was short-lived but still profoundly influential on the Episcopal tradition that was sustained by the non-jurors, and which survives up to the present day in the worship of the Scottish Episcopal Church.

Apart from the sophisticated and ornate court poetry of makars like William Dunbar, there was also a tradition of simpler vernacular religious verse, much of it simply translations from Latin prayers – the *Pater Noster* or the *Ave Maria* – which had a clear and practical purpose. Reciting such prayers carried with it an indulgence, that is a remission from time in punishment in the next life.[15] Thus we find a simple version of the *Nunc*

Dimittis in the collection known as the *Gude and Godlie Ballatis*, ascribed to John, James, and Robert Wedderburn in the middle years of the sixteenth century:

> Lord lat thy seruand now depart,
> In glaidnes, rest and peace:
> I am reioysit at my hart,
> To sé his godlie face,
> Quhome faithfullie thow promeist me,
> Christ Jesus, King of grace.
>
> This present dede salbe full sweit,
> And in to sleip sall changeit be:
> To rest, syne ryis, bot euer my Spreit
> Sall leue, and be alwyse with thé,
> Throw Faith in Christ, my onlie traist,
> Quhome presentlie I sé.[16]

But such essentially simple verse is very different from the highly literary and liturgical poetry of Dunbar, some of which was quite possibly written for quasi-liturgical public performance in the Chapel Royal of James IV in Stirling Castle, an institution designed to match in splendour the English royal chapel at Windsor Castle. Of Dunbar, C. S. Lewis writes that 'he does not deal much in solitary devotional feeling, like the Metaphysicals or the Victorians; he is public and liturgical'.[17] Here, for example, is a part of Dunbar's sophisticated parody of Matins in the Office for the Dead (*'Dirige'*) which contrasts the austere purgatory of the Franciscans with the heavenly joys of the royal court in Edinburgh (Liturgical parodies were not uncommon in the later Middle Ages).[18]

> **Lectio prima**
> The Fader, the Sone, and the Haly Gaist,
> The mirthful Mary, virgene chaist,
> Of angellis all the ordouris nyne,

And all the hevinly court devyne,
Sone bring yow fra the pyne and wo
Of Strivilling, every court manis fo,
Agane to Edinburghis joy and blis,
Quhair wirschep, welth, and weilfaris,
Pley, pleasance, and eik honesty:
Say ye amen for cherite.[19]

Indeed, Dunbar's poetry is saturated through and through with the liturgy and offices of the late medieval Church. His great macaronic poem on the nativity, '*Rorate celi desuper*', draws on the Latin for the liturgy of Christmas Eve and Christmas Day, derived from Isaiah 45. 8 and 9. 6, with echoes also of the *Ave Maria*.[20] Perhaps his best known poem, also macaronic, is on the harrowing of hell and the resurrection, 'Done is a battell on the dragon blak', and ends each verse with Latin words from the first versicle for matins on Easter Day: '*Surrexit dominus de sepulchro*.'[21] At the same time this is a poem written in the medieval romance tradition of chivalric knights and courtly love, a tradition shared by such Scottish court poets as Robert Henryson (c. 1420–c. 1490) and Gavin Douglas (c. 1474–1522) who, with James I (1394–1437) himself, are sometimes known as the 'Scottish Chaucerians'.[22] But in fact, Dunbar's resurrection poem is much more closely allied with William Langland's (c. 1325–c. 1390) deeply theological *Piers Plowman* and to the Mystery play tradition than to the more 'secular' poetry of Geoffrey Chaucer. (William Langland was quite possibly a priest. He has sometimes been identified with William Rokele, a parish priest in East Anglia.)

References to the liturgical offices of the Church are to be found everywhere in Dunbar's poetry. The poem 'I that in heill we and gladnes', traditionally known as the 'Lament for the Makars', ends each verse with the Latin refrain '*Timor mortis conturbat me*', from the Office for the Dead, a line which is used also by Lydgate in his poem 'So I lay this other night'.[23] But there are also signs of later Protestant editing of Dunbar's work that seeks to eliminate these traditional liturgical elements and references. The dream poem, 'Doverrit with dreme, devising in my slummer', ascribed to Dunbar in the Bannatyne MS, but to the pen of Sir James Inglis, 'clerk of the kingis closet', in the Maitland Folio MS, is a poem on corruption in society and Church.[24] It has a reference to the traditional Office for the Dead, 'the deirgey', and the rosary (line 14, Maitland), but is emended to 'the Psalme and the Testament' (Bannatyne) – a Protestant revision that loses entirely the internal rhymes and structure of Dunbar's original.

William Dunbar, then, was a thoroughly late-medieval courtier as well as a cleric and a man of the pre-Reformation Church in Scotland. His writing is saturated in the 'apocrypha, liturgy and legend, which [add] a characteristic medieval enrichment' to his poetry.[25] However, the movement in poetry *from* the liturgical was not merely one way. The poetry also affected the liturgy as it began to emerge from its purely Latin form. Dunbar's deep knowledge of the classical traditions of rhetoric, his linguistic compression, and his use of common phrases helped to establish a tradition of vernacular prayer and devotion that had a clear effect on the *Book of Common Order* in a Scotland (as in England) that was still deeply attached to traditional religious observance and, at least in the earlier sixteenth century, was 'a likely market for English Primers and psalters'.[26] For example, Dunbar's lyric poem 'Now culit is dame Venus brand' makes a contrast between carnal and spiritual love that is a commonplace of medieval courtly literature, found also, for example, at the conclusion of Chaucer's *Troilus and Criseyde* and of Gower's *Confessio Amantis*:

> Now culit is dame Venus brand.
> Trew kuvis fyre is ay kindilland
> And I begyn to understand
> In feynit luve quhat foly bene;
> Now cumis aige quhair yewth hes bene
> And trew luve rysis fro the splene.
>
> [...]
>
> Is non but grace of God, iwis,
> That can in yewth considdir this;
> This fals dissavand warldis blis

> So gydis man in flouris grene;
> Now cumis aige quhair yewth hes bene
> And trew luve rysis fro the splene.[27]

In the same way in England, not only the liturgy of the Sarum rite but also the tradition of vernacular devotion perceived in late medieval poetry and the various versions of the *Primer* had a profound effect on Thomas Cranmer and the English forms of the 1549 *Book of Common Prayer*. Dunbar's Middle Scots poems helped to develop a language that would deeply resonate with the liturgy of a later Protestant Episcopalian Scotland, and that the Catholic Dunbar himself would hardly have recognised. And it was even more than simply a matter of language. In Dunbar's visions of the incarnation and the Passion, events in time and space assume cosmic significance in the here and now. Dunbar's dreamer himself feels the very shaking of the earthquake that accompanies the death of Christ: 'For grit terror of Chrystis deid / The erde did trymmill quhair I lay'.[28] Such an essentially liturgical sense of the presence here and now of the eternal in the time of this mortal life takes us directly to the linking of heaven and earth in the *Sursum Corda* of the 1549 Cranmerian liturgy. Therein, 'it is very mete, righte, and our bounden dutie that wee shoulde at all tymes, and in all places, geve thankes to thee', joining in our singing on earth with angels and archangels in the singing of the heavenly choirs as we all voice at once the earthly and heavenly *Sanctus*.[29]

Unlike Dunbar, Robert Henryson was not ordained. It seems most likely that he was a schoolmaster in Dunfermline, connected perhaps to Dunfermline Abbey. Closer in poetic tone to Chaucer than Dunbar, Henryson is still also thoroughly medieval in ethos while yet acknowledging the existence of corruption and ills in both Church and society. There is in Henryson's poetry a sense of a world that is beginning to change and face reform, though not quite yet. Edwin Muir wrote of him:

> He lived near the end of a great age of settlement, religious, intellectual, and social; and agreement had been reached regarding the nature and meaning of human life, and the imagination could attain

harmony and tranquillity. It was one of those ages when everything,
in spite of the practical disorder of life, seems to have its place;
the ranks and occupations of men; the hierarchy of animals; good
and evil.[30]

Henryson thus remains thoroughly medieval, yet his language betrays this sense of change and offers a vernacular medium for devotion that again resonates as far as the 1637 *Scottish Prayer Book*. Modern literary editors have frequently failed to acknowledge Henryson's deep immersion in the religious profundities of his late medieval courtly tradition. For example, his poem on the annunciation, 'Forcy as deith is likand lufe', begins with a clear reference to the Song of Songs 8. 7, 'Many waters cannot quench love', and the rhythm of its restrained metre and sense of being spoken as liturgy, together with its theological narrative sweep the reader from the annunciation to the resurrection in a great dramatic movement. The poem is a perfect blend of the secular tradition of courtly literature with the religious sense of salvation that brings the poem to a conclusion:

> And syne till hevin my saule thou haist,
> Quhar thi Makar of michtis mast
> Is Kyng, and thow their queen is![31]

But it is Henryson's great poem 'The Bludy Serk' that combines most effectively the image of Christ with that of the courtly love-knight, a tradition in vernacular poetry in English that goes back at least to the theological imagination of St Bernard of Clairvaux and finds its greatest expression perhaps in the fourteenth-century poem 'In a tabernacle of a toure', with its final line of each verse, '*Quia amore langueo*', a poem of both Calvary and courtly love.[32] Like Dunbar, though in a different, perhaps more relaxed style, Henryson writes with both compression and economy of language that readily lends itself to devotional practice. 'The Bludy Serk' is a call to the contemplation of Christ ('Think on the bludy serk'). It draws upon the sermon tradition (which frequently and readily employed as an *exemplum* the image of Christ as the lover-knight[33]) and possibly Henryson's knowledge of an English version of the *Gesta Romanorum* (late thirteenth century). It is deeply, and unselfconsciously, theological: a very liturgical quality.

The final Scottish poet to be considered here is rather different from either Dunbar or Henryson. The slightly later Sir David Lyndsay (c. 1486–1555) was also associated with the Scottish court in the office of herald (essentially a diplomat); his close attachment to James V effectively ending with the defeat of the Scottish forces by the English at Solway Moss in November 1542. After King James's death shortly after the battle, on 14 December 1542, Lyndsay served the Anglophile regency government of the Earl of Arran and its initial policy of church reform and the authorisation of the reading of the Bible 'in the vulgar toung'.[34] Lyndsay was not a profoundly scholarly man, but, despite his reforming tendencies, he was immersed in the liturgy of late medieval Scotland and the rhetorical tradition from which the English liturgies of later non-jurist Anglicanism in Scotland (as in England) developed. Like Henryson he was a layman writing amongst largely poet-clerics, and he shared their knowledge of the Vulgate Bible and the liturgy of the Western Church. In his mockingly self-deprecating 'Answer to the Kingis Flyting' (c. 1535–36), Lyndsay admits his own limitations in response to the King ('Bot I man do as dog dois in his den'), using the words of the penitential Psalm 51. 10, said at lauds on the first Sunday in Lent:

> The mekle Devil may nocht indure your dyting!
> Quharefor, '*Cor mundum crea in me!*' I cry,
> Proclamand yow, the prince of poetry.[35]

The full Latin text runs: '*Cor mundum crea in me, Deus, et spiritum rectum innova in visceribus mei*' ('Create in me a clean heart, O God, and renew a right spirit within me'). Psalm 51 is set to be said at Evening Prayer on Ash Wednesday in the Anglican *Book of Common Prayer*.

Lyndsay's poem 'The Dreme' (c. 1526), a conventional 'dream' poem on the state of Scotland, draws heavily upon Henryson's poems *The Testament of Cresseid* and *Orpheus and Erudices* and has at its heart a vision of heaven (stanza 74ff) where the *Sanctus* is sung before the 'blyssit Trynitie', the poet acknowledging his own infirmities without instruction from the Creed and Scripture, above all St Paul:

> So myne ingyne is nocht sufficient
> For to treit of is heych devinitie.
> All mortal men ar insufficient
> Tyll consider thay thre, in unitie;
> Sic subtell mater I man on neid lat be;
> To study on my Creid it war full fair,
> And lat doctouris of sic hie materis declare.[36]

Lyndsay represents a slightly later stage in the religious history of Scotland from Dunbar and Henryson. Still very much the late medieval courtier and immersed in the Catholic Church of his time, he is moving also towards the Reformation and a sense of the vernacular in worship that is not very far removed from that of Archbishop Cranmer in England.

It is clear that Cranmer's 1549 *Book of Common Prayer* was in fairly wide use in Scotland by the middle years of the sixteenth century after the abandonment of the Latin rite, a fairly commonplace occurrence even before its official proscription in August 1560.[37] In 1559, John Knox remarked that 'the book set forth by godly King Edward' was used in a number of churches where the services were 'the very same or differed very little' from those in England.[38] As we have seen, the *Book of Common Order* dating from 1562, though not a fixed liturgy, took much from the English Prayer Book, and continued to be published until 1644.

The production of the 1637 *Scottish Prayer Book*, however, was a very different matter. The intense opposition to it in Scotland was largely a political and nationalist phenomenon. The book was very much driven by the English King Charles I (and his father James before him) so that it was perceived in Scotland as 'rather an English revision of the English Prayer Book than a book for Scotland'.[39] Changes by James Wedderburn, later Bishop of Dunblane, restored the Communion Service of 1637 to something very like its form in Cranmer's 1549 book, and indeed, this first *Prayer Book* of King Edward VI was very much the model for the 1637 book, a prayer book for Scotland authorised by an English king and, it is generally assumed, under the strong influence of the Archbishop of Canterbury, William Laud. In the blunt words of Geoffrey Cuming, 'To the Scots the book reeked of popery.'[40]

And yet, despite all the radical discontinuities of the Scottish Reformation after 1560, the story of the 1637 book is not quite that simple and its linkage with Archbishop Laud profoundly questionable. Opposition to it in Scotland was very largely nationalistic rather than religious or liturgical, and to some extent it was generated rather than entirely intrinsic. The infamous incident of Jenny Geddes and her stool thrown in St Giles' Edinburgh on the introduction of the book on 23 July 1637 was far from spontaneous, but was, according to George Burnet actually 'a well-organised demonstration led by a number of "rascally" Jenny Geddeses hired by nobles for the purpose'.[41] Burnet continues:

> Except in a broad belt of the country stretching obliquely from Aberdeen and the north-east to Loch Linnhe, and in Nithsdale, where the Service Book was received with varying degrees of pleasure or mild acquiescence, it roused the nation to a pitch of fury which no measure of James VI had ever done. The Scottish people did not object to read prayers or a service-book in itself: they had been accustomed to the Book of Common Order for over seventy years and to the English Prayer Book of 1552 before it.[42]

Opposition to the book of 1637 in Scotland, then, was almost entirely political, rooted in a fear of high-handedness from London and the English Church. It had been 'brought in without warrant from our Kirk', without consultation and against the opposition of the Scottish Parliament.[43]

In fact, however, the true nature of the 1637 Prayer Book was somewhat different. It was far more Scottish than the politics of the time admitted. Gordon Donaldson has carefully pointed out that far from being simply a Laudian and English exercise or 'the [English] King's crowning infatuation', the book was the result of careful efforts on the part of its compilers to conciliate Scottish prejudices.[44] To start with, the King James Version of the

Bible was substituted for the older Geneva Version use in the English *Prayer Book*. In 1633 the Scottish bishops, together with the king himself, objected to the use of the Geneva Version.[45] The same bishops, together with Scottish Presbyterians, had protested against the use of the Apocrypha in the *Prayer Book* and this was now omitted, though not entirely so at the king's particular insistence. The term 'priest' was replaced by 'presbyter'. The terms 'Christmas' and 'Easter' were replaced by the Scottish usage, 'Yule' and 'Pasch'. The doxology was added to the Lord's Prayer at Morning and Evening Prayer.[46] Among a number of other small changes that largely sought to accommodate the more puritan usage in Scotland, perhaps the most important for the Scottish tradition more broadly was the inclusion (alongside the feasts of the Conversion of St Paul and St Barnabas) of a number of feasts of specifically Scottish or Celtic saints, including St Mungo (13 January), St Colman (18 February), St Columba (9 June), St Giles (1 September), St Ninian (18 September), Bishop Adaman (25 September), Queen Margaret of Scotland (16 November), and St Drostane (4 December). Reformers in Scotland, as in England, in the sixteenth century had met with considerable resistance to the reduction of the liturgical year and its place within the rhythm of peoples' lives. Despite the change effected in 1560, and nationalist hostility towards anything imposed upon Scotland from English crown or parliament, the deep underlying piety of late medieval culture remained in Scotland in rather the same way as it has been described by Eamon Duffy in England:

> For the late medieval laity, the liturgy functioned at a variety of levels, offering spectacle, instruction, and a communal context for the affective piety which sought even in the formalized action of the Mass and its attendant ceremonies a stimulus to individual devotion.[47]

Within this tradition late medieval people 'found the key to the meaning and purpose of their lives'.[48]

The Scottish *Prayer Book* of 1637, short-lived though it was in its inception, held something of this deep resonance to the Scottish and Celtic traditions and this is, at least in part, the key to its re-emergence in the survival and re-establishment of the Scottish Episcopal Church in the eighteenth and nineteenth centuries. At the end of the seventeenth century, the High Church English liturgist Edward Stephens described the Scottish *Prayer Book* of 1637 as 'much the best of any modern form whatever', while nineteenth-century liturgical revision in the Scottish Episcopal Church made great use of 1637.[49] It was venerated for both its historical associations and for its clear sense of the real presence of Christ in the sacrament. In the words of Stewart J. Brown:

> In the north, and especially in the north-east, Episcopalians were deeply attached to the Scottish Communion Office, a liturgy based on a modified form of the Scottish Prayer Book of 1637 and formally agreed by the Scottish Church in 1764.[50]

Behind this liturgy, and deeply embedded within its language and ethos is the late medieval Scottish clerical and courtly tradition of poetry that we have examined in this chapter. Just as in England a long tradition of vernacular devotion predates the appearance of the first great 1549 *Book of Common Prayer* of Archbishop Thomas Cranmer, a tradition that embraced a vibrant history of poetry from brief lyrics to Langland's *Piers Plowman* and such works as *The Lay Folks' Mass Book*, so there was a parallel in Scotland. Poets like Dunbar and Douglas wrote within a tradition of classical rhetorical learning and medieval courtly romance as well as within the liturgy and theology of the Western Church that not only finds echoes in Cranmer's liturgical prose, but which is still heard in the continuing tradition of Episcopal worship in Scotland up to the 1929 *Prayer Book* and beyond to the present day.

Endnotes

1 C. S. Lewis, *Poetry and Prose in the Sixteenth Century* (vol. 4 of The Oxford History of English Literature Series) (Oxford: Clarendon Press, 1954), p. 113.
2 See Alasdair A. Macdonald, 'Religious Poetry in Middle Scots', in *The History of Scottish Literature. Vol. 1, Origins to 1660*, ed. R. D. S. Jack (Aberdeen: Aberdeen University Press, 1988), pp. 91–104.
3 *Acts of the Parliaments of Scotland*, ed. T. Thomson (London: 1814), II, pp. 526–34, quoted in George B. Burnet, *The Holy Communion in the Reformed Church of Scotland, 1560–1960* (Edinburgh: Oliver and Boyd, 1960), p. 1.
4 It is notable that the *Oxford Book of Scottish Verse* (1966) contains very little of the surviving religious poetry of the late medieval period. More recent collections have, however, done something to adjust this. For example, *Scottish Religious Poetry: From the Sixth Century to the Present*, ed. Meg Bateman, Robert Crawford, and James McGonigal (Edinburgh: St Andrew Press, 2000), and *The Penguin Book of Scottish Verse*, ed. Robert Crawford and Mick Imlah (Harmondsworth: Penguin, 2006).
5 On tropes as a 'verbal amplification of a passage in the authorized liturgy', see Karl Young, *The Drama of the Medieval Church*, 2 vols (Oxford: Clarendon Press, 1933), I, pp. 179–97.
6 David Jasper, *The Language of Liturgy: A Ritual Poetics* (London: SCM Press, 2018), p. 89.
7 See, for example, the reprinting of the 'Communion Office of the Church of Scotland', taken from 1637, in the widely used manual *The Priest to the Altar, Third Edition, revised and enlarged* (London: Rivingtons, 1879), pp. 205–23.
8 Hary's Wallace, *Vita Nobilissimi Defensoris Scotie Wilelmi Wallace militis*, quoted in James Galbraith, 'The Middle Ages', in *Studies in the History of Worship in Scotland*, ed. Duncan Forrester and Douglas Murray (Edinburgh: T & T Clark, 1984), p. 17.
9 Galbraith, p. 22.
10 Jane Geddes, *Medieval Art, Architecture and Archaeology in the Dioceses of Aberdeen and Moray*. The British Archaeological Association Transactions (London: Routledge, 2016), p. 241.
11 Geddes, p. 36
12 Gordon Donaldson, *The Making of the Scottish Prayer Book of 1637* (Edinburgh: Edinburgh University Press, 1954), p. 60. The objections were that it was too 'English' or 'Canterburian'.
13 See, Eamon Duffy, *Marking the Hours: English People and their Prayers. 1240–1570* (New Haven: Yale University Press, 2006).
14 See *The Lay Folks' Mass Book*, ed. Thomas Frederick Simmons, Early English Text Society (London: N. Trübner & Co, 1879), pp. 148–54.
15 Macdonald, p. 97.
16 *A Compendious Book of Godly and Spiritual Songs Commonly Known as 'The Gude And Godlie Ballatis' Reprinted From the Edition of 1567*, ed. A. F. Mitchell, The Scottish Text Society (Edinburgh and London: William Blackwood and Sons, 1897), p. 58.
17 Lewis, p. 95.
18 See John Harper, *The Forms and Orders of Western Liturgy from the Tenth to the Eighteenth Century* (Oxford: Clarendon Press, 1991), p. 138.
19 Dunbar, *Poems*, ed. James Kinsley (Oxford: Clarendon Press, 1958), p. 99.
20 Ibid., p. 1.

21 Ibid., p. 7.
22 See, Charles Elliot, Introduction to Robert Henryson, *Poems* (Oxford: Clarendon Press, 1963), p. vii.
23 Dunbar, p. 123.
24 The Bannatyne MS is a compilation of poems compiled by an Edinburgh merchant in 1568. The Maitland Folio MS was compiled by Sir Richard Maitland between 1570 and 1585. See Dunbar, xxi.
25 Sarah Carpenter, 'The Bible in Medieval Verse and Drama', in David F. Wright, *The Bible in Scottish Life and Literature* (Edinburgh: St Andrew Press, 1988), p. 75.
26 Gordon Donaldson, 'Reformation to Covenant', in *Studies in the History of Worship in Scotland* (see Forrester and Murray above), p. 35.
27 Dunbar, pp. 68–69.
28 Quoted in J. A. W. Bennett, *The Poetry of the Passion* (Oxford: Clarendon Press, 1982), p. 126.
29 *The Book of Common Prayer: The Texts of 1549, 1559, and 1662*, ed. Brian Cummings (Oxford: Oxford University Press, 2011), pp. 28–29.
30 Edwin Muir, *Essays on Society and Literature* (1949), quoted in Henryson, pp. xxiv–xxv.
31 Henryson, p. 114.
32 See *Medieval English Lyrics*, ed. R. T. Davies (London: Faber, 1963), pp. 148–51; also Bennett, p. 70.
33 See Bennett, p. 117; Donaldson, 'Reformation to Covenant', pp. 37–39; G. R. Owst, 'Fiction and Instruction in the Sermon *Exempla*', in *Literature and Pulpit in Medieval England* (Oxford: Blackwell, 1966), pp. 149–209.
34 Sir David Lyndsay, *Selected Poems*, ed. Janet Hadley Williams (Glasgow: Association for Scottish Literary Studies, 2000), p. xi.
35 Ibid., pp. 98–100.
36 Ibid., p. 21, stanza 78.
37 Donaldson, 'Reformation to Covenant', p. 35.
38 John Knox, *History of the Reformation in Scotland* [1586-7], ed. W. C. Dickinson, 2 vols (London: Nelson, 1949), I, pp. 137–38.
39 Gordon Donaldson, *The Making of the Scottish Prayer Book of 1637*, p. 45. See also Geoffrey Cuming, *A History of the Anglican Liturgy*, 2nd edn (London: Macmillan, 1982), pp. 108–15.
40 Cuming, p. 109.
41 George B. Burnet, *The Holy Communion in the Reformed Church of Scotland, 1560–1960*, p. 95.
42 Ibid., pp. 95–96.
43 John Spalding, *History of the Troubles and Memorable Transactions in Scotland and England from 1624 to 1645*, ed. J. Skene, 2 vols (Edinburgh: Bannatyne Club, 1828–9), I, p. 277.
44 Donaldson, *The Making of the Scottish Prayer Book of 1637*, p. 60.
45 Ibid., p. 62.
46 Ibid., p. 65.
47 Eamon Duffy, *The Stripping of the Altars: Traditional Religion in England, 1400–1580*, 2nd edn (New Haven: Yale University Press, 2005), p. 11.
48 Ibid.

49 W. Jardine Grisbrooke, *Anglican Liturgies of the Seventeenth and Eighteenth Centuries* (London: SPCK, 1958), p. 39. The same was also true, to a degree, amongst High Church Anglicans in England.
50 Stewart J. Brown, 'Scotland and the Oxford Movement', in *The Oxford Movement: Europe and the Wider World, 1830–1930*, ed. Stewart J. Brown and Peter B. Nockles (Cambridge: Cambridge University Press, 2012), p. 59. Cf. Peter B. Nockles, 'Our Brethren of the North: The Scottish Episcopal Church and the Oxford Movement', *Journal of Ecclesiastical History* 47 (1996), pp. 662–63.

4. Post-Reformation Developments in Kirk Attitudes to Scottish Theatre

IAN BROWN

Much has been made historically of the idea that Calvinism in general or, in Scotland in particular, the Presbyterian church – the Kirk – suppressed, even obliterated, theatre for long periods following the 1560 Scottish Reformation.[1] One recognises that such simplifications have a long history. In 1779, Hugo Arnot anathematised the Kirk's views on theatre in his *History of Edinburgh*, often the sole foundation for some later claims in such terms as the following:

> The Church of Scotland, a powerful force in Scottish society, unhesitatingly denounced the theatre as a temple of the devil and threatened potential spectators with dire consequences.[2]

Arnot's views have to be seen in the light of his being both an advocate and a theatre lover: they are not dispassionate. In the twentieth century, one of the most influential followers of such views as Arnot's was Anna Jean Mill. Her important 1927 study of medieval Scottish drama concluded with the assertion that 'the dramatic history of Scotland in the period following the Reformation is that [...] drama as a popular institution and a force in the national life was now dead'.[3] More recent scholarship, including Terence Tobin's detailed 1974 exploration of plays by Scots in the long eighteenth century and the revelatory 1998 *A History of Scottish Theatre*, edited by Bill Findlay, has comprehensively refuted such a miserabilist view.[4] Even as late as 2019, however, it was still possible to find claims that Calvinism long suppressed Scottish theatre.[5] Yet the Kirk was not monolithic, having one single view. It is various through its system of kirk sessions running each parish, presbyteries and synods managing regional matters, and an annual General Assembly debating Kirk-wide issues. Not only do outdated simplifications of Presbyterian attitudes to drama and theatre oversimplify 'Calvinism', they oversimplify drama and theatre. This chapter explores more complex interactions in Scotland of Kirk and theatre.

Playing places and pre- and post-Reformation drama

John McGavin offers a cautionary note against a simplistic conception of 'Scottish theatre' and reminds us of the wider importance of the broader term, 'playing spaces', not least around the time of the Reformation:

> Early Scottish use of the word 'theatre' is usually humanist and does not occur before the sixteenth century. It applies to ancient theatres [… and] is not a word in common use in those records which tell us about actual performances. […] The usual term used at the time for activities we would now define as 'theatre' was 'play', and 'playing place' is used by Gavin Douglas [1474–1522] as the Scots term for a theatre.[6]

The use of such 'playing places' in the incipient Scottish Reformation illustrates Scottish theatre as forming part of a larger religio-political conflict of a kind found in various forms throughout sixteenth-century Europe. Tempting as it has been to lay the impulse to censor theatre at the door of a Calvinist kirk, the position is more interesting and complex. Before the Reformation, as was practice Europe-wide, the Scottish Catholic church used clerks' plays to promote its theology. The reforming playwright and Dominican friar John Kyllour, however, apparently used this form in his play *Historye of Christis Passioun*. His text does not survive but, according to John Knox, it was performed on Good Friday 1535 on the Stirling playfield in front of king, court, and townspeople.[7] It attacked what Kyllour saw as contemporary clergy's blinding, like Pharisees, the people to the real Christ. Accused of blasphemy as a result, Kyllour was hunted down and, after his capture, burned at the stake in Edinburgh in 1539. That same year, James Wedderburn, another protesting dramatist, whose plays had been performed in Dundee's playfield, was also charged with blasphemy. After he fled, no later than 1540, into French exile, the Scottish bishops pressed the bishop of Rouen to arrest him, but he was allowed to remain, dying there in 1553.[8] Kyllour's death and Wedderburn's persecution add resonance to the 1540 performance of the first version of what would become David Lyndsay's *Ane Satire of the Thrie Estaitis*, attacking clerical and political corruption. This version, called an 'Interlude', was performed on Twelfth Night in the great hall of Linlithgow Palace before James V and his court. William Eure describes it in a letter to Thomas Cromwell, saying that, after the performance:

> [T]he King of Scotts dide call upon the Busshope of Glascoe being Chauncelour, and diverse other busshops, exorting thaym to reform thair facions and maners of lyving, saying that oneles thay soe did, he wold send sex of the proudeste of thaym unto his uncle of England [Henry VIII], and, as thoes wer ordoured, soe he wold ordour all the reste that would not amende.[9]

Unlike Kyllour or Wedderburn, Lyndsay was protected: he had been James's childhood mentor and was, as Lord Lyon King of Arms, a senior judge. Given such closeness to the king, who was present at both the Stirling and Linlithgow performances, it is hard not to see the Interlude's reforming (but at the time, not necessarily 'Protestant') content as reflecting the king's views, certainly as expressed in his threat to his bishops. Even after James's death in 1542, Lyndsay remained in place and his play, substantially expanded, was performed on the public playfields of Cupar (1552) and Edinburgh (1554), the Queen-Regent Mary of Guise and the court attending the latter. Such use of playfields, or 'playing places' as McGavin calls them, marks their potential as arenas for the exploration of polemic in public. On Lyndsay's death in 1555, however, the Catholic Church stepped in: in that year, his script was publicly burned at the cross in Edinburgh and the episcopate successfully promoted a parliamentary Act banning theatre. Suppression of Scottish theatre and plays, then, preceded the 1560 Scottish Presbyterian-Calvinist Reformation.

When that Reformation settlement prevailed, based on largely non-hierarchical Presbyterian church government, including, besides ministers, lay members, various forms of theatre flourished, not least in folk, court, and school drama. Bill Findlay identifies most frequent mention of the first in festivities celebrating seasonal change in sixteenth-century records.[10] In the 'May play', sometimes called the 'May game', a mock king was elected, responsible for organising where people in costumes performed, usually with musicians accompanying. Meanwhile, as late as 1599, a Glasgow decree required compulsory attendance at a play on Corpus Christi Day (sixty days after Easter), suggesting continuity with medieval tradition even though, according to Findlay, 'that tradition was by then near to extinction', while the Kirk expunged any Catholic theology plays might still contain.[11]

George Buchanan's (1506–1582) range of playwriting topic and context, both before and after his return to Scotland at the Reformation, demonstrates the fluidity McGavin identifies of Scottish 'theatre'. His masterpieces in Latin, *Jephthes* and *Baptistes* (c. 1540), are innovative integrations of biblical characters and themes with Senecan tragic dramaturgy. Powerfully influential on the development of French neoclassical drama, they were regularly performed across Europe for three centuries. The fact they were initially written for school enactment reminds us of the importance of school drama under the impact of humanist Renaissance thinking. Not only did the Kirk not suppress all theatre (although there was post-Reformation censorship of theological content), Kirk Sessions, while often dilatory in suppressing even pre-Reformation drama, especially seasonal folk drama, actually required drama production in schools. Rather than stamping out theatricality, the Scottish Reformation sought to shape it to its own ends. Margo Todd provides evidence of the Kirk's difficulty in managing, let alone suppressing, dramatic activities, especially those related to older rituals around marriage, death, or seasonal celebrations at May, midsummer, or Christmas.[12] She comments, 'The elders were no fools; they chose their battles carefully, and with the priorities of the larger church and community in mind.'[13] From such subtler, less constantly oppressive, approaches than usual caricatures of a uniformly anti-dramatic Kirk imply, she observes that the evidence suggests that protestantism [sic] may have succeeded in part *because* the sessions enforced their legislation against festivity lightly, flexibly and sporadically. Where a heavy hand might have strengthened the opposition to Reformed doctrine as well as discipline, the elders' sense of the inutility of quashing the useful and harmless allowed for a more gradual but secure cultural reconstruction. [...] session minutes reveal them gradually subsuming old traditions into a new kind of festivity, with new ways of demonstrating individual and corporate status and communal cohesion in the face of both the linear and cyclical passage of time.[14]

McGavin gives an example, among many, highlighting the Kirk's inability to suppress Scottish post-Reformation drama. Discussing the early seventeenth-century Haddington presbytery's failure – or choice – not to suppress annual local plays in Samuelston and Salton, villages near Haddington, twenty miles east of Edinburgh, he observes a pattern of movement

from urban to rural drama [... and] from unthinking pleasures to pleasures pointedly enjoyed in opposition to the kirk. [... The Presbytery's] flurries of activity against rural drama, our only evidence that such drama took place, were all it could manage in the circumstances. By contrast, instances of adultery and fornication were frequently recorded.[15]

Drama and theatre of one kind or another, then, though not always playhouse theatre which we will come to, are found in every part of Scottish society both Lowland and – as Michael Newton has reminded us – Gàidhealtachd.[16] (Indeed, playhouse theatre, largely an urban form, was for economic and demographic reasons until the twentieth century found only on the fringes of the Gàidhealtachd in towns like Greenock, Aberdeen, and Inverness.) Meanwhile, the reformed Kirk, after appropriating many Scottish theatrical impulses, never – although attacking 'heretical' elements in pre-Reformation versions of plays and folk drama – successfully suppressed even the folk drama in its own parishes. As John Jackson wrote in 1793, these 'plays [...]

were exceedingly popular in Scotland, and attempts to suppress them created no small degree of animosity and disturbance'.[17]

The Kirk and varieties of post-Restoration theatre and drama

After the 1660 Stuart Restoration, playhouse theatre quickly gained some urban traction. By 1662, Edinburgh theatre was re-established under Scottish noble patronage at the Tennis Court Theatre at Holyrood, which had been run down in the Cromwellian Puritan period when theatre was indeed formally banned. There, for example, William Clark's (fl. 1663–1699?) *Marciano, or The Discovery* (1663) implicitly celebrated the Restoration through the defeat of a thinly disguised Cromwellian villain: Clark's preface describes theatre as 'this innocent and usefull recreation', condemning 'hell-hounds, assassinats of our liberties [who] snatch'd the very reins of Government [... and voted] down all Scenick Playes [... to suffer] in the same sentence with Monarchy'.[18] This royalist elitism at a time when the Kirk was subject to Episcopalian governance was highlighted during the residence of James, Duke of York and Albany (the future James VII/II) at Holyrood (1679–82). James encouraged plays, bringing over Irish actors for a time, and court masques: in 1681 his daughter Anne, later queen, appeared in Nathaniel Lee's *Mithridates, King of Pontus* (1678) before the Duke and his court.[19] His pro-Catholic milieu's theatrical activity at the beginning of the Killing Time (the period from roughly 1680 to 1688 when Presbyterian Covenanters resisted the Episcopalian direction which Charles II and his brother-successor James VII/II imposed on the Kirk, atrocities being committed by both sides) can only have reinforced any radical Presbyterian's sense that professional or elite theatre was suspect.

Nonetheless, the Kirk continued to support school and university drama, both in Latin and English. Jack McKenzie notes that the Reformation set policies that certainly continued into the 1700s:

> Kirk Sessions and Presbyteries exercised a stricter control, banning Sunday performances, censoring plays, and restricting the choice of subject. School plays were [however ...] used [...] for imparting religious instruction or for revealing the errors of the Roman Catholic faith.[20]

Glasgow Grammar School's 1643 education plan required that 'when the scholars have committed to memory dialogues, speeches, and particularly comedies, they are to assume the characters of the speakers, rehearsing in an imitative fashion in order to acquire the arts of good pronunciation and acting'.[21] When Scotland developed professionalised theatre and Scots wrote for London stages in the eighteenth century, the drivers were largely the professions – including advocates and ministers, the very people to have seen, or participated in, school drama. It is an uncovenanted by-product of the 1706–07 Treaty of Union's maintenance of the independence of Scots education, law, and religion that the interaction of these three spheres should support the later eighteenth-century development of professional theatre in Scotland.

Following James VII/II's 1688 deposition and William and Mary's arrival, there was a lull in Scottish playhouse theatre, though none in other forms of drama, while closet drama scripts circulated, no doubt for private performance. Among these, Archibald Pitcairne's (1652–1713) *The Assembly* (1692), written not long after the Killing Times with their suppression of the Covenanters had concluded, would reinforce possible identification of drama with Jacobite, anti-Presbyterian views. Circulating in manuscript and unpublished until 1722, the play attacks General Assembly pedantry and the obscurantism of both Williamite and Jacobite political sectarianism.[22] It satirises Presbyterian hypocrisy in a subplot of striking frankness, not to say indecency, about perceived ministerial lechery: Solomon Cherrytrees, an Assembly member, counsels Laura in a hidden parodic reference to the *Song of Solomon*:

> [T]hese two fair Breasts of yours evidently prove Parity in the Church-Members [...] Thus and thus they have in brotherly Love and Concord together. Do not imagine that the natural Body there is thus orderly, and that the Wise should suffer such a Blemish in the Mystical (Handling her breasts).[23]

Laura responds, 'Good Mr Parson ye must fetch your *Similies* elsewhere, I'll assure you I'll be neither Parable nor Metaphor to your Kirk-Government.'

Far from being shamefaced, Solomon waxes indignant at the use of the 'Antichristian name of Parson' as prelatic. For him, sectarianism is more important than respect for her as a woman. Pitcairne's main plot plods as he explores intricacies of church politics, but his satirical subplot of Presbyterian double-facedness and love triumphant races along, both plots embodying savage anti-Kirk polemic. Following James VII's 1688 deposition drama, public or closet, retained a lively potential role in politico-religious controversies and marked a polemic strand in Scottish theatre that had apparently prevailed since at least the plays of Lyndsay and Buchanan.

Meanwhile, public performance of school theatre continued. Jack McKenzie identified widespread production, citing performances in Dalkeith, Dumfries, Dundee, Dunkeld, Forfar, Forres, Glasgow, Haddington, Hamilton, Kirkcaldy, Lanark, Leith, Montrose, North Berwick, Paisley, Perth, and Selkirk.[24] Even Lundie, a small village in the Gowrie, produced its play: in 1688, Dunkeld Presbytery, illustrating the manner in which the Kirk did not suppress, but did keep a close eye on, the content of drama, suspended the schoolmaster, William Bouok, for 'acting a comoedie wherein he mad a mock of religious duties and ordinances'.[25] Here, the issue was clearly not theatre's morality, let alone its right to exist, but its use to challenge establishment values. In 1711, Aberdeen Town Council actually required a public theatre to 'be erected in some publict place of the toune, as the theatre shall think fit and there some publict action to be acted by the schollars of the said school'.[26] Unsurprisingly, after school, student-players continued acting at Aberdeen, Edinburgh, and Glasgow universities, sometimes, as in Edinburgh in 1681, *in theatro publico* and occasionally controversially. In 1720, Glasgow university authorities opposed their students' desire to play *Tamerlane* (probably, on the basis of title and timing, Nicholas Rowe's 1701 play), especially their having men dressing as women. The students resisted; some masters supported them; permission to perform, but not on university premises, was finally allowed; the performance happened on 30 December in – appropriately enough – the Grammar School.[27] The role of the Kirk in supplying university staff should be borne in mind when one considers the split that emerged among faculty members in this case. Kirk members and adherents were not uniform in their views, nor of one mind in theatrical matters.

Resistance to eighteenth-century religiose condemnations of theatre

In 1715, after playhouse theatre in Scotland had been discouraged in the Williamite period, an Irish playhouse company visited Edinburgh, and Carrubber's Close Theatre was established as a musical, acrobatic and comedy venue, 'associated mostly with Signora Violante, an Italian performer and singer'.[28] Meanwhile, as Adrienne Scullion observes, though perhaps overstating, as we have seen, the unanimity of attitudes in the Kirk:

> Opposition from the religious authorities was fierce [… one] of the Presbytery's statements in opposition to these players indicates the tone they would continually adopt in confronting theatricalities:
>
> > […] the stage hath been condemned by diverse ecclesiastical Councels and many eminent divines, as a nursery of Impiety and vanity, and […] found to corrupt peoples moralls.[29]

Nonetheless, in 1725, under the aegis of Allan Ramsay (1686–1758), the English actor Anthony Aston was welcomed by the council and social elite, not only as an actor, but as a tutor in newly post-Union 'polite' anglicised speech. In November 1727, however, the Edinburgh Presbytery required an 'Admonition and Exhortation' against stage plays to be read from all the area's pulpits, objecting to plays 'filled with horrid Swearing, Obscenity, and Expressions of a double Meaning, tending directly to Corrupt the minds of the Spectators'.[30] Faced with this and under financial pressure from creditors, Aston decamped in April 1728. Nonetheless, in that October the Edinburgh Company of Players, having a Royal Patent so that throughout 'their stay in Edinburgh, the company never had the least difficulty with either the magistrates or the Church',[31] began playing regular seasons in the Taylor's Hall in the Cowgate, later also touring Dundee, Montrose, Aberdeen, Newcastle, and Scarborough. In this period, Ramsay's importance in theatrical developments was central. Against anglicising models, he wrote in Scots for the stage, publishing an early version of *The Gentle Shepherd* (1725). 1728 saw his *Some Few Hints, in Defence of Dramatical Entertainments*, where he defended 'Dramatick Actions […] which in all

Ages and Nations, have always been esteem'd the most noble and improving Diversions'.[32] His *The Gentle Shepherd* has pro-Stuart/Jacobite, anti-Whig/Calvinist hints as it tells of exile, disguise, true love, honour, and order's restoration. It is now best known in the version performed by Haddington Grammar School boys, directed by their master, Ramsay's friend, John Leslie. Highlighting the seriousness with which such performances were taken in their time and a creative relationship between school drama and professional stage, this full version was premièred on 22 January 1729 in Taylor's Hall, Edinburgh's professional venue. The play became 'the most popular pastoral in eighteenth-century British theatre'.[33] This example suggests only one way in which, in combination with rural and community drama, masters like Leslie developed a seedbed for eighteenth-century Scotland's theatre through a means encouraged by the Kirk in general and despite strong opposition to playhouse theatre by some Kirk members.

One can understand that theatre for some of the eighteenth-century Scottish community might be seen as religiously dubious, not only for the reasons that seventeenth-century English Puritans had condemned it, reflected in the 1727 'Admonition', but also for its earlier link to seventeenth-century High Church oppression of Presbyterianism. This certainly offers a part explanation for eighteenth-century radical Presbyterians' hostility to theatre when, arguably, they offered less substantial opposition to dancing and music. While Ramsay himself was Presbyterian, his milieu was of genteel Presbyterianism. This bridged between the Episcopalian-influenced Kirk of the 1670s and 1680s and the Kirk's later eighteenth-century Moderate movement. Despite opposition from more conservative ministers – who formed an Evangelical movement – and those magistrates under their influence, Moderates tended to support theatre. In the 1730s, the conflict between the two factions reached a new crisis.

When the Players folded in 1736, losing their Patent, Ramsay took over Carrubber's Close Theatre as home for his own permanent company, which included some Edinburgh Company players. The prologue at its November opening with George Farquhar's *The Recruiting Officer* proclaimed, 'Long has it been the business of the stage / To mend our manners, and reform the age'.[34] The claim marked Ramsay's continuing defence of theatre's moral value against any religious and civic opposition. When, after seven months it closed, the direct reason was an injunction quite beyond the context of Edinburgh theatre or its magistrates and ministers, though it gave them succour: Walpole's 1737 Licensing Act, establishing the censorship role of the Lord Chamberlain, forbade theatrical performance of spoken drama without a Royal Patent. Ramsay's theatre had, like others in Britain, to close. Despite attempts by his actors in 1738 and 1739 to re-open the theatre, after a brief re-opening from 5 to 23 January 1739, the new Act finally closed it down. A legal quibble, however, opened a chink. In December 1739, after a concert of music, *The Provok'd Husband* was played 'gratis' as an afterpiece. In December 1741, the precedent now established, Thomas Este began presenting plays regularly in Taylor's Hall under the patronage of the Duke of Hamilton in the guise of music concerts, for which a charge was made, alongside plays which were 'free of charge'. This stratagem proved effective and, on 16 November 1747, complementing Taylor's Hall, the Canongate Concert Hall (in fact a theatre, a name it soon assumed) opened, taking business away from Taylor's Hall. Professional theatre, however, was still to some extent, at least nominally, a hole-in-corner business.

Playhouses were still operating under the terms of 'gratis' performance[35] when the next major conflict arising from the Kirk's divided attitude to theatre emerged. This surrounded the première of John Home's *Douglas* on 14 December 1756 and became a landmark in undermining the power, if not changing the views, of Evangelical Kirk members. The minister of Athelstaneford, Home, was a member of the Kirk's cosmopolitan Moderate wing, alongside church, university, and Enlightenment luminaries like William Robertson, Hugh Blair, and Alexander 'Jupiter' Carlyle, all Kirk ministers, and his play emerged from, and with, their support. It opened in the Canongate Theatre and its development exemplifies linkage between large house amateur drama practice, the reading of closet drama, and the mid-century development of professional playhouse theatre in Scotland. When working on *Douglas*, Home circulated drafts in 1754 for comment, asking for 'corrections'. He sought Hugh Blair's and William Robertson's view on his 'judgement' and the view of Lord Elibank and several women friends on 'taste'.[36] Famously, it was tested in a play-reading by a cast that included Enlightenment luminaries Carlyle, Robertson, Adam Ferguson, David Hume, and Hugh Blair. Its production tied into Kirk politics: earlier in 1756, Moderates had defeated an Evangelical attempt in the General Assembly to excommunicate David Hume.

The importance of the production in the Kirk politics of the time was marked by the local Presbytery's response: it censured ministers who attended it. On 5 January 1757, it uttered another *Admonition and Exhortation*, following the long-held Evangelical line that playhouses were immoral. Yet, where before, as in 1727, such Admonitions had an impact throughout the Presbytery's churches, its power had declined. Ministers who were condemned for attending were not removed from their posts – though the minister of Liberton was suspended for a few weeks – and none suffered any general loss of standing in congregation or community after formally apologising. Having no real effect on theatre, the *Admonition* in retrospect appears a last-ditch attack on drama by the anti-Moderate Evangelicals. Threatened disciplinary proceedings against the playwright-minister were abortive: resigning in June, Home went to London, where David Garrick presented *Douglas*, and he developed a reasonably successful playwriting career. *Douglas* itself was a recurrent success in theatres for the next century. After this point, the Kirk's views on theatre and drama, although it continued to have influence for a time in pockets of the country, became increasingly irrelevant, however much, as the Arnot quotation cited earlier hints, it postured.

Late eighteenth-century and subsequent changes in reception of theatre

This change is underlined by the fact that when in 1739 Lord Glenorchy had introduced a bill to establish an Edinburgh patent theatre, the resistance of the Kirk, university, and magistracy had obliged him to withdraw, while less than twenty years later Robertson, minister and future Principal of Edinburgh University (from 1762) and Moderator of the General Assembly (1763), had supported the production of *Douglas*. The 1767 Act granting Edinburgh Corporation powers to build the New Town included a clause 'to enable His Majesty to grant Letters Patent for establishing a Theatre in the City of Edinburgh, or suburbs thereof'. That would be Edinburgh's Theatre Royal.[37] The rise of theatrical activity in Edinburgh was paralleled by similar interest in Glasgow where in 1762 the Alston Street Theatre opened. Though religious fanatics partially burned it down on the eve of opening, the scheduled play was performed on a temporary stage: Glasgow high society had rallied round to provide costumes and props.[38] The dynamic was again in favour of theatre, and its popularity grew. After the Edinburgh patent was awarded, until the new Theatre Royal, situated at the northeast end of North Bridge, was built, the Canongate Theatre was designated Edinburgh Theatre Royal. The new building opened on 9 January 1769. It became possible for Alasdair Cameron to observe in 1987 in an often-cited passage that 'professional playhouse' theatre in Scotland after the Stuart Restoration

> was limited to short seasons at the Tennis Court Theatre in Edinburgh; it was patronised only by the aristocracy, dominated by English plays and players, and under frequent attack from the Church. By 1800, there were nine permanent theatres [Edinburgh (2), Aberdeen, Glasgow, Dundee, Dumfries, Paisley, Ayr, Greenock] spread throughout Scotland, the theatre was becoming the most popular form of organised entertainment in the country and there were the beginnings of an indigenous tradition of playwriting, acting and management, which paved the way for the 'National Theatre' [usually now called 'National Drama'] at the Theatre Royal Edinburgh in the early nineteenth century.[39]

Meantime, ministerial attitudes varied and changed. John Galt offers in his novel *Annals of the Parish* (1821), set in rural Ayrshire, a wry representation of one fictional minister's attitude to touring theatre when it reached his parish. In August 1795, 'a gang of playactors came, and hired Thomas Thacklan's barn for their enactments'.[40] They play first *Douglas* and *The Gentle Shepherd*, the century's archetypal Scottish plays, then unrecognisable versions of classics like *Macbeth*. The minister is told (for he cannot possibly himself attend, though he permits his daughter to do so) that 'in their parts they laughed most heartily, but made others do the same'. In actuality, although some Kirk elements continued in the nineteenth century to disapprove of theatre as an art form, such disapproval was largely ineffectual and theatre flourished, especially after the arrival of railways permitted more rapid exchange of theatrical practitioners and a widespread and effective touring system developed.

One piquant example of how aspects of Kirk reception of theatre in Scotland had changed by the late nineteenth century is an episode involving the actor Walter Bentley (1849–1927), born William Begg, the fourth son of the Rev. Dr James Begg, a distinguished Free Church Minister (and Queen Victoria's favourite Scottish preacher). Viki McDonnell reports that when Bentley 'met up with his disapproving parent after he had taken to acting, the Rev. Dr Begg greeted him with "So, how is the Son of Satan?" and Walter replied "Fine, *father*, I'm fine".[41] McDonnell continues that Bentley visited the Theatre Royal Greenock for a week in December 1888 to play the Shakespearean roles he specialised in. He invited local ministers, enclosing two gratis tickets and a copy of the text, to his Monday performance as Hamlet to 'influence the people to patronise high-class and other essentially moral dramatic works'. While some were hostile to his offer, at least five ministers wrote back cordially, though declining the offer for a variety of reasons. These included a sense of regard for 'those who sincerely believe the influence of the theatre to be hurtful' and the availability of 'intoxicating drinks' in theatres, while one 'remarked that he held that the stage, when well conducted, was next to the pulpit as a medium of moral training'.

In 1946, the Kirk, having had an actual Edinburgh theatre donated to it, opened the Gateway Theatre. It managed this as a base for a range of dramatic activity including professional, semi-professional, and outreach theatre until in 1953 it reduced its direct involvement in theatre, becoming landlord to the permanent repertory Gateway Theatre Company. When this stood down in 1965 in favour of the current major Edinburgh producing theatre, the Royal Lyceum, whose launch involved many Gateway personnel, the Kirk sold the building to Scottish Television in 1968 to become their Edinburgh studios. It used the bulk of the receipts to build the Netherbow Theatre at the foot of Edinburgh's High Street. This remains an active venue for professional companies and is base for the Scottish Storytelling Centre. In a further rich irony, the Netherbow not only lies within four hundred yards of Playhouse Close, the site of the Canongate Theatre, but also is next door to Carrubber's Close, home of Allan Ramsay's theatre, closed with the approval of many in the Kirk by Walpole's 1737 Licensing Act.

Given the examples this chapter has discussed, the perception that post-Reformation drama was suppressed in Scotland for centuries by the Kirk seems odd. There was indeed substantial opposition from Kirk members to playhouse theatre, particularly in the seventeenth and eighteenth centuries, but it was not always effective. It certainly was not monolithic. One explanation for such views as those of Anna Jean Mill and her followers is, of course, over-dependence on a small range of sources – possibly partisan as in the case of Arnot – accepted at face value. Another is that the lens through which some writers have seen the history of Scottish drama is purely that of eighteenth-century professional building-based playhouse theatre. This is a limited framing of the complexity of Scottish drama provision, not to mention the Kirk's involvement in it, and takes no account of narrower earlier meanings, as McGavin has pointed out, of the term 'theatre' as opposed to the polemical potential in Scotland of 'playing places'. This chapter has demonstrated that there was no halcyon period for theatre, however defined, in the decades before the Scottish Reformation, while developments in attitudes to varieties of theatre in the centuries after that Reformation are complex and ultimately more positive than negative.

Endnotes

1. This chapter draws substantially on and develops material from Ian Brown, 'Cultural Conflict and Versions of Censorship in post-Reformation Scottish Theatre', in Anne Etienne and Graham Saunders (eds), *The Palgrave Handbook of Theatre Censorship* (London: Palgrave Macmillan, forthcoming).
2. Hugo Arnot, *History of Edinburgh* [1779] (Edinburgh: Turnbull, 1816), p. 281.
3. Anna Jean Mill, *Mediaeval Plays in Scotland* (Edinburgh: Blackwood, 1927), p. 112.
4. Terence Tobin, *Plays by Scots 1660-1800* (Iowa City: University of Iowa Press, 1974); Bill Findlay (ed.), *A History of Scottish Theatre* (Edinburgh: Polygon, 1998).
5. See, for example, Mark Brown, 'An Historical Note', *Modernism and Scottish Theatre since 1969: A Revolution on Stage* (London: Palgrave Macmillan, 2019), pp. 30-38.
6. John McGavin, *Theatricality and Narrative in Medieval and Early Modern Scotland* (Aldershot: Ashgate, 2007), p. 2.
7. Bill Findlay, 'Beginnings to 1700', in *A History of Scottish Theatre* (see Findlay above), p. 18.
8. Ibid., pp. 18-19.
9. Greg Walker (ed.), *Medieval Drama: An Anthology* (Oxford: Blackwell, 2000), p. 539.
10. Findlay, p. 3.
11. Ibid., p. 15.
12. Margo Todd, *The Culture of Protestantism in Early Modern Scotland* (New Haven: Yale University Press, 2002), pp. 213-21.
13. Ibid., pp. 185-86.
14. Ibid., pp. 221-22.
15. John McGavin, 'Drama in Sixteenth-Century Haddington', *European Medieval Drama* 1 (1997), pp. 156-57.
16. Michael Newton, 'Folk Drama in Gaelic Scotland', in Ian Brown (ed.), *The Edinburgh Companion to Scottish Drama* (Edinburgh: Edinburgh University Press, 2011), pp. 41-46.
17. John Jackson, *The History of the Scottish Stage* (Edinburgh: Peter Hill, 1793), pp. 408, 415.
18. William Clark, *Marciano, or The Discovery* [1663], ed. W. H. Logan (Edinburgh: privately published, 1871), pp. 5-6.
19. Findlay, pp. 72-74.
20. Jack McKenzie, 'School and University Drama in Scotland, 1650-1760', *Scottish Historical Review* 34 (1955), p. 103.
21. Ibid., p. 104.
22. Ian Brown, *Scottish Theatre: Diversity, Language, Continuity* (Amsterdam: Rodopi, 2011), p. 28.
23. Archibald Pitcairne, *The Assembly* (London: 1722), p. 50.
24. Jack McKenzie, *passim*.
25. Ibid., p. 106.
26. Ibid., p. 104.
27. Ibid., pp. 106-07.
28. Adrienne Scullion, 'The Eighteenth Century', in Findlay (ed.), *A History*, p. 93.
29. Scullion, p. 87.
30. Ibid., pp. 89-90.

31 Donald Campbell, *Playing for Scotland: A History of the Scottish Stage 1715–1965* (Edinburgh: Mercat Press, 1996), p. 8.
32 Allan Ramsay, *Some Few Hints, in Defence of Dramatical Entertainments* (Edinburgh, 1728), p. 2.
33 Scullion, p. 93.
34 Ibid.
35 Findlay, p. 102.
36 Katherine Glover, 'The Female Mind: Scottish Enlightenment Femininity and the World of Letters. A Case Study of the Women of the Fletcher of Saltoun Family in the Mid-eighteenth Century', *Journal of Scottish Historical Studies* 25.1 (2005), p. 17.
37 Donald Mackenzie, *Scotland's First National Theatre* (Edinburgh: Stanley Press, 1963), p. 8.
38 Scullion, p. 111.
39 Alasdair Cameron, 'Theatre in Scotland 1660–1800', in Andrew Hook (ed.), *The History of Scottish Literature, vol. 2 (1660–1800)* (Aberdeen: Aberdeen University Press, 1987), p. 191.
40 John Galt, *Annals of the Parish* [1821] (London: Foulis, 1919), p. 207.
41 Viki McDonnell, *Sugar, Ships and Showbusiness: Entertaining Greenock*, vol. 1 (Greenock: WL Publishing, 2019), p. 138.

5. Eccentrics as Spokespersons for Tobias Smollett on Religion

J. WALTER McGINTY

In his novel *The Adventures of Peregrine Pickle*, published in 1751, Tobias Smollett introduces Cadwallader Crabtree as a misanthrope. Cadwallader recognises something of himself in Smollett's main character Peregrine: 'There is something in your disposition which indicates a rooted contempt for the world.'[1] Cadwallader tells of how one day when he was in Portugal, he got drunk and began 'to broach doctrines on the subject of religion'.[2] His scandalised hearers reported him, and the next day he was dragged off by officers of the Inquisition and confined in their prison.[3] He at first was able to withstand their torture, but on learning from another prisoner that there was soon to be an *Auto da Fé*, 'not at all ambitious of the crown of martyrdom', he recanted and was allowed to go free.[4] As a sign of repentance, he undertook to make a pilgrimage to Rome in his bare feet. After many adventures as a beggar, pilgrim, priest, soldier, gamester, and quack, Cadwallader says:

> I have learned that the characters of mankind are everywhere the same; that common sense and honesty bear an infinitely small proportion to folly and vice; and that life is at best a paultry province. [...] I now appear in the world, not as a member of any community, or what is called a social creature; but merely as a spectator.[5]

So Cadwallader offers his comments on religion as an outsider, an observer. By using this device, Smollett is enabled to express views about religious belief which, if they were associated too closely with him, might land him in trouble with the authorities. This chapter will attempt to trace Smollett's slyly critical portrayals of religious belief and practice through examining the eccentric characters in several of his novels.

'A spirit of contradiction'

Cadwallader is the first eccentric under examination and helps demonstrate Smollett's impatience with religious intolerance. Through Cadwallader's conversation with a fellow prisoner in the prison of the Inquisition, he learns that this man had secretly practised Judaism for quite some time and had been left alone by the church. But he had gradually amassed a fortune, and it was then that the church became interested; he was accused of heresy and incarcerated. Cadwallader is observing as a spectator the corruption and intolerance of the Roman Catholic Church whose Inquisition had been very active in Spain and Portugal in the century that he had come into the world. The persecution of what were called 'New Christians' or '*conversos*' – Jews who had been forced to become Christians – was rife, as they were often suspected of returning to their former beliefs and practices.[6]

The Jewish Synagogue authorities, although not as capable of inflicting as severe punishment as the Inquisition, were just as intolerant of any deviance from what they considered orthodoxy. Notably, the philosopher Spinoza had the distinction of being declared a heretic by both the Synagogue and the Church.[7] Even the Church of Scotland participated in intolerance through its Calvinistic theology, for instance when it was instrumental in causing an Edinburgh University student, Thomas Aikenhead, to be hanged for blasphemy in 1697.[8] Intolerance on many religious fronts was alive and well throughout Europe, and in the time of Tobias Smollett, was well within living memory. The English philosopher John Locke had written his *Letters Concerning Toleration* in 1685, and the subject was still relevant when French theologian Marie Huber's *Letters Concerning the Religion Essential to Man* was translated and published in Glasgow in 1771.

Smollett's eccentric number two is 'A tall meagre figure, answering, with his horse, the description of Don Quixote mounted on Rozinante' – Lieutenant Obadiah Lismahago.[9] He is introduced in the novel *The Expedition of Humphry Clinker*, published in 1771, the same year as Huber's *Letters*. Lismahago is a retired army officer. Smollett wants his readers to remember his name and has his character hand to the hostess a slip of paper with three words on it: Lieutenant Obadiah Lismahago. Lismahago tells the company that he is named after a place in Scotland so called. His opening words to the company are:

> Leddies, perhaps ye may be scandaleezed at the appearance my heed made, when it was uncovered by accident; but I can assure you, the condition you saw it in, is neither the effects of disease, nor of drunkenness; but an honest scar received in the service of my country.[10]

He had, he explains, 'been wounded at Ticonderoga in America' by 'a party of Indians' who had 'rifled him, scalped him, broke his scull with a blow from a tomahawk, and left him for dead'. His adventures had continued: hospitalised by the French, escaped from hospital, captured by 'a party of Miamis', tortured, survived, married to the chief's daughter, and eventually was himself 'elected sachem'.

Obadiah's first religious comment is about the Puritans. He says to Matthew Bramble, totally ignoring the biblical origin of his own name: 'I have a foolish pique with the name Matthew, because it savours of those canting hypocrites, who, in Cromwell's time, christened all their children by names taken from the scripture.'[11] He goes on to tell of how he had lived with the Native Americans for several years and had had a son to his wife, Squinkinacoosta.[12] At this, Matthew's sister, Tabitha, also bearing a biblical name, becomes greatly curious to know all the details of his life. Tabitha exclaims (inadvertently promoting him): 'In the name of God, Captain Lismahago, what religion do they profess?' Lismahago explains:

> As to religion, madam, it is among those Indians a matter of great simplicity – they never heard of any *Alliance between Church and State*. – They, in general, worship two contending principles; one the Fountain of all Good, the other the source of evil. – The common people there, as in other countries, run into the absurdities of superstition; but sensible men pay adoration to a Supreme Being, who created and sustains the Universe.
>
> 'O! what pity, (exclaimed the pious Tabby) that some holy man has not been inspired to go and convert these poor heathens!'[13]

Lismahago then tells of 'two French Missionaries' who came 'to convert them to the catholic religion':

> But when they talked of mysteries and revelations, which they could neither explain nor authenticate, and called in the evidence of miracles which they believed upon hearsay; when they taught, that the Supreme Creator of Heaven and Earth had allowed his only Son, his own equal in power, and glory, to enter the bowels of a woman, to be born as a human creature, to be insulted, flagellated, and even executed as a malefactor; when they pretended to create God himself, to swallow, digest, revive, and multiply him *ad infinitum*, by the help of a little flour and water, the Indians were shocked at the impiety of their presumption.[14]

The 'assembly of the sachems', convinced that the missionaries are cheats, suspects them of being spies, tried them, convicted them of blasphemy, and condemned them to be burned at the stake. Smollett tartly concludes his narrative: 'They died singing *Salve Regina*, in a rapture of joy, for the crown of martyrdom which they had obtained.'

Here, Smollett is tilting at the attitude of the Church which is so small-minded as to think that there is only one way to find, worship, and understand God. He is also pointedly showing how some of the beliefs of the church might be held up to questioning doubt, if not ridicule. Smollett, through Lismahago, is calling attention to a people who lived perfectly contentedly, with no concern for the relationship between church and state – a relationship whose working out had caused much bloodshed, from the time of Constantine down to the more recent Cromwellian and Covenanting times. Even in his own century, by the Patronage Act of 1712, church and state relationships were causing much strife between the ordinary people and those who wanted to assert an authority over them.

At the time *The Expedition of Humphry Clinker* was published, the relationship between church and state had assumed a considerable importance. The church had ceded some of its power to the state. In England, the titular head of the Church of England was the monarch, who had a say in appointing its bishops. The Church of Scotland, although it claimed a freedom to govern itself, was not entirely free of state interference, through some charges having a royal patron, and also by having the date of its General Assembly determined by the monarch through his Lord High Commissioner to the Assembly. As recently as 1712, the state, through the Patronage Act, had interfered with the right of members and elders of the congregations to choose their own minister, breaking the promise of the Act of Security, passed at the time of the Union of 1707, that guaranteed the Churches in the United Kingdom the right of governance over their respective national bodies.[15] Smollett was not merely griping in the manner of the persona given to him by Laurence Sterne as the forever complaining 'Smelfungus'; he was dealing with real issues that were impinging on the life of the church and affecting the practice of religion.[16]

Thus, Lismahago is concerned about the way in which religion could degenerate into superstition, not only in America but also in any country. He is also claiming that religion had descended to the level of superstition among many people who did not test their religious beliefs against their common sense. Lismahago also makes use of words such as 'reason, philosophy and contradiction in terms'; he drops hints that he is a freethinker, and Tabitha is shocked at 'certain sarcasms he threw out against the Creed of Athanasius'.[17] Eusebius, the church historian, describes Athanasius as having 'tenaciously maintained the faith of Nicaea through all vicissitudes'.[18] The Nicene Creed of 325 had an input from the Emperor Constantine, who had insisted on a clause that declared that Jesus was 'consubstantial with the Father'.[19] Writing further on the creed, Eusebius uses words that were later picked up by Smollett: '[o]n this faith being publicly put forth by us, *no room for contradiction appeared*', to which Smollett rejoinders by implying that the Creed is a contradiction in terms.[20] Smollett, through Lismahago, praises 'the great simplicity' of the faith of his Native Americans and holds up the Nicene Creed as an example of a Church making religion much more complex than it needs to be. It could be said that by attempting to spell out the precise relationship between Jesus and God, the Church has entered into an area of thought where there is quite insufficient data to come to an understanding that equates with reality. Matthew Bramble attempts to sum up Lismahago's attitude:

> The spirit of contradiction is naturally so strong in Lismahago, that I believe in my conscience, he has rummaged, and read, and studied with indefatigable attention, in order to qualify himself to refute established maxims, and thus raise trophies for the gratification of polemical pride.[21]

Smollett, through Lismahago, refutes such 'established maxims'.

'A horrid and shocking theology'

Turning now to eccentric number three, Tabitha, the unmarried sister of Matthew Bramble in *The Expedition of Humphry Clinker*, through this character Smollett voices a criticism of the theology of salvation popular in his day. Tabitha, or Tabby as her brother calls her, has a predilection for Methodism. When the Brambles' party is in Edinburgh, Tabitha attends a Wesleyan meeting. (Incidentally, Smollett's fictional journey is set in 1766, when John Wesley was indeed in Edinburgh.) Matthew Bramble's nephew, Jery, recalls that Tabitha was in a bad mood when they left Edinburgh, because of a discussion she had had with a Mr Moffat touching the 'eternity of Hell-torments'. This older gentleman, as he advanced in years, was against the common acceptation of the word *eternal*. He is now persuaded that:

> *Eternal* signifies no more than an indefinite number of years; and that the most enormous sinner may be quit for *nine millions, nine hundred thousand, nine hundred and ninety-nine years of hell-fire*; which term or period, as he very well observes, forms but an inconsiderable drop, as it were, in the ocean of eternity—For this mitigation he contends, as a system agreeable to the ideas of goodness and mercy, which we annex to the supreme Being.[22]

He adds that no person was to be exempted from punishment and 'the most pious Christian upon earth might think himself very happy to get off for a fast of seven or eight thousand years in the midst of fire and brimstone'.[23] Tabitha is indignant at this notion, while Humphry Clinker thinks that it is similar to the Popish doctrine of Purgatory and quotes scripture that said that the fire everlasting was only prepared for the devil and his angels.

Although Moffat and Tabitha's discussion of the duration of 'hell-fire' borders on the farcical, it is being seriously discussed as to what the word *eternity* means, and an attempt is made to quantify the time to be spent amidst hellfire and brimstone. Smollett is presenting an argument carried to its extreme and holds it up to ridicule for all its absurdity. Now, although we may laugh at the argument today, in Smollett's time theological works that engaged in equally ridiculous and inconsequential discussion were still being read.

One such writer was Thomas Watson (c. 1617–1686). His major work, *A Body of Divinity*, was a bestseller.[24] Released posthumously in 1692, it was still being published and discussed at the time in which Smollett's novel is set. Robert Burns, purchasing for the Monkland Friendly Society library, refers to it in a letter to Peter Hill on 2 March 1790: 'This heavy Performance so much admired by many of our Members that they will not be content with one Copy.'[25] But Burns, who in a later letter describes Watson's work as 'trash', instructs Hill to say that he could not procure a copy of the book as cheaply as he had the last time and, with the agreement of Captain Riddle, cancels the request. However, in 17 January 1791, the members again requested Watson's book. Burns ordered it but described it, in company with a few others, as 'damned trash'.[26]

Watson enters into the kind of theological discussion similar to that engaged in by Tabitha, and just as absurd. In a section on 'The Fall', Watson considers Adam's Fall and asks the question, 'How long did Adam continue in Paradise before he fell?' He then goes on to quote various theological authorities:

> Tostatus says, he fell the next day. Pererius says, he fell the eighth day after his creation. The most probable and received opinion is, that he fell the very same day in which he was created. So Irenaeus, Cyril, Epiphanius, and many others.[27]

Watson concludes: 'By which it appears Adam did not stay long in Paradise', adding, 'Adam did not take up one night's lodging in Paradise.' But, as if unwilling to leave his finding, he then warns: 'If Adam, in a few hours, sinned himself out of Paradise, how quickly would we sin ourselves into hell, if we were not kept by a greater power than our own!'

Throughout the eighteenth century, such writings were hugely popular and influential among ordinary people such as the subscribers to the Monkland Friendly Society, but they also formed part of the debate among the more literate. John Goldie (1717–1811) attacked those who took the words of scripture literally and did not allow for what he called a metaphorical interpretation. A literalist view of the Adam and Eve story led to such nonsensical speculation as was indulged in by the likes of Thomas Watson. Goldie also attacked the doctrine of Original Sin that had been extrapolated from that story. He attacks the doctrine that stems from Adam's sin as 'that most horrid doctrine'. He appeals to reason and shows his contempt for ecclesiastical authority when he discusses the case of a child dying on the day of its birth and going to eternal punishment because of Adam's sin. Goldie blames Augustine for the doctrine and says that it is:

> A Doctrine sufficiently coarse to be expressed by the devil himself because it redounds to the dishonour of the great God.
>
> Now what a horrid and shocking theology is this that millions of rational beings, for no fault of their own, but only for an offence committed by another, thousands of years before, [...] should be given up and delivered over to eternal damnation without mercy.[28]

It is no coincidence that there is an echo of this in 'Holy Willie's Prayer':

> O THOU that in the heavens does dwell!
> Wha, as it pleases best thysel,
> Sends ane to heaven and ten to h-ll,
>   A' for thy glory!
> And no for ony gude or ill
>   They've done before thee.[29]

Goldie also attacked the Westminster Confession's attempt at supporting the doctrine of Original Sin by the use of 'proof texts', which were often taken out of context in support of the doctrine being promoted. Smollett, like Goldie, detested what he called 'Priestcraft', and Goldie called that doctrine 'the very soul of priestcraft'.[30] Goldie saw religion as something essentially simple but that had been corrupted by priestcraft. Smollett agreed and through Tabitha's words calls in question the religion that had become concerned with calculating the length of punishment that might have to be endured by sinners.

But Smollett does not just offer criticism. He offers a model of how simple a thing religion might be through another of his eccentric characters, Commodore Hawser Trunnion, in *The Adventures of Peregrine Pickle*. When Peregrine attends the old sea-captain, who is dying, Trunnion's wife is sitting by the fire quietly weeping, and Trunnion says of her: 'She's an honest heart in her own way, and thof she goes a little crank and humoursome, by being often overstowed with Nantz [wine] and religion, she has been a faithful ship-mate to me.'[31] Is Smollett gently saying, 'You can sometimes have too much wine and sometimes too much of religion'? Or perhaps, 'If you want religion, then keep it simple'? Making the arrangements for his own funeral, Trunnion instructs that there be no ceremony other than being carried to the grave 'by my own men, dressed in the black caps and white shirts'. He does not want his tombstone to be inscribed in anything other than plain English:

> When the angel comes to pipe *all hands* at the great day, he may know that I am a British man, and speak to me in my mother tongue. And now I have no more to say, but God in heaven have mercy on my soul, and send you all fair weather, wheresoever you are bound.[32]

'No religion but that of nature'

The complex pieties of these various eccentric characters naturally lead readers to wonder what Smollett's personal religious convictions may have been. In attempting to ascertain Smollett's own religious views, I have consulted two of his nonfictional writings: *Travels in France and Italy* (1766) and *An Essay on the External Use of Water* (1752). The comments on religion in the *Travels*, especially in Chapter Four, tell us more of what Smollett did not believe, than what he did, but from these we can at least glean hints of what he respected in religion. He did not like the Roman Catholic version of the Christian religion, declaring:

> their religion affords a perpetual comedy. Their high masses, their feasts, their processions, their pilgrimages, confessions, images, tapers, robes, incense, benedictions, spectacles, representations and innumerable ceremonies, which revolve almost incessantly, furnish a variety of entertainment from one end of the year to the other. If superstition implies *fear*, never was a word more misapplied than it is to the mummery of the religion of Rome. The people are so far from being impressed with awe and religious terror by this sort of machinery, that it amuses their imaginations in the most agreeable manner, and keeps them always in good humour.[33]

Note that this is not an attack upon Roman Catholics as individuals, but upon the beliefs of the Roman Catholic Church and its organisation. On the very next page, Smollett also attacks Calvinism:

> I know not whether I may be allowed to compare the Romish religion to comedy, and Calvinism to tragedy. The first amuses the senses, and excites ideas of mirth and good humour; the other, like tragedy, deals in the passions of terror and pity. Step into a conventicle of dissenters, you will, ten to one, hear the minister holding forth upon the sufferings of Christ, or the torments of hell, and see many marks of religious horror in the faces of the hearers.[34]

Once again, this criticism is being directed not at the ordinary people, but at the way in which the people are being led and at the doctrines that are being thrust upon them. A letter Smollett wrote while travelling in Nice rails against superstition:

> With respect to religion, I may safely say, that here superstition reigns under the darkest shades of ignorance and prejudice. I think there are ten convents and three nunneries within and without the walls of Nice; and among them all, I never could hear of one man who had made any tolerable advances in any kind of human learning.[35]

Written at a time when there was an explosion of exploration in many areas of learning, this is a condemnation of a religious body that is not, in Smollett's opinion, contributing to the common good and the improvement of understanding.

Another curious reference to religion appears in *An Essay on the External Use of Water*. Before I read this essay, I wondered if Smollett might have used it to comment on the Sacrament of Baptism, which makes an external use of water. The fact that he did not, although this is 'argument from silence', is perhaps an indication that he was not averse to symbolism and not entirely opposed to religious ceremony. Smollett briefly touches on the subject of religion when referring to the belief in the healing power of touch, in this case by the hand of a corpse. He reduces its efficacy on account of the patient being

> a poor diseased wretch, of low station, and weak intellects, prepossessed with the superstitious notion of a delegated power from Heaven, and struck with the *Apparatus*, as well as with the sublime rank of the *Operator*, acting in the double capacity of apostle and king, could not fail to be extremely affected through the whole system of the nerves, and suffer such agitations in the blood and spirits, as might work great changes in the constitution.[36]

The *Essay* concentrates on a discussion of the efficacy of the waters of the spa at Bath and dismisses the Baths as unsanitary, and the mineral waters there as inferior to ordinary water.[37]

In addition to the direct statements in these nonfictional accounts, one of the foremost Smollett scholars, Lewis M. Knapp, has reasoned that Matthew Bramble in *The Expedition of Humphrey Clinker* is the most likely fictional character to reflect Smollett's own views.[38] I have therefore examined the letters that purport to be written by Matthew Bramble in this volume as a source that at least hints at the opinions Smollett held on the subject of religion. Two further factors increase this likelihood. Firstly, a number of historical characters appear in this novel, bringing it to more closely resemble a factual account. Secondly, this is Smollett's last novel, written when he knew that he was dying and had less need to protect himself from possible criticism. These two factors increase the likelihood that Bramble can justifiably be read as a figure representative of Smollett.[39] Following the incident when Humphrey Clinker has just been declared innocent of a charge of highway robbery, Bramble speaks highly of his qualities:

> He has recommended himself in an extraordinary manner, not only by his obliging deportment, but by his talents of preaching, praying, and singing psalms, which he has exercised with such effect, that even Tabby respects him as a chosen vessel. If there was anything like affectation or hypocrisy in this excess of religion, I would not keep him in my service; but, so far as I can observe, the fellow's character is downright simplicity, warmed with a kind of enthusiasm, which renders him very susceptible of gratitude and attachment to his benefactors.[40]

Bramble (and thus arguably Smollett) respects the honest simplicity of a religious person, even if he perhaps does not share their belief. Another, almost off-the-cuff comment on religion by Bramble is on the occasion of meeting a 'Country apothecary called Grieve', of whom he says, 'By his garb, one would have taken him for a quaker, but he had none of the stiffness of that sect.'[41] Again, in this judgement it is implied that religion should be less formal than it is often presented.

On visiting York Minster, Bramble comments on the practice of burying people within the cathedral as having arisen through 'the effect of ignorant superstition influenced by knavish priests'.[42] As in the nonfictional writings, the criticism here is directed not at the ordinary people but at the hierarchy of church professionals. During this same visit, Bramble muses on the architecture, commenting that 'the long slender spire puts one in mind of a criminal impaled with a sharp stake rising up through his shoulder'.[43] This extreme distaste seems to arise from the ostentatious showiness of the shape of the cathedral. Again, by implication, simplicity in the expression of religion is being preferred to ostentation. It is significant that immediately after his account of his visit to the Minster, Smollett recalls that it was here that he met with 'my old acquaintance Hewitt'. William Hewitt (1693–1766) was noted for his advocacy of a simple form of religion, and as Smollett here says, 'the truth is H— owns no religion but that of nature'.[44] This simple, but I think deliberate, juxtaposition in the text is for me compelling evidence of Matthew Bramble being a representative of Tobias Smollett's stance on religion.

It is very difficult to be entirely certain of Tobias Smollett's religious beliefs. As some of these passages have shown, he had an abhorrence of religious ostentation. He detested superstition. He hated hypocrisy. He had no place for fanatically held doctrines, regardless of religious denomination. He did not want reason to be left aside, but for it to be taken into account in religious beliefs. He respected the genuinely held and simply expressed piety held by an ordinary person. He preferred simplicity in the expression of religion. He saw a place for religion, especially the Protestant version of the Christian faith, as one of the factors that helped to hold society together. These are some of the religious views of that complex man, Tobias Smollett, that I think can be teased out from his writings.

We must not, however, come to the conclusion that Smollett's religious beliefs can be fully extrapolated from his eccentric characters. Following the publication of his first novel, *The Adventures of Roderick Random* (1751), he disowned the autobiographical nature of his portrayal of his main character, allowing for the exception of Roderick's experience at the battle of Cartagena.[45] Smollett's role is to hold up to view the things in his society that need to be critically examined, judged, and changed according to the application of common sense, reason, and a generous humanity. Through his eccentric characters Cadwallader, Obadiah, Tabitha, and Trunnion, Smollett is the enlightened spectator, the acute observer, the critical commentator, and the whimsical witness of the religious issues of his time.

Endnotes

1. Tobias Smollett, *The Adventures of Peregrine Pickle* in which are included *Memoirs of a Lady of Quality* (Oxford: Oxford University Press, 1983), p. 383.
2. Smollett, *Peregrine Pickle*, p. 385.
3. Ibid.
4. Ibid., p. 386.
5. Ibid., p. 387.
6. Steven Nadler, *Spinoza: A Life* (Cambridge: Cambridge University Press, 1999), pp. 1–15.
7. Nadler, pp. 120–30.
8. T. M. Devine, *The Scottish Nation 1700-2000* (London: Penguin, 2000), pp. 64–67, 71, 75.
9. Tobias Smollett, *The Expedition of Humphry Clinker*, ed. with intro. Lewis Knapp, rev. Paul-Gabriel Boucé (Oxford: Oxford University Press, 1988), p. 188.
10. Smollett, *Humphry Clinker*, pp. 189, 193.
11. Ibid., p. 191.
12. Ibid., pp. 193–94.
13. Ibid., pp. 195–96.
14. Ibid., pp. 196–97
15. 1706–1707 The Articles of Union; and 1707 Act for Security of the Church of Scotland in *Scottish Historical Documents*, ed. Gordon Donaldson (Edinburgh & London: Scottish Academic Press, 1974), pp. 268–75; 275–77; Patronage Act 1712 in *A Church History of Scotland*, ed. J. H. S. Burleigh (London: Oxford University Press, 1960), pp. 277–79.

16 Tobias Smollett, *Travels through France and Italy* (Oxford: Oxford University Press, 1981), ix; see also Laurence Sterne, *A Sentimental Journey Through France and Italy* (London: T. Becket and P. A. De Hondt, 1768), pp. 51–53, 150 note 13.
17 Sterne, p. 393.
18 *A New Eusebius Documents of the History of the Church to AD 337*, ed. J. Stevenson, based upon the collection ed. B. J. Kidd (London: SPCK, 1957), p. 398.
19 'Letter of Eusebius of Caesarea to his church, on the Creed of Nicaea', in *A New Eusebius*, pp. 365–66.
20 Ibid., p. 365.
21 Smollett, *Humphrey Clinker*, p. 203.
22 Ibid., pp. 236–37.
23 Ibid.
24 Thomas Watson, *A Body of Divinity* (Edinburgh: The Banner of Truth Trust, 1992).
25 *The Letters of Robert Burns*, ed. J. De Lancey Ferguson, 2nd edn, rev. G. Ross Roy, 2 vols (Oxford: Clarendon Press, 1985) II, pp. 20, 66.
26 Ibid. Trash or not, it continued to sell, and my paperback copy was published in 1992. I share Burns's assessment of the work, although would add the words 'historically interesting' to 'damned trash'.
27 Watson, pp. 137–38.
28 John Goldie, *Essays on Various Important Subjects Moral and Divine* (Glasgow, 1779), pp. 22, 189–90, 286–87, 324.
29 *The Poems and Songs of Robert Burns*, ed. James Kinsley, 3 vols (Oxford: Oxford University Press, 1968), I, p. 74.
30 Goldie, pp. 286–87.
31 Smollett, *Peregrine Pickle*, pp. 392–93.
32 Ibid., p. 393.
33 Smollett, *Travels Through France and Italy*, p. 27.
34 Ibid., p. 28.
35 Ibid., p. 147.
36 Tobias Smollett, *An Essay on the External Use of Water in a letter to Dr. ***** (London: M. Cooper, 1752; repr. [n.p.]: Gale ECCO, Print Editions, 2012), p. 11.
37 Ibid., pp. 4–5, 34.
38 Lewis M. Knapp, introduction to *The Expedition of Humphry Clinker*, by Tobias Smollett (Oxford: Oxford University Press, 1988), p. xiii: 'Through the persona of Bramble [...] Smollett revealed much of his own personality'.
39 Cf. Smollett, *Clinker*, pp. 182, 216, 235, 237, 238.
40 Ibid., p. 153.
41 Ibid., p. 166.
42 Ibid., p. 181.
43 Ibid.
44 Smollett, *Clinker*, pp. 182, 365, note 1.
45 See Smollett's letter in the introduction to *The Adventures of Roderick Random* (Oxford: Oxford University Press, 1988), p. xv.

6. A Working-Class Poet from the Eastern Border: Robert Davidson (1778–1855)

BARBARA BELL

In nineteenth-century Scotland, the impact of Christianity on literature cannot easily be divorced from a consideration of 'place'. This chapter examines the religious writing of a peasant poet, Robert Davidson (1778–1855), a day labourer who spent his entire life within sight of the Scottish/English border, working within a landscape and community suffused with religious fervour and controversy.[1] For Davidson, the word 'place' and the term 'Borderer' have relevance in geographical, cultural, and theological terms. It was not simply that he was a Borderer, with all that implies about identity and the expression of identity, but Davidson was also a man caught between the traditions of his dissenting faith, rooted in the land around him, and the ideals of the Scottish Enlightenment. In 1848, Davidson wrote an autobiographical foreword to the final volume of his poetry, describing his working life and the literary sources that first influenced him. We consider those writings and Davidson's treatment both of the Border's religious history and of the personal beliefs of a working man for whom poverty and misfortune were never far away.

Born in Lempitlaw, for much of his life Davidson lived in and around the village of Morebattle in Roxburghshire, close to the site of the celebrated Gateshaw Brae blanket-preachings (1739–c. 1750). By the time of Davidson's birth, the dissenting congregation was well established in a meetinghouse in Morebattle and active in campaigning for the oppressed. Iain Whyte notes that 'The only church petition [anti-slavery petition to Parliament] in 1792 which came from outside the Church of Scotland was from the Dissenting Congregation of Morebattle on 29th February'.[2] Nevertheless, the antipathy between some Church of Scotland clergy and their dissenting neighbours remained. Rev. James Rutherford, who wrote the *Statistical*

Account for the neighbouring parish of Hounam (Hownam) in 1799, said of Gateshaw that there had been 'from the beginning of the Secession, a meeting-house of the wildest kind of Seceders, the Antiburghers, who are zealous in disseminating their principles, not supposed very favourable to morals and true piety'.[3] In 1866, *The United Presbyterian Magazine* published an article which outlined the importance of Gateshaw Brae and the surrounding community to the seceders' struggle for autonomy and sustained growth.[4] Whilst recognising the area's long and suffering Covenanting history and its connections to the Marrow-men – twelve Church of Scotland ministers who caused controversy in the early eighteenth century by insisting repentance was not a prerequisite for salvation – the article made special mention of the continuing religious life of Morebattle. It noted the regular fellowship meetings, particularly the 'female prayer meetings', and it ascribed the 'extraordinary number of ministers' from the village who had 'obtained licence to preach' to the influence of 'these mothers in Israel'.[5] The article then listed nineteen young men whose ministry spread across the globe.

In comparison with those who left the village, Robert Davidson inhabited a world which can appear modest in scope, confined within a rigid geographical and economic round, underpinned by a history centred on narrow, exacting systems of belief. It is not certain why Davidson chose to remain in Morebattle. Three of his sons eventually emigrated to America and did well there, but not quickly enough to save Davidson from Parish Relief at the end. As a young man he may not have been able to raise the funds to transport his family; however, his several poems on the unhappiness of the exile returned to a land now bereft of old companions or ruined by 'improvements' express a fundamental unwillingness to leave his beloved Border hills. Davidson writes in his 'Autobiography' that he was content in the station Providence had allotted him, and it seems fairest to believe him. Nevertheless, the breadth of his writing reveals a shrewd, humorous, humane, sometimes sceptical, often irate, observer of the world around him, and a man who struggled to answer the fundamental questions that his faith and fate asked of him.

The course of Davidson's writings

Davidson initially self-published a small pamphlet of his verses in 1811 during a period of 'wet seasons and late harvests'. He had not intended to make his writings public, but prices had risen to the point where he could not earn enough to feed a wife and six children.[6] No surviving copies of this pamphlet are known to exist. There are currently two extant collections of Davidson's work: a second self-published volume from 1825, and a third, more 'polished' offering from 1848.[7] This chapter works primarily from the 2008 reprint of the 1848 edition, with an added 'Introduction' by historian David Welsh; the page numbers come from this reprint unless indicated otherwise, and in order to get a sense of the poet's emerging views, the date of a poem's first appearance is noted after the initial mention of each title.[8]

The expanded 1848 edition, appearing at the behest of some Jedburgh benefactors and edited by them, represents an attempted rebranding of Davidson mid-century as an idealised 'peasant poet'. Whereas the 1825 edition was simply titled *Poems*, the 1848 volume is gilded with a more picturesque title in *Leaves from a Peasant's Cottage Drawer: being Poems by Robert Davidson, Day-Labourer, Morebattle, Roxburghshire*. The 1848 edition also includes an epigraph from Cowper, a set of editorial notes for the interested reader, and is sized to fit in a coat pocket. Comparing it with the 1825 edition, the poems are re-ordered to emphasise the lyrical. Whereas the 1825 volume begins with 'The Witch's Cairn', a grimly comic rendering of a legend surrounding the trial of a local 'witch', the later edition opens with bucolic merriment on 'The Kirn Day' (1825), which describes the traditions surrounding the finish of a successful harvest. In many respects, 'The Kirn Day' exemplifies Davidson's accounts of rural life in that a keen eye for the value placed on tradition, the sometimes-cruel constrictions of peasant life, and the vitality of rural jollification is set within closely observed descriptions of the landscape and a final, more sombre, analysis of the situation of the poor. In 'The Kirn Day', it is the destruction of communities by the Lowland Clearances which haunts the landscape, unseen by the workers celebrating the harvest.

There is evident in the 1848 edition a tension between the efforts to present the ageing and impoverished Davidson as worthy of patronage for his person, if not his poetry, with Davidson's evident streak of independence. A short, rather hackneyed poem on the peasant-poet taking inspiration from the landscape, 'See Teviotdale romantic charms display' (1825), is cut from the later collection to allow for a dedication page. Davidson's dedication is not, however, addressed to an influential patron but rather to his peers.

TO

THE WORKING MEN OF THE BORDER

THESE POEMS ARE CHIEFLY DEDICATED

AS I AM ACQUAINTED CHIEFLY WITH THE SCENES WITH WHICH

THE COTTAGE ABOUNDS,

AND AM PERSUADED THAT IT CONTAINS

THE VERY SOUL AND LIFE-BLOOD OF OUR COUNTRY

MORE TRUE WORTH OF THE PLEASURES OF THE HEART BEING

FOUND AROUND ITS SIMPLE HEARTH

THAN IN MANY A STATELIER DWELLING

I FEEL THAT, WHILST YOU ARE WORTHY OF A FAR

NOBLER MUSE THAN MINE,

I CAN HAVE NO MORE NOBLE PATRON THAN YOURSELVES

THE WORKING MEN OF THE BORDER.

A number of Davidson's poems display an undercurrent of anger at the mistreatment of the poor: 'The Term Day' (1848), for example, concerns a peasant family packing and leaving their home, driven out by the system of agricultural employment which gives them no security. The poem mixes comic detail with a thread of cold-eyed rage masking as sentiment, as when Davidson describes their final leaving with a solitary calf, 'hawkie, routin', fetches up the rear' and notes bleakly 'She's a' their stock o' either goods or gear' (p. 41, ll. 44–45). This type of poem seems to contradict his declaration in the autobiography that 'I was content with the station in which Providence had placed me' (p. 4). However, the poet's ire is directed in general at those who fail in their duty, temporal and/or sacred, to their fellow man rather than at Providence itself.

The lands around Morebattle had a violent history. Dere Street skirts the parish and from the attentions of Roman legions, English armies, and the interminable cross-border raiding of the Reiving time, the inhabitants of the area had developed a hardy, independent character. Davidson was living through the Peninsular and Napoleonic Wars, and a number of his poems laud the history of Border men as warriors and reiterate the worth of the workingmen to their country in contrast to the 'sons o' affluence': 'They are the nerves that constitute her strength, / Ye're but the feathers waving on her brow' ('The Term Day', p. 42, ll. 66–67).

Davidson was also a farm labourer during a period of upheaval in the Agrarian Revolution. Morebattle in particular was surrounded by agricultural innovators, notably William Dawson of Frogden, who established turnip husbandry in the region in 1753, and James Church at Eckford, who introduced Church's Oats in 1776.[9] In terms of improving yield and feeding the urban population, such innovations were undoubtedly improvements on the old system. The farmed fields around Morebattle are rich agricultural land, which is why smallholdings could support peasant families. Yet it also made them ripe for amalgamation. As a child, Davidson had herded cattle on the unenclosed Border hills whose valleys were peppered with hamlets and fermtouns, but the agricultural improvements prompted widespread depopulation of the area in the Lowland Clearances as the old places were enclosed. Cottars were evicted by the landowners to allow for the amalgamation of smallholdings into large fields, and single tenant farmers, renting from those absentee landowners, often worked several farms together.

The local ministers, writing for the *Statistical Accounts,* regularly deplored the way in which farmworkers' cottages had been razed to make way for sheep-walks and noted that Morebattle had provided a refuge for the displaced. Many young men and some entire families from the area emigrated during the nineteenth century, including three of Davidson's sons who went to America and flourished there. One repeated image that opens Davidson's later poems is that of the now-empty land coming alive as people move within it, changing employment on 'The Term Day', gathering 'baith frae Tyne and Tiviot' for 'The Cheviot Games' (1848; p. 35, l. 17), and mustering for 'The Ordination' (1848). It was an irony that the same improvements that had seen Davidson's family evicted from Lempitlaw gifted the poet an opportunity to work on his verse unseen and undisturbed. Davidson says that he often found himself beginning verses whilst ploughing, but until he was married, with a house of his own and safe from the ridicule of his fellows, 'none of my attempts at poetry were ever written down' (p. 4). The heavier older ploughs needed two farm labourers, one man to guide the horses whilst another held down the plough but, after the introduction of an improved plough suited to the light Border soils, the ploughman worked alone to a steady rhythm for hours at a time.

The short autobiography added to the 1848 edition, while evidencing Davidson's farm-labouring background, also steers the contemporary reader towards key influences on Davidson's writing. In terms of schooling, Davidson shared a similar experience to James Hogg: both men had a scant formal education and depended for further opportunities on the generosity of others. Davidson describes sitting listening to elderly women's songs and stories and adds that 'few cottages were without Boston's and Erskine's works'.[10] The *United Presbyterian Magazine* noted that during the second half of the eighteenth century reading materials were limited for working folk on the Eastern Border; nevertheless, 'the sonnets and sermons of Ralph Erskine, as well as the works of Boston, Hervey, and Owen, were found at many a fireside' (pp. 359–60).

It is rare to be able to read about what a working-class writer encountered in his formative years beyond generalisations. Davidson's 'Autobiography' is strikingly specific about the impact of 'Barry's [sic] Collection'[11] for schools to which Davidson attributes his first experience of 'great writers' (p. 3). This popular school text contained secular pieces, including works by Addison, Shakespeare, Dryden, Thomson, Home, and Miss Christian Edwards. There were also works by two labouring-class poets: Christopher Jones from Crediton, Devon, and John Hoy, Jr, from Gattonside, near Melrose. The selections with explicitly Christian content spanned not only sections from the King James Bible, but also Milton and four hymns by

Isaac Watts. As might have been expected, religious poetry is represented by, amongst others, Grey's 'Elegy', James Hervey's 'Meditations', and Pope's 'Universal Prayer'. Taken as a whole these pieces afford a deal of what Eric Parisot refers to as the 'didactic opportunities afforded by death'.[12] There has been a scholarly tendency to characterise the influence of the Graveyard School of poetry as both pervasive and deadening, and Davidson's poems 'The Poor Man's Funeral' (1848), 'On the Death of Mr. Pringle of Clifton' (1848), and 'Churchyard Musings' (1848) do cover familiar ground, but there is a range of religious writing in Alexander Barrie's *Collection* which goes beyond a simple survey of the Graveyard School. Taken together with the dense theological arguments of Boston and Erskine, Davidson encountered a breadth of writing which tried to express man's path to faith, including works by ministers from Morebattle, notably Robert Culbertson (1765–1823), author of *The Covenanter's Manual* (1808).

Davidson contrasts Barrie's *Collection* with the penny histories and ballads, oral renditions of ghost stories, and ancient songs he had encountered till then. 'I had attempted before this to compose some simple verses, of which [...] I was proud; but I found now that doggerel rhyme and poetry were two distinct things' (p. 3). Like Hogg, Davidson claimed not to have heard of Burns until after the poet's death (p. 3). However, at the age of twenty-one, Davidson was hired to a farmer who had a share in a country library and allowed the ploughman to take out what volumes he wished. This may have been the Morebattle Library, founded on Whitsunday 1797, in which 'membership represented all classes of the community'.[13] Davidson's name appears on a list of subscribers in the mid-nineteenth century. Notes from the library Minute Book support the assessment of the Rev. Walter Morison in the *Statistical Account* of 1845 that the books were 'chiefly in general literature', alongside some noted theological works, and surviving volumes from the library stock include Witherspoon's *Essays on Important Subjects* (1765) and Andrew Thomson's *The Doctrine of Universal Pardon considered and refuted* (1830). Morison described the folk of Morebattle as 'generally sober and industrious [...] of moral and religious habits. Many of them have a taste for reading and are well informed and intelligent' (p. 452). At this time, he estimated that the library contained six to seven hundred volumes. The range of literary works that Davidson encountered is reflected in the breadth of forms and styles that he wrote in.

Davidson's literary background as it influenced his writing

A number of scholars have addressed the linguistic and stylistic origins of working-class writing. In particular, in 2016 H. B. de Groot focused on the way in which Hogg's works 'absorb structural and stylistic aspects of prior texts' becoming 'the source of his metatextual and self-referential narrative style'.[14] In 2009, Kirstie Blair suggested that 'the concept of "hybridity" might be useful in exploring works that blend the voice of a working-class author with more established voices, whether through allusion, quotation, parody, or a less definable sense of linguistic and formal influence'.[15] Blair goes on to point out that whilst the Scottish poets could be read as colonial writers, class is rather more important than nationality to her argument, whilst Ian Brown sees hybridity as a key element of Scottish cultural making, prompted by the country's multiple languages and complex border lines, and determines that 'issues of cultural definition grow, in one dimension, out of the language communities to which one belongs or has access'.[16]

It is certainly the case that Davidson utilises a considerable breadth of verse forms and a selection of English and dialect vocabularies to suit the subject of each poem.[17] He uses at least fifteen different verse forms, including Standard Habbie and Christis Kirk verse. In his religious poetry, Davidson confines himself almost exclusively to the formal English he would have encountered in the religious writings of the period and which his target readership would have expected in discussing serious subjects.

An exception to Davidson's usual habit, however, occurs in the 'Epistle to William Bennet' (1848), where he addresses a fellow day labourer with a survey of their situation, comparing it to that of the rich and offering up a common-sense plan to avoid the pitfalls of drink, greed, and the abuse of power:

> The lee lang day fatigued and toil'd,
> Wi' to the haunches soil'd,
>   Thrang delvin' in a ditch;

> Yet still it's needless to repine,
> Though poor's the lot—it's your's and mine;
>   We canna a' be rich.
> (p. 120, ll. 1–6)

Davidson describes the careworn rich man imagining a rural idyll for the poor, whilst the poor imagine the rich as carefree, and both parties mistake the case, for each has their challenges whilst sharing the bounties 'Dame nature' bestows on one and all:

> A nearer view makes us confess,
> The means of human happiness,
>   Are very equal shared;
> For, when we right consider a',
> We find the differ is but sma'
>   'Tween cottars and the laird.
> (p. 120, ll. 25–30)

However, the poet warns against earthly consolations, such as drink or the love of money, which cannot provide the solid foundation upon which true happiness is built:

> When stern misfortune bends her bow,
> And aims her shafts at me or you,
>   We'll shun what's low an' mean;
> Amidst the stour we'll catch content,
> And scorn each peevish, poor complaint,
>   That ne'er can serve a preen.
> (p. 121, ll. 43–48)

The religious content in Davidson's poetry ranges from coincidental background detail, through the re-telling of historical events and contemporary religious controversy, to the most intimate accounts of the struggle for faith in the face of personal tragedy. At one level, the prompt for 'Lines on the

Falling Down of the Bell of Hownam Kirk' (1848), in which the narrator sees the valley filled with faeries, witches, and warlocks, was a local belief that 'uncanny beings' would be driven away by the tolling of the kirk bell, whilst the editor's notes in the 1848 *Leaves* edition tells the reader that 'The Witch's Cairn' (1825) 'was suggested on seeing a stone [...] which tradition pointed out as the spot where those horrible tragedies of witch-burning were perpetrated amid the pious maxims of our forefathers' (p. 184).

'The Witch's Cairn' was the longest piece in the 1825 publication and utilised a common theme, in suspicion of the Catholic Church and its clergy. The narrator, wondering about the desolate spot known as the Witch's Cairn, meets with a shepherd who recounts the tale, passed down to him, of an old woman, Maggie, who is seized by a mob and brought to trial for witchcraft, before a corrupt judge. A blacksmith, shepherd, and weaver in turn accuse her of fantastical malevolence, in patently absurd accounts of their misfortunes. Maggie almost sways the crowd in her defence, but then a priest appears to tell a tale of sexual misdeeds in a convent and Maggie is doomed. The length may have suggested its position as the first poem in the collection; however, in 1848 it has been moved further into the volume and has also been edited to remove some earthy comments on the character of the Judge, suggestive of a younger, more acerbic spectator of human failings.

> 1825 text:
> The wide fields of science he clearly could scan,
> His study was woman—I dare not say man;
> Nor wit, worth, nor genius can shield from mishap,—
> He'd twice been bewitched, and thrice had the c—!
> His fame as a judge flew o'er land and o'er sea,
> For none came before him that ever got free:
> (p. 17, ll. 129–34)

> 1848 text:
> The wide fields of science he clearly could scan,
> His study was woman—I dare not say man;

His fame as a judge flew o'er land and o'er sea,
For none came before him that ever got free.
(p. 30, ll. 1-4)

Davidson allows the three initial accusers to reveal the absurd character of their complaints through their own mouths, but the humorous tone is tempered by the ignorance of the mob, which would affix the responsibility for a community's misfortunes at the feet of the person least able to defend themselves. Yet Maggie makes a strong defence, based in both logic – 'My couch in the cavern is flinty and hard— / If demons employ me, how poor's my reward!' (p. 31, ll. 180–81) – and sentiment, appealing to their collective memory of and respect for the fallen of Flodden. Davidson allows a moment's pause, with a brief, isolated, four-line stanza after her speech is ended, to show how the crowd could be persuaded by common sense and a shared humanity, if given the opportunity:

When two rushing torrents do thwart in their course,
They're both for a moment bereft of their force!
Swift o'er the wide crowd rose a short broken sigh,
And a mild beam of pity shone in each eye.
(p. 32, ll. 190–93)

Even as reason might prevail a 'friar came forward and spoke in the ring, / Then reason and pity fled both on swift wing' (p. 32, ll. 194–95). He offers the crowd a heady mix of sexual shenanigans and religion, and Maggie's fate is sealed. As final evidence of the tenacious nature of ignorant superstition, the shepherd relating these events to the narrator, evinces Maggie's guilt by the blasted nature of the cairn where her ashes were scattered.

'The Witch's Cairn' is a straightforward imagining of a local legend and offers no particular insight into Davidson's religious beliefs beyond an abhorrence of the religious extremism of the past, which should seem both brutal and ignorant to the Enlightenment reader; however, there are a handful of poems in the earlier collection which grapple with more personal trials. A comparison of the religious poetry in the 1825 volume with that in the 1848 collection reveals a younger man who sometimes struggles to reconcile his faith with the knocks of life that come to him personally amidst a world that seems forever in a maelstrom of change.

The poem 'Epistle to a Rev. Friend' (1825) sees the poet gaze on a world where ostensibly the fall of the French Empire, like that of Greece and Rome before it, should bring about peace and yet 'still there's nothing but perpetual change' (p. 68, l. 32). As grieving parents mourn the loss of their children, and orphans their parents, Davidson appeals to the minister to support his flock through these painful events and look forward to the 'sleep secure' of death until 'nature wakes thee with her parting groan; / When the vain transient things of time are o'er; / And all is fix'd and change shall be no more' (p. 68, ll. 80–82). The editor of the 1848 edition identifies the minister as the Rev. David W. Gordon, the parochial minister of Earlston, in a simple asterisked footnote; however, there is a rather more pointed note beneath the first page of the poem 'Lines Written on Visiting the Grave of a Young Friend' (1825), which states: 'It may interest the reader to know, that the young friend was the author's own daughter, who died of croup, at the age of twelve' (p. 70). This piece is paired with a second poem, 'A Mother's Lament for the Death of an Infant Son' (1825), for which the footnote simply reads: 'The deceased was the author's son' (p. 78). Nowhere does it tell the reader that the children died within six months of one another.

Many of Davidson's commentaries on death are confident declarations of the power of Christian belief, for example 'The Poor Man's Funeral' and, indeed, the 'Mother's Lament' mocks the 'sceptic' who has no hope of a blessed reunion to be his 'pole-star' through life (p. 80, ll. 63–74). However, Davidson acknowledges his own weakness in 'Lines Written on Visiting the Grave'. The poet struggles, repeatedly trying and failing to reconcile his grief with both 'sense' and 'reason'. He seeks to console himself with the thought that his daughter is in heaven, but finds himself weak, trapped by 'the frail bosom, still to sense enslaved' (p. 71, l. 31) and cannot sustain the thought against the agony of 'remembrance'. Then he thinks of the child mourning her dead brother and wonders 'How lost to reason every grief appears / That mourns thy exit from a land of tears' (p. 71, ll. 51–52). Finally, as he remembers her last moments, his account of Christ's redeeming power and the strength she drew from it appears as much to support the poet in the writing as to record the child's experience:

> At the decisive, final, trying hour,
> When vain's the aidance of created power,
> You lean'd on Him whose arm can succour yield,
> Who doth the keys of death's dark mansions wield;
> Whose strong right hand, omnipotent to save,
> Dispels the terrors that begird the grave;
> Streaks death's dark valley with celestial light,
> And shields his friends with uncreated might—
> (p. 72, ll. 73-80)

Davidson views religion in its political context

The 1848 collection shows Davidson both expanding on previous works and addressing some contemporary events. A wryly amusing earlier poem, 'The Gypsy's Rant' (1825), in which a Romany woman laments the impact of the Scottish Enlightenment on the fortune-telling trade, now has a neat companion piece in 'The Constable's Rant' (1848) in which her nemesis, one of the local constables, launches on a drunken tirade, boasting of their prowess in dealing with '[t]ipsy tinkers' wives' (p. 151, l. 20). However, the intervening twenty years also see Davidson grow more inclined to view the articulation of faith in a broader, political context, so that the religious pieces added to the 1848 collection include, for example, 'Religion versus Sect' (1848) and 'The Song of the Patriotic Elector' (1848) which skewers the venality of religious and political institutions.[18] The later volume also contains poems rooted in the history and culture of the surrounding locality, notably 'A Tale of the Covenanters' (1848) and 'The Ordination' (1848).

'The Ordination' is the longest of Davidson's religious works, set around the action of a celebrated Ordination Riot in 1725, when the congregation at Morebattle rebelled against the imposition of a new minister by the 'patron'. It follows a familiar pattern for his narrative pieces whereby Davidson begins by describes the surrounding landscape, the weather, the flora and fauna.

He describes in vivid, sometimes humorous, tones the unfolding events of the day, and ends by stepping back to view the Riot in the context of developments over the succeeding years. Early on the poet admits to working from traditional oral records, 'as legends tell' (p. 89, l. 31), and whilst Davidson would have been familiar with both the theological arguments behind the riot and the accounts handed down within the seceding community, it is doubtful if he would have had access to original documents from the period which reveal the peril in which the rioters stood and the tangle of loyalties which saw seventy of Morebattle's residents hauled before the Jedburgh court. According to letters between Sir William Bennet of Grubbet and the Countess of Roxburgh, the trial was a fractious affair. The Morebattle defendants had secured a lawyer who robustly defended their right to choose their own minister, whilst the authorities, threatening the defendants with the death penalty should any further disturbance occur, could obtain no coherent account of the event itself, although it was clear that the sheriffs had largely ignored the correct procedure for dealing with a riot.

In 'The Ordination', Davidson plainly regarded with contempt the actions of a crown and an elite who thought to control the conscience of the people by statute:

> Of pastor, they no more had choice,
> Since law had hush'd the public voice,
>   And said they must submit;
> 'Twas vain objections, then, to make,
> Since they must for their pastor take
>   Whom e'er his Grace thought fit.
> (p. 89, ll. 37–42)

However, he also deplored the resort of the crowd to 'Border' justice, whilst recognising that the impetus ran deep:

> The crowd are oft less wise than wight,
> And loath to part with public right—
>   Their counsel's rash and vain.

> Despite of Anna's mandate high,
> They were resolved club law to try
> > Their freedom to maintain.
>
> In Scotland's rude and restless days,
> To wait upon the law's delays,
> > Men had but little skill.
> From their own hand to seek remeid,
> Long time had been their border creed—
> > Its spirit lingered still.
> (pp. 89–90, ll. 43–54)

Davidson is particularly critical of the insult offered to the church building itself, once considered a place within which people gathered soberly, respectful of its sacred character, and also identifies in this religious dispute the origin of the current moral decline of the Kirk:

> With clamour now the kirk resounds,
> Each lifts his voice, and sense confounds.
> > What a sad change is there!
> These men once thought it deadly sin
> That sacred pile to enter in,
> > But with a reverend air.
>
> The kirk was then revered, I ween;
> She in broad Scotland sat a queen,
> > By Scotland's favour graced.
> But now in this unhappy hour,
> Dropp'd from her diadem a flower
> > That's never been replaced.
> (p. 93, ll. 153–64)

The position that Davidson finds himself in, balanced between an Enlightenment appreciation of moderation, knowledge, and due process, and the core beliefs of a resilient religious community, conscious of its long history of resistance to persecution, reveals itself in the way in which he deals with the rioters, their fundamental complaint and eventual acceptance of the minister selected for them, swayed by the man's personal piety rather than pressed to it. He introduces the leader of the rioters, Nub of Bowmont/Beaumont, as a reckless, religious zealot:

> Great zeal for Scotland's kirk he had—
> No common zeal, but zeal run mad—
>   As frantic as the wind;
> And when his hobby-horse got head,
> He, scouring off with reckless speed,
>   Left common sense behind.
> (p. 90, ll. 19–24)

However, despite this fiery introduction, the speech Davidson gives Nub, in sixty-eight lines of rhyming couplets, could be seen as more measured in tone than the account of the persecution of the faithful in 'A Tale of the Covenanters'. Nub's address begins with an appeal to 'Ye true border men' and lists the enemies defeated in the surrounding landscape: Romans, Saxons and Danes, the English, and latterly '[s]ome ones of her princes were worse than her foe' (p. 92, l. 104). Nub outlines the struggle against the Stuart who 'attempted to fetter their mind[s]' (p. 92, l. 106), the persecution under the 'bloodhounds of Clavers', and declares that '[n]o tyranny's safe while's religion's unbound' (p. 92, l. 118). Now their hard-won rights are once more threatened; Nub's final call to action is critical of the current generation of clergy:

> For this foul encroachment our clergy we blame—
> Their great predecessors, how different from them!
> Ne'er tempted by lucre, nor scar'd by a frown,
> The rights of the people, they counted their own.
> The times now are alter'd. There's none to contend
> On the side of the peasant, his rights to defend.

> Since now on ourselves our dependence must be,
> I hope we dare venture a blow to be free.
> Be men and stand by me; If right is bereft,
> This day they shall find that our cudgels are left.
> (p. 93, ll. 137–46)

Davidson is able to write characterful voices in local dialect, for example that of the drunken Constable, but for so serious an argument, he reverts to formal English and finds himself unable, or unwilling, to give a distinctive voice to Nub that conveys both the sympathetic narrative of his argument and his avowed character of zealot.

Throughout the riot, Davidson reiterates that no-one was badly hurt and he emphasises the active role played by the intervention of 'a band, like Bruce's', comprising the women of the community (p. 96, l. 223). Davidson's account of the riot itself is dryly humorous, utilising military vocabulary and succinct punctuation to suggest the rhythm of the shifting fortunes in the fight.

> Maids, wives and widows were the band,
> Who nobly then, with heart and hand,
>   On Nubie's side fought keen;
> Nor did they ammunition lack—
> The kirkyard dyke was at their back—
>   They found a magazine.
> (p. 96, ll. 225–30)

[...]

> The clergy now bewail'd the day,
> But had no power to quell the fray,
>   Since blood was hot and high.
> They stood, like cravens on the spot,
> And often jouked a random shot,
>   As stones flew whistling by.

> The guards could now no longer bear
> Those fierce assaults on front and rear,
> > Though little blood was shed;
> But when they saw Nub leading on
> Another charge, with stick and stone,
> > They wavered, reel'd and fled.
> (pp. 97–98, ll. 255–66)

Nub's identification of the clergy as complicit in the hated new law echoes other criticisms of contemporary sacred and temporal powers evident in a number of Davidson's later poems. Davidson deplores the fractious nature of contemporary religious beliefs in 'Religion versus Sect' (1848). He also offers up a stark account of the pressure put on newly enfranchised voters to vote to their landlord's instruction in the days before secret ballots, in 'Lines Suggested by Incidents following the Passing of the Reform Bill' (1848), which portrays the Kirk as perceiving the reform as a threat to its financial interests. A more sympathetic relation between the Kirk and the local community appears in 'Lines Suggested by the Visit of the Cholera' (1848), where the poet lauds a minister, identified by the editors as being Mr Taylor of the Relief Church, Coldstream who, amidst the danger of infection, did not desert his sick and dying charges.

The Border and the Voice

Scholarship around the impact of living on a Border, belonging to a Border people, has often focused on concrete borders; however, Davidson's experience of living as a labouring Borderer, on a divide only clearly marked on the maps of the governing elites, undoubtedly strengthens the impetus to define, record, and celebrate the experience of the places and communities around him. The complexity and duality of the borderer's lived experience is reflected in his ability to seemingly straddle competing powers and pressures and not to see a contradiction in doing so. Kenneth McNeil's work on Walter Scott's *Minstrelsy of the Scottish Border* has addressed the impact of Scott's complex combination of ballad collection, editing, and invention, in an imaginative recounting of the historical and regional parameters that defined the author's own community; and an (in)authentic (auto) ethnography in that it forges, in both senses of the word, a historical and genealogical continuity that is set against the disruptive forces of modernisation.[19]

The impact of change and hopes for change for the good is a recurring theme in Davidson's poetry. His strong attachment to the search for truth and justice within a Christian framework is evident in the final verse of 'Religion versus Sect', which sets out Davidson's vision for a balanced future:

> We hail the dawning of a happier day,
> When bigotry is sinking into decay,
> When education aids the mental sight,
> Amidst the blaze of revelation's light,
> Candid to read that volume from above,
> That teaches peace, good will, and Christian love.
> (p. 126, ll. 75–80)

Davidson's 'own community' is rooted both in the land and the history of the land. The 1866 article in the *United Presbyterian Magazine* characterised the landscape around Gateshaw Brae as playing an active role in sheltering the persecuted faithful, providing lookout points and escape routes for the hunted clergy, alongside ideal acoustics for preaching to a crowd. It is the refuge from where the precious word can emerge, tempered by adversity, so that Davidson's creativity must be assessed not only in terms of the liminality of the borderlands but also for the additional layer of communal history and contemporary beliefs operating on the poet's relationship with the subjects, themes, and structures of his verses. The unenclosed hills of his youth, peopled by folk 'baith frae Tyne and Tiviot', speaking in Border tongues of things lost and won, run in parallel with the roots, ideology, and varied literature of his secession faith.

Endnotes

1. This chapter was prompted by a conference paper, jointly presented with David Welsh, with contributions from Martin Marroni and Rev. Dr I. D. L. Clark, for the ASLS Conference 'Literature and Religion in Scotland' (Glasgow University, 1–2 July 2016).
2. Iain Whyte, *Scotland and the Abolition of Black Slavery, 1756–1838* (Edinburgh: Edinburgh University Press, 2006), p. 81. The United Associate Congregation of Morebattle sent another petition on the same subject in 1831.
3. Rev. James Rutherford, 'Introduction: Alehouses and State of Religion' in *Statistical Account of Scotland 1791–1845: Appendix of Hounam [sic], County of Roxburghshire* (OSA, 1799) XXI, pp. 19–20.
4. 'Reminiscences of Gateshaw Brae' in *The United Presbyterian Magazine New Series – Vol. X* (Edinburgh: William Oliphant, 1866), pp. 354–361.
5. Ibid., p. 358.
6. Robert Davidson, 'Autobiography of Robert Davidson', in *Leaves from a Peasant's Cottage Drawer: being Poems by Robert Davidson, Day-Labourer, Morebattle, Roxburghshire* (Edinburgh: James Hogg, 1848) pp. 4–5.
7. Robert Davidson, *Poems* (Jedburgh: Printed for the Author, by W. Easton 1825); Robert Davidson, *Leaves from a Peasant's Cottage Drawer: being Poems by Robert Davidson, Day-Labourer, Morebattle, Roxburghshire* (Edinburgh: James Hogg, 1848).
8. Robert Davidson, *Leaves from a Peasant's Cottage Drawer: Robert Davidson 1778–1855*, ed. David Welsh, Robert Davidson Committee (Leicester: Matador, 2008). Further citations to this edition given in text.
9. Rev. David Ure, *General View of the Agriculture of the County of Roxburgh*, The Board of Agriculture and Internal Improvement (London: B. Millan, 1794), pp. 30, 34, 52.
10. Robert Davidson, 'Autobiography of Robert Davidson Day-Labourer, Morebattle Written in his Seventieth Year' in *Leaves from the Peasant's Cottage Drawer*, ed. David Welsh, pp. 1–5 (p. 2).
11. Alexander Barrie, *A Collection of English Prose and Verse, for the Use of Schools, Selected from different Authors*, 2nd edn (Edinburgh, Leith: The Author & W. Coke, 1781).
12. Eric Parisot, 'The Work of Feeling in James Hervey's *Meditations among the Tombs* (1746)', *Parergon* 31.2 (2014), pp. 121–135. Project MUSE, doi:10.1353/pgn.2014.0073.
13. J. E. F. C., 'Rural Libraries', Letter to *The Scotsman* newspaper, 21 December 1925, col. 5. The letter was sent by Mrs J. E. F. Cowan, antiquarian, who claimed to have the library Minute Book, now lost, before her as she wrote.
14. H. B. De Groot, 'The Labourer and Literary Tradition: James Hogg's Early Reading and Its Impact on Him as a Writer', in *James Hogg and the Literary Marketplace: Scottish Romanticism and the Working-Class Author*, ed. Holly Faith Nelson (London: Routledge 2016), pp. 81–92 (p. 81).
15. Kirstie Blair, '"He Sings Alone": Hybrid forms and the Victorian Working-Class Poet' in *Victorian Literature and Culture* 37 (2009), pp. 523–41. doi:10.1017/S1060150309090329.
16. Blair, p. 527; Ian Brown, *Scottish Theatre: Diversity, Language, Continuity* (Amsterdam: Rodopi, 2013), p. 24.
17. As part of the 2016 conference paper, Martin Marroni, 'Analysis of Robert Davidson's Verse Forms', revealed that Davidson uses at least fifteen different verse forms: (1) Standard Habbie; (2) Christis Kirk; (3) iambic tetrameter couplets; (4) iambic pentameter couplets; (5) iambic pentameter nonets (ABABCDCDD); (6) quatrains ABAB in trimeter,

(7) tetrameter, and (8) pentameter; (9) quatrains AABB in tetrameter; (10) sestet: 2 x tetrameter + trimeter, e.g. 'The Ordination'; (11) tetrameter triplets + tag; (12) hexameters + tetrameter refrain; and (13, 14, 15) three distinct song forms.

18 For further discussion of Davidson's complex treatment of these themes, and the challenging combination of Davidson's lyrics with the performance format/lyrics of racially charged popular song, see Barbara Bell, 'Robert Davidson', *The People's Voice: Scottish political poetry, song, and the franchise, 1832-1918*, 1 June 2017: thepeoplesvoice.glasgow.ac.uk/robert-davidson-by-barbara-bell/.

19 Kenneth McNeil, 'Ballads and Borders', in *The Edinburgh Companion to Sir Walter Scott*, ed. Fiona Robertson (Edinburgh: Edinburgh University Press 2012), pp. 22–34 (p. 24).

7. Walter Scott's *Religious Discourses*

J. H. ALEXANDER

Of Walter Scott's many acts of personal kindness, the most curious must surely be his composition in autumn 1824 of two sermons for the profoundly deaf 'stickit minister' George Huntly Gordon (1796–1868). Scott had first made Gordon's acquaintance during his visit to the field of Waterloo in 1815 when the young man's father, a major on half-pay residing in Brussels, showed the poet round the site and offered him hospitality. He had taken to the youth with the ear-trumpet, sensing his 'intelligence, accuracy, and organizational powers', and in due course he employed him as his amanuensis and the cataloguer of his library at Abbotsford for extended periods between 1819 and 1826 while Gordon was wrestling with the problem his deafness posed in his quest for a pulpit.[1] In his biography of Scott, J. G. Lockhart gives an account of the genesis of the two sermons:

> [Gordon] was spending the autumn of 1824 [at Abbotsford], daily copying the MS. of Redgauntlet, and working at leisure hours on the Catalogue of the Library, when the family observed him to be labouring under some extraordinary depression of mind. It was just then that he had at length obtained the prospect of a Living, and Sir Walter was surprised that this should not have exhilarated him. Gently sounding the trumpet, however, he discovered that the agitation of the question about the deafness had shaken his nerves—his scruples had been roused—his conscience was sensitive,—and he avowed that, though he thought, on the whole, he ought to go through with the business, he could not command his mind so as to prepare a couple of sermons which, unless he summarily abandoned his object, must be produced on a certain day—then near at hand—before his Presbytery. Sir Walter reminded him, that his exercises when on trials for the Probationership had given satisfaction; but

nothing he could say was sufficient to re-brace Mr Gordon's spirits, and he at length exclaimed, with tears, that his pen was powerless,— that he had made fifty attempts, and saw nothing but failure and disgrace before him. Scott answered, 'My good young friend, leave this matter to me—do you work away at the Catalogue, and I'll write for you a couple of sermons that shall pass muster well enough at Aberdeen.' Gordon assented with a sigh; and next morning Sir Walter gave him the MS. of the 'Religious Discourses'.[2]

On reflection, Gordon realised that he could not pass the sermons off as his own, and in the event, as we shall see, he was able to produce perfectly acceptable substitutes, but he came to appreciate that his disability was incompatible with a clerical career in those days. Three years later, when working in London as a private secretary at the Treasury, he found himself in financial difficulties, and at his request Scott, who was by now himself in straightened circumstances and unable to come up with ready cash, reluctantly agreed to allow him to sell the sermons for publication without formally advertising their authorship:

> As I have no money to spare at present, I find it necessary to make a sacrifice of my own scruples, to relieve you from serious difficulties. The enclosed will entitle you to deal with any respectable bookseller. You must tell the history in your own way as shortly as possible. All that is necessary it to say is, that the discourses were written to oblige a young friend. It is understood my name is not to be put on the title-page, or blazed at full length in the preface. You may trust that to the newspapers.[3]

Accordingly, on 30 April 1828, *Religious Discourses. By a Layman* (identified, pretty transparently, as 'W. S.' of Abbotsford) were brought out by the popular publisher Henry Colburn (Scott called him 'a puffing quack'), to whom Lockhart had directed Gordon, and who paid the fee of two hundred and fifty pounds in line with Scott's estimate of the sermons' commercial value.[4]

That Scott was able to turn his hand to sermon writing for a few hours, and make a decent job of it, is hardly surprising. He was not a regular churchgoer, though he did conduct family worship on Sundays, reading the Prayer Book service.[5] But as a boy he had been familiar, albeit less than enthusiastically, with the family pew at Old Greyfriars Kirk, where the pulpit was occupied Sunday to Sunday by either the historian and moderate William Robertson (1721–1793, collegiate minister from 1761) or his evangelical colleague John Erskine (1721–1803, collegiate minister from 1767). Walter Scott senior expected his family and the servants to rehearse later on Sundays the arguments of the sermons they had heard at their chosen places of worship.[6] Only one of Robertson's sermons was published,[7] but a selection of those preached by Erskine appeared as *Discourses Preached on Several Occasions*.[8] Scott's two discourses have the careful organisation and something of the density of scriptural illustration evident in Erskine's published sermons (though, as the account of his preaching in *Guy Mannering* makes clear, he spoke from notes rather than reading a prepared script).[9] The reviewer of the *Discourses* for the *Athenaeum* has an eminently sensible characterisation:

> They contain nothing novel, either in sentiment or doctrine, are written in a simple and unornamented style, and derive all the illustrations which are employed from the usual sources of pulpit oratory. They will, of course, be less generally attractive, composed in this style, than they would have been had they possessed the graces of originality and ornament. But their excellent author has given a proof of the power of his mind and of his acquirements, greater than any he could have produced by the most laboured attempts at sermon-writing. A man of inferior powers would most probably have flourished away at every point that admitted of his being eloquent; but Sir Walter has explained and defended the doctrines of Scripture with a calm and unruffled seriousness, has spoken like one long experienced in the medium style of such addresses, and appears throughout as too well acquainted with

his subject to confound either the language or sentiment of poetry with that intended to convey instruction t[o] persons of ordinary understanding.[10]

In his account of the genesis of the *Discourses,* Lockhart makes it clear that he is interested in the story, not the sermons:

> I am afraid that the 'Religious Discourses' [...] would, but for the author's name, have had a brief existence; but the history of their composition, besides sufficiently explaining the humility of these tracts in a literary as well as a theological point of view, will, I hope, gratify most of my readers.[11]

Scott himself wrote to Gordon that 'they contain no novelty of opinion, and no attempt at brilliancy of composition': they are merely 'rational and practical' discourses on particular texts; Scott fears that 'those who open this pamphlet with expectations of a higher kind will be much disappointed'.[12] But the *Discourses* have rather more to interest the literary student than Lockhart's comment, or the verdict of the *Athenaeum*, might suggest. Although it would be difficult to make any claims for them as creative works, they contain elements which can usefully be linked with Scott's work as a novelist: firstly, in his choice of texts; and secondly, in certain stylistic touches.

Choice of texts

It may reasonably be conjectured that Scott had a free choice of texts for his sermons, which form a complementary pair. The first may be characterised as doctrinal; the second (somewhat shorter) as practical. The first takes a single verse as its text, while the second offers a commentary on the first psalm.

For the doctrinal sermon, Scott selected as his text a verse from the Sermon on the Mount (Matthew 5. 17), 'Think not that I am come to destroy the law, or the prophets; I am not come to destroy, but to fulfil'. His discourse is in two parts: in the first, he explores the significance of Jesus's assertion at the time it was made, suggesting that it was intended to bring his hearers back to those fundamental principles underlying the minutiae of the law, principles they had lost sight of; in the second, he finds in the life and death of Jesus the ultimate fulfilment of the law.

One can see that Scott's pervasive concern with evolution and mutation in societies, and his rejection of abrupt revolution, would draw him to the fulfilling rather than the destroying of the law. One is bound to link the motif with the negative and inhumane rigidities evident in a certain Christian attitude to Judaism in *Ivanhoe*,[13] where the text Scott was to choose for his sermon is debated, albeit obliquely, by Beaumanoir and Rebecca as he attempts to convert her:

> 'In some sisterhood of the strictest order, shalt thou have time for prayer and fitting penance, and that repentance not to be repented of. This do and live—what has the law of Moses done for thee that thou shouldest die for it?'
>
> 'It was the law of my fathers', said Rebecca; 'it was delivered in thunders and in storms upon the mountain of Sinai, in cloud and in fire. This, if ye are Christians, ye believe—it is, you say, recalled, but so my teachers have not taught me.'[14]

Scott's first discourse asserts that, rather than being 'recalled', the detailed Mosaic institutions continued to be valid, though it is understood they became progressively obsolescent when 'that part of the Church which consisted of Christian Jews or Judaizing Christians, gradually diminishing, merged at length in the great mass of Christianity, and availed themselves of the general liberty' to observe the essence of the law, found in Deuteronomy and confirmed in the Sermon on the Mount, loving one's neighbour as oneself (pp. 36–37).[15]

Another factor drawing Scott to the fulfilment text, or at any rate confirming its appropriateness for him, is likely to have been the opportunity it afforded to discuss a recurring motif in the novels: hypocrisy. This first discourse notes that Jesus's teaching was seen as a threat by the Sadducees and the Pharisees, whom Scott characterises respectively as atheists or epicureans and spiritually proud hypocrites. It is significant that he devotes only one page to the Sadducees whereas the Pharisees occupy several (reflecting the scriptural emphasis), and that he introduces a number of references to other gospel texts, most notably the Pharisee and the publican in Luke 18 and the censure in Matthew 23 of the Pharisees' 'enlarged garments and extended phylacteries, their lengthened prayers, their formal ceremonial, and tithes of mint and anise' and their 'whited sepulchres' (pp. 16–17). There are a number of allusions to these texts in the novels, and it is instructive to compare the straightforward nature of their introduction in the sermons with the complex shifting multivocal patterns in the fiction. Thus the Pharisee is invoked by Henry Warden at the climax of his attack on the youthful and proud self-confidence of Roland in the fourth chapter of *The Abbot*.[16] The much less stable Bridgnorth in *Peveril of the Peak* proclaims that he has been taught by adversity to abandon his 'cold, formal, pharasaical meditations'; as texts take over his discourse in the last chapters, Bridgnorth recalls that 'in the days of [his] nonage' he thought as Julian does now, deeming 'it sufficient to pay my tithes of cummin and anniseed—my poor petty moral observances of the old law'.[17] In other novels, the dominical strictures are appropriated for a wide range of denominational censures: by Burley on Morton, by David Deans on separatism or pharisaism among those of his own persuasion, by Holdforth on Anthony Forster's lingering Catholic impurity, by Sir Henry Lee on Milton, by a Catholic sister in *The Abbot* on Protestant limitations, and by Redgauntlet on Joshua Geddes.[18] Two pharisaical references in *Quentin Durward* match the tone of the discourse closely: the Author's censure of Louis's hypocrisy is contrasted with his appreciation of the fundamental authenticity of Quentin Durward's Catholic devotion:

> its purpose being sincere, we can scarce suppose it unacceptable to the only true Deity, who regards the motives and not the forms of prayer, and in whose eyes the sincere devotion of a heathen is more estimable than the specious hypocrisy of a Pharisee.[19]

While the first discourse is most obviously linked with *Ivanhoe*, the second points towards *The Heart of Mid-Lothian*, and in particular the much-debated concluding moral:

> READER—This tale will not be told in vain, if it shall be found to illustrate the great truth, that guilt, though it may attain temporal splendour, can never confer real happiness; that the evil consequences of our crimes long survive the commission, and, like the ghosts of the murdered, for ever haunt the stapes of the malefactor; and that the paths of virtue, though seldom those of worldly greatness, are always those of pleasantness and peace.[20]

In his practical sermon, Scott introduces a parallel argument dealing with the righteous man of the first two verses of the psalm, and then the unrighteous man of verses three and four. He argues that the righteous man may be blessed with temporal prosperity, since 'tried honesty, approved fidelity, devoted courage, public spirit, the estimation created by a blameless conduct, and the general respect which even the profane bear to a man of conscience and honesty, often elevate to eminence' (p. 66). This, however, he argues, is by no means universally the case, and

> It is safer therefore to view the blessed state of the righteous, as consisting in that calm of mind, which no one can enjoy without the applause of his own conscience, and the humble confidence in which, with mingled faith and hope, the good man throws himself on the protection of Providence. (p. 67)

The unrighteous man prompts a mirror argument: 'If the righteousness of the just is sometimes followed by temporal prosperity, the wickedness of the profane is yet more frequently attended by temporal punishment' (pp. 68-69), but (in the words of Psalm 37) 'we have seen the wicked great in power, and flourishing like a green bay-tree' (p. 70). In the novel, the concluding moral is highly nuanced and qualified, not least because it is not clear who is the moraliser (the Author, or Pattieson, or conceivably

Cleishbotham), and there can be no question of a single correct reading. But the sermon may suggest as one possibility an emphasis on the predictability of the lack of 'real happiness' in the malefactor and an inner 'pleasantness and peace' in the virtuous.

Style

At the beginning of this chapter, it was noted how the *Athenaeum* praised the stylistic decorum of the *Discourses*. This was a view shared by other reviewers, though decorum was not invariably welcomed: the hostile *Monthly Review* thought the sermons flowed on 'smoothly and coldly enough' and the Unitarian *Christian Examiner* in Boston declared that Scott had either 'caught an infectious dullness from his employment' or deliberately assumed it.[21] Scott himself observed to Gordon that '[t]he eloquence of the pulpit should be of a chaste and dignified character; earnest, but not high-flown and ecstatic, and consisting as much in close reasoning as in elegant expression', avoiding Henry Irving's 'species of eloquence, consisting of *outré* flourishes and extravagant metaphors',[22] but in his first sermon he does allow himself to introduce four prominent images. One is a carefully varied use of the standard harvest trope, employing the biblical 'garner' and involving the conversion of the crop of the law to the bread of life (pp. 38-39). Another is also standard, the tree of the law rotten at the heart, but in this case (perhaps for his personal amusement) Scott adds the quoted line 'All green and wildly fresh without, but worn and grey within', pointedly avoiding identifying its source, Byron's 'Stanzas for Music' (p. 23, l. 16). The other two prominent images form a contrasting pair as the sermon reaches its culmination in the ultimate fulfilment of the law in the atonement. Scott uses orthodox language as he approaches 'the great and wonderful mystery of our salvation in the fulfilment of the law of Moses by our blessed Redeemer' (pp. 39-40), and his formulaic account made the reviewer for *The Monthly Repository*

> a little curious to know whether Sir Walter is a sincere believer in the doctrines of the Atonement and Original Sin, as commonly received, or has merely adopted the expressions out of accommodation to the friend for whom he wrote.[23]

It is probable that Scott's Christian belief, for which he was prepared to die, centred on the perceived benefits of the faith to society rather than on personal salvation,[24] but he adds to his orthodox account at the end of the sermon two contrasting images which may, separately or together, carry more weight with some readers than precise dogma. In the first, the atonement is seen as being like the last of

> the parts of some curious machine, wrought separately by the art of the mechanic, but with such accurate adjustment, that no sooner are they put together, than out of detached portions and limbs, there is composed, merely by their union, a whole, working with the most delicate accuracy the purpose for which it was invented. Such is the nature of the fulfilment of the law by Christ Jesus. (p. 46)

In the second image, the Mosaic Law 'may be compared to the moon, which is not forced from her sphere, or cast headlong from the Heavens, but which, having fulfilled her course of brightness, fades away gradually before the more brilliant and perfect light of day' (p. 48).[25] In its quiet beauty that image may be compared to the picture of the righteous man in the opening verse of the psalm being 'like a tree planted by the rivers of water' which Scott commends as 'a beautiful eastern simile' (pp. 64–65) and which in his second sermon he allows to stand unchallenged by any prominent trope of his own.

There is only one passage in the *Discourses* where one may sense something of the novelist's complexity.[26] It occurs in the second sermon, as Scott explicates the last clause of the opening verse, 'Nor sitteth he in the seat of the scornful':

> We are far from terming a harmless gratification of a gay and lively spirit sinful or even useless. It has been said, and perhaps with truth, that there are tempers which may be won to religion, by indulging them in their natural bent towards gaiety. But supposing it true that a jest *may* sometimes hit him who flies a sermon, too surely there are a hundred cases for one where the sermon cannot remedy the

evil which a jest has produced. According to our strangely varied faculties, our sense of ridicule, although silent, remains in ambush, and upon the watch during offices of the deepest solemnity, and actions of the highest sublimity; and if aught happens to call it into action, the sense of the ludicrous becomes more resistless from the previous contrast, and the considerations of decorum, which ought to restrain our mirth, prove like oil seethed upon the flame. There is also an unhappy desire in our corrupt nature, to approve of audacity even in wickedness, as men chiefly applaud those feats of agility which are performed at the risk of the artist's life. And such is the strength and frequency of this unhallowed temptation, that there are perhaps but few, who have not, at one time or other, fallen into the snare, and laughed at that at which they ought to have trembled. But, O my soul, come not thou into their secret, nor yield thy part of the promised blessing, for the poor gratification of sitting in the seat of the scorner, and sharing in the unprofitable mirth of fools, which is like the crackling of thorns under the pot! (pp. 61-63)

That ends with a severity worthy of Henry Warden, who also uses the 'crackling of thorns' from Ecclesiastes 7. 6 in rejecting idle mirth.[27] Its eloquence ('But, O my soul [...]'), unparalleled elsewhere in the *Discourses*, may well be a reaction to the unexpected intrusion of unruly humanity in the previous sentences.

Motivation

Scott's transition in a single short page from the trivial and ludicrous to the deepest seriousness may help in conclusion to answer the question: why did he write the *Discourses*? The answer may seem obvious enough. According to Lockhart's account, as we have seen, Scott, anxious to ease Gordon's depression of spirits, devoted a few hours to providing him with a pair of sermons which would 'pass muster well enough at Aberdeen'. That was certainly the story which went abroad when the sermons were eventually published, and it was not denied in the brief explanatory statement in the Preface that '[t]hey were written [...] with the kind intention of serving a youthful friend, then pursuing his theological studies' ([v]).²⁸ The *Athenaeum* reviewer, well disposed to Scott as he is, pulls no punches on this matter:

> It is not very creditable, under any circumstances, for a minister of religion to offer the results of another's inquiry after truth for his own. If he do it on an occasion, in which he is expected to give a specimen of his ability and professional knowledge, it is still worse, and amounts, in fact, to deception and dishonesty. In a certain degree, his auxiliary ought to share the censure; and, though there is something in the present instance which really increases our admiration of the distinguished writer, we think his kind and amiable feelings would have been better employed in rousing his young friend to fresh and patient exertion.²⁹

In his account of the episode Lockhart does indicate that 'On reflection, Mr. Gordon considered it quite impossible to produce them [the sermons] as his own'.³⁰ But Scott's putting him in the position of having to make that decision, if that is indeed what happened, was, at best, a false kindness.

It is possible, though, to see Scott's action in a less damaging light. In the letter to Gordon authorising publication reproduced in the Preface, he says: 'They were meant, I may remind you, to show that a rational and practical discourse upon a particular text was a task more easily performed than you, in your natural anxiety, seemed at the time disposed to believe' (p. vii). That may be an attempt to cover his (or their) tracks, but it may have at least played a part in his thinking, and if so it seems to have had the desired effect, since Gordon did produce at least one sermon of his own that seemed satisfactory to Scott, leading the author to observe to the young man, who had apparently asked him to make suggestions for its enhancement:

> I would have made some additions to your sermon with great pleasure, but it is with even more than great pleasure that I assure you it needs none. It is a most respectable discourse, with good divinity in it, which is always the marrow and bones of a *Concio ad clerum*

[Discourse to the clergy], and you may pronounce it, *meo periculo* [I will vouch for it], without the least danger of failure or of unpleasant comparisons.[31]

While declining to come up with any changes in Gordon's work, Scott goes on to make suggestions for possible future discourses, which confirm his own familiarity and concern with the subject:

> It occurs to me as a good topic for more than one discourse,—the manner in which the heresies of the earlier Christian Church are treated in the Acts and the Epistles. It is remarkable, that while the arguments by which they are combated are distinct, clear, and powerful, the inspired writers have not judged it proper to go beyond general expressions, respecting the particular heresies which they combated. If you look closely, there is much reason in this. ... In general, I would say, that on entering on the clerical profession, were it my case, I should be anxious to take much pains with my sermons, and the studies on which they must be founded. Nothing rewards itself so completely as exercise, whether of the body or mind. We sleep sound, and our waking hours are happy, because they are employed; and a little sense of toil is necessary to the enjoyment of leisure, when earned by study and sanctioned by the discharge of duty. I think most clergymen diminish their own respectability by falling into indolent habits, and what players call *walking through their part*. You, who have to beat up against an infirmity, and, it may be, against some unreasonable prejudices arising from that infirmity, should determine to do the thing not only well, but better than others.[32]

In the event Gordon's reluctant acceptance that his disability was considered an insurmountable obstacle to his clerical ambition meant that Scott's suggestions remained just that.

There may, however, also have been one unacknowledged factor at work in the composition of the *Discourses*. The 'scorner' passage in the second sermon may remind readers familiar with Scott of his unremitting playfulness. Producing a pair of sermons would be for Scott a modest new challenge, almost a game. And it was a game in which he was well versed. His depiction of the discourse of religious extremism in several of the Waverley novels zestfully imitates the virtuosity of preachers and ranters in the Puritan and Covenanting camp. The discourse in question was marked by four main elements:

> firstly, a continuous context of reference to the Scriptures, particularly the Old Testament; secondly, close imitation of the cadences of the prose of the Authorised Version; thirdly, the constant use of images and metaphors of a very earthy and non-spiritual kind, and finally, an inspirational and rhapsodic tone.[33]

Scott had displayed this particular rhetorical virtuosity first, and perhaps most notably, in *The Tale of Old Mortality*, and in his anonymous self-review of the first *Tales of my Landlord* for the *Quarterly* he recognised his own ability in the tale of Bothwell Bridge to discriminate between different varieties of usage:

> The author of Old Mortality has [...] introduced several characters of their clergy, on each of whom religious enthusiasm is represented as producing an effect in proportion to its quality, and the capacity upon which it is wrought. It is sincere but formal in the indulged Presbyterian clergyman Poundtext, who is honest, well-meaning, and faithful, but somewhat timorous and attached to his own ease and comfort. The zeal of Kettledrummle is more boisterous, and he is bold, clamorous, and intractable. In a youth called Mac Briar, of a more elevated and warm imagination, enthusiasm is wild, exalted, eloquent, and impressive; and in Habbakuk Mucklewrath it soars into absolute madness.[34]

The same discriminating virtuosity, at once ludic and deeply serious, was to be displayed in *The Heart of Mid-Lothian* (David Deans) and *Peveril of the Peak* (Bridgnorth), and in 1825–26 Scott returned to it for a final flourish in *Woodstock*, with the Independent Tomkins, the Presbyterian Holdenough, the crazed Harrison, and the role-playing Cromwell. He was inward with the rhetoric he imitates, with little exaggeration, in all of these novels from his own encyclopaedic knowledge of the Bible, the sermons and tracts in his library at Abbotsford, and the overviews (hostile and admiring respectively) in *The Scotch Presbyterian Eloquence* and Patrick Walker's *Six Saints of the Covenant*.[35] In 1824, imitating the much more restrained pulpit rhetoric familiar to him from his many hours in the family pew at Greyfriars was a less spectacular challenge, but a new one, and one not likely to present itself again.

If the composition of the *Discourses* was indeed in part ludically motivated, their publication, albeit unintended and reluctantly agreed, was conceivably yet another minor move in the long game of transparent anonymity that Scott played with his public – a game which had officially (and unintentionally) come to an end with his acknowledgement of his authorship of the Waverley novels at the Theatrical Fund dinner on 23 February 1827. That is conjecture. It may or may not help the case for the defence. But even Henry Warden might have preferred a crackling of thorns to the encouragement to practise a serious deception on an occasion demanding total integrity.

Endnotes

1. See Jane Millgate, '"Litera scripta manet": George Huntly Gordon and the Abbotsford Library Catalogue', *The Library*, 6th series, 20 (1998), pp. 118–25 (p. 123).
2. J. G. Lockhart, *Memoirs of the Life of Sir Walter Scott, Bart.*, 7 vols (Edinburgh, 1837), VII, p. 101 (henceforth referred to as 'Lockhart').
3. *The Letters of Sir Walter Scott*, ed. H. J. C. Grierson and others, 12 vols (London: Constable, 1932-37), X, pp. 350–51 (p. 350): 28 December 1829 (henceforth referred to as '*Letters*').
4. For 'a puffing quack', see the entry for 25 January 1828 in *The Journal of Sir Walter Scott*, ed. W. E. K. Anderson (Oxford, 1972), p. 419 (henceforth referred to as '*Journal*'). For Scott's suggestion of the fee, see *Letters*, 10, p. 352n, and p. 353: to Robert Cadell, 2 January [1828]. Lockhart thought the two hundred and fifty pounds 'a good deal too much—as they are so short': *Journal*, p. 419n. Colburn produced a second edition identical with the first, on 4 September 1828, and the discourses were printed the same year in New York, Philadelphia, Kingston (Canada), and Paris. See William B. Todd and Ann Bowden, *Sir Walter Scott: A Bibliographical History 1796–1832* (New Castle, DE: Oak Knoll Press, 1998), pp. 673–74.
5. Lockhart, II, p. 190.
6. Lockhart, I, p. 106.
7. See the article by Jeffrey R. Smitten in the *Oxford Dictionary of National Biography*: Robertson's solitary published sermon was *The Situation of the World at the time of Christ's Appearance, and its Connexion with the Success of his Religion, Considered: a sermon, preached before the Society in Scotland for Propagating Christian Knowledge, at their anniversary meeting in the High Church of Edinburgh, on Monday, January 6, 1775* (Edinburgh, 1775; frequently reprinted).
8. The second edition, in two volumes, was published at Edinburgh in 1801–04.
9. *Guy Mannering*, ed. P. D. Garside, *The Edinburgh Edition of the Waverley Novels* (henceforth referred to as '*EEWN*'), 2 (Edinburgh: Edinburgh University Press, 1999), p. 212: 'The sermon was not read—a scrap of paper containing the heads of the discourse was occasionally referred to, and the enunciation, which at first seemed imperfect and embarrassed, became, as the preacher warmed in his progress, animated and distinct; and although the sermon could not be quoted as a correct specimen of pulpit eloquence, yet Mannering had seldom heard so much learning, metaphysical acuteness, and energy of argument, brought into the service of Christianity.'
10. *Athenaeum*, 7 May 1828, pp. 435-37 (p. 435).
11. Lockhart, VII, p. 98.
12. *Letters*, X, p. 352: 2 January 1828.
13. The connection has been made briefly by Lionel Lackey: 'Vainly Expected Messiahs: Christianity, Chivalry and Charity in *Ivanhoe*', *Studies in Scottish Literature* 27 (1992), pp. 150-66 (pp. 150-51)
14. *Ivanhoe*, ed. Graham Tulloch, *EEWN*, 8 (1998), p. 330.
15. In the sermon, Scott does not follow Henry Warden's insistence that the love for one's neighbour is conditional, whereas love for God is unconditional: *The Abbot*, ed. Christopher Johnson, *EEWN*, 10 (2000), p. 12.
16. Ibid., 10, p. 41.
17. *Peveril of the Peak*, ed. Alison Lumsden, *EEWN*, 14 (2007), pp. 104, 440.
18. For Burley on Morton see *The Tale of Old Mortality*, ed. Douglas Mack, *EEWN*, 4b

(1993), p. 237; for Deans on separatism see *The Heart of Mid-Lothian*, ed. David Hewitt and Alison Lumsden, *EEWN*, 6 (2004), p. 179; for Holdforth on Forster see *Kenilworth*, ed. J. H. Alexander, *EEWN*, 11 (1993), p. 69; for Lee on Milton see *Woodstock*, ed. Tony Inglis with J. H. Alexander, Alison Lumsden, and David Hewitt, *EEWN*, 19 (2009), p. 279; for the Catholic sister see *The Abbot*, ed. Christopher Johnson, *EEWN*, 10, p. 78; for Redgauntlet on Geddes see *Redgauntlet*, ed. G. A. M. Wood with David Hewitt, *EEWN*, 17 (1997), p. 197.
19 *Quentin Durward*, ed. J. H. Alexander and G. A. M. Wood, *EEWN*, 15 (2001), pp. 311, 196.
20 *The Heart of Mid-Lothian*, *EEWN*, 6 (2004), p. 468.
21 *Monthly Review*, new series, 8 (June 1828), pp. 271-72 (p. 271); *Christian Examiner and Theological Review* 5 (1828), pp. 346-47 (p. 346). The favourable judgment of the *Athenaeum* was supported by: *Monthly Repository and Review*, new series, 2 (September 1828), pp. 623-24 (623); *New Monthly Magazine* 24 (June 1828), pp. 243-44 (p. 243); *New-York Mirror, and Ladies' Literary Gazette* 6.1 (12 July 1828), p. 1; and *Repository of Arts*, third series, 12 (1 July 1828), p. 39.
22 *Letters*, IX, pp. 72-73 (p. 72): 12 April 1825.
23 *Monthly Repository and Review*, new series 2 (September 1828), pp. 623-24 (p. 623).
24 See the assertion prompted by his consent to publication of the discourses in the entry for 18 December 1827 in *Journal*, p. 399: 'I would if calld upon die a martyr for the Christian religion, so completely is (in my poor opinion) its divine origin proved by its beneficial effects on the state of society. Were we but to name the abolition of slavery and of polygamy how much has in these two words been granted to mankind by the lessons of our saviour.'
25 The image was censured as illogical, and an example of Scott's 'tawdry and conceited' illustrations, by the hostile *Monthly Review*: new series 8 (June 1828), pp. 271-72 (p. 271), but it was quoted with implied approval by the generally lukewarm *Literary Gazette*, 3 May 1828, pp. 277-78 (p. 277).
26 Lionel Lackey, op. cit., p. 151n, senses 'a disparity between the conforming tone of these sermons and the more rationalistic tenor of the Waverley narrator': for 'rationalistic' one might suggest 'rationalistic and complex', or even just 'complex'.
27 *The Abbot*, *EEWN*, 10, p. 12.
28 It is not known whether Scott or Gordon was responsible for these words. On 19 February 1828, Scott wrote in his *Journal*: 'The proofs of my sermons are arrived but I have had no time saving to blot out some flummery which poor Gordon had put into the preface' (*Journal*, p. 429). On 29 February, he seems to have paid more attention to revision as he 'corrected the Discourses for Gordon' (*Journal*, p. 435).
29 A slightly garbled version of the story is treated with similar disapproval, with a transatlantic twist, in the *Christian Examiner and Theological Review* 5 (1828), pp. 346-47.
30 Lockhart, VII, pp. 101-02.
31 *Letters*, XI, pp. 72-73 (p. 72): 12 April 1825.
32 Ibid., pp. 72-73. The ellipsis is present in the *Letters* and in the source in Lockhart, VII, p. 105, indicating an omission.
33 Robert Hay Carnie, 'Scottish Presbyterian Eloquence and Old Mortality', *Scottish Literary Journal* 3.2 (December 1976), pp. 51-61 (p. 51).
34 *Quarterly Review* 16 (1817), pp. 430-80 (p. 464).

35 See the contents of Press M as listed in Catalogue of the Library at Abbotsford, compiled by J. G. C[ochrane] [and George Huntly Gordon] (Edinburgh, 1838), pp. 63–84. The second edition of *The Scotch Presbyterian Eloquence* (London, 1693: an Episcopalian compilation by 'Jacob Curate', pseudonym of Gilbert Crokatt and John Monroe) is listed on p. 65, and Walker's *Covenanting biographies in three volumes* (Edinburgh, 1727–32) appear on p. 73: the latter were edited as *Six Saints of the Covenant* by D. Hay Fleming, 2 vols (London: Hodder and Stoughton, 1901).

8. 'The Sermon Pump': Failed Preachers in George MacDonald's Fiction

JOHN PATRICK PAZDZIORA

On 17 January 1851, George MacDonald (1824-1905) wrote to his father that 'very few sermons can I hear with pleasure [...] Most preaching seems to me greatly beside the mark—that only can I prize which tends to make men better—and most of it "does na play bowf upo' me"'.[1] MacDonald was a competent and studious reader of Greek; his wording here suggests he may have known that the verb ἁμαρτάνω ('hamartano'), frequently glossed in scriptural texts as 'to sin' or 'to transgress', can also mean to 'miss the mark'.[2] The Christian use of the term was perhaps informed by Aristotle's use of ἁμαρτία (*hamartia*) in his *Poetics* to define the flaw in the tragic hero's understanding of an action resulting in the play's unintended catastrophe, so that opportunity for greatness instead leads to apparently inevitable downfall. MacDonald's assertion about preaching is perhaps theological wordplay: he seems to be saying that most preaching is iniquitous, a negligent failure to spiritually and morally uplift the listening congregation.

Sermons, preaching, and the life of church ministers generally were matters of some urgency for MacDonald at the time. In 1851, he had but recently graduated from his theological studies at Highbury College in London and accepted a call to become the minster of Trinity Congregationalist Church in Arundel, Sussex. He was also newly married, and his wife Louisa was pregnant with their first child. But MacDonald's recurring struggle with lung disease had rendered him an invalid for the winter of 1850-51 – a minister unable to preach or otherwise serve.[3] About a year later, the church deacons would compel him to resign over his audacity in challenging the Westminster Confession on the question of hell, leaving him with a young family and no steady income. He was only twenty-eight at the time.

It hardly seems surprising that the life-altering events of these years find resonances throughout his later literary work.[4] The bitter reality of having been *a stickit minister* – even if through no fault of his own – seems to have rankled him deeply. At some level, MacDonald remained convinced of his ministerial calling, preaching in churches when invited and publishing multiple volumes of his sermons. Moreover, he repeatedly drew from his own experience of the church in his novels, writing about ministers with the shrewdly sympathetic insight of a practitioner. Indeed, the sheer variety of religious experience that MacDonald portrays – established and dissenting churches, occultism and spiritualism, Calvinists and Broad Churchmen, mystics and academics, the faith experiences of small children and the syncretism of Christianity with folk religion – renders him indispensable reading for understanding the interplay of religion and literature in Scotland.

This chapter can only begin examining a small corner of this far-ranging, under-researched, and complex topic in MacDonald's work.[5] There are, of course, many fine and even edifying sermons throughout his writings. Failed preachers and *stickit ministers*, however, also recur with engaging frequency in his novels, ranging from comic asides to complex narrative motivators. MacDonald evinces fascination with preaching as a distinctly literary artform, which, when done correctly, offers performative possibilities that allow communication of people's deepest, truest selves. Failure in preaching, however, appears in MacDonald's view to be tantamount to failure of self: the donning of a hypocritical mask, as it were, concealing truth rather than revealing it. What emerges in his portrayals of failed preachers are sketches of weak-willed, small-minded men (and they are all men) whose sermons can only be said to succeed in revealing the hollowness of their character. MacDonald suggests that failure in preaching can be an experience of catharsis – a public opportunity not merely to express oneself but to undergo a redemptive purgation.

'Jesus or Balaam'

A backhanded glimpse into MacDonald's understanding of preaching appears in *Alec Forbes of Howglen* (1865), arguably his finest novel. Throughout the book, MacDonald portrays rivalry between the Church of Scotland and the Missionar Kirk in the small, Aberdeenshire village of Glamerton, a thinly disguised version of his native Huntly. The Church of Scotland minister, Mr Cowie, is portrayed as a tender-hearted old man, hobbled by the austerity of his Calvinistic theology. His natural personal empathy, rather than any particular spiritual acumen, wins him the devotion of his congregation.[6] By contrast, the Missionar minister, Mr Turnbull, is an 'eloquent' preacher, attracting even Mr Cowie's parishioners. Indeed, despite Mr Turnbull's provincialism and unforgiving Calvinism – 'the influences of a thousand theological ancestors' (II, p. 194) – he can preach.

> In that ugly building, amidst that weary praying and inharmonious singing, with that blatant tone, and, worse than all, that merciless doctrine, there was yet *preaching*—that rare speech of a man to his fellow-men whereby in their inmost hearts they know that he in his inmost heart believes. (II, pp. 195–96)

MacDonald distinguishes between the doctrinal content of the sermon and the act of preaching itself. He describes preaching as the expression of the preacher's 'inmost heart'. Even when the 'tone' and 'doctrine' are as ugly as the building, the sermon itself still holds potential to create a spiritual connection between the speaker and the hearers and to convey the profundity of personal belief to the gathered community of faith. This view anticipates MacDonald's comments in his sermon 'The New Name', published in his collection *Unspoken Sermons* (1867):

> Truth is truth, whether from the lips of Jesus or Balaam. But, in its deepest sense, *the truth* is a condition of heart, soul, mind, and strength towards God and towards our fellow—not an utterance, not even a *right* form of words; and therefore such truth coming forth in words is, in a sense, the person that speaks.[7]

In describing Mr Turnbull's preaching, MacDonald emphasises the rarity of such speech but also recognises it as more vital than ordinary communication. Preaching is more than a right order of words. This suggests a conception of preaching being akin to poetry as elevated speech, giving verbal form to spiritual faith as poetry does to image and emotion.

It is helpful to consider how to approach sermons as a distinct literary form. The religious historian William Gibson has identified four distinguishing features of sermons as a performance text:

> First, they were produced for liturgical use. Secondly, as confessional performance texts, with the audience palpably involved, there was only a single speaker. Thirdly, they were often critical acts—exegetical exercises on Scriptural texts—whether composed as ethical teaching or as an expression of collective worship and confession [...]. Fourthly, occupying the central ground in a largely Protestant society, they had an extraordinarily miscellaneous nature: within the defined contextual limits of liturgy and pastoral ministry there was hardly an area of contemporary human concern or enquiry which was unexplored in terms of the Church's spiritual mission.[8]

Several salient observations emerge from this. The extraordinary miscellany of subject which Gibson notes was, on the one hand, simple practicality. Gibson calculates that some twenty-five million individual sermons were preached in the British Empire between 1689 and 1901, a number which seems to necessitate sermons about every conceivable topic that chanced across clerical minds.[9] On the other, this topical scope is of a piece with the totalising claims of Christianity to first explain and then transform every aspect of human experience. Elsewhere, Gibson suggests that 'the essential element' of the sermonic form 'was its confessional purpose: teaching, exposition, exhortation, and the propagation of the Christian faith.'[10] Yet implicit within the concept of *confession* is what might be termed *withness*, the manifold voices of church and congregation speaking together as a unity; the words of the confession create a single communal identity. Moreover, the basic tenets of Protestantism – *sola scriptura, sola fide, sola gratia* – place significant emphasis on the scriptural text as the primary mediator of that confession, rooting faith in Christ and the experience of the grace of God resolutely in comprehension of the scriptural text. The community of faith is in this sense a primarily textual construct. Thus, for the transformative work of grace to be brought to bear pastorally on any aspect of congregational life, public or private, it must be somehow explicated through the scriptures. Within this framework, the role of the preacher and the liturgical function of the sermon is to perform that explication. As Gibson's second point notes, the preacher must somehow accomplish this through solo performance which manages to meaningfully involve the entire congregation, both as individual faithful and as members of the textual-confessional community.

Arguably, preaching can be said to have *stickit* when it fails at one or more of these four points. Taken together as criteria for competence, however, they place the individual preacher under significant pressure. One does not need to listen to twenty-five million sermons to suspect that not all of them succeed on all four points equally well. One may, indeed, be forgiven for suspecting that many of them failed on one point or more. Thus Margaret Oliphant (1828–1897), writing for *Blackwood's Magazine* in 1862, tartly remarks:

> To expect from some thousands of men of all classes and descriptions that they shall each emerge from the work-day week on every Sunday morning with something worthy of being presented, by way of spiritual nutriment, to the many thousands who *must* listen to them, is an utterly inhuman and inconceivable fallacy.[11]

Oliphant describes the Sunday sermon as 'a piece of nauseous and unprofitable taskwork, hard for [the preacher] who becomes in spite of himself a kind of authorised charlatan, hard for us who are forced into imposture and a solemn make-believe of attention'.[12] The 'young clergyman', she says, 'if he bears a conscience', feels burdened with the 'perpetual presence' of 'the dead incubus of that weekly sermon which he has to deliver whether he will or not'.[13] The difficulty, as Oliphant sees it, is that the peculiar skillset required of the sermon reduces too many otherwise capable ministers into second-rate mountebanks.

> Thrust the victim back into his academical gown, harness him with what particoloured emblems of his literate condition he may have

won, and set him up there to teach us, albeit we are very sceptical about his power, and indeed do not intend to be taught, but only to hear what he has to say for himself. This is what we do week after week, thinking it all very good and pious.[14]

Oliphant's proposed solution for such appalling sermonary is 'to re-distinguish the old offices—to accept our ministering Priest, without asking him to be a perennial preacher—and to receive our Preacher when he comes with gratitude, as the holder of a special office', thereby resulting in 'a much smaller number of sermons, but an incomparably greater amount of instruction'.[15]

While MacDonald would likely have been in sympathy with Oliphant's critique, his own approach was more nuanced. His works question not simply the excess number of sermons spouted on a Sunday morning but the essential nature of the genre itself. Daniel Gabelman, consistently one of MacDonald's most incisive commentators, has written at some length about the complex literary game MacDonald engages with the readers of *Unspoken Sermons*.[16] Gabelman points out the 'slippery' signification of 'unspoken', which

> could also mean 'not spoken of' as in a phrase like 'unspoken rules', that which is forbidden or secret. 'Unspoken sermons' might, therefore, be 'taboo sermons': clandestine missives that unruly pupils circulate behind the backs of their masters, perhaps encoded just in case they are intercepted.

Intriguingly, he suggests that MacDonald's written sermons can be read as acts of *unspeaking*:

> MacDonald frequently unsays things in these sermons, so there is a sense in which they are self-deconstructing discourses. He also unsays many of the dominant, oppressive doctrines of his day; thus, there is a further sense in which the sermons that are 'unspoken' might not be MacDonald's but those of hegemonic religious leaders [...]

Here the 'confessional performative text' posited by Gibson becomes instead a 'self-deconstructing discourse', the tacitly participatory faith community replaced by Barthesian *imprévision*, 'la possibilité d'une dialectique du désir' ('the possibility of the dialectic of desire' [my translation]).[17] Gabelman argues that MacDonald patterns his own process of biblical exposition on 'Jesus' unconventional method' of 'imaginatively reading scripture into new contexts [...] sweeping away accrued doctrines and mummified readings to reimagine and revivify the words of the Bible.' The key concept here is *imagination* as MacDonald himself limns it: 'that faculty which gives form to thought – not necessarily uttered form, but form capable of being uttered in shape or in sound or in any mode upon which the sense can lay hold'.[18] This emphasis on sensory ways of meaning distinct from utterance seems to accord with the idea of unspeaking. Jesus's sermonic reimagination involved unspeaking the text and commentary of the Hebrew Scriptures into extratextual forms directly linked from the everyday lives of his hearer – a technique he startlingly insists is meant to *conceal*, rather than reveal, divine truth.[19] The poetic imagination in Jesus's sermonic method offers the possibility of creating a community of faith in which faith and grace, both singly and in congregation, are active possibilities of encounter with the divine rather than lessons to be poured into uncom-prehending little vessels.[20]

'As Chaucer in the hands of Dryden'

This thought seems to animate the depictions of sermons in MacDonald's first novel, *David Elginbrod* (1863). Descriptions of preaching and Sunday services recur with curious frequency throughout the text, and MacDonald is quick to contrast the formal dogmatism of the Church with the natural piety of the title character, a venerable Aberdeenshire crofter, as witnessed by his friend Hugh Sutherland, an eager-minded student from Aberdeen University.[21] In a chapter entitled 'A Sunday Morning', Hugh goes with the Elginbrod family to services at a church 'perched on a barren eminence, that it might be as conspicuous by its position, as it was remarkable for its ugliness' (I, p. 93). MacDonald is playing here with double meanings: the 'eminence' of the location implies the church's self-assumed religiose grandeur, while its 'position' perhaps refers to theological as well as topographical views. The narrator remarks:

> One grand aim of the reformers of the Scottish ecclesiastical modes, appears to have been to keep the worship pure and the worshippers sincere, by embodying the whole in the ugliest forms that could be associated with the name of Christianity. (I, 93)

The marked, almost angry sarcasm of this passage is typical of the narrative voice MacDonald uses to describe failed preaching. He seems both able to discern the ludicrousness of the situation and vexed with indignation at how deeply the underlying doctrines misrepresent the teaching of Christ. Thus here the narrator associates outward ugliness of the building directly with the 'degeneracy' of the Scottish Calvinist theology, which requires people 'to love that which is unlovable, or worship that which is not honourable—in a word, to bow down before that which is not divine' (I, p. 93).

The minister addresses the doctrine of justification by faith, and after the service, David Elginbrod remarks to his wife that 'the minister, honest man, near-han' gart me disbelieve in't a'thegither wi' his gran' sermon this mornin"' (I, p. 95). While holding the minister himself in regard, he says that 'my quarrel [is] wi' a' thae words an' words an' airguments, an' seemilies as they ca' them, an' doctrines, an' a' that—they just haud a puir body at airm's length oot ower frae God himsel"' (I, p. 96). Alongside its theological significance, this is a forceful indictment of the sermonic form: in Elginbrod's telling, it is fully possible for a good minister to give a grand sermon that pushes congregants away from God, festering moral and spiritual ugliness. This could be glossed as the sermon's failure on the point of textual criticism – a misapprehension of how the scriptures reveal God. It could also be described as a failure of imagination, mistaking the textual-critical act of the sermon, however finely done, for revelation of God. The arguments, doctrines, and similes, David Elginbrod declares, 'raise a mist an' a stour' in front of God, so 'the puir bairn canna see the father himsel' stan'in' wi' his airms steekit oot as wide's the heavens, to tak' the worn crater,—and the mair sinner, the mair welcome—hame to his verra hert' (I, pp. 96–97). It is not better textual criticism in the sermon that will calm the stour but rather a sermon intended to 'jist get fowk persuâdit to speyk a word or twa to God him lane' (I, p. 97) – in other words, to encourage the congregants to discover God for and through their own inmost selves. In a sense, Elginbrod is advocating sermons which unspeak themselves out of existence: they are not performances meant to educate and inform but point beyond themselves to the solitude of direct divine encounter. Greville MacDonald has suggested that David Elginbrod is a character sketch of MacDonald's own father, George MacDonald Sr.[22] Another possibility is that Elginbrod is a riposte to Douce Davie Deans in Walter Scott's *The Heart of Mid-Lothian* (1818): MacDonald's narrator remarks that David Elginbrod 'was looked upon as a *douce* man' (I, p. 98, emphasis in original) and the speech quoted here seems something of a repudiation of the disputations of which David Deans is so fond.

MacDonald does not restrict his criticism to ugly churches in Aberdeenshire. When Hugh Sutherland finishes his studies, he takes a position as a tutor for a well-to-do family in England. Gothic mystery and a disastrous love affair soon follow, but more pertinent for this chapter is the country church where Hugh's employers worship: 'one of those which are, in some measure, typical of the Church itself: for it was very old, and would have been very beautiful, had it not been all plastered over, and whitened to a smooth uniformity of ugliness' (II, p. 95). This description alludes to Jesus's condemnation of religious 'hypocrites' as 'whited sepulchres, which indeed appear beautiful outward, but are within full of dead men's bones, and of all uncleanness'.[23] The narrator compares the whitewashed ugliness of the building – it 'had fared as Chaucer in the hands of Dryden' – with the 'desecration and ruin' which the sermon wreaks on Christianity itself (II, p. 96). The clergyman preaches with 'indubitable condescension' on the concept that 'God is no respecter of persons', despite the church itself containing 'three platforms of position', with 'the loftiest, in the chancel, occupied by the gentry', the middle platform for 'the tulip-beds of their servants' and the lowest for 'the common parishioners' (II, p. 96). The narrator remarks that 'there was not much inconsistency' between the sermon and its surroundings, since the sermon

> found[ed] its argument chiefly on the antithetical facts, that death, lowering the rich to the level of the poor, was a *dead leveller*; and that, on the other hand, the life to come would raise the poor to the level of the rich. It was a pity that there was no phrase in the language to justify him in carrying out the antithesis, and so balancing his sentence like a rope-walker, by saying that life was a *live leveller*. (II, p. 97)

This preposterous sermon is a literary production meant to retrench the socio-political inequalities apparent in the physical form of the church. The narrator explains that the clergyman merely reads out the cleverness of a 'sermon-wright whose manuscript he had bought for eighteen pence— I am told that sermons *are* to be procured for that price—on his last visit to London' (II, p. 95). As Dryden crammed Chaucer into the mangle of heroic couplets, so any divine truth about the equality of humankind before God has been moulded into a fashionable shape that flatters the tasteless sensibilities of wealthy congregants. The inmost heart of the minister is revealed only by accident through his ease with dissonance of his surroundings and his scriptural text.

The worst sermon in *David Elginbrod* is given at a dissenting congregation in suburban London. A well-to-do family ask Hugh Sutherland to attend church with them at Salem Chapel, in order to determine whether he would be a suitable tutor for their children. They are preparing one of their young sons for the dissenting clergy and so wish to test Sutherland's religious purity (III, pp. 82ff). The sermon proves a test of some rigour: 'a strange, grotesque, and somewhat awful medley [...] worthless, save as gravel or chaff or husks have worth' (III, p. 100):

> The text was the story of the good Samaritan. Some idea, if not of the sermon, yet of the value of it, may be formed from the fact, that

> the first thing to be considered, or, in other words, the first head was, 'The culpable imprudence of the man in going from Jerusalem to Jericho without an escort.' (III, p. 100)

This appalling exegesis, victim-blaming the man robbed and beaten on the Jericho Road, is not merely a failure of textual criticism but an indictment of the minister's character. It is informative to contrast this with MacDonald's own comments on the parable, where he emphasises that its 'endless story' is continually manifested 'in active kindness, that is, the recognition of kin, of *kind*, of nighness, of *neighbourhood*; yea, in tenderness and loving-kindness' (emphasis in original).[24] The 'somewhat awful' sermon is due to the minister's arrogance, exuding 'all the solemnity of the self-elect':

> He was just old enough for the intermittent attacks of self-importance to which all youth is exposed, to have in his case become chronic. He stood up and worshipped his creator aloud, after a manner which seemed to say in every tone: 'Behold I am he that worshippeth Thee! How mighty art Thou!' Then he read the Bible in a quarrelsome sort of way, as if he were a bantam, and every verse a crow of defiance to the sinner. (III, p. 98)

The biblical allusions in this passage are subtle and vicious. The minister's posture evokes Jesus's parable about the pompous, self-righteous Pharisee who 'stood and prayed thus with himself, God, I thank thee, that I am not as other men are', and whose vainglorious prayers go unheard.[25] Moreover, his 'quarrelsome' reading is compared to a crowing bantam: the rooster's crow is traditionally associated with St Peter's three denials of Christ on the night of his crucifixion.[26] The sound wakes St Peter's conscience and turns him to confession and repentance. Here, however, the minister crows in 'defiance', actively embracing his arrogant betrayal of Christ and refusing sympathy with the Man of Sorrows. Instead, he floats on the swollen balloon of his unjustified ego: 'After the prayer, [the minister] spread abroad his arms as if he would clasp the world in his embrace, and pronounced the benediction in a style of arrogance that the pope himself would have been ashamed of' (III, p. 102). Considering that this is a dissenting chapel, the comparison with the pope is particularly pointed. Though rejecting hierarchal church authority, MacDonald suggests, chapels such as these have raised the minister's ego and arrogance in its place. The preacher's blinding arrogance creates an authoritative enslavement of its hearers which is worse than their favourite bogey of papism. The narrator gloomily remarks, 'the whole affair was suggestive of Egyptian bondage' (III, p. 103). The arrogance of the preacher has a blighting effect on the whole chapel; alternatively, his self-importance simply reflects the arrogance and complacency of his congregation. What it reveals of his inmost self and the religious belief of his chapel is, the narrator says, mere 'fungous growth', noxious outcroppings indicative only of underlying decay (III, pp. 102f).

'Cauld kail het again'

Arrogance also brings the failed preacher in *Alec Forbes of Howglen* to ruin. Murdoch Malison, the schoolmaster – called Murder Malison by his students – is a dour and unimaginative man, whose enthusiasm for corporal punishment borders on sadism; he beats the students regularly with his tawse, 'a long, thick strap of horse-hide, prepared by steeping in brine, black and supple with constant use, and cut into fingers at one end, which had been hardened in the fire' (I, p. 60). The details of this description and its physical effects on the children are alarmingly realistic; indeed, the character is apparently based on MacDonald's own schoolmaster, who seems to have been both sadistic and mentally unstable.[27] Notably, the narrator claims that Malison's Calvinism is 'the theological subsoil' from which his brutality springs (I, p. 241). His heavy use of beatings was, the narrator explains, customary to his time and his country:

> There is not to be found a more thorough impersonation of his own theology than a Scotch schoolmaster of the rough old-fashioned type. His pleasure was law, irrespective of right or wrong, and the

reward of submission to law was immunity from punishment. He had his favourites in varying degrees, whom he chose according to inexplicable directions of feeling ratified by 'the freedom of his own will.' These found it easy to please him, while those with whom he was not primarily pleased, found it impossible to please him. (I, pp. 239–40)[28]

Malison's characterisation in this passage offers a scathing depiction of the Calvinist doctrine of double predestination – the notion that God divinely chooses both those souls who will be elected for salvation and those who will be damned to hell. The phrase 'the freedom of his own will' echoes *The Freedom of the Will* (1754), a famous tract on the doctrine of total depravity by Jonathan Edwards (1703–1758), whom MacDonald detested.[29] It also appears to be a direct quotation from the Canons of the Synod of Dort (1618–19), an important theological document which first codified Calvinist doctrine into five points against the rival system of Arminianism.[30] Perversely, in the Canons the phrase refers to Adam's prelapsarian innocence, indicating that this freedom led him to collude with the devil and rebel against God. Malison is thus implicated as being, in a sense, akin to the justified sinner in James Hogg, arrogantly convinced of his own election. This belief leads him to become a type of the Calvinist God in his classroom, using his self-assumed sovereignty to elect some helpless children for cosseting and others for abuse. Malison's theological hidden pedagogy of favouritism and brutality, at once legalistic and arbitrary in its derivation from double predestination, provides a depraved spiritual formation for the children in Malison's care. At one point in the narrative, Malison beats a student so viciously that the boy is permanently disabled. The protagonist, young Annie Anderson, witnesses this cruelty with horror: 'The feeling that God was angry with her grew upon her; and Murdoch Malison became for a time inseparably associated with her idea of God, frightfully bewildering all her aspirations' (I, p. 244). This, MacDonald suggests, is a direct result of belief in double predestination: believing that divine goodness is reflected in God's capricious choice to damn others but not oneself engenders Malison's spiritual arrogance and cruelty. But serious consideration of the possibility of one's own arbitrary damnation results in Annie's bewildered terror before an inexplicably angry God. Malison's brutishness and Annie's fear are thus two sides of the same theological coin.

Malison's ambition is to succeed the benevolent Mr Cowie as parish minister. So, when Mr Cowie goes to his reward, Malison is invited to preach. He decides to employ 'the fashion of preaching so much in favour amongst the seceders and missionars', that is, 'he would be a *Jupiter tonans*, wielding the forked lightnings of the law against the sins of Glamerton' and preach on the plague of locusts foretold by the prophet Joel (II, p. 214). Apparently, his administration of law in the classroom carries over to his ideas of popular preaching. It also reveals the turpitude of his own inner beliefs. Malison has been corrupted by unthinkingly accepting whatever has been the custom of the moment, whether the Calvinistic use of the tawse or the Missionar stylings of hellfire and brimstone. It does not seem coincidental that MacDonald compares this theological attitude to a famously erratic, pre-Christian Greek deity.

Malison also decides to commit his sermon to memory 'and deliver it as like the extempore utterance of which he was incapable as might be—a piece of falsehood entirely understood, and justified by Scotch custom' (II, p. 214). This detail is historically correct: Gibson offers several attestations of this practice and notes that it made supreme demands on the preacher's intellect and endurance.[31] MacDonald himself would refer to the practice again in *The Marquis of Lossie* (1877), when another over-ambitious young schoolmaster candidates for the pulpit:

> The custom of the time as to preaching was a sort of compromise between reading a sermon and speaking extempore, a mode morally as well as artistically false: the preacher learned his sermon by rote, and repeated it—as much like the man he therein was not, and as little like the parrot he was, as he could.[32]

The attempt ends in instant and immediate humiliation; when the young man rises to speak:

he failed—failed utterly, pitifully. His tongue clave to the roof of his mouth; his lips moved, but shaped no sound; a deathly dew bathed his forehead; his knees shook; and he sank at last to the bottom of the chamber of his torture.[33]

Malison's fate is, if anything, even more excruciating. A clever man, the root of his hubris is not an overestimation of his ability. The narrator remarks:

> if he could have read his sermon, it would have shown itself a most creditable invention. It had a general introduction about the temporal punishment of sin; one head entitled, 'he completeness of the infliction;' and another, 'The punishment of which this is the type;' [...] These two heads had a number of horns called *particulars*; and a tail called an *application*, in which the sins of his hearers were duly chastised, with vague and awful threats of some vengeance not confined to the life to come, but ready to take present form in such a judgement as that described in the text. (II, pp. 215–16)

Malison's sermon demonstrates technical homiletic proficiency. Yet two horned heads and a tail can either create a creditable sermon or one of the fiercer animals, and by attempting to make a model sermon, Malison has created a grotesquery. Malison mounts the pulpit and declaims

> with sweeps of the hands, pointings of the fingers, and other such tricks of second-rate actors, to aid the self-delusion of his hearers that it was a genuine present outburst from the soul of Murdoch Malison. For they all knew, as well as he did, that his sermon was only 'cauld kail het again.' (II, p. 216)

This is hypocrisy in its most literal sense: play-acting, mask-wearing, mountebanking. Malison assumes the role of the fervid preacher, gripped with a prophetic warning and call to repentance, while the congregation assumes the part of the enthralled, chastened supplicants, in fear for their souls. There is not an iota of genuine feeling in all the elaborate pageant.

What struts and frets its hour in the pulpit is not any inmost belief, but simply Malison's hubristic confidence that he somehow deserves to preach. The sermon is a sham.

Malison is out of his depth, and

> as he approached the second head, the fear suddenly flashed through his mind that he would not be able to recall it; and that moment all the future of his sermon was a blank. He stammered, stared, did nothing, thought nothing—only felt himself in hell. (II, p. 216)

Perhaps by doing and thinking nothing, Malison is truly testifying to his inmost belief. He plunges his hand to his pocket to retrieve the manuscript and his dignity: 'Horror of horrors for the poor autocrat!—the pocket was as empty as his own memory; in fact it was a mere typical pocket, typical of the brains of its owner' (II, 217). Murdoch Malison simply has nothing to say: no original thought and certainly no spiritual conviction to impress on his hearer. He has nothing beyond a text in the wrong pocket – he keeps checking the same one and never finds it – and a pompous play-acting role which he is unable to maintain. In desperation, he attempts 'to bring his discourse down the inclined plane of a conclusion':

> 'In fine,' he stammered, 'my beloved brethren, if you do not repent and be converted and return to the Lord, you will—you will—you will have a very bad harvest.'
>
> Having uttered this prediction, of the import of which he, like some other prophets, knew nothing before he uttered it, Murdoch Malison sat down, *a stickit minister*. (II, pp. 217–18, emphasis in original)

Malison has failed, utterly and pitifully. If the act of preaching requires deep spiritual conviction to be successful, then a preacher like Malison, like the nameless pastor of Salem Chapel, is manifestly inadequate to the task. It becomes a poetic justice: the narrator remarks drolly that Malison 'found that to hear boys repeat their lessons and punish them for failure, did not necessarily stimulate the master's own memory' (II, p. 215). The schoolmaster's humiliation teaches him both a pedagogical and a moral lesson. Pedagogically, beating his little pitchers full of rote-memorised facts, like a sadistic Gradgrind, is ineffective for its own task; morally, the physician cannot heal himself. Malison's redemption begins from the realisation that he himself cannot attain the standard he set for his students.

In consequence, Malison stops beating his students: 'How could he punish failure who had himself so shamefully failed in the sight of them all?' (II, p. 231). He undergoes a change of heart nearly as dramatic as Ebenezer Scrooge, vowing to 'spend his days in making up for the hardness of his heart and hand' and that 'he would henceforth be [the children's] friend, and let them know it. Blessed failure ending in such a victory! Blessed purgatorial pulpit!' (II, pp. 232–33). Through his failure, the preacher has been forced to acknowledge the paucity, hypocrisy, and self-centredness of his inmost belief and to form a new one: 'The heart of the master was forced to yield, and the last state of that man was better than the first' (II, p. 233). (The allusion here is a puzzling inversion of Matthew 12. 45.) Malison's shift from cruelty to becoming a friend and support of little children seems to repudiate the severe narrowness of his old Calvinistic theology to embrace the compassion of Christ. Malison, indeed, becomes a Christ-figure, dying in a self-sacrificial attempt to save one of his young pupils – the same boy he had injured so badly – from drowning. Through the catharsis of the purgatorial pulpit, Malison's hubris is replaced with both a more profound spiritual praxis and greater human decency.

'Pieces of a literary mosaic'

The cathartic potential for publicly failing at reading a sermon serves as an engine of crisis in a later novel, *Thomas Wingfold, Curate* (1876). MacDonald begins in a mode reminiscent of Anthony Trollope, offering an introspective character study of the weak-willed Wingfold, 'a curate of the church of England who knew positively nothing of the foundation upon which that church professed to stand'.[34] Wingfold undergoes a crisis of belief after a conversation with a hearty atheist, finding himself unable to articulate a defence of Christianity against the atheist's good-humoured, sherry-and-cigar-laden arguments. Wingfold laments:

> I pass my examinations with decency, distinguish myself in nothing, go before the bishop, am admitted a deacon, after a year am ordained a priest, and after another year or two of false preaching and parish work, suddenly find myself curate in charge of a grand old abbey church; but as to what the whole thing means in practical relation with myself as a human being, I am as ignorant as Simon Magus, without his excuse. (p. 140)[35]

His crisis deepens when a spiritually astute parishioner – Joseph Polworth, a natural mystic of a type with David Elginbrod – recognises the text of one of his sermons as having been cribbed from the work of Jeremy Taylor (1613–1667), a notably eloquent cleric whose writings remained popular throughout the nineteenth century. The discovery is all the more appalling for Wingfold in that the sermon in question is not his composition. His uncle, Jonah Driftwood, D.D., has bequeathed him 157 handwritten copies of his own sermons 'with the feeling probably that he was not only setting him up in sermons for life, but giving him a fair start as well in the race of which a stall in some high cathedral was the goal' (p. 95, cf. 129). Wingfold himself 'had never made a sermon' and 'since his appointment had not once preached a sermon of his own' (p. 116). He simply reads from his uncle's manuscripts, quietly concealing the fact from his congregation. It thus occasions severe annoyance to learn that sermons he has been reading 'could all be pieces of a literary mosaic' (p. 115). Wingfold commences a prolonged internal argument:

> What had he to be ashamed of? […] Did not everybody know that very few clergymen really made their own sermons? Was it not absurd, this mute agreement that, although all men knew to the contrary, it must appear to be taken for granted that a man's sermons were of his own mental production? Still more absurd as well as cruel

was the way in which they sacrificed to the known falsehood by the contempt they poured upon any fellow the moment they were able to say of productions which never could have been his, that they were by this man or that man, or bought at this shop or that shop in Great Queen Street or Bookseller's Row. (p. 118)

It is, he concludes, 'the old Spartan game of—steal as you will and enjoy as you can' (pp. 117–18). He finds his state of mind appalling, however, and so appeals to Polwarth, who tells him, 'There is no law that sermons shall be the preacher's own, but there is an eternal law against all manner of humbug' (p. 164). Thus chastened, Wingfold confesses his fault to the congregation the following Sunday and resorts to reading careful selections from various books of sermons, clearly introducing the source of each extract (pp. 169–71). Nor is the opprobrium he feared forthcoming, with many in his congregation remarking 'it was the most interesting sermon they had ever heard in their lives—which perhaps was not saying much' (p. 172).

At this point, MacDonald seems to weary of the Barsetshire-esque world of his novel so far and abruptly veers into a sensationalist narrative of lust, betrayal, drug-fuelled deliriums, and hot-blooded murder, set in the confines of a ruined mansion, thereby bringing the prosaic world of sermons, bishops, and clerical office into collision with an entirely different literary genre. The shift subverts the entire sermonic genre by decontextualising preaching from its liturgical and confessional context, placing it instead amid the nightmare unrealities of Gothic fantasy. When the young murderer, Leopold, screams in panicked horror, 'Oh that I could enter a second time into my mother's womb and never be born! Why are we sent into this cursed world? I would God had never made it. What was the good?' (p. 199), he performs an act of unspeaking truer to his inmost belief than Wingfold's 'literary mosaic' or the atheist's cheerful cant. Leopold's cry reverses the rhetorical question Nicodemus poses Jesus – 'How can a man be born when he is old? Can he enter the second time into his mother's womb, and be born?' – into Job's lamentation 'Why died I not from the womb?'[36] Here Jesus's own riddling teaching that 'Ye must be born again'[37] is aggressively unspoken, both in the sense that MacDonald seems to expect his readers to recognise its echo and that it is transmuted into a semi-delirious death-wish. The cry goes further to wish for the world's unmaking; as God created the world through speaking and calling it good, here the young murderer declares a wish to uncreate it – that is, through unspeaking. Perversely, this is perhaps the first act of genuine *preaching* in the book. Leopold is conveying his inmost belief through performing a textual-critical act on the text, deeply involving his audience – in this case, his terrified sister. In a moment of brilliant insanity, he declares truth *de profundis*. There is a symmetry between his actions – unmaking a human life through violence – and his exposition of the world as unbirth and uncreation.

The fantastic mode offers a destructive counterpoint to the sermonic form, allowing the truth conveyed through preaching to take a non-discursive, unspoken form. Surely the most bizarre failure of preaching in MacDonald's oeuvre occurs in *The Princess and Curdie* (1883), a fairytale book for children. In this story, the brave young miner, Curdie, sets out to the royal city of Gwyntystorm to aid his friend the Princess Irene, who had previously rescued him from the goblins. The princess and the king are being threatened by a rebellion of corrupt royal ministers; Curdie routs the lot, with the help of his horde of grotesque goblin creatures.

The narrator then explains how this remarkable, carnivalesque rout was turned into fodder for sermons:

> Now that same day was Religion day, and not a few of the clergy, always glad to seize on any passing event to give interest to the dull and monotonic grind of their intellectual machines, made this remarkable one of the ground of discourse to their congregations.[38]

The first priest of the kingdom takes as his text: 'Honesty is the Best Policy'. This is rank hypocrisy: 'they talked ever about improvement at Gwyntystorm, all the time they were going downhill with a rush'.[39] Despite 'being considered a very eloquent man', there is little beyond pompous vacuity in the first priest's sermon:

> The main proof of the verity of their religion, he said, was, that things always went well with those who professed it; and its first fundamental principle, grounded in inborn invariable instinct, was, that every One should take care of that One. This was the first duty of Man. If every one would but obey this law, number one, then would every one be perfectly cared for—one being always equal to one.[40]

Here, again, the preacher emphasises narcissism over neighbourliness. This being a fairy tale, his judgement swiftly assumes grotesque physical form, when one of the goblin creatures brings an abrupt end to the sermon. Fittingly, the creature who punishes the blustering first priest is the legserpent, described 'like a boa constrictor walking on four little stumpy legs near its tail. About the same distance from its head were two little wings, which it was for ever fluttering as if trying to fly with them.'[41] Waddling along earthbound on four stumps, it imagines itself flying gracefully aloft – an apt symbol of pulpit hubris. As the hapless first priest warms to his subject, expanding on how the chief benefit of kindness to one's neighbour is how smugly comfortable it makes oneself, the legserpent looms up from the congregation, dropping down on him like a silly nemesis.

> Horror froze the sermon-pump. He stared upwards aghast. The great teeth of the animal closed upon a mouthful of the sacred vestments, and slowly he lifted the preacher from the pulpit, like a handful of linen from a wash-tub, and, on his four solemn stumps, bore him out of the temple, dangling aloft from his jaws. At the back of it he dropped him into the dust-hole amongst the remnants of a library whose age had destroyed its value in the eyes of the chapter. They found him burrowing in it, a lunatic henceforth—whose madness presented the peculiar feature, that in its paroxysms he jabbered sense.[42]

Endnotes

Many thanks to Eric M. Pazdziora, a veritable editor's editor, for relentlessly correcting this chapter in manuscript.

1. 'Letters of George MacDonald to Family 1851–52', in New Haven, Beinecke Rare Book and Manuscript Library, George MacDonald Collection, Gen Mss 103: box 3, folder 150. Cp. Glenn Edward Sadler, *An Expression of Character: The Letters of George MacDonald* (Grand Rapids: Wm. B. Eerdmans, 1994), p. 49. Sadler's dating of the letter as 16 January is incorrect; the rendering of 'bouf' rather than 'bowf' similarly looks to be an error.
2. 'ἁμαρτάνω' in *A Greek-English Lexicon*, ed. Henry George Liddell and Robert Scott, rev. edn (Oxford: Clarendon Press, 1940), *Perseus Digital Library*: www.perseus.tufts.edu/hopper/text?doc=Perseus%3Atext%3A1999.04.0057%3Aentry%3Da(marta%2Fnw.
3. Sadler, p. 40 [November 15, 1850].
4. For a full discussion of MacDonald's oft-misunderstood expulsion from Trinity Congregationalist Church and its effect on his later writings, see John Patrick Pazdziora, *Haunted Childhoods in George MacDonald* (Leiden: Brill Rodopi, 2020), pp. 30–39.
5. For a thoughtful analysis of how MacDonald integrates his own sermons into his fiction, see Martin Dubois, 'Sermon and Story in George MacDonald', *Victorian Literature and Culture* 43.3 (2015), pp. 577–87: www.doi.org/10.1017/S106015031500008X.
6. See George MacDonald, *Alec Forbes of Howglen*, 3 vols (London: Hurst & Blackett, 1865), I, pp. 247–49. Further citation given in the text.
7. George MacDonald, *Unspoken Sermons* (London: Alexander Strahan, 1867), p. 103. Emphases in original.
8. William Gibson, 'The British Sermon 1689–1901: Quantities, Performance, and Culture', in *The Oxford Handbook of the British Sermon 1689–1901*, ed. Keith A. Francis and William Gibson (Oxford: Oxford University Press, 2012), pp. 3–30 (p. 3).
9. Ibid., pp. 6–7.
10. Ibid., p. 6.
11. Margaret Oliphant, 'Sermons', *Blackwood's Edinburgh Magazine* (August 1862), pp. 202–20 (p. 204).
12. Ibid.
13. Ibid., pp. 204, 205.
14. Ibid., pp. 204–05.
15. Ibid., p. 209. Oddly, a similar division of pastoral labour has been implemented in many present-day Protestant megachurches, with certain members of the church leadership team designated as 'teaching pastors'; see Amy Florian, 'My Neighbor, the Evangelical Megachurch', *Liturgy* 19.4 (2004), pp. 25–32 (p. 30); Scott L. Thumma and Warren Bird, 'Megafaith for the Megacity: The Global Megachurch Phenomenon', in *The Changing World Religion Map: Sacred Places, Identities, Practices and Politics*, ed. Stanley D. Brunn (Heidelberg: Springer Dordrecht, 2015), pp. 2331–52 (esp. p. 2338).
16. Daniel Gabelman, '"Ἔπεα Ἄπτερα. Children in the Midst: A Deadly Playdate with MacDonald and Derrida. An Unspoken Talk' (details forthcoming), n.p. All subsequent quotations refer to this edition.

17. Roland Barthes, *Le Plaisir du Texte* (Paris: Éditions du Seuil, 1973), p. 11.
18. George MacDonald, 'The Imagination: Its Functions and Its Culture', 1867, in *A Dish of Orts. Chiefly Papers on the Imagination, and on Shakespere*, enlarged edn (London: Sampson Low Marston & Company, 1895), pp. 1–42 (p. 2).
19. Matthew 13. 13–14, 34–35; cp. Mark 4. 33–34; Luke 8. 10; John 10. 6; et al.
20. Cf. Willis Barnstone, trans., *The Poems of Jesus Christ* (New York and London: W. W. Norton, 2012).
21. George MacDonald, *David Elginbrod*, 3 vols (London: Hurst & Blackett, 1863). Citations to this edition are given in the text, preceded by the relevant volume number.
22. Greville MacDonald, *George MacDonald and His Wife* (London: George Allen & Unwin, 1924), p. 323.
23. St Matthew 23. 27.
24. MacDonald, *Unspoken Sermons*, p. 194.
25. Luke 18. 11.
26. Cf. Matthew 26. 34, 74–75; Mark 14. 30, 72; Luke 22. 34, 61; John 13. 28, 18. 27; et al.
27. See Greville MacDonald, p. 60.
28. Cp. *Alec Forbes*, I, p. 127: 'for *law* having been, and still, in a great measure, being, the highest idea generated of the divine by the ordinary Scotch mind, it must be supported, at all risks even, by means of the leather strap'.
29. MacDonald's clearest statement of his contempt for Edwards occurs in ″Επεα Ἄπτερα. *Unspoken Sermons: Third Series* (London: Longmans, Green, & Co., 1889), pp. 161–62: 'I love the one God seen in the face of Jesus Christ. From all copies of Jonathan Edwards's portrait of God, however faded by time, however softened by the use of less glaring pigments, I turn with loathing.' A similarly dismissive reference, closer chronologically to the works discussed here, is found in *Robert Falconer*, 3 vols (London: Hurst and Blackett, 1868), I, p. 182, where the narrator describes the Calvinism of the dour Mrs Falconer as 'implicit faith in the teaching of Jonathan Edwards', quoting John Milton's reference in *Areopagitica* (1644) to 'Protestants and professors who live and dye in as arrant an implicit faith, as any lay Papist of Loretto.' For which see *The John Milton Reading Room*, ed. Thomas H. Luxon (1997–2022): milton.host.dartmouth.edu/reading_room/areopagitica/text.shtml.
30. The phrase 'the freedom of his own will' appears to have been the standard translation of the original Latin '*libera sua voluntate*' in MacDonald's lifetime; see Philip Schaff, *The Creeds of Christendom with a History and Critical Notes*, 4th edn, 3 vols (New York: Harper and Brothers, 1877), III, pp. 564, 587–88; cp. *The Psalms and Hymns with the Catechism, Article of Faith, Canons of the Synod of Dort, and Liturgy of the Reformed Protestant Dutch Church in North America* (Philadelphia: William G. Mentz, 1847), section 2, p. 44.
31. Gibson, p. 16.
32. George MacDonald, *The Marquis of Lossie*, 3 vols (London: Hurst & Blackett, 1877), I, p. 246.
33. MacDonald, *The Marquis of Lossie*, I, p. 247.
34. George MacDonald, *Thomas Wingfold, Curate*, 3 vols (London: Hurst & Blackett, 1876), I, p. 104. Further citations given in the text.
35. The reference is to Acts 8. 9–24.

36 John 3. 4; Job 3. 11. See the whole of Job 3 for the complete poem on this theme; cp. Job 10. 18ff.
37 John 3. 7, et al.
38 George MacDonald, *The Princess and Curdie* (Philadelphia: J. B. Lippincott, 1883), p. 215.
39 Ibid.
40 MacDonald, *Curdie*, pp. 215–16.
41 Ibid., p. 98.
42 Ibid., p. 217.

9. Margaret Oliphant in a Land of Death: Representations of Other-Worlds in Nineteenth-Century Scottish Writing

REBECCA McLEAN

Margaret Oliphant (1828–1897) was a prolific author, critic, and historical writer. However, upon her death the executors of her estate were dismayed to find a highly fragmented collection of diary entries comprising the material which was to be her autobiography.[1] The first entry of the collection is an undated musing on Oliphant's decision to remain single following the death of her husband, while the second entry contains the raw emotion from the day Oliphant suddenly lost her daughter Maggie. Her diary ends with her reflecting on the death of her son Francis, her last surviving child, and the reflection 'And now here I am all alone / I cannot write any more'.[2] Given that the deaths of her children so prominently frame the biographical narrative that Oliphant had begun to construct in her fragmentary biography, Oliphant's diary entries allow us an unprecedented insight into her thoughts on death. Oliphant would go on to create works of fantasy that explore the tensions between the worlds of the living and the dead; her supernatural fiction contains a number of tales that offer representations of other-worlds that are accessible after death.

These emotions found a poignant imaginative expression in the texts gathered in Oliphant's *Tales of the Seen and Unseen* (1857–97), a collection of texts that contain supernatural elements or are set in the afterlife.[3] While the Seen is the ordinary, realistic world, the Unseen represents a world inhabited by spirits. The Unseen becomes uncanny when real and spirit worlds are brought together. Ilona Dobosiewicz contends that 'it took [Oliphant] fourteen years to discover for herself a form through which [she] could convey her feelings and anxieties concerning God, the dead and the living'.[4] This existential anxiety underlies the *Tales of the Seen and Unseen*; indeed, M. R. James classifies the tales as 'the religious ghost story'.[5]

John R. Reed argues that the collection is in part a reaction against the increasing materialism and aestheticism of the Victorian age: 'Underlying all of Mrs Oliphant's stories of the seen and the unseen was the desire to affirm the existence of a transcendental, Christian creator and the immortality of the soul against the increasing materialism and aestheticism of her time.'[6] The concepts of a transcendental divinity and the endurance of the soul beyond death are clearly expressed in the deathscape Oliphant develops in the *Tales of the Seen and Unseen*. This chapter argues that with an understanding of the deeply personal modes of mourning expressed in her diary entries, a selection of her supernatural fiction, *A Beleaguered City* (1879), *The Little Pilgrim* series (1882–88), and 'The Land of Suspense' (1897), can be identified as key examples of how Oliphant used her writing to express aspects of her mourning process via the development of secondary world-building in the development of imagined afterlives. There are two distinct strands to Oliphant's literary deathscape examined in this chapter. First, the four aspects of the divine highlighted in the interaction of the living with the dead will be used to identify Oliphant's world-building in *The Little Pilgrim* series. Second, the theology which underpins the representation of the deathscape will be discussed.

Oliphant's modes of mourning

Oliphant's personal life was one of immense tragedy and loss. She outlived her husband and all six of her children. Following the death of her husband in October 1859, the then six-months-pregnant Oliphant and her two surviving children were left in a precarious fiscal situation with one thousand pounds of debt.[7] Oliphant's writing became the only means by which to provide an income for the family. The extent of Margaret Oliphant's fiscal responsibilities for her family continued to grow as she financially supported her alcoholic brother Willie and became responsible for supporting the son of her bankrupted brother Frank, sending him to Eton College along with her sons, and taking in one of his daughters. She also added a distant cousin to the household, Annie Louisa Coghill (*née* Walker), who later edited Oliphant's autobiography. Following the death of Frank in 1875, Oliphant adopted his two younger daughters, Margaret and Janet.[8]

Further tragedy struck five years later, in 1864, with the sudden death of Oliphant's only daughter, Maggie, at the age of ten. Oliphant's diary entry on the day of Maggie's death shows the extent of her loss: 'God have pity upon me, who have thus parted with the sweetest companion, on whom unconsciously, more than on any other hope of life, I have been calculating.'[9] Somewhat jarringly, the wording here suggests a transactional element in Oliphant's relationship to her daughter, wherein she expected and planned for Maggie to be a lifelong companion, presumably caring for Oliphant as she grew older and in some way filling the gap left in Oliphant's life following her decision to remain single after her husband's demise (which, of course, is the subject of the preceding diary entry). Maggie's death appears to have increased Oliphant's attachment to her two surviving sons. She spared no expense in their education, moving to Windsor and sending her sons to Eton College from 1865 as day students.[10] As her comments on Maggie's death indicate, Oliphant's children were the centre of her life. She doted on the boys, and a family acquaintance, Janet Story, said of them:

> they were being educated at Eton, a great mistake, as they would have been much better at a more ordinary school. But their mother thought an Eton education the only one suitable for a gentleman and was prepared for any sacrifice on her part for what she fondly imagined the good of her boys.[11]

Oliphant's ambitions for her sons were never fulfilled. She hoped her oldest boy, Cyril, would become a lawyer, having attended Oxford University.[12] Cyril, however, never appeared keen to take on any career.[13] Oliphant's inflated opinion of her son and blindness to his faults is clearly displayed in her bemusement when editors proved unwilling to offer Cyril or Francis work. She declared that Leslie Simpson, editor of the *Cornhill* magazine,

> might have given my Cecco [Francis] work on the National Biography which he would have done so well he did not do so I could never imagine why. No one indeed, however good they may have been in

professions towards me ever did anything to help me in that chief care of my life.[14]

Following Cyril's death aged thirty-three in 1890, and Francis's death aged thirty-four in 1894, Oliphant was left alone and devastated. After the boys' deaths, Oliphant herself appears to realise that she may have sheltered her children too much. In a footnote added to her autobiography she muses on the impact this has had, especially on Cyril:

> I had so accustomed them [the boys] to the easy going on of all things, never letting them see my anxieties or know that there was a difficulty about anything, that their minds were formed to that habit, that it took all thought of necessity out of my Tiddy's [Cyril's] mind [...] the sentiment [...] was in a way forced upon him, partly by my own insouciance [...] And my Cecco [Francis], who had not these follies but who was stricken by the hand of God [...] I seem sometimes to feel as if it were all my doing, and that I had brought by my heedlessness both to an impasse from which there was no issue but one. It was a kind of forlorn pleasure to me that they had never wanted for anything but this turns it into a remorse.[15]

Oliphant's fragmentary autobiography broadly maps on to the times when she loses members of her family or close friends. The first biography entry follows her husband's death, and the second consists of an outpouring of grief at the death of Maggie in 1864. It is poignant that her entries stop a full twenty years before Oliphant's own death. The editor of her autobiography and close friend, Annie Louisa Coghill, describes it as a thread of narrative that 'finally breaks off after the death of both her sons'.[16] Oliphant's accounts include emotionally raw descriptions of her mourning in the immediate aftermath of her children's deaths, including suicidal ideation, questions regarding her faith, understanding of God, and brief imaginative forays into where her deceased children may now be.

By understanding Oliphant's fantasy writings as forming a response to and as part of her mourning process, an underlying theological leaning appears. Jenni Calder notes that Oliphant 'was a believing Christian, but not an unquestioning one, and her faith did not offer easy consolation'.[17] Oliphant was brought up in Scottish Dissenter communities and continued to be an active member during her time in England. As such, she was aware of Calvinist understandings of the afterlife, based on the inherent depravity of humanity and the predestination of an elect few to be saved. It is clear that Oliphant engaged in theological reflection beyond those teachings.

Oliphant held close friendships with a number of theologians and was clearly capable of holding her own in theological conversation. John Tulloch, the principal of St Mary's College, the School of Divinity at the University of St Andrews, and his family were travelling companions of Oliphant and were in Rome with her when Maggie died. Another notable friend was the Christian Socialist, Frederick Denison Maurice. This acquaintance came about through Oliphant's friendship with Maurice's sister. Oliphant reviewed his 1853 *Theological Essays*, in which Maurice argues that unrepentant sinners are not condemned to eternal suffering, for *Blackwood's* magazine in 1855. She later described him as 'pre-eminently Christian' in *The Victorian Age of English Literature*.[18] Following Maggie's death she wrote to Maurice

> [a]sking him if he knew any explanation of this terrible enigma God had given me to read—a vain question to ask of anyone. He [...] tells me that he thinks it is my work in the world to tell truths which are not likely to be welcome to my contemporaries and that this is a baptism of fire—this is the last desperate shift of human consolation.[19]

Oliphant has clearly sought advice about why Maggie has been taken from her, but Maurice's response is much broader. Oliphant's development of a deathscape that addresses questions of God surrounding the death of a loved one and the structure of an afterlife is in some respects an attempt on Oliphant's part to tell truths which may not have been welcomed by those around her.

Yet to see these works only as ghost stories or religious statements overlooks the deeply personal aspects of Oliphant's life that can be recognised in the tales. As Coghill notes in her preface to Oliphant's autobiography:

> there remains one of the most wonderful set of writings in our language – that which began very simply and sweetly with 'A Little Pilgrim,' and went on through various 'Stories of the Seen and Unseen,' reaching a strange poetic power and beauty in 'A Beleaguered City,' and finding, to those who were near enough to her life to guess the thoughts with which it was written, a most fitting end in 'The Land of Suspense.'[20]

Coghill here confuses the publication chronology of Oliphant's works. *A Beleaguered City* was published in 1879, while the *Little Pilgrim* series was published between 1882 and 1888, and 'The Land of Suspense' is the last known tale written or published by Oliphant, appearing in 1897. However, Coghill also hints at the reasons why these three examples from this wider grouping are of particular significance when she speaks of the poignancy of these tales to those close to Oliphant. In fact, Oliphant's thoughts do not need to be guessed at, as deceased family members are represented in all three of the tales Coghill highlights. In *A Beleaguered City*, the character Marie holds parallels with Oliphant's daughter Maggie. The protagonist of 'The Land of Suspense' is based on her son Cyril and features her son Francis. While these two texts provide a glimpse into Oliphant's mourning process, her *Little Pilgrim* series offers a more fully realised representation of the afterlife. Oliphant based the eponymous Little Pilgrim largely on her neighbour and good friend Ellen Clifford, who was an honorary 'Aunt Nell' to the children and whom Oliphant affectionately called 'Little Nelly'.[21] In 1882, Clifford died unexpectedly in her sleep at only fifty-eight. Her death moved Oliphant deeply, both in its unexpectedness and its peacefulness, and she later wrote in her *Autobiography* that it 'put the story, if story it can be called, of "The Little Pilgrim" in my mind'.[22] Oliphant wrote the first

Little Pilgrim story over the following weeks, seemingly as a way of processing her and her children's grief.[23]

The tales host a variety of figures from Oliphant's life and close family and provide a backdrop for her to explore some of the emotions arising from the loss of Maggie. The setting is later reused as a means of processing the deaths of Cyril and of Francis and allows Oliphant to explore her own mortality.

Processing of grief in deathscapes

Oliphant expresses two key sentiments that can be traced in her later work in an emotionally charged early fragment of her autobiography, written in Rome in 1864 shortly after Maggie's death. It reveals her own emotions relating to God as the orchestrator of Maggie's death: 'Whatsoever you shall ask in my name seemed to come to me like a mockery.'[24] This reference is to St John 14. 13–14: 'And I will do whatever you ask in my name, so that the Father may be glorified in the Son. You may ask me for anything in my name, and I will do it.' Oliphant is clearly hurt that her prayers to glimpse Maggie safely in Heaven remain unanswered, and thus she feels that the promise of Christ to his followers is not fulfilled. Despite, if not because of, this challenge to Oliphant's faith, she begins to question what exactly the afterlife may entail:

> Where, then, are they, those who have gone before us? Some people say around us, still seeing, still knowing all that occupies us; but that is an idea I cannot entertain either. It would be happiness but pain to be beside those we love yet unable to communicate with them, unable to make ourselves known. Where are you, oh my child, my child. I have tried to follow her in imagination […][25]

Oliphant does not appeal to scriptural passages or prayer to answer questions of the afterlife, but rather is dealing with her own feelings on the matter, stating she 'cannot entertain' some suggestions and relying on her imagination to understand the afterlife that Maggie may have entered. Elisabeth Jay notes that Oliphant is 'allowing the imagination to create a liminal world, where past, present, and future can coexist permit[ting] the unseen a point of entry'.[26] This imaginative engagement with potential concepts of the afterlife and the idea of the deceased still being present in the world of the living are both evident in *A Beleaguered City* when the ghosts of loved ones take over the city of Semur as a perpetual twilight descends on the town: 'This was the sensation that overwhelmed me here—a crowd: yet nothing to be seen but darkness.'[27]

The spectral presence of the deceased penetrates *A Beleaguered City*: Oliphant's real-life grief over the loss of Maggie, leaving her unable to say her child's name. After the death of Cyril, Francis insisted on using his brother's name in conversations and this allowed Oliphant to begin using Maggie's name.[28] Maggie, although not directly represented in *A Beleaguered City*, haunts the text through the figure of Marie Dupin, the deceased daughter of the mayor and one of the ghosts inhabiting the town. Her mother sees Marie and understands the purpose of her appearance, at one point echoing Oliphant's own desire to see Maggie once more:

> [I]f you will submit your hearts they will open the gates, and they will go back to their sacred homes: and we to ours [...] Would they harm me that love us? I would but give our Marie one kiss.[29]

There is an acceptance of Marie's place in the afterlife and a sense of consolation that her mother knows she is well. This understanding of and reaction to the ghostly invasion contrasted with the reactions of the mayor to his daughter: 'They came near to me who were my own, and it was borne in upon my spirit that my good father was with the child; but because they had died I was afraid.'[30] This mimics Oliphant's expression of discomfort at the thought that the spirits of the deceased constantly surround us. The uncanny appearance of eerie, unseen crowds of ghosts jostling the menfolk of the town is discomforting, and the recognition that these ghosts could be loved ones adds another layer of disquiet to their presence.

The contrasting responses of the men and women of Semur, while offering a critique on gender, also become a means for Oliphant to express her own wide-ranging and sometimes contradictory feelings of grief. Her fear of the dead and discomfort at the thought of spirits haunting the living is embodied by the men, while her maternal desire to see and engage with her daughter once more is expressed by the women of the tale. The figures interacting with the dead themselves are complicated, as Esther Schor argues: 'For Oliphant's haunted interpreters, confronting the unexplained figure often leads to an uncanny exchange of roles: as the ghostly figure assumes authority, the interpreters take on an aura of the irrational.'[31] Thus Oliphant, when representing her conflicting desires regarding contact with the unseen, is also critiquing those desires through the inversion of power and the depiction of both living perspectives (male and female) as irrational.

A Beleaguered City also examines the function of the afterlife and explores the role of God in this interaction between the living and the dead. Oliphant expresses her frustration with God in her autobiography:

> Oh my darling Maggie. I feel as if I could go down on my knees and pray for her not to forget her poor mother and as for the other prayers, my heart seems crushed and stifled [...] God has taken her away out of my arms and refuses to hear my cry and prayer. My heart feels dead.[32]

The desire to ensure that Maggie still remembers her mother is hauntingly recalled when the women of Semur have been escorted from the city and seek to re-enter, crying out to the ghosts of their loved ones: 'Open to us, open to us, our most dear! Do you think we have forgotten you? We have never forgotten you.'[33] This statement preserves the uncertainty which Oliphant expresses in her autobiography whilst highlighting the scale of the divide between living and dead. The crowd no longer knows what these ghosts remember or think of their living loved ones. The gulf between the living and the dead is starkly depicted as the living project their fears on the unspeaking dead. The idea that the dead think they have been forgotten by the living is an inversion of the fear Oliphant expresses: that her daughter will forget her mother as she enters into the afterlife. On a strictly interpersonal level this gulf is unbridgeable, and it is at this point that Oliphant, while developing these ideas through a work of imagination, returns to her understanding of God to develop a potential means of bridging this divide between the living and the dead.

Once the inhabitants have been removed from the city, the mayor calls at the gates 'Open, open in the name of God', and a voice responds 'Closed—in the name of God'.[34] The closing of the doors cuts off any form of conversation between the living and the dead and is symbolic of the deaths which had already separated them. By viewing this moment as an abstract representation of death, the power dynamics of the living and the dead are clear. While both sides call on the name of God, it is never suggested that it is God who responds in the form of the 'voice' that the mayor hears. Rather it appears that this is the voice of one of the spirits in the city. The perception that God is ignoring the prayers of the living is voiced by Oliphant when grieving each of her children; *A Beleaguered City*'s response to this is to display a power dynamic between the living and the dead. The dead are imbued with a higher level of moral authority: '[C]ome not in anger but in friendship: for the love they bear you, and because it has been permitted',[35] and later we are told 'They [the dead] have other work, which has been interrupted because of this trial'.[36]

Oliphant develops these ideas about the afterlife further in her *Little Pilgrim* series and in 'The Land of Suspense'. First, the interaction between the seen and unseen or the living and the dead is interpersonal in nature and does not directly include the divine. (When referring to the divine, I intend any aspect of the Christian Trinity, though it is specifically the Father and Son which are anthropomorphised in Oliphant's afterlives.) Secondly, it is because of the deceased memories and love for their living relatives that they interact with the living world. Thirdly, this can only happen with the approval of the divine and is depicted as a 'trial' for the dead. Fourthly, in the afterlife the deceased have meaningful work beyond the scope of the living world. These four aspects of the afterlife will form the basis from which Oliphant's theological world-building of the afterlife will be examined in the next section.

What *A Beleaguered City* provides is a depiction of 'the moment when the Unseen was thus, as it were, brought within our reach'.[37] The text represents Oliphant's first speculative foray into the intersection of life and death and allows her to explore some of the questions and emotions which arose from the death of Maggie. Oliphant's own reaction to the tale hints at the positive and cathartic experience of writing it: 'It is a story which I like—a thing which does not always happen with my own productions—and I should like to republish it.'[38] This catharsis seems to have prompted her to continue writing the *Little Pilgrim* stories, using 'The Land of Suspense' to process her concerns about Cyril's reckless lifestyle and to imagine what both her children would encounter in the afterlife.

World-building, theology, and deathscape

The term *deathscape* invokes 'both the places associated with death and for the dead, and how these are imbued with meanings and associations'. (I am using the term *deathscapes* as defined by Avril Maddrell and James D. Sidaway.[39]) For the purposes of this chapter, deathscapes are Oliphant's notional landscape of death, a projected landscape in which the dead reside. This landscape is not referred to as Heaven, Hell, or Purgatory by Oliphant, although there are occasional references to Dante's *Divine Comedy*. Oliphant's deathscape is coherent across a number of tales, especially that depicted in the *Little Pilgrim* tales and in 'The Land of Suspense', considered here as part of the same large landscape of the dead.

Oliphant's foreword to the first *Little Pilgrim* book, *The Little Pilgrim in the Unseen*, says that the text 'sprang out of those thoughts that arise in the heart, when the door of the Unseen has been suddenly opened close to us; and are little more than a wistful attempt to follow a gentle soul [...] into the New World.'[40] At its heart, it is an attempt to imagine the afterlife as a way of mourning the loss of a close friend. In so doing, it returns to the four aspects of the afterlife which were exposed in *A Beleaguered City*, namely: interpersonal engagements independent of interaction with the divine; the relationships between the living and the dead; Divine approval and trials; and specific meanings and purpose attributed to the afterlife. A short examination of how each of these is developed provides the building blocks on which Oliphant's deathscape is built.

The interaction between the seen and unseen in *A Beleaguered City* was based on the interaction of individuals, not through the voice or personage of the divine. A similar omission is found in *The Little Pilgrim*. Oliphant does not depict the Godhead directly. There are references to the Father and the Son, but any meetings between Oliphant's protagonists and these figures are not shown but may be later reported to others. There is also a specific sense of calling that directs the eponymous little Pilgrim in her journey through the deathscape which could be representative of the Holy Spirit. The main interactions are between the Pilgrim and other dead souls. This allows Oliphant to present continually developing understandings of the afterlife from those who have been there for varying amounts of time. Oliphant's questions and speculation are vocalised in the narrative, while workable solutions to these issues are presented in this imagined deathscape.

One of Oliphant's enduring concerns during her mourning is that her loved ones in the afterlife will forget her. This is reflected in the Pilgrim's concern for the living she has left behind, but is also demonstrated through other family members coming to visit the newly arrived little Pilgrim. The earthly bonds of love between humans are not lost in death, however this love is changed as the dead's proximity to the divine allows these relationships to be less all-encompassing than they may have been on earth. The love which the dead have for the living is in part what motivates the little Pilgrim's initial task of meeting the newly arrived.

In the third book of the *Little Pilgrim* series, *The Little Pilgrim in the Seen and the Unseen*, the interaction between the living and the dead in the real world is explored from the perspective of the deceased. The Pilgrim returns to earth as a ghost of sorts. Although shown from the opposite side to that developed in *A Beleaguered City*, the ground rules for the interaction are similar and her visitation is seen as being divinely directed work.

The Land of Darkness provides an exemplar of the importance of work in the afterlife, an outlier of the *Little Pilgrim* series as it does not follow the journey of the little Pilgrim, but rather an unnamed man as he progresses around the land of darkness which has previously been shown as an image in *The Little Pilgrim Goes Up Higher* and is alluded to in *On the Dark Mountains*. The lack of any meaningful work for the Pilgrim to do in *The Land of Darkness* is starkly contrasted with the little Pilgrim's journey which is full of purpose and tasks that assist others. In this land, the inhabitants do entirely as they will with no thought for the divine, but when God's name is uttered, the inhabitants are gripped by a momentary anguish.[41] As they require no sleep or food and heal from all injuries over time, the key motivations for work are removed. Without a clear purpose to their time in the land, or a desire to help one another, the occupants of the land roam around the landscape. Oliphant uses the setting to depict excesses found in Victorian society through the eyes of a traveller. We are shown a busy city devoted to commerce, an authoritarian city, mines worked by slaves, a hedonistic town always feasting, and an industrialised place where the workforce are being replaced by machines.

Moving away from the aspects that tie Oliphant's deathscape together as a cohesive whole, it is clear that she is also using the deathscape as a space for theological reflection. In *A Little Pilgrim in the Unseen*, Oliphant counters the Calvinist afterlife of judgement and damnation when the little Pilgrim meets a soul who believes they have been sinful and expects to enter Hell. This first soul argues that she should fear the divine: 'Oh, should not I fear Him who can send me away into—the lake that burns—into the pit.'[42] A second soul appeals to Dante's version of Hell as a deathscape with nine circles of torment, asking for someone 'to tell us which is our circle, and where we ought to go.'[43] Having found that he is not being directed anywhere, he brings up the idea of divine judgement:

> 'I did not think', he said, 'that I should have found such ignorance here. Is it not well known that we must all appear before the judgement seat of God?'
>
> These words seemed to cause a trembling in the still air, [...] and some of those who had just entered heard the words, and came and crowded about the little Pilgrim.[44]

Oliphant counters these beliefs through the little Pilgrim's foregrounding of the paternalistic and loving aspects of God:

> 'Oh,' she said, 'I do not know anything about a judgement seat. I know that our father is here, and that when we are in trouble we are taken to Him to be comforted [...] When you see Him it comes into your heart what you must do.'[45]

As Margaret Gray has observed, Oliphant's tales provide a 'theology of her own, a simple faith in which God's existence was affirmed [...] as a God of Love, an ever-forgiving, consoling deity'.[46] Oliphant's deathscape allows her to imagine a space in which her loved ones are safe and receive greater care and love than she could provide on earth. The pain and grief associated with no longer being able to look after her daughter finds a solace in this paternalistic version of the divine.

The development of Oliphant's deathscape in the *Little Pilgrim* series addresses some of the questions and issues that arose after the deaths of Maggie and Aunt Nell. However, when faced with the death of her two adult sons, especially Cyril, whose behaviour on earth, while not entirely debauched, was at best self-centred, Oliphant was faced with the task of imagining her boys in that deathscape. This imaginative endeavour to follow her children into an afterlife is clearly at the heart of 'The Land of Suspense', where a further refined version of the afterlife is presented. The tension between an approach to the afterlife as a place of punishment and the deathscape, however, is most clearly bridged in *The Land of Darkness*, which depicts a connected but different section of the deathscape, in which the divine remains distant and the occupants do as they please in an industrial landscape.

The lower levels of the deathscape in the *Land of Darkness* are not represented, but all souls appear to be placed in the same idyllic rural landscape. Those who are closer to or further away from the Divine are distinguished in two ways. First, those closer to the Divine are visible and solid and, second, those people live in towns and cities. The invisible inhabitants of the world roam in groups, seeking knowledge of the universe and denying that there is a god, with some claiming that this disembodied state is a perfect life.[47] The tale follows a nameless young man who bears a strong resemblance to Cyril. This man discovers that he is invisible and unable to enter the town he feels he belongs to. What follows are his journeys throughout the deathscape. As he struggles to come to terms with his exclusion from the town, he needs to accept the divine will before he can progress. He meets his father, who is a resident of the town and seeks to help his son accept the divine will. The arrival of his brother (once more unnamed but generally thought to be Francis), who is welcomed into the town, proves to be a setback to that acceptance. It is at this point that he sees a vision of his mother mourning, alone.[48] Struck by pity for her, he goes to ask God to let her forget him to reduce her suffering. By 'praying for another' he becomes visible and is able to join his brother in the city.[49]

Oliphant has a direct presence in this tale, interjecting as a third-person narrator to explain the peculiarities of the traveller's thought processes and to urge caution. She refers to herself as a 'restraining consciousness'.[50] Not only is Cyril's mother present in this narrative, but his father provides him with advice. Oliphant's concern for her child leads to an imagined afterlife where he can continue to be parented as he works towards moral improvement. There is no direct punishment or judgement in this deathscape, and no state is shown as being permanent. In a final moment of wish fulfilment in this deathscape, it is Oliphant's love for her son that saves him as he remembers her love of him and so intercedes with God on her behalf. However, this leads to the final sentence of the tale: 'As for the prayer which he made, and which was answered in a way he asked not, it is still unfulfilled: yet they know it is not forgotten, for nothing is forgotten, before God.'[51] This returns to Oliphant's original painful questioning of the purpose of prayer when her daughter died: 'Whatsoever you shall ask in my name seemed to come to me like a mockery.'[52] Here, in Oliphant's final attempt to develop a deathscape that can respond to this sentiment, she provides a half answer. She remains in the land of the living with her grief and the memories of her children. Her solution to the question of unanswered prayers is quite simply that God does not forget them, even if he does not respond as the supplicant expects.

Conclusion

Examination of the deathscape found in Oliphant's *Tales of the Seen and Unseen* alongside her autobiographical expressions of grief shows that the loss of her children, which structure her autobiographical writings, are also a significant underlying feature of her representation of the afterlife in her fantasy writing. Oliphant's fiction becomes a means of working through the deeply personal modes of mourning and understanding of death as relayed in her diary entries. *A Beleaguered City* contains the initial roots of this process, focusing on the relationships between the living and the dead. The five books of the *Little Pilgrim* series provide us with a developing cohesive deathscape that can both contain and respond to the fact of death by creating core aspects of the interaction between dead and living in the series. Oliphant's deathscape reaches its fullest form in 'The Land of Suspense', when in addressing the death of her sons, Oliphant's more personal theological reflections and responses to death move towards some form of resolution in this fantasy setting. There is a wealth of connection and insight to be gleaned when Oliphant's autobiography is read alongside her fiction. Her world-building of deathscapes in the *Tales of the Seen and Unseen* reveals not only how Oliphant's personal life shaped her writing, but also how she was using her writing as a means of therapeutically processing the bereavements through which she defined her entire life's narrative. In the construction of her tales, Oliphant seems very aware of her children's presence, whether living or dead. It is perhaps most fitting to end this chapter with Oliphant's closing words from her *Autobiography*, 'And now here I am all alone / I cannot write any more'.[53]

Endnotes

1. The difficulties this caused her executors, who had anticipated a fuller manuscript, is discussed by Elisabeth Jay in her 'Introduction' to *The Autobiography of Margaret Oliphant*, ed. Elisabeth Jay (Ormskirk: Broadview Press, 2002), pp. 7–23 (p. 7).
2. Margaret Oliphant, *The Autobiography of Margaret Oliphant*, ed. Elisabeth Jay (Ormskirk: Broadview Press, 2002), p. 203.
3. From the collection, 'Old Lady Mary' (1884), 'Dies Irae' (1895), 'The Land of Suspense' (1897) and the five *Little Pilgrim* stories: *A Little Pilgrim in the Unseen* (1882), *The Little Pilgrim Goes Up Higher* (1882), *The Little Pilgrim in the Seen and Unseen* (1885), *The Land of Darkness* (1887), and *On the Dark Mountains* (1888) are all set in or feature the afterlife.
4. Ilona Dobosiewicz, '"Though I was alone with the unseen, I comprehended it not": The Relationship Between the Dead and the Living in Margaret Oliphant's *A Beleaguered City*', *Anglica Wratislaviensia* 55 (2017), pp. 27–36 (p. 29).
5. M. R. James, 'Some remarks on Ghost Stories', in *The Bookman,* December 1929.
6. John R. Reed, *Victorian Conventions* (Athens: Ohio University Press, 1975), p. 464.
7. Anne E. Scriven, 'Introduction', in Margaret Oliphant, *Kirsteen*, ed. Anne M. Scriven (Glasgow: ASLS, 2010), pp. 1–18 (p. 2).
8. For more details see Jay, 'Introduction', pp. 7–23.
9. Oliphant, *Autobiography*, p. 36.
10. Jay, 'Introduction', p. 10.
11. J. L. Story, *Later Reminiscences* (Glasgow: James Maclehose & Sons, 1913), p. 49.
12. Oliphant, *Autobiography*, p. 197.
13. Jay, 'Introduction', p. 11.
14. Oliphant, *Autobiography*, pp. 199–200.
15. Ibid., fn. 3. p. 163.
16. Mrs Harry Coghill, 'Preface' to *The Autobiography and Letters of Mrs Margaret Oliphant*, ed. Mrs Henry Coghill (Old Woking: Leicester University Press, 1974), p. ix.
17. Jenni Calder, 'Introduction', in Margaret Oliphant, *A Beleaguered City and Other Tales of the Seen and the Unseen* (Edinburgh: Canongate, 2000), p. viii.
18. Oliphant, *The Victorian Age of English Literature* (London: Percival and Company, 1892), II, 334.
19. Oliphant, *Autobiography*, p. 45.
20. Coghill, p. vii.
21. Oliphant, *Autobiography*, p. 171.
22. Ibid.
23. Cf. Merryn Williams, *Margaret Oliphant: A Critical Biography* (New York: St Martin's Press, 1986), pp. 104, 124.
24. Oliphant, *Autobiography*, p. 37.
25. Ibid., p. 39.
26. Elizabeth Jay, *Mrs Oliphant: A Fiction to Herself* (Oxford: Oxford University Press, 1995), p. 170.
27. Oliphant, *A Beleaguered City* (London: Macmillan, 1880), p. 33.
28. Oliphant, *Autobiography*, pp. 85–86.
29. Oliphant, *A Beleaguered City*, pp. 109–10.
30. Ibid., pp. 90–91.

31 Esther H. Schor, 'The Haunted Interpreter in Oliphant's Supernatural Fiction', in *Margaret Oliphant: Critical Essays on a Gentle Subversive*, ed. D. J. Trela (London: Associated University Press, 1995), pp. 91–92.
32 Oliphant, *Autobiography*, pp. 36–37.
33 Oliphant, *A Beleaguered City*, pp. 78–79.
34 Ibid., p. 72.
35 Ibid., p. 125.
36 Ibid., p. 126.
37 Ibid., p. 88.
38 Oliphant, *The Letters and Autobiography of Mrs. Margaret Oliphant*, ed. Mrs Henry Coghill (Leicester: Leicester University Press, 1974), p. 286.
39 Avril Maddrell and James D. Sidaway in 'Introduction: Bringing a Spatial Lens to Death, Dying, Mourning and Remembrance', in *Deathscapes: Spaces for Death, Dying, Mourning and Remembrance* (Farnham: Ashgate, 2010), p. 5.
40 Oliphant, *A Little Pilgrim in the Unseen* (London: Macmillian and Co., 1882), p. v.
41 Oliphant, 'The Land of Darkness', in Margaret Oliphant, *A Beleaguered City and Other Tales of the Seen and the Unseen* (Edinburgh: Canongate, 2000), p. 322.
42 Oliphant, *A Little Pilgrim in the Unseen*, p. 58.
43 Ibid., p. 64.
44 Ibid., pp. 67–68.
45 Ibid., p. 68.
46 Margaret K. Gray, 'Introduction', in Margaret Oliphant, *Selected Short Stories of The Supernatural* (Edinburgh: Scottish Academic Press, 1985), p. xi.
47 Oliphant, 'The Land of Suspense', in *Blackwood's Magazine* 161 (1897), pp. 131–57 (p. 149).
48 Ibid., p. 154.
49 Ibid., p. 156.
50 Ibid., p. 135.
51 Ibid., p. 157.
52 Oliphant, *Autobiography*, p. 37.
53 Ibid., p. 203.

10. 'If Heaven is a' that man can dream': Religion and Scottish Poetry of the First World War

SILVIA MERGENTHAL

Looking back upon the First World War more than a century after the Armistice, it is almost impossible *not* to assume that its participants would have responded to its horrors with anything but a comprehensive loss of faith: loss of faith in military and civilian authorities, but surely also in a Christian God whom they had been taught to revere as both omnipotent and benevolent. This assumption, namely, that the experiences of the First World War resulted in a widespread sense of disillusionment – an assumption derived not least from canonical war literature – has long been pivotal to how the Great War has been encoded in British cultural memory (though arguably to a lesser degree in the cultural memories of some other nations involved in the conflict).

However, in the last three decades, so-called 'revisionist' historians have begun to insist, ever more vocally, that though perhaps very few combatants (or, for that matter, non-combatants) remained entirely unscathed by what happened to them during the war, the war did not inevitably constitute a chasm separating their pre-war selves from their war selves, and their war selves from their post-war selves.[1] J. M. Winter concludes:

> The upheaval of war led not to a rejection or recasting of attitudes about spiritualism, but to the deepening of well-established Victorian sentiments and conjectures concerning the nature of the spiritual world. Some of these practices and beliefs were superstitious. Others entered the realm of the uncanny, the paranormal, the necromantic, or the mystical. All shared a tendency to slide from metaphors about remembering those who had died to the metaphysics of life after death. The 1914–18 conflict certainly did not create these modes of thought, but neither did the war discredit or destroy them.[2]

Indeed, there is ample evidence of a remarkable continuity between pre-war, war, and post-war attitudes and values – evidence that can also be uncovered from the large body of contemporary texts dedicated to exploring the relationship between 'The Army and Religion' (which is the title of what was probably the most wide-ranging of these investigations).[3] Hence, as Philip Jenkins has remarked,

> the First World War was a thoroughly religious event in the sense that overwhelmingly Christian nations fought each other in what many perceived as a holy war, a spiritual conflict. Religion is essential to understanding the war, to understanding why people went to war, what they hoped to achieve through war, and why they stayed at war.[4]

In what follows, I shall first discuss two 'Army and Religion' texts from 1917, both of which foreground the mid-war situation of the two main Presbyterian churches of Scotland. The first of these is the 'Statement on the Spiritual Issues of the War', written by a sub-committee of the Church of Scotland Commission on the War (which was convened in May 1916 and reported to the General Assembly a year later). The second, *As Tommy Sees Us*, is an essay by A. Herbert Gray, a United Free Church minister who served as a temporary chaplain on the Western Front between November 1915 and December 1916.[5] In the second part of this chapter, I shall survey a number of Great War poems written by combatant as well as non-combatant Scottish poets, and show how some of the themes addressed by the 1917 'Army and Religion' texts are reflected – and indeed refracted – in these poems. I shall conclude with a reading of one particular poem, John Buchan's 'On Leave'.

Scottish churches and the First World War

When the war broke out in 1914, the Scottish churches and, with very few exceptions, their ministers were as ardently supportive of the war effort as their brethren south of the border. Like them, they played a prominent role in recruitment drives, for instance by delivering sermons and addresses in support of Britain's war effort. Also, during the first several months of the conflict, around two hundred parish ministers of the Church of Scotland offered themselves as military chaplains, while around ninety per cent of clergymen's sons who were of military age volunteered for military service.[6] Interpreting the outbreak of the war, Scottish Presbyterians emphasised that it was fought in self-defence, in support of a small nation, Belgium, which had been invaded by its powerful German neighbour, and in order to preserve Christian values against that neighbour's brutal paganism. Furthermore, the war was to bring about a new national unity, and the rejection of the materialism and selfishness of the previous century:

> 'Surely,' proclaimed the Church of Scotland minister, John Muir of Paisley, in a sermon on 9 August 1914, 'if ever in the history of mankind there has been a just war, it is this war.' 'Perhaps there has never been a war,' observed the Church of Scotland magazine, *Life and Work*, in October 1914, 'on which the British nation entered with a clearer conscience than the conflict in which we are now engaged with Germany.'[7]

By 1917, however, the predominant mood in the country – and in its churches – had become much more sombre.[8] Concomitantly, in the 'Statement on the Spiritual Issues of the War', the origins of the war are no longer sought in German aggression alone but are attributed to the religious and moral state of Western civilisation more generally:

> The war arose from the materialization of our Western civilization, the declension of religious belief, and the weakening of restraints which Christianity lays on human passion and desire. These tendencies have affected Christendom generally, and all their nations have been involved in their operation.[9]

Therefore, the war is a divine visitation, at once 'judicial' and 'remedial': it is judicial in that it is an indictment of the selfish individualism, materialism, and aggressive nationalism that pervade the West; it is remedial in that it summons the Scottish people to repentance and reform, not only as individuals but also as a nation.

With this call to repentance – which was, at least initially, unheeded as many congregations throughout the land could not quite see why they should be held responsible for a war which had already claimed so many lives from among them – the churches also tacitly acknowledged that the war had not led to the spiritual awakening they had confidently predicted (nor, for that matter, to national unity across class and denominational divides). Although the early months of the war had indeed seen a rise in church attendance, thus fuelling hopes of a religious revival, this trend had been quickly reversed: the number of active communicants in the Church of Scotland fell by eleven per cent between 1914 and 1918, far fewer marriages were solemnised in religious ceremonies (minus seventeen per cent), and even fewer children were baptised in the Church of Scotland and the United Free Church of Scotland (minus twenty-two per cent).[10] Similarly, the churches had had to accept that, although a small minority of soldiers retained their connections to their religious communities, the vast majority – 'the average male Britisher', as Gray puts it – did not have any affiliations to any church, established or otherwise. Contemporary guestimates put the figures of those who did have church ties at around twenty per cent in Scottish regiments and around twelve per cent in English regiments (though with considerable variations depending on their respective catchment areas).[11]

The reasons given for this state of affairs are manifold. There is, of course, as Gray points out in *As Tommy Sees Us*, the conventional, or rather doctrinal, explanation, namely that soldiers are

> in self-will refusing to submit to God, that they are worldly in mind, that they love pleasure more than God, that they continue in sin by definite choice, and shun religion because of its moral restraints. Alas! there is truth in these charges.[12]

However, he continues, it is also the churches themselves that are to blame, not least because of what he regards as their gender and class biases. Hence, Gray contrasts the perceived 'effeminacy' of the clergy (and by extension, as it were, of Christ himself) with the 'robust manhood' of the 'Tommy' and also claims that the social and cultural gulf between the class to which most army chaplains belonged and the working-class background of most private soldiers had been deepened by the former's officer status. In a rhetoric which attempts to cross class barriers, Gray insists that the church must be re-masculinised, with heroism – the heroism of a newly re-masculinised Christ – a crucial part of this project. In line with nineteenth-century models of Christian manliness such as David Livingstone – and following Thomas Hughes's hugely influential portrait of Christ as a muscular Galilean peasant in *The Manliness of Christ* (1879) – Gray insists that Christian meekness is not a weakness but a sign of strength, the strength of humility and self-denial.

At the same time, soldiers' disaffection with the churches need not imply, and again contemporary observers concurred, that they did not have any religion at all: the problem, for the churches, was rather that, according to a frequently quoted statement by Anglican army chaplain Neville Talbot, 'the soldier has got religion. I am not so sure he has got Christianity.'[13] For the religion of the soldier, army chaplains employed the rather derogatory expressions 'trench', 'emergency', or 'funk' religion to cover such diverse phenomena as 'wind-up prayer' (that is, extempore prayer in situations of danger), the use of amulets (including rosaries, holy medals, and the Bible itself – the latter considered less a source of consolation than as a talisman supposedly bestowing supernatural protection), coping rituals, a fatalistic belief in 'the bullet with one's name on it', and rather colourful visions of the afterlife.[14] According to Michael Snape, these phenomena may be expressions of what he calls 'diffusive Christianity', that is, indicative of an ethically based, non-dogmatic form of Christianity which was characteristic of pre-1914 Britain as a Christian society; this Christianity, he argues, was nurtured through education as socially useful and character-building, but it was not theologically informed.[15]

While Gray, like other chaplains, is wary of emergency religion because it appears to be unrelated to long-term Christian commitment, he does insist that soldiers possess and exhibit Christian values such as courage, endurance, good fellowship, and selflessness. Hence, the ordinary soldier appears to be nearer to Christ than he himself realises, sacrificing, as he does, his own life so that others may live. By contrast, Christianity for 'Tommy' is synonymous with restrictive moral codes. As to the churches, they – and in particular home front pulpit anti-German bellicosity – appear to soldiers to be dissociated from real life, and from their sense of solidarity with their fellow victims on the other side of no man's land. In the words of yet another Scottish divine, Norman MacLean, who would later become Moderator of the General Assembly:

> Courage, selflessness, loyalty—these are the virtues that are being brought back from the blood-stained fields by the men, who offer their bodies to be broken that we may be safe. They are not angels, nor do they look it. They are not saints; and often those who grieve most at their failings are themselves. But one thing they are, and that is men. And it is a Church in which manhood of that sort will find a congenial atmosphere that must await them when they come home.[16]

Scottish poetry of the First World War

In the early decades of the twentieth century, poetry was still a highly visible medium of public communication and at the same time remained accessible to many individuals as a vehicle of self-examination and self-expression. Thus, canonical war poems associated with war poets such as Siegfried Sassoon, Robert Graves, Isaac Rosenberg, or Wilfred Owen represent only a tiny percentage of the enormous overall output of First World War poetry. Public war poetry was frequently written for propagandistic purposes, while the private or personal war poem tended to be, according to Elizabeth Marsland, either 'poet-centred' or 'poem-centred'. Poet-centred texts are often confessional in nature, and traditional and easily understood in their form, whereas the poem-centred text strives for detachment by employing experimental literary techniques; additionally, it demonstrates an obvious conscious concern with the functioning of the medium as an art form.[17] In other words, as Marsland, following in the footsteps of Paul Fussell's *The Great War and Modern Memory* of 1975, reminds us, war poetry is shaped less by the reality of war as experienced by poets than by their literary education or, perhaps more broadly, by their cultural environment.[18]

As has been demonstrated above, Christianity – albeit perhaps only of the 'diffusive' kind – is still a prominent feature of this cultural environment; thus, it does not come as a surprise that a number of Scottish First World War poems do address, either implicitly or explicitly, religious issues, or employ religious motifs. In terms of their engagement with Christian belief systems, these poems range from deeply felt and strongly articulated religious belief to an almost casual (indeed 'diffusive') use of religiously inflected language. Among the first group, those components of Christianity which are most frequently referred to are the figure of Christ – for instance in John MacDougall Hay's 'Their Sons' (1918), and in Charles Hamilton Sorley's 'All the Hills and Vales Along' (1916) – and visions of the afterlife, as in John Buchan's 'Fisher Jamie' (1917) – 'If Heaven is a' that man can dream' – and in Patrick MacGill's companion poems 'The Night Before and After the Charge' and 'A Vision' (1917). A third issue, displayed most prominently in Roderick Watson Kerr's 'Faith' and 'Denial' (1919), is submission to God's will.

Thus, Hay's 'Their Sons' – one of the Christ poems – compares the 'cross of wood' erected over the graves of fallen soldiers to the cross on which Christ died, so that it becomes 'the supreme symbol of a nation's sacrifice; the bond that / joins them as brothers to the Son of God' (ll. 22–23). Taken from Hay's 1918 collection of poems, *Their Dead Sons*,[19] 'Their Sons' opens with the startling image of a vast number of dead women's bodies – 'Thousands of graves of young girls side by side in a foreign soil' (ll. 1–2) – a sight which the poem claims would be 'piteous and appalling', whereas the spectacle of thousands of dead young men is, by contrast 'tragic and glorious', their role, in death, to serve as 'keepers of the altar of humanity' and as guardians of Golgotha, and their only reward the cross (ll. 13–14).[20] In another section of the volume, 'The Consolation of the Cross', Hay extends the *imitatio Christi* to women, juxtaposing the 'Spartan Mother' as a pagan symbol of patriotic courage with the poem's dominant Christian imagery to suggest that bereaved mothers should embrace their sons' deaths gladly, as an opportunity to display their own Christ-like sacrifice and heroism.

A similar link between the sacrifice of the soldier and that of Christ is established in the second and third stanzas of Charles Hamilton Sorley's 'All the Hills and Vales Along', although the references here, for example in stanza 3, serve, paradoxically, to both affirm the soldier's Christ-like victimisation *and* to criticise the rhetoric which exploits this victimisation for propagandistic purposes. In this respect, Sorley's song-like, mock-pastoral poem, published posthumously in 1916 – Sorley had been killed by a sniper during the Battle of Loos in 1915 – reads like a pre-emptive strike against Hay's combination of Biblical and classically inflected registers:

> Earth that never doubts nor fears,
> Earth that knows of death, not tears,
> Earth that bore with joyful ease
> Hemlock for Socrates,
> Earth that blossomed and was glad
> 'Neath the cross that Christ had,
> Shall rejoice and blossom too
> When the bullet reaches you.
> (ll. 19–26)

War equals death – which is neither sleep nor a joyful reunion with nature, but the inevitable, and heartless, consequence of war: 'So be merry, so be dead' (ll. 30 and 44).

Moving on to the second key topic, visions of afterlife, these visions include John Buchan's humorous re-masculinisation of conventional notions of a Christian heaven in his elegy *cum* affectionate character study 'Fisher Jamie'. The eponymous hero, commemorated by his friend, will not be able to join the heavenly choir, as he 'lo'ed nae müsic, kenned nae tünes' (l. 10). He will also be uncomfortable wearing a golden crown instead of his 'kep of dacent tweed' (l. 15) but will be able to bond with some of the apostles (fishers themselves), though even they will not manage to cure him of his 'poachin' whim' (l. 29). More commonly, the afterlives of soldiers are envisaged, for example by MacGill in 'The Night Before and the Night after the Charge' and 'A Vision', as ghost-like visitations: revenants rising from their graves 'where comrade and foe are blent / In God's own peaceful churchyard / When the fire of their might is spent' ('A Vision', ll. 14–16), to fight their old battles all over again. Or else, and particularly poignantly, in a commemorative poem by J. B. Salmond, 'The Unveiling', soldiers live on as 'those who placed for us / The light upon the hill' (ll. 11–12). And: 'God help us give in Peace the thousandth part / Of what they gave in war' (ll. 19–20).

Finally, as has already been mentioned, the question of God's will and how best to submit to it is at the centre of Watson Kerr's poems 'Faith' and 'Denial'. Both are as ambivalent in tone as Hamilton Sorley's 'All the Hills and Vales Along', and the second, furthermore, is a savage parody of Rupert Brooke's 'The Soldier', as well as a rejection of the Christ-like role assigned to the soldier:

> If I should die—chatter only this:—
> 'A bullet flew by that did not miss;
> I did not give life up because of a friend;
> That bullet came thro'—and *voilà*, the end.'
> (ll. 1–4)

Most strikingly, however, 'Faith' and 'Denial' demonstrate that the line between doctrinally orthodox submission to God's will, that is, a Christian view of providence, and a fatalistic belief in the randomness of the brutal material forces of modern artillery may be difficult to draw. Or, as Joseph Lee's poem 'The Bullet' has it:

> Every bullet has its billet;
> Many bullets more than one:
> God! Perhaps I killed a mother
> When I killed a mother's son.
> (ll. 1–4)

Lee's 'The Bullet' is, of course, an example of the kind of Scottish war poems in which religiously inflected language – 'God! Perhaps I killed a mother' and so on – is profanely employed, as is also the case for E. A. Mackintosh's 'Recruiting':

> Girls with feathers, vulgar songs—
> Washy verse on England's need—
> God—and don't we damned well know
> How the message ought to read.
> (ll. 9-12)

Additionally, Lee's and Mackintosh's poems indicate that there is another scale along which war poems can be ranged: on this scale, poems either construe the gulf between the home front and the battle front as ultimately unbridgeable, or else stress the interconnectedness, indeed permeability, of these two spaces. In Lee's 'The Bullet', the emphasis is clearly on interconnectedness, as the speaker speculates upon the effects his 'bullet' will have on the dead foe's mother far behind the lines. By contrast, the first six stanzas of Mackintosh's 'Recruiting' are a scathing indictment of civilian warmongering: represented by profiteers who hypocritically deplore the fact that they are exempt from war service because of their age ('Can't you see them thanking God / That they're over forty-one?', ll. 7-8), by women handing out white feathers, and by the press. While this seems to suggest that communication between home front and battle front is impossible, in the second half of the poem the voices of the soldiers make themselves heard across the gulf. Leaving 'the harlots still to sing / comic songs about the Hun' and 'the fat old men to say / Now *we've* got them on the run' (ll. 29-32), the soldiers appeal to their own gender and age cohort back home 'to share their martyrdom' (l. 28). The same movement from a sense of estrangement to a feeling of interconnectedness is performed in Hamish Mann's 'To-day':

> A rifle fired ... a groaning man sank down to die ...
> An anguished prayer to his white lips leapt ...
> Far on a highland hill where browsing cattle lie
> A waiting woman wept.
> (ll. 1-4)

Close reading: John Buchan's 'On Leave'

Yet another home-front/battle-front poem, John Buchan's intensely private, poet-centred 'On Leave', from his 1917 collection *Poems, Scots and English*, consists of twenty-two loosely cross-rhymed four-line stanzas in Scots, which are divided into five sections.[21] The first of these sections and its seven stanzas summarise the physical as well as spiritual journey which the speaker will have undertaken by the end of the poem and already conclude with the line 'I made my peace wi' God'. The next four sections – of four, four, two and five stanzas each – provide the details of this journey, and once again close on 'I made my peace wi' God'.

As the poem opens, the speaker, a soldier hailing from the Lammermuirs who has spent the past eighteen months at the front, has returned home, presumably on compassionate leave: on the third day after his return, he has had to bury his child. While his wife sits at home and grieves, he himself is so traumatised by his experiences at the front that he is unable to feel anything. In fact, these experiences have followed him home as a kind of sensory hallucination, so that, having climbed up to the 'Lammerlaw' in the twilight and settling down, quite appropriately, on a cairn, he still smells gas, sees blood, and hears a voice tempting him to curse his Maker. This is, perhaps, an allusion to the Mount of Temptation of Matthew 4. 8, 'Again, the devil took him to a very high mountain and showed him all the kingdoms of the world and their splendour.' The vision which the soldier is granted on his mountain in the second section of the poem superimposes two locations one upon the other: the Scottish hills which stretch into the nocturnal distance before his eyes and the mounds under which his friends are buried at Loos, the sun setting in the West and the flashes and noise of guns on the Western Front: 'There was naething in life but death, / And a' the warld was a grave' (ll. 39–40).

At this point, which marks the emotional nadir of the poem and of the speaker's journey, his immediate environment is beginning to exert a powerful influence on him: its clean, summery smells drive out the reek of gas and also remind him of the carefree boyhood spent playing in the hills. Hence, at the end of this third section, the speaker is prepared to admit that, even if all the hills he sees are graves, it is still possible for both those already dead and those still alive to feel a sense of peace, and perhaps of budding life amidst death. As a result, in the fourth and shortest section, it is now also the sound – in addition to the smells and sight – of battle which is driven out by the beauty of nature. After this ritual of cleansing, the way is thus paved for a communion with God: this begins with the speaker's fervent prayer, which is answered by the voice of God, a voice which grants him peace as he is given to understand that, yes, battles are fought at home as well as at the front, and yes, people die in these battles, and yes, the world is a grave. But the grass on the grave is green, the gravestones are the building-blocks of homes, and children play between them.

> Kneelin' aside the cairn
> On the heather and thymy sod,
> The place I had kenned as a bairn,
> I made my peace wi' God.
> (ll. 85–88)

In many respects, the Scottish war poems which have been discussed in this chapter are dependent on what MacDonald Daly has called 'a combination of English literary models and English literary temperament' so that a 'corresponding growth in conscious [Scottish] poetic nationalism is hardly detectable in it'.[22] It is, thus, also difficult to gauge whether there are, in Scottish war poems with a pronounced religious dimension, any doctrinal nuances which align them more closely with Presbyterian rather than Anglican or Catholic belief systems. Even so, it is by poems like Buchan's 'On Leave' that a specifically Scottish audience is hailed, and a specifically Scottish, as distinct from British, patriotism is appealed to: not only because it is written in Scots but more importantly because it is, after all, to Scottish landscapes to which poets, or their soldier personae, return in their imagination when they want to gauge the distances between their pre-war and wartime selves.

Endnotes

1. On the continuity of (and changes in) belief systems, see J. G. Fuller, *Troop Morale and Popular Culture in the British and Dominion Armies* (Oxford: Clarendon, 1990), pp. 154–59; see also J. M. Winter, 'Spiritualism and the First World' War', in *Religion and Irreligion in Victorian Society: Essays in Honour of R. K. Webb*, ed. R. W. Davis and R. J. Helmstadter (London and New York: Routledge, 1992), pp. 185–200.
2. Winter, p. 197.
3. *The Army and Religion: An Enquiry and its Bearing Upon the Religious Life of the Nation*, ed. D. S. Cairns (London: Macmillan, 1919). This is the report of an interdenominational fact-finding commission which, in 1916, sent out questionnaires and elicited more than three hundred memorandum-type responses from officers, chaplains, nurses, and so on.
4. Philip Jenkins, *The Great and Holy War: How World War I Changed Religion For Ever* (Oxford: Lion Hudson, 2014), pp. 4–5.
5. See for the first *Reports on the Schemes of the Church of Scotland, with Overtures or Draft Acts Sent to Presbyteries for Their Opinion, and Legislative Acts Passed by the General Assembly 1917* (Edinburgh: Blackwood, 1917). For the second, see A. Herbert Gray, *As Tommy Sees Us: A Book for Church Folk* (London: Arnold, 1917). The attitudes of the Scottish Presbyterian churches to the war are discussed most comprehensively in Stewart J. Brown, '"A Solemn Purification by Fire": Responses to the Great War in the Scottish Presbyterian Churches, 1914–19', in *Journal of Ecclesiastical History* 45 (1994), pp. 82–104. For a discussion of Gray's life and work, see Sue Morgan, '"Iron Strength and Infinite Tenderness": Herbert Gray and the Making of Christian Masculinities at War and at Home, 1900–40', in *Men, Masculinities and Religious Change in Twentieth-Century Britain*, ed. Lucy Delap and Sue Morgan (Basingstoke: Palgrave Macmillan, 2013), pp. 168–96.
6. Brown, 'A Solemn Purification', p. 82.
7. Ibid., p. 84.
8. See on this development Brown, 'A Solemn Purification', pp. 96–97. Brown quotes Church of Scotland minister H. J. Wotherspoon, writing in 1917: 'The whole world has come into judgment and we with it.'
9. 'Statement on the Spiritual Issues', pp. 742–43.
10. Clive Field, 'Keeping the Spiritual Home Fires Burning: Religious Belonging in Britain during the First World War', in *War and Society* 33 (2014), pp. 244–68 (pp. 256–57).
11. These figures are given in *The Army and Religion*, pp. 189–91.
12. Gray, *As Tommy Sees Us*, p. 16.
13. Quoted for instance in Alan Wilkinson, *The Church of England and the First World War* (London: SPCK, 1978), p. 161.
14. For nuanced discussions of these and other phenomena and coping mechanisms, see: Wilkinson, *The Church of England*; see also John Wolffe, *God and Greater Britain: Religion and National Life in Britain and Ireland 1843–1945* (London and New York: Routledge, 1994); Michael Snape, *God and the British Soldier* (London and New York: Routledge, 2005); Edward Madigan, *Faith Under Fire: Anglican Army Chaplains and the Great War* (Basingstoke: Palgrave Macmillan, 2011).
15. Snape, pp. 19–28.

16 Norman MacLean and J. R. P. Slater, *God and the Soldier* (London: Hodder and Stoughton, 1917), pp. 145–46. However, Madigan argues, in *Faith Under Fire*, that 'unconscious Christianity was a construct. Chaplains, as men who were inclined to view the world in religious terms, naturally interpreted the positive qualities they observed as "Christian" qualities' (p. 195).
17 It is one of the strengths of the anthology *From the Line: Scottish War Poetry 1914–1945* that it includes public as well as private war poetry, and from among the latter, poet-centred as well as poem-centred texts. Even so, and for obvious reasons, the focus of the anthology is on private war poetry which, 'like the poetry of other combatant nations […], is significant for what it shows of the means by which poetry began, albeit hesitantly and tentatively, to find ways of articulating appropriate, measured, and sometimes very moving responses to an unprecedented experience'. *From the Line: Scottish War Poetry 1914–1945*, ed. David Goldie and Roderick Watson (Glasgow: Association for Scottish Literary Studies, 2014), p. xvi.
18 Elizabeth A. Marsland, *The Nation's Cause: French, English and German Poetry of the First World War* (London and New York: Routledge, 1991); Paul Fussell, *The Great War and Modern Memory* (Oxford: Oxford University Press, 1975).
19 John MacDougall Hay, *Their Dead Sons* (London: Erskine MacDonald, 1918).
20 See Elizabeth Vandiver, *Stand in the Trench, Achilles: Classical Receptions in British Poetry of the Great War* (Oxford: Oxford University Press, 2010), pp. 180–81.
21 John Buchan, *Poems, Scots and English* (London and Edinburgh: T. C. and E. C. Jack, 1917).
22 MacDonald Daly, 'Scottish Poetry and the Great War', in *Scottish Literary Journal* 21 (1994), pp. 79–95 (p. 81).

11. Approaching God in Scottish Renaissance Poetry

DOMINIQUE DELMAIRE

The world's darkening never reaches
to the light of Being.
We are too late for the gods and too
early for Being.
—Martin Heidegger[1]

Out of the four Scottish Renaissance poets examined in this essay – Hugh MacDiarmid (1892–1978), the founding father, and George Bruce (1909–2002), Norman MacCaig (1910–1996), and Iain Crichton Smith (1928–1998), who belong to the next generation – three claimed to be atheists; the fourth, Bruce, though a member of the Church of Scotland, was nevertheless, like the others, a fierce critic of hard-line Calvinism. Starting from the idea that *renaissance* – whether of Scottish literature or European culture – is, as P. M. Pasinetti rightly points out, bound up with a 'preoccupation with this life rather than the life beyond'[2] (a stance confirmed by MacDiarmid's zestful assertion: 'I find inexhaustible riches in the life of everyday. […] Back to the eager appetites of the Renaissance!'[3]), I will take the poets' claim as my working hypothesis, bearing in mind, however, that the matter is still largely open to debate. For instance, Edwin Morgan sees Iain Crichton Smith more as an 'antitheist' than the atheist Crichton Smith claimed to be, because, 'marked by an inheritance he could never shrug off', he 'still uses capital letters for "He" and "Him" when talking about God, and no self-respecting atheist would do that'.[4] Similar remarks can be made about Norman MacCaig and his 'ingrained Calvinism that casts a pall over much of his poetry'.[5] MacDiarmid himself, generally taken at his word when he insists that he is 'a materialist and an atheist', seems, in G. S. Fraser's view, to be 'preoccupied with death in what is essentially a religious way'.[6] Likewise, Baudelaire's *ennui* and 'morbidity of temperament' had struck T. S. Eliot as a form of

Christian *acedia*, while 'genuine blasphemy' – or any forceful refutation or defiance of the faith such as 'satanism itself' – was, in his opinion, 'a way of affirming belief'.[7] In other words, denial is often predicated on adhesion – be it to an ideal form of religion – especially if the rejection is as vocal and censorious as MacDiarmid's.[8] In fact, Catherine Kerrigan, Alan Bold, and other critics have acknowledged the importance of religion in MacDiarmid's poetry.[9] For A. H. Beveridge, it is even essential for the interpretation of his work,[10] although he admits that 'there might appear to be a certain absurdity in speaking of MacDiarmid as a religious poet'.[11]

Naturally, much depends on what is meant by *religion*. Between the 'extreme Calvinism' detected by Scott Lyall in 'On a Raised Beach'[12] – a Calvinism so extreme that it no longer has anything to offer but what Alan Riach sees as a 'secular, Godless universe'[13] – and the Eastern mystical traditions which, in Beveridge's view, provide the unifying pattern behind much of MacDiarmid's poetry, the term's polysemy might actually prove to be more of a hindrance than a help in this discussion. To say nothing of the 'religion' of communism, in which the poet may have sought 'God's purity'.[14] What is undeniable and may warrant a spiritual, rather than a strictly religious (in the sense that spirituality seems to imply the pursuit of a transcendent truth that does not necessarily posit the existence of a deity nor abide by religious rites or observances) perspective on these poets' works is that the Reformation was largely perceived by them, and many others as well, as having destroyed poetry's connection with God and the concomitant sense of wonder that had suffused Scottish poetry since St Columba's *Altus Prosator*.[15] Yet their poetry, as Douglas Dunn has noted about MacCaig, 'affirms a genuine sensation of wonder before the abundance and beauty of life'; it is 'both profane and sacramental, secular and sacred, agnostic and in its own way devotional'.[16] But how can a poetry which is sacramental, sacred, and devotional possibly ignore the Christian God? This is what I now propose to investigate.

Calvinism and the modern commodification of the world

In this task, Martin Heidegger, an almost exact contemporary of MacDiarmid (MacDiarmid's poems demonstrate his familiarity with Heideggerian terminology – 'Zeitlichkeit', 'Augenblick', 'Zuhandenheit', 'the inauthentic life', and so on),[17] can provide invaluable help, for at least four reasons. Firstly, he too abandoned his religious faith: although he was raised a Roman Catholic, entered a Jesuit seminary in preparation for the priesthood, and then studied theology at university, he renounced his Catholicism at the age of thirty. Secondly, that decision led him to shift his quest from God to *Being* – the 'one question' which, according to him, 'never was raised' in Western thought except in ways that, as noted by George Pattison, 'construe Being and therewith God in terms of beings'.[18] By not confusing Being, which he maintains to be 'earlier than beings', with either metaphysics' 'first being' or theology's 'Supreme Being', that is, by avoiding the age-old trap of ontotheology, Heidegger was able to approach it in a both non-phenomenal and non-theological manner.[19] In fact, his conception became more and more spiritual, with suggestions of mysticism.[20] Thirdly, he entered into dialogue with poetry and demonstrated that poetry and philosophy share similar ontological concerns. As Gilbert J. Shaver puts it:

> the thinker states Being and the poet names the holy, i.e., '*das Licht des Seins*' (the light of Being). Both thinker and poet share the responsibility of bringing Being home by forging language which, as Heidegger insists, is the 'House of Being'.[21]

Lastly, the latter's strictures on technology are at least as trenchant as those of some Scottish Renaissance poets. To take but one example, echoed by George Mackay Brown (1921–1996) who, though not included in the present selection as he is a self-declared Catholic, nevertheless speaks for his generation, Heidegger's mention of the 'world's night', resulting from what he describes as the 'attack of atomic physics on the phenomena of living matter',[22] seems to foreshadow the sinister 'Black Star' project of the novel *Greenvoe*, itself an instance of what may happen when

> Under the rational sun
> The black mushroom is sprouting
> By which we are undone.[23]

Brown was undoubtedly one of the most scathing standard-bearers for the ferocious criticism of both Calvinism and technological progress. In 'The Broken Heraldry', he declares that during the Reformation 'the old heraldry began to crack, that the idea of "progress" took root in men's minds',[24] brought about by 'the rational sun', an emblem of the crippling, tyrannical dichotomies of our Cartesian philosophical and religious systems. As MacDiarmid had noted before him,

> reason, used or misused,
> Usurps man's consciousness;
> Life's other and greater tide flows unseen
> And its presence men hardly guess.
> (HMD, CP, p. 412)

By contrast, Brown goes on, '[i]n earlier times the temporal and the eternal [...] were not divorced, as they came to be after Knox'.[25] But with 'the violent change to Calvinism [...] the old music and poetry died out' and '[p]oets followed priests into the darkness'. Although, as Michel Serres avers, 'Western reason went off to conquer the universe',[26] people became enslaved to what MacDiarmid called the 'Treadmills of rationalising' (CP, p. 413). The rift that ensued, not only between humankind and the world – now reduced to its use-value – but also between humankind ('the temporal') and God ('the eternal'), was an effect of what Heidegger saw, more broadly, as the ontotheology that has plagued metaphysics since Plato. For that 'bad ontology and bad theology', as Mary-Jane Rubenstein encapsulates it, by conflating God and Being on one hand, and Being with beings on the other, has led precisely to the reification of God and to the concurrent commodification of the earth, while Being gradually disappeared from view since 'Being isn't an object'.[27]

A fitting illustration of this rationalist, dualist, and materialistic philosophy in its relation to nature can be found in Iain Crichton Smith's poem 'Johnson in the Highlands', where the scholar shows a 'tough reasoning mind' which makes him so 'contemptuous of miracles' that all he can see is 'water falling, and some meagre deer', while the 'huge hard light' of his intellect 'falls across shifting hills'.[28] The same could be said about MacDiarmid's 'Scotland Small?' section of *Direadh I*, in which the 'fool' famously sees 'Nothing but heather!' (HMD, *CP*, p. 1170). Like the people of Lewis in Crichton Smith's 'Poem of Lewis' (ICS, *CP*, pp. 2-3), these characters 'have no time for the fine graces / of poetry'. One could go on with Bruce's lament that 'Our kind's productivity deal takes over— / the dead gull's wing weighted with oil'.[29] (One will note how the mimetic effect of the slow consecutive stresses combined with the sustained assonance of the semi-vowel makes the stickiness of the oil almost tangible.) As Crichton Smith puts it in his own way, 'Greed opens its maw', and instrumentalises the natural environment. What is at work here is the 'limited philosophy of utility' denounced by MacDiarmid in 'The Kulturkampf' as the product of 'the puritan-industrial-Anglicised rhythm' which '[d]evitalised church and university, buried Gaelic culture', '[d]iscarded the inner life of man' (HMD, *CP*, pp. 698-99), and, in a more immediately shocking way, brought the 'darkness of industrialism' to Edinburgh in the form of 'the monstrous pall' (*CP*, p. 646) choking the city.

Countless are the victims of this wholesale exploitation. The fate of the daffodil - a common symbol of freedom, life, and even resurrection in Scottish poetry[30] - could alone emblematise what Heidegger meant when he said that 'the humanness of man and the thingness of things dissolve into [...] calculated market value'.[31] Indeed, in Crichton Smith's 'Crofter's Wife',

> Prices are going up
> year after year,
> soon even the harmless daffodil
> will be valued in gold.
> (ICS, *CP*, p. 352)

Worse, in another of his poems, a stern, utilitarian Presbyterian old woman 'steadily stamp[s] the rising daffodil' (*CP*, p. 47), just as the distant, ruthless God of Scottish Calvinism might be expected to crush one's vital force, freedom, and the 'inner life' mentioned by MacDiarmid. All that because in the Cartesian *Weltanschauung*, and particularly in the religion of John Knox (Scotland's special brand of ontotheology, as it were) as it is perceived by the poets selected here, 'a thinking subject represents beings as objects' – 'literally, "what is set before" (*ob-jectum*) a subject' – and then goes on to subjugate the world.[32]

The major spiritual upshot of this state of affairs is that 'now that the whole earth has been made into a stockpile for humanity's techno-calculative will toward global domination, modernity is incapable of wonder'.[33] For not only is wonder incompatible with certainty and mastery, but it presupposes the kind of decentring of the self that will allow acceptance of otherness and, sometimes, perplexity or bewilderment. A case in point was the young Theaetetus who, in Plato's eponymous dialogue, confessed that the mathematical puzzles being submitted to him by Socrates set him 'wondering' – that is, struck with astonishment or admiration – to the point of making him 'quite dizzy'. This 'perte d'équilibre' ('loss of balance'), this 'perte vertigineuse des repères' ('dizzying loss of bearings'), as Michael Edwards describes it,[34] is what prompts Socrates to declare that '[t]his sense of wonder is the mark of the philosopher'.[35] In Heidegger's view, the pre-Socratic thinkers, unhampered by a modern subject-based, objectifying relation to nature, were even more remarkably gifted with a quasi-Keatsian 'Negative Capability, that is when man is capable of being in uncertainties, Mysteries, doubts, without any irritable reaching after fact and reason'.[36] It allowed them to have an immediate (that is, unmediated by reason) experience of the presence of all beings and things, and to be awed by them: 'The Greeks name the relation to this thrust of presence *thaumazein*' (wonder, astonishment), says Heidegger.[37]

That is precisely what the later MacDiarmid's 'poetry of facts' seems to fail at.[38] Nancy Gish has remarked that, 'lacking the power of revelation, [...] [p]oetry is to be factual, [...] because to MacDiarmid the facts are not open to question'.[39] Similarly, according to Crichton Smith, the poet 'has only seen with his mind, not felt with his heart'.[40] Elsewhere, he notes that 'feeling and intuition' have been replaced by 'scholarship' and 'the cult of the intelligence as aggressive and logical'.[41] MacDiarmid's urge to collect, amass, catalogue, categorise, itemise – his well-known 'grim business of documentation' (HMD, *CP*, p. 653) – goes far beyond the 'gluttony of the particular' and 'the piling up of detail' which G. Gregory Smith considered to be a distinctively Scottish literary trait and which may be relevant to a poem such as 'Scotland Small?', with its 'celebration of life's abundance'.[42] It is a literary bulimia that aims at no less than the 'mastery by the spirit of all the facts that can be known' (*CP*, p. 899) in an '[a]ttempt to express the whole' (*CP*, p. 652) which sounds hubristically Promethean:

> The protean blind obstructions of nature
> Within us and without, will not prevail
> Against the crystallising will, the ordered, solvent knowledge,
> The achieved clear-headedness of an illuminated race.
> (*CP*, p. 785)

The speaker of the poem, however, is fully aware that the endeavour is chimerical because, even though language is 'the instrument / For the progressive articulation of the world / In spatial and temporal terms' and 'speech actually shapes and extends our experience' (*CP*, p. 794), '[w]e know that total speech is impossible, of course' (*CP*, p. 742). Yet his awareness of the medium's limits seems to further fuel his prolixity, in what sounds like an ultimate show of defiance:

> —If the book's ultimate realisation
> Is the impotence of language
> In the face of the event,
> This abdication is announced
> With a power of words wholly inaccessible
> To those never overpowered and speechless.
> (*CP*, p. 776)

This bravado amounts to a denial of the otherness and resistance of reality: the 'facts' (*CP*, p. 899), the 'protean blind obstructions of nature' (*CP*, p. 785), the 'event' (*CP*, p. 776), and so on. As Adolphe Haberer has argued, 'Le poète est celui qui accepte de *faire* avec les limites, […] de *faire* avec l'altérité du réel' ('the poet is the one who agrees to *make do* with limits, [...] to *make do* with the otherness of the real'.[43] Hugh MacDiarmid's vociferous self-assertion leaves little room to the 'other'. On the contrary, his poetic self seems to expand and swallow up more and more of the world: 'So I have gathered unto myself / All the loose ends of Scotland' (*CP*, p. 652), which he then controls by 'naming' them. This 'celebrative extension of selfhood' makes him, as G. S. Fraser concludes, 'a poet of the "egotistical sublime"'.[44]

Having, as John Baglow argues, shifted 'from *being* [...] to *knowing*' (author's emphases),[45] the poet has swapped poetic wonderment for the materialistic collecting of wonders – in the sense of the early-modern age practice of maintaining 'cabinets of curiosities'.[46] Heidegger claims in *Being and Time* that 'curiosity has nothing to do with the contemplation that wonders at being, *thaumazein*, it has no interest in wondering to the point of not understanding. Rather, it makes sure of knowing, but just in order to have known'.[47] In 'What are poets for?', he explains that poetry 'does not consist in a clutching or any other kind of grasping, but rather in a letting come of what has been dealt out'.[48] This requires the humility to abandon precisely what Norman MacCaig denounces as 'the greed for knowing' (NMC, *CP*, p. 325) – Freud's *Wissbegierde*, or epistemophilic drive – in order to develop, instead, a *relational* approach to beings and the world, both in the literal and in the phenomenological sense.

Wonderment as the knowledge of Being

The kind of relation posited by phenomenology is intentionality; it transcends the Cartesian subject/object division by, according to Maurice Merleau-Ponty, abolishing the very concepts of 'subject', 'mind', or 'ego' by means of which 'le philosophe veut me distinguer absolument des choses' ('the philosopher would absolutely distinguish me from things').[49] This is what the earlier MacDiarmid experiences when he writes in 'Stony Limits': 'I can feel as if the landscape and I / Became each other' (HMD, *CP*, p. 422). Similarly, Norman MacCaig, in 'Gale at Stoer Point', compares himself to a moorhen, wondering if he too has 'Longtoed green legs with neat red garters' (NMC, *CP*, p. 442). More precisely, it can be described as an active-passive movement in which consciousness, by directing itself toward an object, allows the latter to appear in the space thus hollowed out in its environment. Typically, in 'Painting—"The Blue Jar"', the speaker 'sink[s] into [his] surroundings, / leaving in front of [him] a fictitious space / where [he] can be invented' (possibly by the jar itself, owing to the reversibility of the seer and the seen that underlies this kind of relationship[50]) while '[t]he blue jar jumps forward / thrust into the room / by the colours round about it' and 'helplessly / presents itself' (*CP*, pp. 195–96). This is a most apt illustration of how representation (of an object by a subject) has given way to that object's 'thrust of presence', which, as MacCaig writes in 'Still life',

> [...] keeps on bursting, one burst, on and on:
> A new existence, continually being born,
> Emerging out of white into the sombre
> Garishness of the spectrum [...]
> (*CP*, p. 104)

But the idea of relation can also be taken in the literal sense. Heidegger thought that the ancient Greeks owed their sense of wonder to the fact that they 'resided in the midst of phenomena'; they had understood that '*Dasein* is [...] a "being in the world"'.[51] This is exactly what the four poets studied here do when they depict themselves sharing quarters with the humblest creatures, as George Bruce recalls from his childhood:

> We lived in between with the
> Worms, forkies, shell-fish, crabs —
> All things that crept from stones,
> And with the daisies for company.
> (GB, *CP*, p. 84)

Norman MacCaig, for his part, 'love[s] them all. Earwigs, grasshoppers, toads ... people' – the latter not even having pride of place in the list – and he has a personal relationship with them, going as far as to 'pat slaters on their heads and call earwigs by their first names',[52] or sit 'amongst spiders in chinks' (NMC, *CP*, p. 305). These, along with heather (*CP*, p. 361), 'baby mussels' (*CP*, p. 230), crows (*CP*, p. 166), and many more, are part of those 'unemphatic marvels – that woman, child, horse' (*CP*, p. 176) which the poet has singled out and made special; they testify to what Crichton Smith has identified in him as 'a lust of the particular' which makes him 'concerned [...] with the individual toad or frog'.[53] But Crichton Smith himself can be heard addressing ravens (ICS, *CP*, p. 280) or blackbirds (*CP*, p. 198). As for Bruce,

> each stone was shaped to be itself and none other,
> each shell to be itself and none other,
> each creature to be itself and none other
> (GB, *CP*, p. 88).

Again, this respectful attention to the otherness of the thing or being contemplated allows these to manifest their presence dynamically, as they did to the Greeks:[54]

> on the white bed each stone,
> insisting on its difference, presents
> itself for the first time,
> surprising us with the shock of light
> (*CP*, p. 136).

A lesson is to be learned from these stones, as they are a direct product of the earth and are thus etymologically related to humility (*humble* comes from *humus* – the ground, the earth); hence 'It makes no difference to them whether they are high or low', writes Hugh MacDiarmid in 'On a Raised Beach' (HMD, *CP*, p. 425). This may have deep spiritual implications, something his lament that 'We have lost the grounds of our being / We have not built on rock' (*CP*, p. 431) seems to suggest in itself, but also because, if indeed '[t]hese stones go through Man, straight to God, if there is one' (*CP*, p. 427), they may, conversely, symbolise God's kenosis, his humble self-emptying through the Incarnation which Gerard Manley Hopkins (1844–1889) would also have had in mind when he addressed

Christ as, precisely, 'Ground of being, and granite of it' in 'The Wreck of the Deutschland'.[55] It follows that to contemplate the stones is to learn humility. This is what the speaker of 'On a Raised Beach' realises as he relinquishes the Cartesian mode of investigation and 'like a blind man run[s] / [His] fingers over' them, acknowledging that he 'know[s] little about them' (*CP*, pp. 422–23). Therefore, he concludes, '[w]e must be humble', for we 'do not realise that these stones are one with the stars' (*CP*, p. 425). This non-egotistic acceptance of uncertainty is precisely what Heidegger implied with the phrase, taken from a late Hölderlin poem, 'poetically, man dwells', when, as he added, poetry 'remains a listening'.[56]

Crichton Smith, Bruce, MacDiarmid and MacCaig all seem to have unawares heeded his advice, for while Crichton Smith's persona is 'listening to the empty quietness' (ICS, *CP*, p. 181), Bruce's astronomer, having 'placed his warm heart on stone faces', 'listens to the faint illiterate stars' (GB, *CP*, p. 180). With MacDiarmid this becomes an entreaty:

> [...] Listen.
> Each star has its rhythm and each world its beat.
> The heart of each separate living thing
> Beats differently, according to its needs,
> And all the beats are in harmony.
> (HMD, *CP*, p. 871)

Now can the poet finally be attuned to the mystery of things. In fact, at 'the gate / Which separates the earthly from the eternal', Hugh MacDiarmid can declare: 'Our wonderment will have no end' (*CP*, 871).

It is important to note that for all four poets this wonderment originates in the contemplation of each particularised object, animal, plant, or person – 'each separate living thing', as MacDiarmid puts it – and leads to the apprehension of what Duns Scotus would have named *haecceitas*, that is, a given entity's 'thisness' or 'eachness', its peculiar form of being. As a matter of fact, these terms as well as Hopkins's 'inscape', which designates not only the distinctive quality of a thing or being but also its intuitive apprehension by the observer, happen to be used by the Scottish poets. In 'The Point of

Honour' MacDiarmid marvels at the river Esk's 'instant inscapes of fresh variation' (HMD, *CP*, p. 388), and in 'On a Raised Beach' he similarly comments on the 'haecceity' of the stones (*CP*, p. 423). Bruce, for his part, knows exactly that, quoting from Duns Scotus, 'objects may possess individualities / peculiar to themselves' and that these are called 'thisness' or '*haecceitas*' (GB, *CP*, p. 119), a concept he was bound to have had in mind when he titled another poem 'City Inscape' (*CP*, p. 274). MacCaig's 'love' for each being and thing apparently yields the same kind of knowledge, for '[i]f you love something, surely it gives you an entry into their nature'[57] – 'nature' meaning here the set of inherent characteristics that make that thing or being specifically what it or he or she is.

The word 'nature', however, may also suggest something more generic, a commonality of character which answers more the question of the 'whatness' (i.e. essence), rather than that of the 'thisness', of the object or being in question. The scholastic philosophers would, in this case, have spoken of *quiddity* (the Latin term for 'whatness') and not so much of *haecceitas*. Such is the case when MacCaig wonders about 'the steadiness that makes the stone steady' (NMC, *CP*, p. 39) or when he recognises the '[i]dea of goatishness made flesh, pure essence' (*CP*, p. 71). Similarly, when MacDiarmid waits for the fog '[t]o quicken into perfect quidditas' (HMD, *CP*, p. 387), or when Crichton Smith avers that '[t]he fact of water is unteachable' (ICS, *CP*, p. 171), or, equally, that he can see 'the water running as the water runs' (*CP*, p. 27), they too extend *haecceitas* into *quiddity* or essence.

But, be it in its individualised or generalised form, what is pondered or contemplated by these poets is always, to phrase it more loosely, the *being* – either *haecceitas* or essence – of specific entities. Thus Bruce, watching a bird in winter, can conclude:

> the red burns upon the breast,
> bringing into the ordinary dying light
> into my constructed code
> your being [...]
> (GB, *CP*, p. 105).

This being is very often intuited – or 'instressed', in Hopkins's vocabulary – in a Joycean epiphany, as, to use Stephen Hero's words in the eponymous novel, 'we recognize that it is that thing which it is. Its soul, its whatness, leaps up to us from the vestment of its appearance', and as it does so, the 'soul of the commonest object [...] seems to us radiant'. Typically, just as 'the red burns upon the breast' of Bruce's bird, MacCaig's kingfisher, a 'resplendent Samurai' 'jewelling upstream', 'gulps / into its own incandescence' (NMC, *CP*, p. 315) and MacDiarmid's 'instant inscapes of fresh variation' reveal '[d]elights of dazzle and dare' (HMD, *CP*, p. 388), likewise in Bruce's 'The Stones of Iona and Columba' each stone is, as we remember, 'surprising us with the shock of light', and in spring there appear 'bluebells shining mile on mile, / vivid creation of the dullest earth' (GB, *CP*, pp. 136, 141). As underscored by Heidegger, in those moments 'beings stand in a luminosity, in a light, and allow free access and entrance—they are lighted'.[58] Hence, for instance, the 'treasury of radiances, of insights' to which Crichton Smith likened MacCaig's *Collected Poems*, concluding he has been 'dazzled by the world that he sees', drily noting that 'it is certainly not the fallen world of the Calvinists'.[59]

While this may not quite be the overtly theophanic world of Hopkins – a world 'charged with the grandeur of God' where 'Christ plays in ten thousand places',[60] 'inscape' being for the Victorian poet 'not only the this-ness of nature, but [...] God himself'[61] – it is nonetheless, in Crichton Smith's words, a world of 'fine spiritual graces / descending from the heavens in luminous dress' where the poet can

>   sense a vast connection, spiritual things
>   bodying forth material, material too
>   bodying forth the spiritual
>   (ICS, *CP*, pp. 139, 141)

Bruce describes it as 'a land of the strange and the common' (GB, *CP*, p. 65), where the mundane or insignificant becomes extraordinary; one may also think, in this respect, of MacCaig's 'building site' where '[e]xtraordinary pools appeared' (NMC, *CP*, pp. 113–14). And that is exactly what wonder

(Heidegger's 'highest disposition, the one open to the uniquely uncanny fact: that there *are* beings, rather than not'[62]) does: it 'reveals the strangeness of the everyday',[63] whose miraculous character becomes visible in the coming-into-view (*Ereignis*) of all beings and things, which are thus bathed in what Heidegger depicts as 'the golden splendor' of Being, glimpsed in 'the very *presencing itself* of everything' (author's emphasis).[64] Being and light are bound up together, as suggested by Heidegger's choice of the term *Ereignis* (from the archaic German word *Eraügnis*).[65]

This process, called 'unconcealment' (*alêtheia*), constitutes the ultimate goal of ontological investigation. It affords, in Heidegger's very words, the 'apprehension of being' *per se* – as opposed to the being of *individual* entities, on which the emphasis has hitherto been laid – through '*phenomenological reduction*', namely 'the leading back or reduction of investigative vision from *a* naively apprehended being to being' (author's emphasis).[66] It is, in other words, the unveiling of *Being* with a capital B, namely Being as 'transcending the phenomena in which it or by means of which it is made known'.[67] And this is made possible because, in turn, 'Being [...] unfolds the landscape (all beings)',[68] as MacCaig understood when he wrote about

> [...] the ordinary communion
> of all sounds, that are
> Being expressing itself – as it does in its continuous,
> its never-ending creation of leaves,
> birds, waves, stone boxes – and beliefs,
> the true and the false.
> (NMC, *CP*, p. 230)

The evanescence of Being

But, as Rubenstein insightfully points out, the revealing of the concealed 'means both the revealing of that which was concealed and the revealing that concealment itself does, by remaining concealed'.[69] Thus in 'Drenched field and bright sun', MacCaig goes beyond the mere visible expression of Being through the 'unfolding of all things'[70]:

> I saw a crow swallow a silver worm
> On a ploughed field so dazzled that it was
> A puzzle to make a ploughed field out of – and
> Then find the crow. The one thing that was clear
> Was the stretched worm, the twirl, the thing not there.
> As though a little chaos of colours tossed
> A flake in the air, the crow flopped up and turned,
> Suddenly black, into what made him black.
> He cawed Brother! and, shrugging his graceless shoulders,
> Ambled away behind some happening trees.
> (*CP*, p. 166)

Here the 'silver worm' is reduced to a 'twirl', that is, a motion or a shape – in other words, the presence-absence of 'the thing not there' (line 5), 'that strangest thing, / that being that was and now no longer is', as Crichton Smith reflects in 'On Looking at the Dead' (ICS, *CP*, p. 135), like Bruce who notes that '[o]n the white-sheeted table / lay what had been a being' (GB, *CP*, p. 261). Yet, like Bruce remembering 'a blue butterfly / that rose from dry grasses' and, 'lifted airy over granite edge, / [...] / in the beam of the sun' was suddenly 'gone' (*CP*, p. 87), the speaker is here contemplating another dimension of Being, which, in Richard Capobianco's words, is 'the No-thing that nonetheless *shines out brightly* to those who can "see" in this special way'.[71] MacCaig, when he notices how the 'kingfisher jewelling upstream / seems to leave a streak of itself behind it / in the bright air' (NMC, *CP*, p. 315), could well be one of the lucky few. For few indeed are those who can achieve that, unless they are prepared, like the poet, to learn from 'a collie [that] stares / at nothing at all, and sees it, teaching [him] to do the same'.[72]

As a matter of fact, 'Can something like being be imagined?', Heidegger asks. 'If we try to do this, doesn't our head begin to swim? Indeed, at first we are baffled and find ourselves clutching at thin air',[73] like the 'blank-puzzled cliff-hanger' of Norman MacCaig's 'In Everything' (NMC, *CP*, p. 305). 'A being – that's something', Heidegger continues, 'a table, a chair, a tree, the sky, a body, some words, an action. A being, yes, indeed – but being? It looks like nothing – and no less a thinker than Hegel said that being and nothing are the same.' In George Pattison's words, '[n]othingness is no longer something to flee, but the ground on which we might first come into relation to being-as-a-whole'.[74] Interestingly, Edwin Muir (1887–1959) seems to echo this view in 'In Love For Long': 'It is not any thing, / And yet all being is.'[75] It is this incomprehensible reality that leaves MacCaig's cliff-hanger unable to decide whether that 'space in space', the 'eagle-shaped space [...] left, stamped on the air' by the bird flying off, is '[a]bsence or presence' (*CP*, p. 305). That uncertainty only confirms Heidegger's intuition that, as Bruce V. Foltz phrases it, 'being also inclines toward self-withholding and that presence itself can be understood only in its interplay with absence', in what Rubenstein describes as 'a ceaseless double movement of revelation and concealment', like MacCaig's clouds 'bright with their own opaque selves' (*CP*, p. 230).[76] This is why 'being cannot be grasped by a subject' and, therefore, also why 'the thinker herself must be displaced – transported out of herself and into what looks like nothing, into the terrifying withdrawal of being'.[77]

Yet it only looks so. For 'being is becoming'.[78] Both in its revelation (*Ereignis*)[79] and in its withdrawal, 'being takes places. Being occurs.'[80] Angela Leighton, commenting on Auden's famous phrase, 'Poetry makes nothing happen', also notes that 'nothing is neither a thing, nor no thing, but a continuous event: "a way of happening [...]"'.[81] (The phrase quoted by the author is, like the other one, from the second stanza of Auden's 1940 poem, 'In Memory of W. B. Yeats'.) It is difficult to think of a better illustration of this than the crow in MacCaig's 'Drenched Field and Bright Sun' that 'ambled away behind some happening trees', its very disappearance causing the viewer to become aware of the emerging presence of the trees. Such an epiphany results from having maintained the right disposition, what Heidegger terms 'ecstatic instanding', consisting in 'keeping oneself open to the self-concealing event of being'[82] – in this case, the blending of the crow into its environment ('the crow flopped up and turned, / Suddenly black, into what made him black'), as well as the transient material presence of the worm. Without this acceptance of the intermittent withdrawal of presence, MacCaig wonders in 'In Everything', 'How can there be a revelation / In a world so full it couldn't be more full?' (*CP*, p. 305). This, as Pattison puts it, is 'Being made manifest even in the midst of its ceaseless coming-into-being and passing-away'.[83]

Presence thus conceived in terms of the 'constant interplay of Being and nothingness' is largely Eastern in its inspiration.[84] It contradicts Western metaphysics' 'understanding of being as constant presence',[85] as well as the conception of presence as static, which, as noted above, Heidegger contrasts with the pre-Socratic philosophers' capacity to perceive *presencing* (that is, Being as, in his own words, 'the No-thing, the manifesting process itself [...] which allows all beings to come to presence'),[86] and more specifically 'the passage from presencing to absencing, from arriving to departing, from emerging to passing away, that is, movement'.[87]

To be sure, movement plays a major role in MacCaig's poetry: 'I find myself to be fascinated by movement, I love the movement of creatures and grasses, anything.'[88] Movement in this sense designates life's essential characteristic in a world where, for the poet, grass is 'Not grass but grasses rippling like the sea' (*CP*, p. 90). Life as *process*, as opposed to the deathlike immobility of Calvinist 'tall black men and their women [...] in tight-locked streets', also defines Crichton Smith's perception (ICS, *CP*, p. 24), and 'the endless process of the roses' or the worms of 'The White Air of March' are some of its ambassadors:

> At midnight the worms dance on the lawn
> transforming recreating
> altering
> (*CP*, p. 157)

By being attuned to the 'changing tones / of water swarming over lucid stones / and salmon bubbling in repeated suns' (*CP*, p. 138) or to various essentialised 'swishings: sousings' (*CP*, 208), the poet is, as Hopkins puts it, in the right attitude to 'study inscape in the spraying of trees, for the swelling buds carry them to a pitch which the eye could not else gather'.[89] Bruce's exhortation to 'See Spring come / again and again in the green shoots: / See the flush of Summer in the rose' (GB, *CP*, p. 234) or to pay attention to 'wintry thunderings' (*CP*, p. 64) and 'sudden lightnings'[90] partakes of the same pursuit.

Yet 'movement' in Heidegger's quotation has more to do with the fluctuations and impermanence of phenomena which those processes of emergence, transformation, variation, development, or change tend to denote. Crichton Smith, for instance, evokes a 'wave's random glintings' (ICS, *CP*, p. 64) while Bruce writes about 'the wavering music of the wind'.[91] Thus, if Crichton Smith is right in stating that 'Poetry has to do with misty mornings / and beginnings, beginnings', then those beginnings are but fugitive 'tremblings':

> Beginnings, tremblings ...
> Poetry will move among
> the morning shadows. All is transient
> nothing is permanent.[92]

That is what Hugh MacDiarmid also realises in 'the tiny hardly visible trembling of the water' of 'The Glass of Pure Water' (HMD, *CP*, p. 1041) or in the endless, subtle movements of the river Esk:

> Pride of play in a flourish of eddies,
> Bravura of blowballs, and silver digressions,
> Ringing and glittering she swirls and steadies,
> And moulds each ripple with secret suppressions.
> (*CP*, p. 388)

These 'suppressions' are, indeed, an integral part of the rippling, and together with it they image the flickering, or vacillation, of Being itself, traceable only through its own fading: 'As it leaves, it becomes absent, absences; but in its absencing it stays, as absent, and this is its presencing as having been.'[93]

Thanksgiving

Such a fine awareness of the elusiveness and evanescence of Being is a far cry from MacDiarmid's doomed attempt to 'circumjack' (i.e. catch, capture)

Cencrastus, 'or the Curly Snake' of change and movement. It enables the poet to maintain Heidegger's 'highest disposition', which, as we have seen, is 'the one open to the uniquely uncanny fact: that there *are* beings, rather than not', with the corollary that these can vanish at any moment. Bruce is acutely aware of that in 'Camelia in the Snow', as he marvels at

> that strange world
> that blossoms in the snow,
> growing where no life should
> grow on this short winter day.
> (GB, *CP*, p. 102)

The attendant feeling of gratitude for the gift of life prompted the German philosopher to recast his phenomenology in terms of donation and thanking – a direction recently adopted in his own work by a phenomenologist like Jean-Luc Marion in France. More precisely, in interpreting 'there is' ('*Es gibt*') literally as 'it gives', Heidegger suggests that 'the task of the philosopher is transformed from thinking upon Being to giving thanks for what gives Being', remaining, however, evasive about the nature of the 'it' in question, so much so that Jacques Derrida saw him as a theologian in disguise, despite his strong claims to the contrary.[94]

If the parallel sketched throughout this study between Heidegger and the four Scottish poets is to be followed through to its conclusion, what are, then, the implications for the latter's spirituality? Indeed, how long can one walk such a fine line without confessing a belief in the giver of life, otherwise known as God? But maybe that is a step which these poets, still hurting from their Knox-inflicted wounds, are forever unwilling, or simply have no need, to take. They exhibit, instead, a remarkable capacity to maintain the 'highest disposition' and remain, as Esther de Wall puts it, 'lost in wonder' over the miracle of Being,[95] on the cusp of what Douglas Dunn identified as the sacramental, the sacred, and the devotional, but leaving God unnamed all the while. As Heidegger himself declared, 'god-less thinking is more open to Him than onto-theo-logic would like to admit'.[96]

Endnotes

1. Quoted in Martin Heidegger, 'What are poets for?', in *Poetry, Language, Thought* [1971], trans. and intro. Albert Hofstadter (New York: Harper and Row, 2001), p. 4.
2. Cited in Cherien Lennie, 'Past, Present and Future in Poetry: MacDiarmid and the Scottish Revival', *Alif: Journal of Comparative Poetics* 9 (1989), pp. 50–69 (p. 56).
3. Hugh MacDiarmid, *Complete Poems: Volumes 1 & 2*, ed. Michael Grieve and W. R. Aitken (Manchester: Carcanet Press, 1993 and 1994), p. 832.
4. Edwin Morgan, 'The Contribution of Iain Crichton Smith', *ScotLit* 23 (Winter 2000), available at: asls.org.uk/the-contribution-of-iain-crichton-smith-scotlit/.
5. See Dominique Delmaire, 'The "Zen Calvinism" of Norman MacCaig', *Ranam* 36 (2003), pp. 147–59 (p. 147). Note, for instance, his treatment of time as a possible 'metaphor for the exacting God of the Old Testament to whom man is in perpetual debt' (p. 148).
6. G. S. Fraser, 'Hugh MacDiarmid: The Later Poetry', in *Hugh MacDiarmid: A Critical Survey*, ed. Duncan Glen (Edinburgh; London: Scottish Academic Press, 1972), pp. 211–27 (pp. 221, 227).
7. T. S. Eliot, *Selected Essays* [1932] (London: Faber & Faber, 1951), pp. 421–23.
8. See in particular MacDiarmid's essay 'Religion and Art', in *The Thistle Rises*, ed. Alan Bold (London: Hamilton, 1984), pp. 265–66.
9. Catherine Kerrigan, *Whaur Extremes Meet* (Edinburgh: Mercat Press, 1983); Alan Bold, *MacDiarmid: The Terrible Crystal* (London: Routledge and Kegan Paul, 1983).
10. See Alexander Hutchison Beveridge, 'Hugh MacDiarmid and Religion: A New Approach to the Poet's Work through a Study of his Recondite Spirituality' (University of Edinburgh, unpublished PhD thesis, 1985), p. 4: 'religion [...] has a claim to be considered as of central, and even supreme, importance, for the interpretation of MacDiarmid's work as a whole'.
11. Beveridge, p. 27.
12. Scott Lyall, 'MacDiarmid, Communism and the Poetry of Commitment', in *The Edinburgh Companion to Hugh MacDiarmid*, ed. Scott Lyall and Margery Palmer McCulloch (Edinburgh: Edinburgh University Press, 2011), pp. 68–81 (p. 80).
13. Alan Riach, 'Hugh MacDiarmid', in *The History of Scottish Literature Vol. 4, Twentieth Century*, ed. Cairns Craig (Aberdeen: Aberdeen University Press, 1987), pp. 75–83 (p. 79).
14. Lyall, p. 80.
15. Carl MacDougall, *Writing Scotland: How Scotland's Writers Shaped the Nation* (Edinburgh: Polygon, 2004), pp. 130–31.
16. Douglas Dunn, '"As a Man Sees..." – On Norman MacCaig's Poetry', *Verse* 7.2 (Summer 1990), pp. 55–67 (p. 67).
17. See Hugh MacDiarmid, *Complete Poems*, ed. Michael Grieve and W.R. Aitken, 2 vols (Manchester: Carcanet Press, 1993 and 1994), pp. 622, 624, 884 [henceforth abbreviated as HMD, *CP*].
18. 'Interview: 'Martin Heidegger: Interview with a Monk (English Subtitles)', 0.26'–0.48', YouTube, www.youtube.com/watch?v=4WK8PJvkzGo (accessed 24 January 2022); George Pattison, *God and Being: an Enquiry* (Oxford; New York: Oxford University Press, 2011), p. 16.
19. Martin Heidegger, *The Basic Problems of Phenomenology*, ed. and trans. Albert Hofstadter (Bloomington: Indiana University Press, 1988 [1982]; German edition: 1975), p. 20.

20 On the later Heidegger's mysticism, see John D. Caputo, *The Mystical Element in Heidegger's Thought* (Bronx, New York: Fordham University Press, 1986), p. 27; Mary-Jane Rubenstein, *Strange Wonder: The Closure of Metaphysics and the Opening of Awe* (New York: Columbia University Press, 2008), pp. 9, 28–31.
21 Shaver, p. 746.
22 Heidegger, *Poetry, Language, Thought*, pp. 92, 109. See also his essay on Nietzsche, where '[b]ecause it is willed out of the essence of being, nature appears everywhere as the object of technology': Martin Heidegger, 'Nietzsche's Word "God is Dead"', in *Off the Beaten Track*, ed. Julian Young and Kenneth Haynes (Cambridge: Cambridge University Press, 2002), p. 191.
23 George Mackay Brown, *Greenvoe* (London: The Hogarth Press, 1972); George Mackay Brown, 'The Rational Sun' [undated MS], Orkney Library & Archive, BOX D31/30/2, probably written between 1945 and 1950.
24 George Mackay Brown, 'The Broken Heraldry', in *Memoirs of a Modern Scotland*, ed. Karl Miller (London: Faber and Faber, 1970), p. 145.
25 Brown, 'The Broken Heraldry', p. 145.
26 Michel Serres, *The Natural Contract*, trans. Elizabeth MacArthur and William Paulson (Ann Arbor: University of Michigan Press, 1995), p. 32.
27 Mary-Jane Rubenstein, 'One Way up through the Way back into the Out of Ontotheology', *'In Theory' Lecture Series* (2011) pp. 20, 26: works.bepress.com/mary_jane_rubenstein/31/
28 Iain Crichton Smith, *Collected Poems* (Manchester: Carcanet, 1995), p. 51 [henceforth cited as ICS, *CP*].
29 George Bruce, *Today Tomorrow: The Collected Poems of George Bruce 1933–2000* (Edinburgh: Polygon, 2001), p. 131 [henceforth cited as GB, *CP*].
30 In Iain Crichton Smith's poetry alone, one can think of 'the early daffodil, purer than a soul' (*CP*, 3); 'the free daffodils / wave in the valleys and on the hills' (*CP*, 47); 'unless perhaps we are resurrected / like an astronomy of daffodils / changing into a yellowness of stars' (*Ends and Beginnings* (Manchester: Carcanet, 1994), p. 8). Another poet would easily come to mind: George Mackay Brown, for whom daffodils are 'Three Marys at the cross' ('Daffodils', *CP*, 35), and 'daffodil-shining dove-winged words' can be spoken by pure hearts ('Halcro', *CP*, 27).
31 Heidegger, 'What are poets for?', p. 112.
32 Rubenstein, 'One Way up', p. 5; Bruce V. Foltz, *Inhabiting the Earth: Heidegger, Environmental Ethics, and the Metaphysics of Nature* (New Jersey: Humanities Press, 1995), p. 12.
33 Rubenstein, *Strange Wonder*, p. 32.
34 Michael Edwards, *De l'émerveillement* (Paris: Fayard, 2008), pp. 15 and 16 [my translation].
35 Plato's *'Theaetetus'*, ed. and trans. Francis M. Cornford (London: Routledge & Kegan Paul, 1934; repr. Indianapolis and New York: Bobbs-Merrill, 1959), archive.org/details/theaetetusooplat/ [accessed 21 May 2022], 155c, p. 43.
36 John Keats, *Selected Poems and Letters*, ed. Douglas Bush (Boston: Houghton Mifflin, 1959), p. 261.
37 Cited in Richard Capobianco, *Heidegger's Way of Being* (Toronto: University of Toronto Press, 2014), p. 44.
38 MacDiarmid, 'Poetry and Science', *Collected Poems*, p. 630.

39 Nancy Gish and Hugh MacDiarmid, 'An Interview with Hugh MacDiarmid', *Contemporary Literature* 20.2 (1979), pp. 135-54 (p. 146).
40 Iain Crichton Smith, 'The Golden Lyric', in *Hugh MacDiarmid: A Critical Survey*, ed. Duncan Glen (Edinburgh; London: Scottish Academic Press, 1972), pp. 124-40 (p. 128).
41 Iain Crichton Smith, *Towards the Human* (Edinburgh: MacDonald Publishers, 1986), pp. 150, 152.
42 G. Gregory Smith, *Scottish Literature: Character and Influence* (London: Macmillan, 1919), p. 6; Alan Riach, 'Hugh MacDiarmid', p. 80.
43 Adolphe Haberer, 'Théorie et pratique de la poésie impure dans l'oeuvre de Louis MacNeice', in *La Lyre du Larynx. Poétique et poésie moderne* (Paris: Didier érudition, 2000), pp. 49-74 (p. 64, my translation).
44 Alan Riach, 'The Later MacDiarmid', in *The History of Scottish Literature Vol. 4, Twentieth Century*, ed. Cairns Craig (Aberdeen: Aberdeen University Press, 1987), pp. 217-28 (p. 226); G. S. Fraser, p. 213.
45 John Baglow, *Hugh MacDiarmid, the Poetry of Self* (Kingston: McGill-Queen's University Press, 1987), p. 107.
46 Rubenstein, *Strange Wonder*, p. 14.
47 Cited in Rubenstein, *Strange Wonder*, p. 28.
48 Heidegger, 'What are poets for?', p. 222.
49 Maurice Merleau-Ponty, *Le visible et l'invisible* (Paris: Gallimard, 1964), p. 76 [my translation].
50 See Merleau-Ponty, pp. 175, 181.
51 Heidegger, cited in Foltz, p. 28.
52 Cited in *The Poems of Norman MacCaig*, ed. Ewen McCaig, intro. Alan Taylor (Edinburgh: Polygon 2009), p. xlix.
53 Iain Crichton Smith, 'A Lust of the Particular: Norman MacCaig's Poetry', *Chapman* 2.45 (1986), pp. 20-24 (p. 21).
54 See Capobianco, p. 40.
55 On G. M. Hopkins's incarnational theology, see Walter J. Ong, *Hopkins, the Self and God* (Toronto: Toronto University Press, 1986).
56 *Poetry, Language, Thought*, pp. 214, 221.
57 In Ewen McCaig, p. xlix.
58 Martin Heidegger, *Basic Questions of Philosophy: Selected 'Problems' of 'Logic'*, trans. Richard Rojcewicz and André Schuwer (Bloomington: Indiana University Press, 1994), p. 178.
59 Smith, 'A Lust of the Particular', pp. 24, 22.
60 In respectively 'God's Grandeur' and 'As Kingfishers Catch Fire', in *The Poems of Gerard Manley Hopkins*, ed. W. H. Gardner and N. H. Mackenzie (Oxford: Oxford University Press, 1970), pp. 66, 90.
61 Brian Willems, *Hopkins and Heidegger* (London, New York: Continuum, 2009), p. 5.
62 Heidegger, *Basic Questions of Philosophy*, p. 3.
63 Rubenstein, *Strange Wonder*, p. 30.
64 Capobianco, p. 34.
65 See Willems, p. 41.
66 Heidegger, *Basic Problems of Phenomenology*, p. 21.
67 Pattison, p. 16.

68 Capobianco, p. 34.
69 Rubenstein, 'One Way up', p. 26.
70 Capobianco, p. 34.
71 Ibid., p. 35.
72 'View with no prospect', in Ewen McCaig, p. 385.
73 Heidegger, *Basic Problems of Phenomenology*, p. 10.
74 Pattison, p. 300.
75 'The Voyage' (1946), in Edwin Muir, *Collected Poems* (London: Faber & Faber, 1984), p. 159.
76 Foltz, p. 6; Rubenstein, 'One Way up', p. 27.
77 Rubenstein, 'One Way up', p. 27.
78 Willems, p. 27.
79 Hofstadter, *Poetry, Language, Thought*, p. xviii.
80 Ibid., p. 26.
81 Angela Leighton, *On Form: Poetry, Aestheticism, and the Legacy of a Word* (Oxford University Press, 2007), p. 145.
82 Rubenstein, 'One Way up', p. 28.
83 Pattison, p. 109.
84 Ibid., p. 305. Pattison refers in particular to the Kyoto School of philosophy.
85 Foltz, p. 25.
86 Matthew Rumbold, 'Interview with Richard Capobianco', *Figure/Ground*, 20 May 2013 figureground.org/fg/interview-with-richard-capobianco [accessed 24 January 2022]. On the use of 'presencing' by Heidegger, see also Capobianco, pp. 34–40.
87 Cited in Capobianco, *Heidegger's Way of Being*, p. 40.
88 Ewen McCaig, p. xlix.
89 Hopkins, cited in Willems, p. 23.
90 Bruce, *Ends and Beginnings*, p. 65.
91 Ibid., p. 108.
92 Bruce, 'The Young Girls', *Ends and Beginnings*, p. 115.
93 Hofstadter, cited in Willems, p. 27.
94 Pattison, p. 309; see Jacques Derrida, *Of Spirit: Heidegger and the Question*, trans. Geoffrey Bennington and Rachel Bowlby (Chicago; London: University of Chicago Press, 1989), p. 2.
95 Esther de Waal, *Lost in Wonder: Rediscovering the Spiritual Art of Attentiveness* (Norwich: Canterbury Press 2003).
96 Cited in Rubenstein, 'One Way up', p. 21.

12. George Mackay Brown and the Disenchantment of Orkney

LINDEN BICKET

In Act One of George Mackay Brown's (1921–1996) play *A Spell for Green Corn* (1970), a group of 'shore people' fix their eyes on the sea. The action takes place on the fictional island of Hellya, in an imagined medieval past that Brown's stage directions describe as 'the age of saints and fish and miracles'.[1] The famished islanders train their gaze on the boat of their best fisherman, Erik, but soon a wave consumes him and he perishes. Into this crowd comes a monk, Brother Cormac, who admonishes the islanders gently for their reliance on the sea's scarce reward. Calling the sea 'a miser and a murderer', the monk implores the islanders to 'take part in the good dance of agriculture [...] That is God's will for you' (p. 11). When the islanders refuse his gift of stones gathered from the shoreline, Brother Cormac mutters ruefully, 'you're not all saints and poets, I suppose', before blessing the stones and transforming them miraculously into fresh haddock (p. 12). This austere scene ends with the recitation of 'The Ballad of John Barleycorn' – a rural song of agricultural ritual in which Brown draws parallels between Christ's sacrificial death and fruitfulness of God's kingdom. In this way, the opening act of *A Spell for Green Corn* introduces its audience to a drama in which cycles of famine and feast recur over centuries, from the spiritual hunger of pre-Christian times to the bounty of the medieval 'age of saints and fish and miracles', and from the darkness of Reformation Orkney ('a time of witches and ploughs and kirk sessions') to the mechanised, secular, post-industrial present – an 'age of machines and numbers and official forms' (pp. 16, 54).

A Spell for Green Corn offers a starting point for this chapter's exploration of Brown's enduring preoccupation with patterns of devotion and doubt throughout the sweep of Orcadian history. In particular, this study of

Brown's place as a Scottish Catholic writer will consider the significance of his post-Enlightenment, potentially Weberian notion of the Protestant Reformation as 'a milestone on the road towards modernity and secularization, a landmark in the narrative of progress' and the scourge of 'magical and supernatural forces in the world'.[2] In his first poetry collection, *The Storm* (1954), Brown announced that it was the task of 'poet and saint' to re-spiritualise a disenchanted, 'Knox-ruined' Scotland.[3] This refrain is echoed by Brother Colm in his admonishment of the sceptical 'shore people', and indeed it reverberates and evolves in much of Brown's subsequent short fiction and poetry, before finally appearing afresh, though matured, in his valedictory last novel, *Beside the Ocean of Time* (1994). This chapter's ensuing discussion will trace the evolution of Brown's Catholic thought about Orkney's 'disenchantment' though a diachronic survey of key moments in his poetry, short fiction, a mid-career play, and final novel. Recurring characters, patterns of sacred imagery and ritual, and pre-Reformation ruins all feature in Brown's depiction of the effects of Scottish religious change over centuries. These creative leitmotifs demonstrate not only the evolution of Brown's thought about the 'disenchantment' of Orkney, but also reveal the relationship between Brown's writing and other works of Scottish and Catholic fiction more broadly.

In her highly valuable overview of the 'desacralisation' thesis, Alexandra Walsham outlines Max Weber's description of the Reformation as 'the disenchantment of the world':

> Weber argued that, especially in its more ascetic forms, Protestantism fostered a fundamental rejection of sacramental magic as a mechanism for aiding salvation and prompted the evolution of a transcendental and intellectualised religion in which numinous forces were removed from the sphere of everyday life.[4]

Yet Walsham rightly observes that any notion of the Reformation as a swift and decisive break between a medieval Catholic, 'superstitious' understanding of the world, and a 'Protestant ethic' of rationalism, fails to do justice to patterns of devotion and supernatural belief throughout what is increasingly recognised by historians as the 'Long Reformation'.[5] Similarly, historian Andrew Keitt has pointed out that 'the Weberian model approximates at face value many of the same polemical categories used by the sixteenth-century reformers themselves' even as it 'projects nineteenth-century confessional stereotypes about the "rationality" of Protestantism back onto the Reformation era'.[6]

The Weberian thesis of disenchantment is a powerful feature of the output – both critical and artistic – of the so-called twentieth-century Scottish Cultural 'Renaissance'.[7] Nowhere is this more palpable than in the writings of Edwin Muir (1887–1959), whose resentment of the Reformation is an intensely prevalent strand within both his poetry and literary criticism. Muir's derision for 'King Calvin with his iron pen / And God three angry letters in a book' in 'The Incarnate One' (1956) denounces the word-centred Scottish Reformation's swift obliteration of the sacralised world.[8] As discussed fully elsewhere, Muir's view was eagerly adopted by his student, the Catholic convert and fellow Orcadian, George Mackay Brown, and it is a powerful driver in Brown's own work about religious change in sixteenth-century Orkney.[9] In *An Orkney Tapestry* (1969), Brown writes that '[t]he Orkney imagination is haunted by time; it is Edwin Muir's great theme, and in this matter he is the poet who speaks for all of us'.[10] The notion of the Scottish Reformation as spiritual and cultural affliction is a consistent theme in much of Brown's early poetry and prose. Muir notes in *Scottish Journey* (1935) that in Scotland 'one has to dig for history beneath a layer of debris left by the Reformation and the Industrial Revolution'.[11] In Brown's work too, the excavation and retrieval of ancient faith is a key priority, and he signals this through repeated invocation of 'the remains of pre-Reformation chapel and monastery' and 'the rose-red Cathedral of Saint Magnus the Martyr in Kirkwall' in his poetry and prose.[12] Brown's frequent criticism of what he calls 'the new religion, Progress, in which we all devoutly believe' is often noted by critics as a sign of his conservatism – particularly given his rural location – but in fact it might be better understood as part of the Weberian historiography of Protestant disenchantment that he inherited from Muir.[13]

The 1950s–1960s: poetry and short fiction

'Chapel Between Cornfield and Shore', a poem included in Brown's second collection *Loaves and Fishes* (1959), traces the time-haunted Orcadian landscape to the religious turmoil of the sixteenth century. Musing on the ruins of a pre-Reformation chapel, the speaker reflects on the 'ascetic forms' of (Scottish) Protestantism identified by Weber as removing the numinous from everyday life:

> Above the ebb, that gray uprooted wall
> Was arch and chancel, choir and sanctuary,
> A solid round of stone and ritual.
> Knox brought all down in his wild Hogmanay.[14]

These lines identify the ruin as an Orcadian Tintern Abbey – a permanent reminder of the medieval past in the landscape of the present, and a catalyst for internal reflection on the lost devotions of Catholic Orkney. But unlike the titular abbey of Wordsworth's poem, this ruin was not created by the dissolution of the monasteries; rather, the architect of the chapel's demolition is the Reformer Knox, his 'wild Hogmanay' a specifically Scottish form of iconoclasm akin to the 'carnivalesque rituals of defilement and desecration' of early modern Europe.[15] The sudden end-stop of the poem's fourth line subdues the speaker's imaginative leap into the chapel's lost liturgical life. But the inertia threatened by this pause is overcome in the next stanza by Brown's hopeful description of 'new ceremonies', which will transform the chapel's barren resting place (its 'thrawn acre') and catalyse resurrection 'after the crucifixion of the seed' (ll. 6, 8). By the close of the poem, the speaker imagines a future in which the chapel surges with new life, and a 'fisher priest' offers the body of Christ as 'spindrift bread' (l. 13). In this poem, the loss of ritual and the Eucharistic sacrifice is presented as merely a historical anomaly. Eventually, suggests Brown, after many centuries of liturgical and devotional famine, God's grace will completely re-enchant the world.

The 'fisher priest' of 'Chapel Between Cornfield and Shore' appears again, much fleshed out, as the narrator of 'Master Halcrow, Priest', a tale included within Brown's first short story collection, *A Calendar of Love* (1967). This character clearly appealed to Brown, as this is the first of two short stories in which he appears. 'Master Halcrow, Priest' is a first-hand testimony of the Orcadian Reformation, written 'on a harvest evening in the year of Our Lord 1561'.[16] Despite Brown's claim that 'realism is the enemy of the creative imagination', Halcrow's account of the 'stripping' of his Orcadian altar does, at first glance, seem to comply reasonably well with what we know of the Reformation in Orkney (though a comprehensive study of this has yet to be attempted).[17] The old priest Halcrow makes a careful note that the day's events have been the culmination of 'things that have come upon us this ten years and more' (p. 124) – a statement which reflects the fact that the move towards Reform in Orkney and elsewhere 'was not a single event but a long and acrimonious process of transition', as Jocelyn Rendall asserts.[18] However, the description of Orcadian religious change at grassroots level is perhaps more open to question given the charismatic timbre of the new street preaching witnessed by the islanders. Master Halcrow recalls 'a man come to the town of Kirkwall that preached under the sky like a friar, his texts the Scarlet Woman and Anti-Christ and the Whore of Babylon out of the Apocalypse' (p. 126). The new preaching raises the spectres of 'shrieking, babbling, seeing of visions and speaking in tongues', and men respond by 'sob[bing] and declar[ing] their sins openly in the streets' (p. 126). This 'blasphemous clowning' disturbs Halcrow, and rightly so, as it proves to be a precursor to the story's crisis, in which he is cast out of his chapel by the new Protestants and returns to rescue the blessed sacrament amid iconoclasm carried out by 'powerful and angry men' (p. 128).

The hysterical evangelism and cold ferocity of the Reformation in this story has, arguably, a much more literary than historical basis. The street preaching and frenzied conversions described by the old priest are strikingly reminiscent of the late nineteenth-century evangelical revivals in Orkney that Muir describes in *An Autobiography* (1954), in which he describes a Revivalist preacher ('a thin, tense young man called Macpherson') and a 'conspicuous groaner' who 'burst into a loud and rapid prayer, as if he were already resolved to make a record in the world of the saved'.[19] Muir notes that his mother attended a revival as a young woman, at which 'people fell down in fits in the church and rolled on the floor'.[20] The strangely modern quality of the Reformation in Halcrow's Orkney might have its roots in the revivals recounted by Muir, who himself saw them as 'communal orgies, such as were probably known long before Christianity came to these islands', and which he thought had 'very little to do with religion'.[21]

Indeed, Brown's imaginative recreation of religious change in Orkney did not rely on meticulous historical research. The later stages of the Reformation in seventeenth-century Orkney did witness 'scarred walls and ravished [church] interiors', and '[t]he Kirkwall Presbytery ordered the statue of St Peter in St Peter's Kirk in South Ronaldsay to be burnt', but Brown's depiction of thrown-down statues, a broken crucifix, and smashed candles in 'Master Halcrow, Priest' (and the 'blows and smashing and dilapidation' he describes in *An Orkney Tapestry*) were the polemical devices of an eager convert.[22] As Brown himself admitted in his posthumous autobiography, '[a]t the Reformation there was none of the violence and burning in Orkney that afflicted shrines in other parts of Scotland; St Magnus' Cathedral sailed intact through the tempest'.[23] Indeed, Rendall writes that Orcadian Reform was directed by the 'frail, cultured, intellectual bishop, Adam Bothwell', who ensured the Cathedral's safety, and met with only moderate popular resistance. She notes:

> Resistance did not last long, however. The 'commonis' do not seem to have given trouble for long, and although there is no evidence that there was any great fervour in Orkney for 'reforming' religion, the landowners enthusiastically welcomed the opportunity to enrich themselves and their families with property confiscated from the Church. [...] In fact, there was a surprising degree of continuity, because most of the Orkney clergy 'conformed' to Protestantism and remained in their parishes.[24]

Grasping landowners do not receive the wrath of Halcrow's pen in Brown's short story. His troubled priest lays the blame for religious change squarely at the door of the Reformers, and at Catholic clergy weak enough (in Halcrow's view) to conform, accept positions as ministers, take wives, and read 'German and Swiss books' (p. 127). The religious 'continuity' described by Rendall agrees broadly with recent accounts of the age of Reformations in Europe, which counteract Weber's 'disenchantment' narrative by stressing 'continuities and homologies between medieval and Protestant mentalities'.[25] And although Brown's fictional Reformation is dramatic and brutal in 'Master Halcrow, Priest', he makes sure to hint at these continuities too, not least when an apostatised priest, Master Anderson, saves the blessed sacrament from destruction, and agrees to deliver the last rites to Halcrow in secret at the hour of his death.

However, the most powerful and effective element of 'Master Halcrow, Priest' is not Brown's attempt to manufacture a historically accurate voice, though Halcrow is a compelling narrator. Nor is it broader historical authenticity which, as noted above, Brown was not wholly committed to, writing that 'the reality of history and the reality of literature are quite different, each being one facet of the truth'.[26] The richest component of the story is the collision between the new, 'improved' and de-sacralised world and Halcrow's sacramental universe, in which every created thing is a visible sign of God's presence. Halcrow confesses that he is a sinner. He admits, 'I fish too long at the rock, I pray only a little, I drink too much of the dark ale that they brew on the hill' (p. 124). And yet, he is content to accept his fallenness. Indeed, Halcrow's appeal as narrator stems from his very human combination of frailty and strength, and in this he reflects something of the characters of Brown's fellow literary convert, Graham Greene (1904– 1991). J. C. Whitehouse points out that in Greene's work, 'holiness and faith are of greater importance to human beings than piety',[27] and the same might be claimed of Brown, whose Halcrow can be read as an Orcadian echo of Greene's 'whisky priest' – the hero of *The Power and the Glory* (1940), described by Brown in his autobiography as 'a hunted and driven priest, and in many ways a worthless one, who nevertheless kept faith to the end, as better martyrs had done in other places'.[28] Thus Brown transplants the persecution of the clergy in 1930s Mexico to an Orcadian early modern milieu in this short story. In Greene's novel, the anticlerical secular state pursues a renegade padre. In Brown's text, the flawed but heroic, determined priest is persecuted as part of the Orcadian stripping of the altars – the process of 'disenchantment' that, according to Enlightenment thinking, 'interpreted the Reformation as part of a long-term process of rationalization and secularization, an interpretation further reworked by the historiography of the nineteenth century until it constructed our modern view of the Reformation'.[29]

Halcrow earns our sympathy because he sees the world in beautiful ways, and he is redeemed by his imaginative gifts – poignant indicators of an older, magical universe. The old priest's frequent similes speak of his defiant understanding of the world as enchanted by the divine: he holds 'nine haddocks […], a cold silver bunch like a silent bell' and views his beleaguered kirk 'like a foundering ship in long windy surges of corn' (pp. 126, 129). The stones of his chapel, taken from the shore, 'shine with wetness like dark mirrors' for 'these stones (as it seems) remember the element of water out of which they have been taken' (p. 131). Halcrow's lyrical language expresses his trust in God's active participation in human life through the sacraments of the Church (and especially through the sacrament of the Eucharist) but also through her sacramentals – candles, statues, the kirk's crucifix, its gleaming stones, and Orkney's surging cornfields – materials noted by Robert Scribner to have 'earned the designation of "the magic of the late-medieval church"' and which 'attracted the scorn and hostility of the Protestant Reformers of the sixteenth century'.[30] Brown's narrator is regarded as drunken, idle, idolatrous, and blasphemous by the men who invade his kirk and hurl down its statues, but his vulnerability, bravery, and appreciation of the celestial qualities of the everyday both rouse the reader's compassion and pit imagination against the severity of disenchantment. By the end, Halcrow, 'like an old wounded beast, hard beset, that groaned and laboured under the yoke', is a frail, but heroic narrator (p. 133).

The reference to Halcrow's 'yoke' – perhaps deliberately referencing Christ's utterance 'my yoke is easy, and my burden is light' in Matthew 11. 30 – chimes with other references in Brown's work to the 'yoke' as an agricultural implement as well as a metaphor for Christ's cross, as in 'Stations of the Cross', from *Winterfold* (1976), which states, in its second stanza ('Cross'): 'Lord, it is time. Take our yoke / And sunwards turn.'[31] The Reformation comes to Orkney, then, as the old priest's Passion play. As with the Biblical Passion, this story suggests that death is not the end; resurrection, or re-enchantment, will overcome it. Gavin Miller argues persuasively that this story proposes that faith 'can be driven underground by institutional religion', but older forms of belief might survive, 'preserved and maintained in a covert religious life of the folk'.[32] Halcrow's testimony is the first of many of Brown's works which insist that pre-Reformation Catholicism cannot be fully erased from communal life, making this text a rather more nuanced appreciation of religious change than we might expect from Edwin Muir's early student. In this text, the beauty of Catholic ritual and places of worship are deeply inscribed into the psyche of the people, and the history and landscape, of Orkney. God continues to disclose his presence through land, sea, and other matter.

Of course, during the long Reformation, 'Protestantism, in no sense, rejected the notion that the sacred could intervene in the world', as Walsham rightly asserts. She adds, 'In the guise of the doctrine of providence, it placed fresh emphasis on the power and omnipotence of God and defended vigorously the precept that he interceded to warn, punish, chastise, try, and reward individuals and communities alike'.[33] This is an idea that is dramatised – arguably somewhat polemically, again – in the second of Brown's 'Father Halcrow' stories, 'The Treading of Grapes'. This tale appears in his second collection, *A Time to Keep* (1969), and it presents the reader with three historical sermons preached on the wedding at Cana (from John 2. 1–11) in the kirk of St Peter's, Orkney – the same church which features in 'Master Halcrow, Priest'. The first sermon is delivered by the Rev. Garry Watters, a modern-day Presbyterian minister, whose homespun preaching style and matter-of-fact exegesis are wholly lacking in mysticism. Watters understands the miracle of water into wine as an act of thrifty expediency in which Jesus smooths over a foolish administrative error: 'the foresight of Jesus more than compensated for the steward's blundering. […] Think, in the wider sphere, what a brilliant business executive, what a wise ambassador, what a competent minister of state [Jesus] would have made!'[34] The sermon reaches its ironic climax with Watters's announcement that a ballot will be taken to decide whether the congregation would prefer a non-alcoholic wine for future sacraments, 'in keeping', he suggests, 'with the seemliness of our devotions' (p. 67). In this way, Brown suggests, the miracles of Jesus and the wonder of the incarnation have been entirely neutralised in the present day. Watters's sermon lays bare his rather trite interpretation of the miracles and person of Jesus and exposes worship in modern-day St Peter's to be a polite and rather douce obligation.

There is no such neutrality in the next sermon, a crude and thunderous rant delivered by the Rev. Dr Thomas Fortheringhame, St Peter's eighteenth-century minister, who warns his parishioners darkly against taking John's account as an excuse to make 'drunken beasts' of themselves. 'It is the devil of hell that has put such a thought into your minds', he rages, before announcing the formal process of public rebuke for the father of a 'bastard child' and reminding one man, James Drever, to deliver a keg of brandy to the manse (pp. 67, 70). Fortheringhame is of course a hypocritical 'justified sinner' in the tradition of Robert Burns's Holy Willie and James Hogg's Robert Wringhim. As his sermon takes shape, the Cana narrative functions merely as a prompt for the preacher's punitive warnings and chastisements. Fortheringhame robs Jesus' miracle of its joy and uses it as an instrument with which to amplify his congregation's fear of eternal punishment (p. 69).

The final sermon, delivered by Master John Halcrow, is from 'the second Sunday after Epiphany in the year 1548' (p. 64). It is, therefore, a pre-Reformation reflection on the miracle at Cana, which takes place thirteen years before the events of 'Master Halcrow, Priest'. Halcrow's homily takes the form of a series of 'stations', all of which lead his listeners through the miracle described in the Gospel of John. But Halcrow's exegesis expands the contours of the wedding at Cana. Not only does he situate the beginning of his reflection long before the wedding takes place, he sees the story as one which is continually revealed in the lives of his parishioners through their celebration of the sacraments. Halcrow's congregants hear him speak of 'the vine', the beginning of the life of the grape, which is nurtured by 'the quick merry blood of the earth', before becoming, through the processes of cultivation (and transubstantiation) 'the miracle' – the blood of Christ which nourishes the faithful (p. 70). Halcrow understands the wedding at

Cana as a prefiguration of 'the marriage of Christ with His Church' in the Eucharist. He exclaims:

> *And where will this marriage be?* you ask. Everywhere, I answer, but in particular, lords and princes, in this small kirk beside the sea where you sit. *And when is it to be, this wedding?* you ask me. Always, I answer, but in particular within this hour, now, at the very moment when I bow over this bread of your offering, the food, princes and lords, that you have won with such hard toil from the furrows, at once when I utter upon it five words HIC [*sic*] EST ENIM CORPUS MEUM. (p. 74)

With these words ('this is my body'), Halcrow situates the eternal sacrifice of Christ within the temporal lives of his Orcadian flock, and he exhorts them to rejoice in their Eucharistic celebration. This transforms them from ordinary men and women into 'dear children' and revelling 'princes and ladies', beloved by God (pp. 73, 74). Moreover, the body of Christ – the Eucharist – nourishes the people of God, who themselves become the body of Christ in the Pauline metaphor of 1 Corinthians 12. 12–14. This is the spiritually sublime reflection of a more assured Father Halcrow than we saw in Brown's earlier short story. In Brown's earlier depiction, the old priest is troubled and apprehensive, a lone voice of dissent in the face of bigger and more powerful historical forces. In 'A Treading of Grapes', published two years later, Halcrow acts *in persona Christi* as a fluent and ecstatic messenger who glorifies God through lyrical agricultural analogy. The Reformation has not yet taken hold and desacralised the world, as per Weber's paradigm, and the sacramental system of the medieval church nourishes the body and souls of the faithful.

Brown's theme of eternal life through Eucharistic encounter is reinforced by the story's coda, in which a present-day narrator tells us '[t]he sea shattered and shattered on the beach' (p. 75). As in 'Chapel Between Cornfield and Shore', where resurrection is hinted at through the line, 'The Wave turns round', Brown uses the sea as a metaphor which suggests eternally recurring patterns of goodness and salvation (l. 5). And it is no accident that the prompt for reflection on the three sermons of 'A Treading of Grapes' is the ruined chapel of St Peter's, first mentioned in 'Master Halcrow, Priest'. As in Brown's earlier work, 'older anonymous stones' again function as a catalyst for imaginative journeying into the past in this short story (p. 63). Brown's modern narrator introduces the story's frame tale by gazing at the parish church of St Peter's, built in 1826. He muses, 'there were churches there before the present church was erected', and he goes on to describe the medieval remains of an older kirk:

> Among the clustering tombstones is a piece of wall with a weathered hole in it that looks as though it might have been an arched window, and slightly to one side an abrupt squat arrangement of dressed stones that suggests an altar (p. 63).

Once again, the scattered remains of pre-Reformation material culture and architecture – specifically, the ruined chapel – is a literary device that allows Brown to travel backwards in time and reflect on the past riches of Orcadian popular devotion and ritual.

In this second collection of short fiction, then, Brown demonstrates his continued preoccupation with cyclical patterns of spiritual erosion, renewal, and Catholic re-enchantment. The Rev. Dr Thomas Fortheringhame is used by Brown as the (rather blunt) agent of erosion in 'A Treading of Grapes'. Our narrator tells us that he 'says curtly',

> There is in the vicinity of the Kirk remnants of a popish chapel, where the ignorant yet resort in time of sickness and dearth to leave offerings, in the vain hope that such superstition will alleviate their sufferings; the which Romish embers I have exerted myself to stamp out with all severity during the period of my ministry. (pp. 63–64).

Of course, Fortheringhame's efforts to subdue residual ex-voto offerings are shown to be largely fruitless, as despite their dilapidated state these

Catholic ruins possess a palpable spiritual and imaginative power for parishioners, from the eighteenth century to the present-day narrator of Brown's text. But Brown's depiction of the lingering popular appeal of old Catholic rites, prayers, and practices in the post-Reformation era is, as already noted, historically grounded, as are Fortheringhame's attempts to rid his parish of such practices. Rendall notes that '[o]n the surface, Orcadians were turned into Protestants with remarkably little resistance, but old beliefs endured, underground, and survived generations of ministers' attempts to extirpate the "dregs of popery" from the isles'.[35] This endurance of belief provided rich fodder for Brown's imaginative exploration of religious change. Although Reformation desacralisation has ushered in clerical narratives of both eighteenth-century hellfire and brimstone and benign modern uniformity in Brown's text, the holy can never be entirely erased from the world, and it broods, waiting and ready to re-enchant the hearts and imaginations of those who seek it.

The 1970s: drama

The survival of deep-rooted ritual and belief is also the haunting theme of Brown's already-mentioned, mid-career play *A Spell for Green Corn* (1970). In this play, Brown suggests a correlation between the blighted crops and the by now completely Calvinist, disenchanted landscape of mid seventeenth-century Orkney. In the midst of looming famine, a young woman, Sigrid, and a fiddle player, Storm Kolson, secure the fecundity of the land through a 'spell': they make love in the laird's cornfield. Soon afterwards, a group of crofters dance ritually around a bonfire to Storm's fiddle music. His airs, 'A Spell for Water', 'A Rune for Ripeness', and 'A Prayer for Good Ale', provide the musical accompaniment for their mysterious, liturgical-sounding chants which take place in secret, away from the prying eyes of the Kirk Session. These acts function as fertility charms and suggest that Brown knew of and understood concepts such as the medieval 'charming of the fields' or Rogationtide processions with banners and bells, which were, according to Eamon Duffy, 'designed to bring good weather and blessing and fertility to the fields'.[36]

Indeed, these customs lingered long after Reform began, and Scribner notes that in Lutheran and Calvinist parts of early modern Germany,

> The inability of Protestant authorities to prevent rogation day processions which sought divine protection for ripening crops against pests or damaging storms led to the creation of a distinctively Protestant form of the *Hagelfeier* ('hail ceremony'), a procession around the fields with hymns and prayers instead of a Eucharistic procession.[37]

Brown's Eucharistic 'spell' for green corn is not so fanciful as it might then initially appear; this 'cold act of beauty (in default of sanctity)' to 'flush the hill with ripeness' refers directly to the idea that Catholic enchantment could not be fully erased from an Orcadian collective unconscious even when Catholicism was no longer officially practiced (p. 62). This is also another instance of Brown's frequent pairing of agricultural fertility and human sexuality in his work. Both are seen to stem from God's hands as gifts to be cherished.

The Reformed kirk responds to Sigrid and Storm's 'spell' with bitter fury in Brown's play, in keeping with Brown's frequent depiction of Reformation-era clergy as fundamentalist, domineering and cruel. In the play's fourth act, we find that unmarried Sigrid is pregnant and appears before the Kirk Session to answer for her 'sin'. Through the cunning of one of the Session's elders, Sigrid is found guilty not only of fornication, 'a most serious crime against God and his kirk', but also witchcraft, due to magical associations of the 'spell' and the subsequent disappearance of Storm Kolson (p. 38). The factor and elder, John Rosey, seethes:

> Who put the blight on the oats at the start of summer? – so that, until the prayers of God's elect revived them, we were faced with stark famine this present winter. You ken well what she did on midsummer night, on the summit of Kierfea, you were all there. Men, I'm saying now that this entire parish is enchanted with witchcraft.

In the centre of the web stands this woman. The yeast of hell is working strong in her. [...] Dare you deny it, witch? (p. 41)

Again, Brown's depiction of the Session and its equation of the fertility 'spell' with witchcraft has much historical grounding, though this complicates Weberian thought about 'desacralisation'. As Scribner points out, 'Far from further desacralizing the world, Calvin and the reformed religion intensified to an even higher degree the cosmic struggle between the divine and the diabolical'.[38] Notably, the Kirk Session's interrogation of Sigrid and first accusation of witchcraft comes in Act IV, 'The Wrong Word'. Earlier, Storm Kolson declares that Hellya's crop failure occurs because 'the word is lost, it's forgotten' (p. 29). Here, Storm clearly refers to the lost Logos – or body of Christ – and the hunger for sacramental nourishment in a desacralised Orkney. The Kirk Session, by comparison, focuses exclusively on the word of scripture, to the neglect, Brown suggests, of true and full communion with the divine.

Perhaps Brown's depiction of the Kirk Session in a disenchanted Orkney veers rather near to caricature in this play. While Reformation-era Sessions were certainly an important instrument of church discipline and punishment, as David Fergusson points out: 'in the sixteenth and seventeenth centuries the best friend to an unmarried pregnant woman was often the Kirk Session. It was they who would ensure that errant fathers would make provision for the maintenance of mother and child.'[39] The 'poor fund' is mentioned briefly during the elders' interrogation of Sigrid during the Session. Nevertheless, one of Brown's elders, Manson, says uncharitably, 'Bad enough it'll be to feed her bastard, without the expense of burning her at the Market Cross of Kirkwall' (p. 40).[40] And although one of the others, Corrigall, shows Sigrid some sympathy, he does not defend her, and so the young woman is killed in the next act. Her death in front of a jeering crowd in Kirkwall recalls Calvary, and her final walk towards the hangman becomes Sigrid's *via crucis*. As she faces her death like Christ, she chants words from the Song of Solomon, revealing her firm knowledge of scripture and her trust in a just and loving God. Notably, the next and final act is called 'Resurrection' – signalling that Sigrid and Storm's Eucharistic 'spell' has brought fecundity back to the land, and Sigrid's death has in some way atoned for the sinfulness of the barren Calvinism of seventeenth-century Orkney. Despite her wordless horror when she is first accused of witchcraft in the Kirk Session, Sigrid recognises early on that in order to prevent the island's crops from dying 'there must be a sacrifice' (p. 28). Her death is thus a re-enactment of Christ's original sacrifice, and in this way, Sigrid restores the Logos to the famished Orcadian landscape.

A Spell for Green Corn is not regarded as one of the most successful or sophisticated of Brown's works; Donald Campbell writes that 'it reads as if it had been written for an ambitious community project'.[41] Brown's small corpus of plays were often performed by community groups, but this is hardly a weakness, given that Brown was eager for Orcadians to act in his stage dramas. *A Spell for Green Corn*'s appendix is written mainly in prose, and its detailed, rather literary stage directions indicate that Brown was more creatively at home with prose than with drama. But the play does mark a milestone in Brown's thinking about ritual, sacrifice, and time – themes that he went on to perfect in his novel *Magnus* (1973), published three years later.[42] Sigrid functions, then, as a significant precursor to the figure of Orkney's patron saint in Brown's later novel, which he regarded as his best work. Unlike St Magnus, Sigrid is not a pre-Reformation character who signals the riches of Orkney's Catholic past. Instead, she actively resists the Calvinist landscape of Orkney in the age of Reformations and is offered as a sacrificial antidote to disenchantment. And she does not disappear entirely from Brown's oeuvre at the close of the play.

The 1990s: Brown's final novel

Sigrid is in fact an important forerunner of Sophie, the female protagonist of Brown's final, Booker-Prize nominated novel, *Beside the Ocean of Time* (1994). Although the novel's central character is Thorfinn Ragnarson, the dreamy boy turned novelist (who is often read as proxy for Brown himself), Sophie is an important literary descendant of Sigrid and she highlights Brown's interest in resurrecting existing characters, like Father Halcrow, for further development and augmentation in later works. Unlike the other texts discussed here, this novel is not entirely historical. Though it travels back in time through the daydreams of its protagonist, Thorfinn, its main time setting is an Orkney of the 1920s up until the end of the Second World War. However, despite Brown's dispensing with Reformation-era Orkney as a backdrop in this last novel, religious disenchantment is once more an important, though subtle, undercurrent within the text, and one that is irrevocably wound up with the forward march of 'progress'.

Sophie is not introduced into *Beside the Ocean of Time* until relatively late, but she is the main focus of 'The Muse', a chapter which focuses largely on the island of Norday's Presbyterian minister, Rev. Hector Drummond, and Sophie, his half-sister. The attentive reader of Brown might by now expect Drummond to be either a hellfire preacher, a drunken hypocrite, or a common-sense but rather uninspired churchman. Certainly, the Norday community has experienced its share of 'strict and puritanical' ministers, but in general the parish has been led by 'kindly indulgent men, well loved by most of the islanders'. We are told that 'if a nod and a wink might pass between a minister and the innkeeper, concerning the nocturnal delivery at the back door of the Manse of a case of brandy [...] nobody minded'.[43] The community is a harmonious one then, and Drummond is portrayed as a slightly eccentric bachelor who is looked upon fondly by his parishioners. He counsels them wisely, listens with empathy, and exhibits a deep and moving faith. His face 'shone with joy' at Christenings. At funerals, writes Brown,

> it was as if their minister was sending the dead person out on the last voyage into timelessness, with a blessing on him or her [...] In the kirkyard, at a funeral, even the coarsest islander was touched with a certain awe or wonderment (p. 100).

Through Drummond, Brown might be said to be quietly promoting a celibate priesthood as the Christian ideal, and, in a moment of delicate satire focalised through the perspective of the rather gossipy island community, we are told that the minister chats amiably with travellers, 'even though [they] were Catholics who had come originally from Ireland at the time of the great potato famine' (p. 98). Religious rigidity (and prejudice) seems to come more from the islanders themselves, rather than travelling top-down from the clergy in this novel.

Indeed, Norday seems at first glance to be far removed from the 'Knox-ruined nation' that Brown diagnosed in his first collection of poetry. The Reformation has not been a complete cultural or spiritual calamity for the island, robbing the islanders of mystery and miracle. And the sacramental principle of worship does not seem to have been lost entirely, as the kindly, celibate Drummond, with his 'ascetic face', functions as the island's Halcrow-esque priest (p. 99). However, there is a certain religious torpor in Norday, and this is – Brown hints again – the ultimate consequence of Reformation disenchantment. One of the 'rationalists and agnostics in the smithy', Ben Hoy, declares: 'it's all nonsense, of course, no need of kirks or ministers at all, the time's not far off when the human race'll rid itself of superstition once and for all, and that time can't come soon enough' (p. 96). Ben's contempt for 'superstition' lays bare modern Norday's potentially fatal separation from the numinous, his modern rationalism and secularism a sign of Ben's own estrangement from Brown's immanent, Catholic God.

As in Brown's first novel of environmental disaster, *Greenvoe* (1972), the threat of apocalypse looms over the narrative, as the island is eventually cleared of its inhabitants so that it can be used as an air force base. In an echo of the hysteria-inducing Reformation preaching in 'Master Halcrow, Priest', one old wife exclaims that 'it was all prophesied long ago in Revelations, and in the book of Daniel too' (p. 166). Brown hints once more that the ultimate consequence of desacralisation is sterility – even war. In parallel with another Catholic writer, J. R. R. Tolkien (1892–1973), who notably 'link[s] mechanization and the exultation of technology generally with environmental degradation and political tyranny is one of the hallmarks of his fiction', Brown's apocalyptic focus is not simply a sign that he is 'a reactionary writer, in the deepest sense of the word'.[44] Instead, the recycled theme of environmental and spiritual collapse signals that Brown is a Catholic artist who finds humanity's dislocation from nature the sign of a much wider spiritual alienation.

Into this setting comes Drummond's sister, Sophie, who arrives with great fanfare and immediately signals a kind of renewal of the spirit. It is she who must restore Norday's sacramental magic. Like Sigrid, Sophie bestows fecundity on the island. She is referred to by her brother as Persephone, as 'it always seems to be springtime where she is', and indeed she brings new life and fruitfulness in the manner of the queen of the underworld escaped from Hades (p. 115). She delivers daffodils to sick parishioners, swims in the sea, and delights in watching the island's birdlife. She also resurrects the minister's garden so that it is full of butterflies, hums with bees, and is – in a nod to Christ's radiance upon the mountain in the gospels – 'transfigured' (p. 110). But Sophie is not simply a spring goddess. She is attracted to 'a very old ruin on the side of the hill […] that seemed to have some religious roots; the remains of a round arched window could be seen. And two indecipherable tombstones were sunk in the floor' (p. 110). The ruins of 'Chapel Between Cornfield and Shore' and 'A Treading of Grapes' thus meet strikingly with the spell-maker of Brown's *A Spell for Green Corn* in this chapter of his final novel.

As with Sigrid, Sophie's unconscious recusancy allows her to re-enchant Norday with the spell of ripeness and fertility. However, while agricultural rebirth and renewal were secured by Sigrid's sacrifice in *A Spell for Green Corn*, there seems to be no requirement for a sacrificial victim in *Beside the Ocean of Time*. Instead of typologically re-enacting Christ's saving passion through execution and death, Sophie's presence in the novel functions instead as midrashic exposition on the moment of Christ's birth.[45] In a clear suggestion of the nativity, she is happened upon 'under the first star', by a shepherd (p. 110). She is not found in a stable, but within the island's ruined chapel:

> It was a windless night. The lappings of ebb on shore, the hush in the shallows, the distant Atlantic sonorities, rounded out the silence. The sun was down, every hollow was brimming now with shadows. The light in the ruin shone like a ruby.
> William looked carefully inside. A candle was burning in a niche. A shadow stood in the near corner, turned away, folded in silence.
> A new sound came from the sea, like a struck harp. The ebb-tide had reached its mark, some time ago, and made a pause. And now, with this harp stroke, the flood-tide was beginning. (pp. 110–11)

This is a key episode in Brown's novel, and one which nicely draws together and embodies the tropes and motifs of dis- and re-enchantment found in Brown's earlier works. William has stumbled upon a moment of sacramental re-enchantment, which, in its visual and aural symbolism, indicates the closest thing to the celebration of the Mass that the island can offer. The candle shining 'like a ruby' in the niche acts as a red altar lamp, indicating the presence of Christ in the tabernacle. Meanwhile, the sudden, harp-like sound of the sea, which interrupts the congregation-like whisperings of the Atlantic, sounds in place of an altar bell in the moments before the consecration of the host. The ruined chapel is situated, like its literary antecedents, by the sea, Brown's great symbol of time and consolation. Given the presence of the shepherd, Will Simpson, the ruin is also likely to be near to the cornfield, the place of threshing and sacrifice, or 'Bethlehem', Hebrew for 'house of Bread'. And the shepherd is led 'under the first star' to a most surprising Christ Child – a young woman who brings new life and the promise of rejuvenation. The 'flood-tide', Brown hints, is the beginning of the island's re-enchantment, just as 'Chapel Between Cornfield and Shore' promised, with its description of 'new ceremonies', 'when the flood / Sounds all her lucent strings, its ocean dance'. This moment of re-sacralisation has been set in motion by Sophie, who is both the babe in the manger and the chapel's effective 'fisher-priest'. It is striking just how deeply Brown mines his own creative corpus in this episode. Here, he draws on the vocabulary and symbolism of a poem from his first poetry collection, recalls his short fiction of disenchantment from the 1960s, and recycles elements of a play from 1970 in which the promise of spiritual replenishment came with a young woman's sacrifice. In *Beside the Ocean of Time*, decades of thought on the disenchantment of the world swarm together and coalesce in one spiritually sublime moment.

Conclusion

Ultimately, any assessment of Brown's poetry, fiction, and drama as it evolved and matured over the decades would find that his engagement with the Weberian notion of 'disenchantment' is far from straightforward. On the one hand, Brown's work seems to find powerful stimulus in Edwin Muir's gloomy indictment of a disenchanted, de-spiritualised modern Scotland, which has its roots in a destructive religious revolution. Brown's work proposes that the stripping of Orcadian altars was spiritually harmful and led to a de-sacralised world where humanity became increasingly estranged from the sacramental potential of ordinary matter.

Brown's disenchantment narratives interpolate history with a wide range of intertextual literary references, allusions, and influences. In an inflection of Vatican II, his work focuses specifically on place, and on the religious history of that place, but his reference points take in a broader body of Catholic literary works which transcend national boundaries, and which share an incarnational focus.[46] Like Tolkien, he did not believe that 'God's creative activity is something that happened a long time ago and then ceased'.[47] His view is much more hopeful than that, and indeed it chimes with modern historical reassessments of disenchantment. In 'A Treading of Grapes', the dour Rev. Dr Thomas Fotheringhame identifies 'remnants of a popish chapel, where the ignorant yet resort in time of sickness and dearth to leave offerings' – a pilgrimage site that he is very much determined to obliterate (p. 63). Brown's writing, with its fondness for cycles, seasons, and patterns throughout history, offers the suggestion that such iconoclastic efforts have been in vain.

Endnotes

1. George Mackay Brown, *A Spell for Green Corn* (London: The Hogarth Press, 1970), p. 9. Further citations given in the text.
2. Alexandra Walsham, 'The Reformation and "The Disenchantment of the World" Reassessed', *The Historical Journal* 51.2 (2008), pp. 497–528 (p. 497). Walsham's reassessment of the legacy of Max Weber's theory of Protestant disenchantment is both comprehensive and authoritative. It will be drawn on throughout the current chapter.
3. George Mackay Brown, 'Prologue', *The Collected Poems of George Mackay Brown*, ed. Archie Bevan and Brian Murray (London: John Murray, 2005), p. 1, ll. 14, 15.
4. Walsham, p. 498.
5. Ibid., p. 501.
6. Andrew Keitt, 'Enthusiasm, the Spanish Inquisition, and the Disenchantment of the World', *Journal of the History of Ideas* 65.2 (2004), pp. 231–250 (p. 248).
7. For more on broader currents of anti-Reformation feeling in modern Scottish literature, see Linden Bicket, *George Mackay Brown and the Scottish Catholic Imagination* (Edinburgh: Edinburgh University Press, 2017), pp. 4–12.
8. Edwin Muir, 'The Incarnate One', in *One Foot in Eden* (London: Faber and Faber, 1956), pp. 47–48 (p. 47), ll. 10, 11.
9. See for example, Peter Butter, 'George Mackay Brown and Edwin Muir', *Yearbook of English Studies* 17 (1987), pp. 16–30; Linden Bicket, *George Mackay Brown and the Scottish Catholic Imagination* (Edinburgh: Edinburgh University Press, 2017); Simon Hall, *The History of Orkney Literature* (Edinburgh: John Donald, 2010); Sabine Schmid, *'Keeping the Sources Pure': The Making of George Mackay Brown* (Oxford: Peter Lang, 2003).
10. George Mackay Brown, *An Orkney Tapestry* (London: Victor Gollancz, 1969), p. 26.
11. Edwin Muir, *Scottish Journey* [1935] (Edinburgh and London: Mainstream Publishing, 2017), p. 45.
12. George Mackay Brown, 'Foreword', *A Calendar of Love* (London: The Hogarth Press, 1967), n.p.
13. Brown, *Tapestry*, p. 28.
14. George Mackay Brown, 'Chapel Between Cornfield and Shore', *Collected Poems*, p. 35, ll. 1–4. Further citations given in the text.
15. Walsham, p. 507.
16. Brown, 'Master Halcrow, Priest', *A Calendar of Love* [1967] (London: The Hogarth Press, 1970), p. 124. Further citations given in the text.
17. George Mackay Brown, *For the Islands I Sing* (London: John Murray, 1997), p. 180.
18. Jocelyn Rendall, *Steering the Stone Ships: The Story of Orkney Kirks and People* (Edinburgh: Saint Andrew Press, 2009), p. 68.
19. Edwin Muir, *An Autobiography* [1954] (Edinburgh: Canongate, 2010), pp. 76, 78.
20. Ibid., p. 79.
21. Ibid., pp. 79–80.
22. Rendall, p. 75; Brown, *An Orkney Tapestry*, p. 42.
23. Brown, *For the Islands I Sing*, p. 49.
24. Rendall, p. 69, pp. 70–72.
25. Walsham, p. 499.
26. Brown, *For the Islands I Sing*, p. 179.

27 J. C. Whitehouse, 'Men, Women, God and So Forth', *Logos: A Journal of Catholic Thought and Culture* 4.1 (2001), pp. 54–75 (p. 71).
28 Brown, *For the Islands I Sing*, pp. 54–55. See Linden Bicket, *Scotnote: The Short Stories of George Mackay Brown* (Glasgow: ASLS, 2014) for more comparisons between Halcrow and Greene's 'whisky priest' (p. 11).
29 Robert Scribner, 'The Reformation, Popular Magic, and the "Disenchantment of the World"', *The Journal of Interdisciplinary History* 23.3 (1993), pp. 475–94 (p. 492).
30 Ibid., p. 480.
31 *Collected Poems*, p. 178.
32 Gavin Miller, 'George Mackay Brown: "Witch," "Master Halcrow, Priest," "A Time to Keep," and "The Tarn and the Rosary"', in *A Companion to the British and Irish Short Story*, ed. Cheryl Alexander Malcolm and David Malcolm (West Sussex: Blackwell, 2008), pp. 472–79 (p. 474); cf. Walsham, p. 514.
33 Walsham, p. 508.
34 George Mackay Brown, 'A Treading of Grapes', *A Time to Keep* [1969] (London: John Murray, 2000), p. 66. Further citations given in the text.
35 Rendall, p. 72.
36 Eamon Duffy, *The Stripping of the Altars: Traditional Religion in England 1400–1580* (New Haven and London: Yale University Press, 1992), p. 136.
37 R. W. Scribner, *Religion and Culture in Germany (1400–1800)*, ed. Lyndal Roper (Leiden, Boston, Koln: Brill, 2001), p. 327.
38 Scribner, 'The Reformation, Popular Magic, and the "Disenchantment of the World"', p. 483.
39 David Fergusson, 'Calvin in Scotland', *Theology in Scotland* 17.2 (2010), pp. 67–81 (p. 74).
40 Brown, *A Spell for Green Corn*, p. 40.
41 Donald Campbell, 'Greenness in Every Line: The Drama of George Mackay Brown', *International Journal of Scottish Theatre and Screen* 1.1 (2000) ijosts.ubiquitypress.com/articles/255/
42 For which see Timothy C. Baker, *George Mackay Brown and the Philosophy of Community* (Edinburgh: Edinburgh University Press, 2009), p. 75.
43 George Mackay Brown, *Beside the Ocean of Time* [1994] (Edinburgh: Polygon, 2004), p. 92. Further citation given in the text.
44 Smith, p. 83. Ian Bell, 'Breaking the Silence', *Scottish Review of Books*, 7 May 2006, pp. 14–15 (p. 15).
45 For more on midrash and literature, see 'Reading and Re-writing: Midrash and Literature', in Alison Jack, *The Bible and Literature* (London: SCM Press, 2012), pp. 127–45. The current discussion takes its definition of midrashic exposition from this study, which defines midrash as 'personal retellings of biblical stories in fictional texts', p. 133.
46 See Bicket, *George Mackay Brown and the Scottish Catholic Imagination*, p. 177.
47 Smith, p. 75.

13. A Post-Religious Incarnation in Alan Warner's *Morvern Callar*

MIKE KUGLER

Alan Warner's *Morvern Callar* (1995) caught many readers with a portrait of the amoral and hedonistic rural youth of modern Scotland.[1] Morvern is a well-known young woman among a small circle of locals making the rounds of work, drink, pub talk, and shenanigans in 'the port'. She is an orphan with no blood relatives, friends with people whose sexual betrayals seem like second nature. And she is a school-leaver indifferent to promotion at her clerking job. She is obsessed, instead, with the details of makeup and nail polish. She solipsistically attends to music on her Walkman and at raves. While in Spain, she pays close attention to getting a solid tan. She will not even read her dead boyfriend's manuscript because it is just a bunch of words that eventually end (p. 82).[2] She seems unable to mourn her boyfriend's suicide deeply or properly, and at first opportunity she seizes 'His' assets, including passing off 'His' manuscript as her own. She appears to forget she hid 'His' corpse in the attic until, suddenly fearful of discovery, she efficiently dismembers and disposes of the body in trips to the Highland wilderness. Flush with money, and rid of 'His' body, she, like many other figures in Scottish fiction, flees home for better climes, returning only when broke. Duncan Petrie emphasises Morvern's understandable psychological distress in the brutal economic and social circumstances of 'the port', and also notes that Morvern's Spanish epiphany is largely about leisure and happiness abroad. Even given the power and sympathies of Lynn Ramsay's adaptation of the novel, it could be argued that her film concentrates on Morvern as a wanderer borne along by events, in a kind of 'trance' before the hypnotic effects of travel and raves. Matthew Wickman suggests that outside the Scottish Highlands, Morvern discovers emotion's limited access to meaning when lost in the sweaty, beat-driven sensuality of the rave.[3]

This Morvern wandered through her life caring about little more than drink, raves, and opportunistic sex (Ortwin de Graef calls her a 'frivolous Nietzschean').[4] But this reading does not do justice to the novel's heartfelt sympathy for working-class Scots, their near-desperation in seeking meaningful work and decent lives, made worse for young women like Morvern who have even narrower prospects and who are also the targets of sexually aggressive, sometimes violent men. The travail of the single woman in a man's world, the strong woman fighting for her independence, and the abuse of women in everyday life haunts modern Scottish fiction. This story line runs throughout Warner's other novels, following of course Lewis Grassic Gibbon's *Sunset Song* (1932), Muriel Spark's *The Prime of Miss Jean Brodie* (1961), and Duncan McLean's *Bunker Man* (1995).

I have a vivid memory of *Morvern Callar* the first time through; I had never before read such a terrifying account of a frail young person experiencing horror, loss, utter emotional solitude, facing the sheer open horizon of opportunity. It seemed anything but a gonzo Tom Wolfe portrait of the rootless amoral youth at the end of the millennium, or some grotesque celebration of moral anarchy in a Scotland suffering social collapse. First reviewers seem to have been shocked that a young woman could respond with such apparent calculation – 'callar' in Scots means 'fresh, cool' – cutting up a corpse, disposing of it, and vacating Scotland for the warmth of Spanish coastal raves and sexual adventures. In several interviews, Warner has instead emphasised Morvern was shocked numb from the ratcheting desperation of her life, by betrayals from friends, and deep loneliness.[5] It is a morally earnest book, self-consciously intended like James Kelman's *The Bus Conductor Hines* (1984) to create a recognisable, observant working-class person sinking into desolation. Recently, Jordana Brown took this path with a convincingly close examination of the novel's recurring religious imagery. Instead of a glassy-eyed youth drifting from one mindless high to another, Morvern was a religiously illiterate stranger seeking faith in an even stranger land.[6]

I would go further. Morvern is a sojourner seeking a New City, a home for her confused, grief-stricken heart. Her restless soul seeks peace but in Warner's late twentieth century Scotland, its Reformation long evaporated, what little remains is just the gathered silt of churches, holidays, symbols and ceremony few even recognise let alone observe. In the first half of the novel especially, Morvern associates her boyfriend not just with pronoun intimations of God, but with incarnational and Christological imagery. While Christie L. March argues that the pronoun 'He'/'His' testifies to Morvern living under her boyfriend's shadow, from which 'His' suicide has now liberated her, I would suggest that Warner's use of the pronoun is more fruitfully ambiguous.[7] Through Morven's point of view, we watch her grope for some way to explain her boyfriend's suicide and the horizon that 'His' death opens for her. Unlike the educated middle classes who only 'discuss', answer their own questions, and talk over one another, she struggles to tell a story of her liberation, more like a classic pilgrimage or odyssey (p. 164). Warner has been quite explicit about his intentions for Morvern as a serious, intelligent narrator of a working-class myth. But scholars disagree over the character of her myth, be it post-religious (Petrie), religiously eclectic (Brown), or pagan (LeBlanc). In her half-remembered or partly conscious way, I argue, Morvern stumbles to recruit the mythological tradition associated with Jesus for the sake of 'His' significance to her alive, dead, and in memory.[8]

Every mountain

Warner's self-consciousness about growing up in Connel, up the coast from Oban, links him to a long distinctive Scottish literary tradition, part of the context for such sacramental and theological language.[9] Since at least the Jacobite risings, the following concepts have taken hold in popular culture: the British government's refashioning of the Gaelic-speaking regions, the age of Clearances and depopulation, and the differences characterising Highlands from Lowlands. The religious and moral burdens of these ideas are most strongly enshrined in Alexander Carmichael's 1900 *Carmina Gadelica*, his highly stylised collection of translated Gaelic prayers, blessings, incantations, hymns, and folkloric poetry: a particular kind of 'Celtic' spirituality associated with the Highlands.[10] Later, some regions of the Highlands became associated with strict expressions of the Presbyterian faith. The result became a tradition of confessional differences colouring political conflict, social legitimacy, and moral judgement: a tradition that shaped the Scottish literature Warner knows well. Through Morvern's story, Warner narrates some lingering religious comprehension of life and place surviving long after the receding tide of religious confession and conflict.

After the 1745 Rising, the Highlands, no longer full of 'savage' rebels – and after the Clearances, no longer full of anyone – evolved into a retreat for modern citizens struggling with the anxieties and contradictions of urban claustrophobia and technological triumphs over nature. Unlike 'the city', the now-tamed 'wild' Highlands were safe for cultivated, educated tourists and intellectuals to speculate on the vaguely religious, certainly spiritual, sublime meanings of what they perceived to be an undomesticated nature. More recently, from the portrait of Eric Liddell in *Chariots of Fire* (1981) to Diana Gabaldon's *Outlander* series (1991–ongoing) and its television interpretation, the Highlands are a sacred place far closer to the original Creation than modern cities like Edinburgh, Glasgow, or Dundee. Highlanders – for after the nineteenth century in popular culture outside Scotland, all Scotland is Highland and all Scots Highlanders – intuitively recognise the sacred in that place and feel in their heart the voice of God, of some holy power. In popular imagination, the Highlands are dangerous enough to make adventure possible, and visitors there know their proper place in the cosmos as mountains and waters speak an appropriate sublime awe beyond comprehension.[11]

Morvern Callar's principal landscape, however, is not a romanticised Highlands but is modern, urban, and commercialised. Morvern's boyfriend grew up in a nearby mountain village, thirteen years older than her. She met 'Him' at sixteen years old. Their relationship angered her foster father and cooled her friendships with other young women (p. 10). Though self-conscious that she was an orphan, Morvern's intimate affection with 'Him' seemed to give her some deeper confidence (p. 19). In their five years together, she adopted 'His' eclectic musical tastes; she had helped him build the model railroad of 'His' village (p. 52). 'He' seems to have encouraged her taste in so-called European art movies like Michelangelo Antonioni's *The Passenger* (p. 53) and, in her friend Lanna's phrase, 'weirdy horror films' and shocking movies like *The Thing, Ms .45/Angel of Vengeance*, and *Bad*

Lieutenant (pp. 49, 71, 50, 83) – each of which highlight a conversion of some kind. *The Passenger* (1977) has the main character assume a dead man's identity. Abel Ferrara's *Ms .45* (1981) sees its mute rape victim become a vigilante killer. In *Bad Lieutenant* (1992), Harvey Keitel's character is a psychologically tortured Catholic and a corrupt cop. In John Carpenter's 1982 *The Thing*, an alien secretly assumes the form of different humans and undergoes grotesque transmutations. Warner also makes brief references to other horror films, like *The Hills Have Eyes* (Wes Craven 1977). We learn little about 'Him' though, aside from the facts that 'He' is middle class and well travelled, college educated, and a novelist. Aside from adopting certain of 'His' tastes, Morvern seems to know little of 'Him' or 'His' writing.

Abide with me

Early readers of the novel, though, quickly noticed Warner's convention of referring to Morvern's boyfriend using capitalised forms of the pronoun 'He'.[12] 'He' – Morvern's lover, friend, and mentor – was so central to her that the stylisation suggests a pseudo-divine presence in her inner life. In the English-speaking world, perhaps the oldest and most widely recognised version of this convention is orthodox Christianity, most commonly employed in liturgy, Christian publications such as sermons, commentaries, and popular works of theology. As with this subtle yet significant pronoun usage, Warner's religious imagery throughout the novel also is often quite subtle. Consider, for example, the puzzling decision that while killing himself, 'He' has tried to cut off his hand with a meat cleaver. This is puzzling until we learn later that Lanna and 'He' had an affair just before the suicide. In Jesus's Sermon on the Mount, he claimed about adultery, 'And if your right hand causes you to sin, cut it off and throw it away; it is better for you to lose one of your members than for your whole body to go into hell' (Matthew 5. 30, cf. Mark 9. 43).[13]

Morvern seems to be Catholic, or to have been raised with enough Catholic or Anglican ritual to recognise the Virgin Mary and the Apostles, to know to cross herself with holy water when she enters the church and to genuflect before sitting (though she watches another woman to see which knee is proper), and she recognises the Eucharist (pp. 164–65).

Reading back to this from Warner's later novel, the young women in *The Sopranos* are students in a Catholic school who knew Morvern, perhaps from class or church.[14] She prays in the London parish and in the Tree Church back in 'His' village (pp. 165, 228). But while Morvern is sensitive to religion generally, and to its solemn demands in sanctified spaces, she has only a superficial sense of the Christian faith. Warner's 'port', Oban, has at least one church, recalling an older, more pious past, now in almost complete disintegration. Morvern typically mentions the name Jesus when slagging her 'creeping' supercilious manager at the superstore. The harsh, often grotesque challenges Morvern will face expose her spare religious sensibilities.

Her first grotesque challenge is where the novel begins, when Morvern finds 'His' body. It is Christmas Eve, and the room is lit by the flashing tree lights reflecting off the wrapped, now 'useless presents' (p. 1), a phrase from Dylan Thomas's *A Child's Christmas in Wales*. She tries to move around the body. 'His' blood is everywhere; stepping in it, she swears an oath (p. 2). Almost four hours go by before her shock subsides. Why not call the authorities, as she first thought? Trauma and fear provoke strange behaviour. Opening the Walkman gift, that first personal music device which will inaugurate Morvern's retreats from the world into a controlled inner rhythm, she breaks down. 'I started to greet again as I stepped in the blood and knelt' (p. 3), simultaneously reverent and blasphemous, as if 'His' blood might cleanse her but violating the body. Bloody imagery recurs repeatedly in the novel, from Morvern's well-worn tale of the injury that gave her 'the glittery knee' and the blood gushing everywhere (pp. 18–19), the horrific accidents described by others (pp. 66–67), to another injury while swimming in Spain (p. 212). Warner's description here seems purposefully, equivocally, shocking, a moment exhibiting Morvern's stumbling, grief-stricken loss and inept reaction. Yet the Eucharist itself can be a shocking assertion of divine grace. When in the Gospel of John (6. 48–70) Jesus tells his listeners that they must eat his flesh and drink his blood, most of them abandon him.

Very slowly, with Christmas all around, Morvern grabs at a jumble of ideas or symbols to give her some kind of emotional perspective on her loss and the monstrous circumstances of 'His' death. She had primed herself beforehand, though with fantasies of a violent death and her reactions. 'A sort of wave of something was going across me', she says. 'There was fright but I'd daydreamed how I'd be' (p. 1). Had Morvern fantasised 'His' death? 'His' suicide? More narcissistically, her reaction to 'His' death is not clear. This relatively young man who meant so much to her – who helped guide her into young adulthood – now violently dead, begins to take a new shape. 'His' central presence in her life becomes an echo for a while, later gradually rising as a sort of teacher-saviour in Morvern's mind. In some Christological reflections, the Cross cast a shadow over the manger where the child lay, an image of the man born to die for others. Such reflections are often rooted in Luke 2. 19, 'But Mary treasured all these words and pondered them in her heart,' and 2. 35, 'so that thoughts from many hearts may be revealed – and a sword will pierce your own soul too'. In the novel, Morvern's stepping in 'His' blood and kneeling before 'His' body recalls the confusing ways that Christmas can be celebrated, a holiday for an infant Saviour come to die for the world. In a parallel form of confusing demands, contemporary Western celebrations of the holiday promise joy, gratitude, and family reunions when circumstances often conspire against them. In this first part of the novel, Morvern moves through a landscape marking Christmas but with no attention to anything other than a commercialised holiday for drunken parties.

Morvern finally collects herself and carefully gets ready to walk to work. Miles Davis's 'He Loved Him Madly', written following Duke Ellington's death, gives her a 'feeling' that pushes her past the phone box where she could call the police (p. 5). This is her first impulse to consider 'Him' a kind of dead Jesus-presence and immediately contrasts her reaction at work to the person she disliked most, her 'Creeping Jesus' boss. Her dead boyfriend haunts her mind and heart; her boss haunts her boring, repetitive work. At the superstore, she remembers working with meat in the butcher section and how the old blood smell got in everything and ruined your clothes (pp. 12–13). But she had no similar revulsion to 'His' blood back at the flat, which sets 'Him' apart from the mundane males in her life, like 'Creeping Jesus', her boss.

At a party that same night, Morvern meets two young men named 'John and Paul, like disciples' (p. 23). But what kinds of disciples? Warner sets this reference in the midst of a vaguely titillating portrait of a young woman's sexual appetite and subservience. We have just met Morvern, so it is especially shocking after her cruel loss that following work and a night's heavy drinking she and Lanna attend a party which ends with a foursome that includes Lanna, Morvern, and the two strangers. Later that morning Morvern retreats to Couris Jean's, Lanna's grandmother. Couris Jean asks Morvern about her man, and Morvern explains that 'He' was thirty-four years old, had built an exact model railroad replica of 'His' home village in their flat's attic, was unemployed but had money from somewhere, and was writing a novel. 'He's always saying', Morvern tells Couris Jean, 'He doesn't have much time'. This is perhaps a faint echo of Jesus saying his time was short (John 7. 11), but what is more certain is that 'He' was clearly good to Morvern, as Jean says 'He' should be: 'you look like an angel come to earth' (pp. 38–39). Yet later, 'His' suicide makes Morvern rethink his goodness: 'I thought He was a good thing but evidently not' (p. 44).

Here Morvern begins conceiving a plan and, more importantly, hearing a story in which the plan makes sense. This story is Couris Jean's mythological tale of years before when, a Gael from 'the island' of Mull, she married at sixteen, the same age as Morvern when she met 'Him'. Couris Jean recalls to Morvern how she swam nude in the sea at midnight, 'getting a real feeling in my tummy, all awful alive'. This was a portent of the conception of a new life to come, and, faintly, an echo of the Annunciation, but without an overt symbolic tie to Mary. We can understand this because the reader is in Morvern's mind; Couris Jean's story would be more real to her than the Virgin Mary's. Couris Jean, in her tale, confesses a sensuous response Morvern will imitate later in Spain. The howling of dogs in the 'bluey light' heralds something in Couris Jean's story: she sees 'the great white horse' rise from the sea, followed by dozens of others. Sitting in the sea with her arms wrapped around herself, these horses galloped past her as she 'got this feeling so strong for the first time ever' – she was terrified – and after her brothers found her, she 'went silent' for four years, only speaking on her wedding night, and later only talking in Gaelic to her newborn child (pp. 39–40).

Morvern is fascinated with Couris Jean's tale. Brutally hungover and grief-stricken, she visits her foster father, Red Hanna. She tells him that 'He' is gone, at which point Red Hanna tries to console her. Do not fight against the unfairness or injustice of 'His' death, he says, you cannot presume you will be happy. The poor, like Morvern, have few comforts and little dignity. Warner's description of human power twisting desire into a ceaseless vibration of hungers never stilled, and often destructive, is remarkably Augustinian. 'Every desire', her foster father tells her, 'is transformed into sour dreams. [...] The law as brute force has to be worshipped as virtue. Theres [sic] no freedom, no liberty; theres just money. Thats the world we've made and no one tells me to find more to life when I've no time or money to live it.' Any money Red Hanna might come into now at this late age would, he says, destroy the contentment he has fought to achieve (pp. 44–45). Wage-slavery in the town, even with an occasional vacation, leaves 'no much room for poetry there, eh?' (p. 44).

Morvern in these last two scenes is told the meaning of life from two elderly Scots, lifelong residents of 'the port'. One, Couris Jean, describes in archetypal images the sea at that ritual moment of midnight when she sat, naked as a conjuror, and saw that herd of running horses and left mute until she passed the boundary into womanhood, marriage, and childbirth. The other, her foster father, denies the mythopoetic; this scene hammers Morvern with the idea that it is a mistake to have dreams beyond 'the port'. There is no poetry in this world for the working classes, contra Couris Jean's story, not even the poetry of deep emotional satisfaction and love. Couris Jean suggested how an otherwise inexplicable event changed everything in her life afterwards. Even if the horses had only escaped a capsized ship, their appearance was terrifyingly apocalyptic. Red Hanna's story, in contrast, warns Morvern that her boyfriend 'leaving' is just the first of a lifetime of disappointment. Only a wall of wealth protects us from deep frustration, protects the rich from the 'law' binding everyone else. Such is the 'scripture' of the latter scene.

Broken for us

Bearing these different stories back to her flat, Morvern begins to map out a story of her own to permit her to deal with 'His' death and life beyond it. She is inspired by Couris Jean's mythic impulse, but salted by Red Hanna's realism. 'His' death shocked her toward a cleansing, a clarity about her cramped and limited (if not cruel) circumstances, faintly lighting a path of escape for her from the port. Something aches, scratches and whispers behind Morvern's emotionally mute response to 'His' gruesome suicide, her loss of 'Him'. First, Morvern must get the corpse off the kitchen floor. So, she winches 'His' body through the attic entry and drops it onto the model village. This does not seem like a practical option, but perhaps it is. Like Mary Magdalene bringing spices to anoint Jesus's body (Mark 16. 1), Morvern memorialises 'His' body in this scene, reminiscent of the resurrection and ascension stories – in which she raises 'His' corpse to the attic, where 'He' swings suspended above 'His' lovingly created world, which, Morvern notes, looks 'exactly like the real thing' (pp. 37, 51).

Morvern drops 'Him' onto the model, shattering 'His' dad's motel and, significantly, the Tree Church (pp. 52–53). 'His' body lies across the length of the model, crushing the world 'He' created. Unlike the Christian tradition, in which Christ is the Word of God through which the Creator spoke the cosmos into being and sustains it (John 1. 1–3), this monstrous collapse of creator onto creation recalls a story Primo Levi told of rabbinic commentary in Genesis 1. 2.[15] The space between verse one, 'In the beginning when God created the heavens and the earth', and verse two, 'the earth was a formless void and darkness covered the face of the deep, while a wind from God swept over the face of the waters', suggests that the awful presence of God, hovering just above, crushed his creation into the *tohu va-bohu* ('formless void'). This vindicates Red Hanna's brutally honest declaration that there is no enduring comfort for the poor. Disaster will have its victory over the nearly mythic hopes of redemption and consolation. This bizarre, even surreal image recalls the reader again to Morvern's shocked, numbed state.

Morvern again winches the body so it rests, suspended, above the model. After doing so she listens to one of 'His' records, Stravinsky's Orpheus ballet, prefiguring her dismemberment of the corpse later, melding the Greek myth of the artist's cruel death with the breaking of Christ's body (p. 53). Immediately after, she discovers nearly seven thousand pounds in 'His' account, perhaps the seed of her plan to leave 'the port' (pp. 53–54). 'His' body remains, hovering above the wrecked model, in the attic through the winter. Labourers on the adjoining roof startle Morvern one day and she has to dispose of 'His' body. So, she cuts up 'His' corpse. Morvern's menstrual blood joins 'His', and again the two become one, perhaps also echoing the creation of Eve in Genesis 2. 23. She reads the suicide note addressed to her, in which 'He' clearly wants to free her. In the letter 'He' suggests that 'His' father's death prompted 'His' act, yet 'He' might have killed 'Himself' for multiple reasons, including 'His' depression (p. 81). 'His' depression would have condemned Morvern to a harsh life with him (p. 82). Perhaps 'He' killed 'Himself' because 'He' could no longer bear the guilt of 'His' affair with Lanna. But Morvern violates 'His' request in the note, 'I'll settle for posthumous fame as long as I'm not lost in silence' (p. 82). 'Callar', Spanish for 'silent' or 'silenced', implies that 'His' memory dissolves into Morvern's claim of authorship on his manuscript. She takes 'His' story as her own, as her means of living her own story caught between Couris Jean's myth and Red Hanna's realism. At thirty-four, 'He' had told her 'He' didn't have much time; one year older than the traditional age associated with Jesus at his death (who also told his friends 'my time is short'), 'He' had possibly failed to fulfil 'His' calling.

Warner's 'port' – Oban disguised – is perhaps modern Scotland in miniature, like the trainset in the attic. Morvern's acquaintances work with her at the superstore, on fishing boats, the railway. If her account is any measure, the 'port's' residents are self-conscious, perhaps a bit proud, of being from there, and some of being Gaels. Morvern immediately notices accents from the 'south' or 'Central Belt'. Her recognition is usually the first symptom of contempt, whether for her supercilious boss 'Creeping Jesus' or the snobbish upper-middle-class customers at the superstore (pp. 6, 10–11, 17, 22). When she is tramping in the mountains above 'the port' to dispose of her boyfriend's body, Morvern is content in solitude with her music, at times celebrating the silence of a wilderness that happens in the late spring to be filled with sunlight. 'All this loveliness', she says, 'It's just silence isn't it?' (p. 104). Her boyfriend's hobby of building a miniature version of 'His' nearby Highland birthplace fascinates Morvern at these times, as if it were an entirely appropriate celebration of 'His' affection for the place of 'His' birth (pp. 36–37, 50–53). Startled by Morvern's contentment in the Highlands, though, Lanna asks if she fears rape in such a remote spot, if being alone out there 'spooks' her. She cautions Morvern with advice from her grandmother Couris Jean, who from her Highland youth held onto the suspicion that 'the hills have eyes' (pp. 98–99), pointing to Wes Craven's 1977 exploitation shocker about wilderness cannibals. Even though it is Couris Jean, through Lanna, who warns Morvern about the dangers of the solitary Highland wilderness, it is Morvern who is there to dispose of a dismembered body.

Other writers on the novel have noted Warner's association of the Highlands with violence, especially in light of the scene in which Morvern carries 'His' dismembered body into the mountains above 'the port'.[16] The literary, if not memorialised, landscape in which Morvern scatters 'His' body is weighted by and soaked in blood. This scene yokes the region with the grotesque and with the bloodshed endured in Walter Scott's Highland novels, not to mention the tradition and legacy of Highland military recruitment and service or popular history obsessed with the region's noble Jacobites, its famous battles, its heartless and cruel landowning chiefs and theirs hunts, as well as the general struggle of agrarian people in an unforgiving landscape.

But Morvern's inspiration for her grotesque/Romantic act is not Highland history or literature, but a slasher movie. She almost certainly got the idea of cutting 'Him' into pieces from Ferrara's cult exploitation movie *Ms .45/ Angel of Vengeance*, a favourite which Lanna gave her at Christmas (p. 49). In it, a mute woman is raped twice, and after killing her second attacker she cuts up the body and hides it throughout New York City. Ferrara's movie, and his *Bad Lieutenant* (1992), which Morvern watched just before raising 'His' body into the attic, feature psychologically tortured Catholics obsessed with death, guilt, and redemption. They are violent movies, full of crucifix images. This combination of religious ideas and Catholic symbols in such disturbing stories helps Morvern imagine what she must do. Like a priest she 'breaks' the body of her beloved. Travelling into the Highlands more than once to complete the terrible job, she scatters 'Him' in the mountains above her home, saying the flesh will nourish the landscape (pp. 89, 90–91). Breaking the bread and distributing it to communicants is among the oldest acts of the faith, and is found in several Christian liturgies including contemporary English forms. The first-century Christian liturgy *The Didache, The Teaching of the Twelve Apostles*, states 'Creator of all, just as this broken bread was first scattered upon the hills, then was gathered and became one so may your church be gathered from the ends of the earth into your kingdom'.[17] Throughout English-language liturgies, 'broken' refers not only to Jesus's crucified body and the Eucharist: the Christian tradition also points to a world 'broken' by sin, families and societies 'broken' by conflict, and individuals 'broken' by isolation and self-destructive behaviour. In typical Christian atonement theologies, God uses the 'broken' body to heal, reknit, and redeem 'broken' hearts and communities, mystically joining the life of the suffering world. In the novel, we read echoes for such liturgy: Morvern's menstrual blood joined 'His' blood, and 'His' body joined the Highland landscape. Morvern's only consolation, it appears, comes in these fleeting moments of communion in her memory of 'Him' when returning 'His' body to the Highlands.

Go in peace

After she has entombed 'His' body, Morvern's discovery of the bank account immediately sends her to the travel agency to book her first Spanish holiday. As Red Hanna warns her, this will be the test for Morvern, a test if the money 'He' has left behind will truly free her. 'His' death does appear to liberate her from their relationship, freeing her from enduring condemnation in 'the port' so she can seek the 'City of Light,' a promised land, in Spain. 'His' death has given Morvern access to more money than she has ever seen, and financial liberation becomes a kind of salvation. Knowing nothing of 'His' death, Red Hanna tells Morvern that losing 'Him' is like 'All the love in the world rising up leaving just hate' (p. 44). Morvern's increasingly Christological myth surrounding 'His' death and body is her attempt to see how 'His' love rising into that attic tomb strangely enough left behind 'His' love for her. She seizes this salvation to win what Red Hanna says is impossible. In this way she defies her foster father's realism, setting off into her own story – her own myth – as full of portent and light as Couris Jean's story of the horses on the beach. Only Morvern's thunder is the bass thud of rave music, not the horses' hooves on a Mull beach.

Spain is an important pilgrimage site, in particular the St John path. It is wholly different than 'the port', a country full of sun and light, in which Morvern is anonymous, liberated from demands and expectations. But the resort's drunken coupling competitions leave her cold. She begins pulling away from the abandoned libertines, and into solitude. Like a pilgrim, she flees to a small resort (pp. 144–49). Preparing there for her first night out, she puts on a peel-off mask with cucumbers, and she watches a glowing sunset, looking in the mirror and then peeling away the 'mask of my face shape', Pauline-like scales falling from eyes now able to see a new life before her. She tosses that old self – the mask – in the toilet (p. 152). And the next day she follows a procession into a church. The phrase 'All Hills Are Calvary' is engraved in many languages above the door (p. 153–54), again echoing the *Didache* liturgy. After Morvern buried 'His' body in the mountains above 'the port,' this liturgical line is vividly true for her.

Her love of music and 'His' gift of the Walkman open the way for her retreat into a solitary world of rhythm and typically mythic, dark or aching lyrics. But she retreats further into the techno music in the raves she attends, which draws Morvern into the trance of the dance floor, where she experiences a kind of mystical loss of self. Those retreats into her silent, inner life inspire a kind of transcendence, felt faintly in Scotland. Morvern accepts the moving, sweating community of the dance floor, but resists amorous offers, maintaining her solitude, her retreat into herself. Readers who emphasise Morvern's amoral sensuality perhaps fail to recognise, after abandoning Lanna, just how solitary and relatively celibate she is. Spain's light and hypnotising music scenes envelop her in something like a discipline. At the end of the novel, when she announces her pregnancy, it seems far more like Morvern's choice than the result of just another one-night stand. She returns home with her rave-conceived child, as if submitting herself to the discipline of that dance culture, receiving the gift of that mystical other life.

Conclusion

Following 'His' death, Morvern finds herself in churches a few times. In her first trip to Spain, a Catholic procession draws her inside a small parish church. Morvern observes that sitting below the church's ceiling is like being in an overturned boat, 'with the light filtering in you were already drowned' (p. 155), as if she were drowning in light. There she sees the statue of a 'virgin saint girl', her same height, being carried out, set on a raft, and burned. Morvern sees herself in the statue (p. 154–56), seeing herself finally in Scotland as a Mary returning with her child. Spain, so full of sunlit days and cloudless nights, is nothing like 'the port'. Yet Morvern seems drawn to the contrast of light and dark, often at night. Back home, the circular McCaig's Folly on a rise above Oban, 'the port', lets her look out over the Highlands with some perspective (p. 13). After finding 'His' body, she climbs to the attic and switches on 'Nighttimeness' to light the village as if at night (p. 51). At the novel's end, back in Scotland, Morvern hikes to 'His' actual village, utterly dark from an outage. She hears the generator kick on and, leaving the Tree Church, she walks into the darkness. Money was 'His' means of grace for Morvern's salvation, but she exhausted the gift. We might be saved, but not for long. Though we walk a time in myth's light, we return to our dark realities, and for Morvern, this is 'the port', her post-religious Scotland, Red Hanna's reality.

Throughout *Morvern Callar*, the religious images make the most sense as echoes, reverberations, rather than strong, life-altering epiphanies as in Flannery O'Connor's short stories. Morvern's own bare religious literacy, perhaps our own, makes this incarnational reading of the novel quite strange. In her cycles of ecstasy and crash, myth and reality, she pursues transcendent escape in a Scotland and Spain still haunted by their Christian pasts.

I recently taught a course on the evolution of Scottish ideas of national identity, assigning fiction alongside historical documents to lower story's flesh onto what might seem the bare abstractions of political debate. Halfway through *Morvern Callar*, one of the students burst into my office, waving the novel, and in ragged gasps announced that it was the most disturbing book she had ever read. Reading it hurt her heart and soul, she said, and she intended to burn her copy to rid the world of such grotesquery.

I only barely talked her out of burning that book. Of course, this student was quite sensitive and a devout evangelical Christian. That explains some of her reaction. But I think her jagged nerves testify to Warner's success describing this young woman's plight, the starkness of her limited world and her options. *Morvern Callar* leaves a mark. But this book's depictions of sexual licence, drunken excess, and apparent indifference to moral principle – filled with characters holding no discernible theological convictions – could not possibly be *religious*. The 'natural' reading of Warner's first book gives us a decadent contemporary Europe in its Scotland and Spain. The novel is a sign in the secular apocalyptic, a road marker on the downhill slide of Western Civilisation. Finding anything religious in the novel other than as satire, an empty cathedral with long dead metaphors, would seem foolish if not perversely forced. But I have argued here that not only is this an intensely moral story, it is also remarkably pierced through with ideas and images from the Christian tradition, especially the faith's central figure, the person of Jesus. Morvern's story gradually, fitfully, and awkwardly depicts her boyfriend's death: someone powerful and ever-present, not 'creeping' but surely haunting. And because of this haunting she treats 'His' body and memory and interprets 'His' actions as if 'He' were a wise saviour who loved her, whose death made her freedom possible. 'He' becomes myth for her, a kind of Christ, and sets her free from her literal poverty, and the emotional poverty she would have experienced had she stayed with 'Him'. 'His' suicide reveals 'His' frailty, which in her grief exposes Morvern's own. Yet that offers her an unanticipated, odd healing only possible through 'His' death.[18]

Throughout the novel, Morvern struggles to find a moral language that can express and explain her grief and solitude. She processes awkwardly through rituals and liturgical signs of a post-Christendom, for comfort, hope, and guidance in a modern society within which those references are at best obscure and vague. This seems a powerful conviction in a strand of modern literature, from Conrad's *Heart of Darkness* to Cormac McCarthy's

No Country for Old Men. Morvern seems to hope there is a God in the world, one who hears prayers, blesses the sacraments, and saves the hopeless. Maybe. At best Morvern bears 'Him' with her, the dead boyfriend whose relationship seemed to draw her from teenage ignorance and alienation to some kind of education beyond 'the port' and to love and trust. She was 'His' disciple in this sense. 'He' betrayed her, of course, as Christendom has the poor throughout its brutal history. But 'His' suicide included 'His' hope that 'His' death would save her from the condemnation of a life in 'the port' with no other experiences, no other contrasts to the rounds of rainy grey days, drinking, pub talk, and alcohol-fuelled, lonely sex.

'His' death jarred Morvern into escape. After 'His' death she takes risks: criminal risks, in fact. Time is marked in vague terms in the novel after 'His' death, but Morvern's myth-lit journey to a City of Light sets real-time to rhythms of repetitious drama-rave as ritual.[19] 'His' time was short, and 'His' death gave Morvern the freedom and money to buy all the time she might need, bringing to an end typical Red Hanna's realist, working-class time marked by work, pub, family, sleep, sex, and work. Morvern disposes of 'His' body and is later bathed in Spanish sunlight and retreats into an almost anchoritic solitude, in which she returns to Scotland, as a kind of Virgin Mary, returning to 'His' birthplace with *her* unborn child. Here, at this point in the story, Morvern stumbles to find a story in which 'His' death, her responses, and her new-found liberty make sense. When in Spain she would not even sleep, afraid to miss one moment of 'that happiness that I never even dared dream I had the right' (p. 210). Her contentment survives her return home, pregnant and broke, refusing to cast herself on friends or family, which suggests that she has few (if any) regrets. This kind of story explains the meaning of what has happened in the last few years, as well as providing a path for her. We must here imagine Morvern happy.

Often and rightly compared to Camus's *The Stranger*, Warner's novel retains one important difference.[20] In the Algerian's novel, the priest provokes a violent response from the prisoner, who in that cathartic outrage learns that the universe is empty of purpose, utterly indifferent to him. All the religious and moral responsibility falls away and he is left to consider himself alone, responsible, free to create his purpose. Morvern seems to seek, even by novel's end to find, some moral purpose and meaning. Morvern makes no attack on the false piety of religion, the empty fakery of ritual, the hypocrisy or cant of religious moralism. Morvern treats churches and Christian ritual with an innocent longing, curiosity, and respect. At times she is much closer to someone Pascal or C. S. Lewis might have described: one to whom the sacraments and ritual speaks and for whom, for a moment, those ancient rhythms groove into their own. One can imagine St Augustine's claim, 'our heart finds no peace, until it rest in you', resonating with Morvern.[21] If there is substance to my argument, the Christ-references in *Morvern Callar* recall the portrait of Jesus in Shūsaku Endō's *Silence* (1966) and the later theological reflections of Dietrich Bonhoeffer. Still, while 'He' might be a Christ figure capable of accompanying Morvern through suffering, 'He' is powerless to save her.

And yet Morvern seems to be drawn to solitary places, with some aura of tradition, age, and solemnity. The circular folly in 'the port' is a common destination for her, to see out to the mountains and the Hebridean sea. She is especially caught by Couris Jean's life as a Gael, and her beautifully mythic tale, as if in Couris Jean's life an ancient Scotland still lives, possibly pre-Christian, whose gravity and wisdom confronts ATMs and supermarkets and driving lessons and strip clubs and even that foursome with Lanna and the two lads from town. The Highlands are beautiful to Morvern; their silence and the rare gift of sunlight on their heather and waters moves her, as light moves her in the Spanish raves on the surface of the Mediterranean Sea. It is probably more consistent with the spirit of Warner's entire novel that Morvern seeks roots and sustenance from *anything* older, gentler, and more trustworthy than the capitalist, industrialised shell of a Scotland left to her and her generation.

Endnotes

1. I owe thanks to the conveners of the conference for the Association for Scottish Literary Studies (now the Association for Scottish Literature) held at the University of Glasgow in July 2016 for permitting me to read the first draft of this paper. The participants in that session had especially helpful comments. My friend and colleague Sam Martin not only talked with me at length about the project, but the chapter was also greatly improved by his close reading.
2. All references to the novel are from Alan Warner, *Morvern Callar* (London: Vintage, 1996).
3. Duncan Petrie, *Contemporary Scottish Fictions: Film Television and the Novel* (Edinburgh: Edinburgh University Press, 2004), pp. 98–99; On the film, see Robert Morace, 'The Devolutionary Jekyll and Post-devolutionary Hyde of the Two *Morvern Callars*', *Critique* 53 (2012), pp. 115–123; Mathew Wickman, *The Ruins of Experience: Scotland's 'Romantick' Highlands and the Birth of the Modern Witness* (Philadelphia: University of Pennsylvania Press, 2007), pp. 188–89.
4. For this label, and the novel's intensely self-referential portrait of the death of the Author/God, see Ortwin de Graef, 'Grave Livers: On the Modern Element in Wordsworth, Arnold and Warner', *ELH* 74.1 (Spring 2007), p. 166. Among such reviews, see Jordana Brown, 'Finding Her Religion: The Search for Spiritual Satisfaction in Alan Warner's *Morvern Callar*', in *Ethically Speaking: Voice and Values in Modern Scottish Writing*, ed. James McGonigal and Kirsten Stirling (Amsterdam and New York: Rodopi, 2006), pp. 99–101; Sophy Dale, *Alan Warner's* Morvern Callar (New York and London: Continuum, 2002), pp. 68–75; Carole Jones, 'The "Becoming Woman" – Femininity and the Rave Generation in Alan Warner's *Morvern Callar*', *Scottish Studies Review* 5.2 (2004), pp. 56–68.
5. Dale, p. 35, and throughout.
6. Brown, 'Finding Her Religion', pp. 99–116. A few other scholars have touched lightly on Warner's turn in the novel to religious language and images: Berthold Schoene, 'Alan Warner, Post-feminism, and the Emasculated Nation', in Berthold Schoene (ed.), *The Edinburgh Companion to Contemporary Scottish Literature* (Edinburgh: Edinburgh University Press, 2007), p. 256; Wickman, *The Ruins of Experience*, 191; Scott Lyall, 'The Kailyard's Ghost: Community in Modern Scottish Fiction', in Ian Brown and Jean Berton (eds), *Roots and Fruits of Scottish Culture: Scottish Identities, History and Contemporary Literature* (Glasgow: Scottish Literature International, 2013), pp. 92–93.
7. Christie L. March, *Rewriting Scotland: Welsh, McLean, Warner, Banks, Galloway and Kennedy* (Manchester: Manchester University Press, 2002), p. 71.
8. Dale, *Alan Warner's* Morvern Callar, pp. 66–67; Petrie, *Contemporary Scottish Fictions*, pp. 96–101; Schoene, 'Alan Warner, Post-feminism, and the Emasculated Nation', in *The Edinburgh Companion to Contemporary Scottish Literature*, p. 256; Brown, 'Finding Her Religion', pp. 106, 113; John LeBlanc, 'Return of the Goddess: Contemporary Music and Celtic Mythology in Alan Warner's *Morvern Callar*', *Revista Canaria de Estudios Ingleses* 41 (2000), pp. 145–53.
9. On Warner's superficial resemblance to Morvern's 'He' – an author in his 30s, growing up in an Argyll village to a hotelier, travel in Spain – see Dale, ch. 1. Brown builds this into an identification of Warner, 'He' and God: 'Finding Her Religion', p. 105.

10 For idealised expressions of Scottish Celtic Christianity, see Esther de Waal, *The Celtic Way of Prayer: The Recovery of the Religious Imagination* (New York: Image reprint, 1999), and Mary Low, *Celtic Christianity and Nature: The Early Irish and Hebridean Traditions* (Edinburgh: Edinburgh University Press, 1996). But in response, see Donald E. Meek's careful and substantial review of Low in *Studies in World Christianity* 5.1 (1999), pp. 98–101. Meek develops this critique in *The Quest for Celtic Christianity* (Edinburgh: The Handsel Press, 2000); and, see Ian Bradley, *Celtic Christianity: Making Myths And Chasing Dreams* (Edinburgh: Edinburgh University Press, 1999).
11 Malcolm Chapman, *The Gaelic Vision in Scottish Culture* (Toronto: University of Toronto Press, 1978); Murray G. H. Pittock, *The Invention of Scotland: The Stuart Myth and the Scottish Identity, 1638 to the Present* (London: Routledge Press, 2014).
12 For example, de Graef, and Brown, pp. 105–06.
13 All Scripture references are from the New Revised Standard Version.
14 *The Sopranos* (New York: Farrar, Straus, and Giroux, 1999).
15 Primo Levi, *The Drowned and the Saved*, trans. Raymond Rosenthal (New York: Vintage, 1989), p. 85.
16 For instance, Morace, 'The Devolutionary Jekyll and Post-devolutionary Hyde of the Two *Morvern Callars*', p. 120; for a subtle reading, see Wickman, *The Ruins of Experience*, pp. 190–91.
17 *Didache*, 9. 4. The passage is from Glen Cary's translation, based on the Greek text published by Michael W. Holmes, *The Apostolic Fathers* (Grand Rapids: Baker Books, 2005, 1992), pp. 246–69 reformedforum.org/the-didache/
18 For a depiction of moral decency as less about effort, will, or character, and much more to do with the good fortune of birth and education, see Martha Nussbaum, *Fragility of Goodness: Luck and Ethics in Greek Tragedy and Philosophy*, 2nd edn (Cambridge: Cambridge University Press, 2001).
19 For a reading of Morvern's hope and liberation from regular time as utopian, see Jones, p. 64.
20 Petrie, p. 98; Wickman, p. 189.
21 *The Confessions*, trans. R. S. Pine-Coffin (Penguin Press, 1961), p. 21.

14. Edwin Morgan's Last Things: Eschatology and his Post-Millennial Poetry

JAMES McGONIGAL

Jesuits, actual or imagined, are a puzzling presence in the earliest and in the final works of Edwin Morgan (1920-2010). His first post-war poem in a British journal, 'A Warning of Waters at Evening', appeared in May 1950 in *The Month* 3.5, a periodical of the English Province of the Society of Jesus.[1] Under a new editor, Philip Caraman S. J., it had begun from 1948 to publish cultural articles by such figures as Graham Greene (1904-1991), Evelyn Waugh (1903-1966), Edith Sitwell (1887-1964), Muriel Spark (1918-2006), and Thomas Merton (1915-1968). This Catholic milieu seems an odd debut for a Scottish poet of Protestant background whose anti-authoritarian and anti-ecclesiastic views clashed with the Churches on, for example, issues of homosexuality and the law.

Morgan's interest in *The Month* was probably focused on the writings of Gerard Manley Hopkins S. J. (1844-1889). Becoming a junior lecturer in English in the late 1940s after war service in North Africa and Palestine (1940-45), Morgan identified quite strongly with Hopkins in his conflicted personal identity, the constant burden of academic assessment, and a sense of alienation from colleagues.[2] Perhaps the appearance of Morgan's own poem in *The Month* was a sly revenge on a journal whose former editor, Father Henry Coleridge S. J., had refused 'The Wreck of the Deutschland', submitted in May or June 1876. There may also be a glance at sexuality: 'A Warning of Waters at Evening' is a dark poem with themes of guilt and pursuit that have a gay undercurrent.

Hopkins's poetry had made an early impact on Morgan in his teens when it appeared in *The Faber Book of Modern Verse* (1936). His own lectures on Hopkins mention that publication, and praise the poet's innovative yet also realistic attitude to poetic language as 'the current language heightened'.[3] In Morgan's later poetry, Hopkins appears in his professional role in Glasgow as an assistant parish priest in September 1871, warming to the 'Dark tough tight-belted / drunken Fenian poor ex-Ulstermen' in his pastoral care (*Sonnets from Scotland*, 1984).[4] The aesthetic sustenance that Hopkins found in Duns Scotus is also revisited in Morgan's final collection, *Dreams and Other Nightmares* (2010), published just months before his death aged ninety on 19 August 2010.

Can a theological perspective help us to reflect upon his late writings, without attempting to trap him within any dogmatic structure? The branch of theology that deals with the end of life and whatever follows is eschatology – traditionally, the Four Last Things of Death, Judgement, Hell, and Heaven, although concepts such as the soul, immortality, and predestination are also involved. Now the 'four last things' of a poet would be his four final collections of poetry; in Morgan's case these were all published after 2000, and, crucially, in the context of a cancer diagnosis with the prognosis of an uncertain (but most probably brief) period left to complete his work. So, we find the poet writing against the clock and exploring time not only within the context of his own lifespan but also of the immeasurable reach of the cosmos. His four last things and the traditional Four Last Things coalesce in interesting ways. But since Morgan was rarely drawn to the traditional, I will come to focus on a more radical analysis of eschatology, developed in a damaged post-war Europe by two continental theologians of Hopkins's order, Karl Rahner S. J. (1904–1984) and Ladislaus Boros S. J. (1927–1981).

Morgan's poetry was not religious in any conventional sense. For example, the title 'Message Clear' of an 'emergent' concrete poem on Christ's crucifixion is meant to suggest the idea of a message being communicated with difficulty but coming through clear in the end. The seemingly hesitant manner in which the poem is set out suggests the scanning of a text electronically, with the mechanism picking out in an exploratory way all the component letters of the final sentence in their correct order, trying to make sense of its material. While the text seems to begin by referring to the wounds of crucifixion ('there and here and here and there'), it soon moves on down through other dimensions of place, history, and mathematics, catching at information as it proceeds. Its final emergent message, however, may be spoken at the moment of death, or just after, as it moves beyond earthly time: 'i am the resurrection and the life' (*CP*, p. 159, l. 55).[5] (The reference is to John 11. 25.)

Other radical poems about Jesus recur throughout Morgan's creative life. There is 'The Fifth Gospel' in *From Glasgow to Saturn* (1973, *CP*, p. 259): 'Give nothing to Caesar, for nothing is Caesar's' (l. 24). (The reference is to Matthew 22. 21.) In *Sonnets from Scotland* we find 'Pilate at Fortingall', speaking a mad Latin 'harsh with Aramaicisms' (*CP*, p. 439, l. 1). 'Testament' (*Grafts/Takes*, 1983, p. 28) and the late 'Conversation in Palestine' (*A Book of Lives*, 2007, p. 105) also attest to a decades-long puzzled exploration of the character of Jesus. This was continued in the controversial *A.D. A Trilogy of Plays on the Life of Jesus* (2000), on which Morgan was engaged when he received his cancer diagnosis. Advance media misinformation garbled the trilogy, which was wrongly supposed to feature a gay Jesus. There was local disapproval, too, that the action of the final play seemed to end with the crucifixion, lacking any hint of resurrection.[6]

In fact, the trilogy is opened and closed by Middle Eastern magi, who meet in a mountain observatory in Persia before the birth of Jesus, and speak reflectively after his crucifixion. They are less concerned with any individual death than with the mystery of interplanetary reaches beyond human suffering and destiny. These are the trilogy's final lines:

> The stars and planets in their glorious courses
> Awaken thoughts that pass eternity.
> The bones of Jesus lie in Palestine.
> If they have light, let it join all our light.[7]

Like the magi, these plays move across time. Their setting recalls Morgan's war service in Palestine, as earlier explored in the multi-linear, multi-temporal narrative of 'The New Divan', where precursors of these magi appear in the superhuman figures of stanza 81, meeting 'in full divan' or council 'in the anteroom of heaven', above the human fray. The *A.D.* trilogy ends in deliberate mystery, looking beyond the hour of death into wider-arching perspectives of light, space, and time. This sets the scene for the poetry that would follow.

Challenging Death in *Cathures*

Death was the first eschatological motif to be reworked in the new century. In *Cathures* (2002), we find Morgan not only responding humanly to the shock of his cancer diagnosis but challenging the very idea of death, both in recent European history during the years of Nazi persecution and locally through the charismatic voices of 'Nine in Glasgow', whose visionary and non-conformist viewpoints are matched by poetic sightlines on the city from unexpected angles – often from above, as viewed from its hills and chimney-tops.

Cathures is an ancient Celtic name for Glasgow. The collection contains civic poetry written in Morgan's role as Glasgow's Poet Laureate from 1999–2001: poems about city bank buildings re-purposed as restaurants, about new crayfish competing with salmon to inhabit the cleaner waters of the River Clyde, about a severed hand (the bloody result of gang violence) being carried cheerily on to a bus by the victim, and such like, all done with black humour, clever rhyme, and the sort of brash streetwise energy that in Glaswegian dialect is called 'gallus'.[8] Such details of city life are in conflict with a personal sense of impending death. Morgan describes a seagull landing on the window ledge of his flat and coldly inspecting the furnishings of his life, a scavenger ('A Gull', p. 45). In 'Gasometer' (p. 46), he sees from his kitchen window a familiar but soon-to-be-demolished structure on the skyline with its 'gaunt frame' still standing out defiantly – strong and dark and 'constructivist to the core', an aged emblem of the endurance that he might himself hope for.

Death is also viewed historically, in the central placing of 'The Trondheim Requiem', with Morgan's text commissioned by the composer Ståle Kleiberg for performance in Trondheim Cathedral in 2002. It is written '[f]or the victims of Nazi persecution' in three parts: the Yellow Triangle for Jews, the Brown Triangle for Roma, and the Pink Triangle for homosexuals. The sense of personal and cultural loss is haunting, each poem ending in a cry to be remembered, as here the Roma victims:

> We're saddled still through earth and heaven,
> Faithful to what we were and are.

> Remember us! Our horse's forehead
> Keeps its unconscionable star.
> (p. 64, ll. 29–32)

But generally in *Cathures*, death is countered not by memorial or piety but by tough nonconformity. At the start, in 'Nine in Glasgow' we hear the charismatic voices of nine 'Glaswegians', visitors from across the centuries: Pelagius the heretic theologian, Merlin the magus, Thennoch the mother of Mungo (Glasgow's patron saint), George Fox the Quaker preacher, John Hunter the scientist, Vincent Lunardi the pioneer balloonist, John Tennant a forward-thinking industrial chemist, Louis Kossuth the Hungarian patriot and national leader, and Enrico Cocozza, a Glasgow University lecturer in Italian and amateur filmmaker, an isolated gay man. None of these conforms. Each of them is a part of Morgan: in fact, the name Pelagius is a Latin form of this heretic theologian's British name, 'Morgan' (meaning sea-farer):

> I, Morgan, whom the Romans call Pelagius,
> Am back in my own place, my green Cathures
> By the frisky firth of salmon, by the open sea
> Not far, place of my name, at the end of things,
> As it must seem.
> (p. 9, ll. 1–5)

It may seem the end, but defiantly is not. This Pelagius/Morgan had also been in Palestine and North Africa. Merlin, the second 'Glaswegian' ('I made some rough magic for King Roderick. / He fed me in his court on Dumbarton Rock', p. 12, ll. 6–7) was entranced by Morgan le Fay, sister of King Arthur, and Edwin Morgan had adopted her name early as an ironic persona, sending his friend W. S. Graham (1918–1986) a poem in 1951 called 'A Little Ballad of Morgan Lefay'.[9] We discover Merlin at work 'in my house of glass / On Cathkin Hill, above the twinkling lights'. Like the magi in *A.D.*, he tracks the stars, helped by his sister who is compared to Ada, Byron's mathematically gifted daughter: 'We donate our spirit / To that gallus city' (p. 13, ll. 18–19; 29–30).

The range of Morgan's artistic concerns is revealed in 'Nine in Glasgow' through the interplay of poetry with science, technology, and daring human flight; and with Hungarian history and cultural life (he was awarded the Order of Merit of the Republic of Hungary in 1997 for his translations of Hungarian poetry); and with the necessarily secretive but creative life of other Glaswegian gay men, such as Enrico Cocozza. (Morgan claimed never to have met Cocozza, though their employment in Glasgow University overlapped, but he knew of his work as a filmmaker.) George Fox presents a radical religious voice that is resolutely ignored by the populace of 'this vale of darkness', but his tetchy reaction contrasts with Morgan's warm identification with the city and his ability to move between its darkness and light.

These nine are all visionaries of sorts, speaking out of different epochs. They gaze down from the post-glacial 'drumlins' or small hills on which Glasgow was built: Blythswood Hill, Cathkin Hill, Gilmore Hill. Or they rise above it: Lunardi floating above the Trongate in his balloon, or John Tennant gazing down from Tennant's Stalk, the great chimney of his chemical works near Sight Hill. The latter was both a capitalist and a social reformer, providing medical care and education for his workers and their children.

The anti-establishment energy of *Cathures* thus reaches across times and cultures. Pelagius argues with St Augustine in Carthage about the nature of grace and original sin, his own heretical view being that salvation can be achieved by the exercise of human powers:

> My blessing breathes with the earth.
> It is for the unborn, to accomplish their will
> With amazing, but only human, grace.
> (p. 11, ll. 16–18)

This 'voluntarist' tendency in Pelagius/Morgan accords with what Alexander Broadie in *The Shadow of Scotus: Philosophy and Faith in pre-Reformation Scotland* (1995) identifies as an instrumental view of practical reason in Scottish thought, where the reason's proper function is not to determine which are the proper ends of human action (as articulated by Aquinas) but to identify the best means to achieve a goal fixed by our own desires and preferences. Broadie traces this view from Duns Scotus onwards through the Calvinist theologians of the Scottish Reformation and on to David Hume in the Enlightenment. For Morgan, of course, what is always to be contested is a narrow cultural legacy of original sin and predestination.

'I spoke, I had crowds, there was a demon in me', Pelagius proudly declares (p. 9, l. 16). To disturb the established spiritual order is also the task of the Demon, expressed in the twenty sharp monologues that close the collection: 'My job is to rattle the bars. It's a battle. / The gates are high, large, long, hard, black.'[10] And he drives the guard dog wild by dragging an iron shaft along the gates' length. Not so much a demon as a daemon, or guardian spirit of a place or person, he is a rebellious presence. He distances himself from Lucifer and identifies instead with Frankenstein's monster as 'a fellow spirit and a sufferer'. The angelic powers of heaven want this man-made creature dead, and so the Demon rouses him to fight against death. In other monologues he visits Auschwitz and Albania and Glasgow's occasionally threatening Argyle Street (all places that Morgan too had recently visited, signalling a sense of identification between the poet and his spirited creation). Last of all we find the Demon 'at the walls of time', climbing and climbing until he sees the stars, determined not to give up but to read 'the writing on the wall' (p. 115, l. 38). So, balancing the Nine visionaries gazing down on the historical city in different centuries, the Demonic vision here moves upwards from below, to somewhere beyond time. Against any hapless predestination of the damned to Hell, against Calvinistic negativity, the Demon speaks in a voice that is by turns sarcastic, defiant, humorous, challenging, sharply intelligent, and self-aware. His presence and placing in *Cathures* serve to intensify the eternal perspective, stretching it beyond the play with time in 'Nine in Glasgow'.

This perspective is caught in the collection's epigraph from Lucretius's *De Rerum Natura*:

> *Nec refert quibus adsistas regionibus eius:*
> *usque adeo, quem quisque locum possedit, in omnis*
> *tantundem partis infinitum omne relinquit.*

The epigraph is un-glossed, but comes from Book I, ll. 965–67, and in Morgan's own manuscript translation reads: 'It does not matter in what regions of the universe you set yourself: the fact is that whatever spot anyone may occupy, the universe is left stretching equally unbounded in every direction.'[11] As time and space are bound together within the universe, then one spot, call it Cathures or Glasgow, may be connected to all times.

This pan-cosmic perspective may also echo in 'At Eighty', written for the poet's birthday on 27 April 2000: 'Push the boat out, compañeros, / Push the boat out, whatever the sea' (p. 69, ll. 1–2). Morgan's 'compañeros' recalls the 'Camerado' of Walt Whitman's (1819–1892) 'Song of the Open Road'.[12] In his 1963 essay 'A Glimpse of Petavius', Morgan quotes from Whitman's preface to *November Boughs* of 1888: 'the true use of the imaginative faculty of modern times is to give ultimate vivification to facts, to science, and to common lives.'[13] Here was an early validation of Morgan's incipient sense of the poet as a mediator between the technological world and ordinary people who inhabit that world without seeing their place in it as having any significance. Whitman was to be contrasted with Yeats, Pound, and Eliot in their high-Modernist disregard of facts, science, and common life.

Somewhere in the poem's background there may also be Gerard Manley Hopkins's self-identification with Whitman: 'I always knew in my heart Walt Whitman's mind to be more like my own than any other man's living. As he is a very great scoundrel, this is not a pleasant confession.'[14] For Morgan, the identification appears not to be merely one of homoerotic reference. Whitman the American scoundrel was everywhere alert and responsive to the energy of technological invention and scientific discovery. Similarly, in his lectures on Hopkins, Morgan linked the Victorian poet's linguistic and technical experimentation with the new physics of Einstein, relativity, and particle theory: 'as if the universe has moved from a noun to a verb', he suggests, when substance becomes activity, mass turns into energy and everything is flux or process, 'not in space at a certain point in time but in spacetime'.[15] So the interconnection of Whitman, Hopkins, and Morgan may be sensed as an engagement with 'all-at-oneness', whether in a quasi-mystical or a scientific way. Hopkins had found this in religious meditation and Whitman in more unorthodox ways that were attractive nonetheless to someone trained in the Ignatian Spiritual Exercises. Traces of past and future within the present, the spiritual energy of the material world, and of ordinary people at work in that world, along with the challenge too to conformist religious practice, all seem part of Morgan's creative consciousness now in the face of death, sustained by the insights and memories of lifetime's reading.

Death-defying *Tales from Baron Munchausen*

Tales from Baron Munchausen (2005) challenges death not through intellectual combat or literary reflection but through narrative and creative re-imagining. Having outfaced death once before in war, Morgan was drawn to the idea of retelling for dramatic performance the tall tales of the eighteenth-century Hanoverian military man. It was commissioned by Benno Plassmann, a German director and actor interested in exploring the borderlines between storytelling, lies, and madness. Hidden among these 'genuine' Munchausen tales there are two stories completely invented by Morgan but un-signalled in the text.

In the background was Morgan's own war story. Voyaging round the Cape of Good Hope in 1941, en route to North Africa as a young recruit among a 'band of brothers', he could identify with the epic *Beowulf* that he had left behind with other favourite Old English voyager texts, midway through his undergraduate studies.[16] When in 2002 Carcanet re-launched his translation of *Beowulf* (in print almost continuously since its publication in 1952), Morgan explicitly called it his own war-poem 'of conflict and danger, voyaging and displacement, loyalty and loss' (Introduction, p. xx). And now, hidden amidst the 'genuine' Munchausen tales, he adds two others related to his own war service in Egypt and to *Beowulf*. In the Introduction, he recounts a love affair with Leila ('my Sheherazade') who not only entranced him with her stories from *The Thousand and One Nights*, but also bore him a son in Egypt – by now a grandfather, nearing retirement from his scholarly work as an archaeologist in Cairo Museum. This story of the gay poet's wartime son made good publicity copy in the Scottish press and was never denied. But it is a lie, of course.

The second invented tale, 'Danish Incident' (pp. 24–25), revisits *Beowulf* territory on the coast of Denmark. Swimming to cool off in the summer heat, the storyteller encounters a ten-foot snake which he wrestles, ties in a knot, and pushes down to the seabed. Beowulf also fought off a sea monster while competing in swimming against Breca.[17] Now pushing on towards an off-shore island, Munchausen/Morgan discovers a clutch of baby sea-snakes behind a rock:

> Even at that age they spat at me.
> I admired their spirit. I am not cruel.
> I left them hissing there in their stony crèche.
> Some would survive to give other travellers
> A useful shock.

Shocks are 'useful' because of what can be learned in trying to overcome them. In his frequent lectures on *Paradise Lost*, Morgan would stress that if the Fall had brought history and fate into the world, it had also brought fighting spirit and human inventiveness. His lecture notes emphasise the pathos and human dignity of Adam and Eve (new emblems of epic heroism) stepping out with new understanding and self-determination into the earthly world.[18] Against the disaster of cancer, Morgan's Munchausen tales challenge the moribund and revel in energetic movement. The shock has been useful to that extent. As in *Cathures*, much of the action reaches beyond the earth – it is 'death-defying' in that sense, refusing to be earth-bound or chained by common sense. The final tale is 'My Day among the Cannonballs', when Munchausen jumps astride a cannonball to carry out a spying mission over enemy lines – and transfers mid-air onto an enemy cannonball being fired back towards his own lines. But the climax of the journey is 'an unearthly duet' that he sings with an eagle, which comes shrieking at this 'usurper of that space / Between ground and sky, between friend and foe' (pp. 29–30, ll. 46–47). To keep his spirits high, we might say, as his being hovered precariously between existence and afterlife, Morgan had to keep singing. No matter where the cannonball might come to earth, the storyteller must survive, skipping aside to recount his tall tale.

Judgement in *A Book of Lives*

The motif of death defied appears to shift in *A Book of Lives* (2007) towards aspects of the afterlife and judgement. The personal Judgement that in traditional Christian eschatology follows immediately after death seems adumbrated in 'Love and a Life', an autobiographical sequence of fifty linked poems. These are written in the 'Cathurian stanza', a deftly rhyming poetic form invented for *Cathures*.[19] The dexterity of this form balances confessional aspects of the text, which explores experience of love in many aspects – homosexual and heterosexual love and desire, opportunistic encounters and missed opportunities in cinema or aeroplane, the mystical love of St John of the Cross and St Theresa of Avila. There is defiant self-exposure in some poems, for example in the late senex-puer relationship of Morgan and a young heterosexual student. Such past and present varieties of love appear alongside the unnerving experience of CT scans and bone scans to track his cancer's progress, as if determined to mete out a personal judgement on himself, bones and all:

> [...] Skull, ribs, hips emerge from the dark like a caravan
>   Bound for who knows where
>   Stepping through earth or air
> Still of a piece and still en route, beating out the music of tongs and bones
>   while it can.

(p. 94)

The 'tongs and bones' echo Bottom's basic choice of music when prompted by Titania in *A Midsummer Night's Dream* (IV.1.27) and possibly assert an earthy energy against high-tech medicine. In its ironic range, tenderness, and technical adroitness the sequence defies judgement. The religious term 'soul' does appear, 'our feeble but our dearest soul', but is re-defined as 'Touch' (p. 85), with the body as 'the means of greatest grace'. Loved people from the past persist in memory, but also 'in clouds in streets in trees'. Memories are moments, but caught and preserved by 'friendless friendly time'. And memory itself is scoured by the unearthly gaze of 'cosmic harvesters' in search of 'sheafs and tracks of love' left since time began

('Tracks and Crops', p. 83). So 'Frank, Jean, Cosgrove, John, Malcolm, Mark – loves of sixty years' in the opening line are joined by Egyptian dancer Leila and one of her magical tales, by Morgan as the *Beowulf* poet, 'old in many winters', and by others encountered in a long life, all within an eternal perspective – the all-at-onceness of presence in memory and art.

This sequence is an apologia, but also a challenge: Who dares judge another person's life, or the kinds and depth of love, or of honesty or regret? *A Book of Lives* explores other forms of judgement too: of Scotland's legislators in 'For the Opening of the Scottish Parliament, 9 October 2004', of kings and emperors from James IV to Charles V and Hirohito, and of the law's own prejudice in the case of Oscar Wilde (pp. 9, 21, 52, 54, 53).

Politicians await the judgement of poetry or history – but is there life after history? In 'Planet Wave', a work written for Scottish saxophonist Tommy Smith to be performed with his jazz orchestra, the afterlives of whole epochs are observed by a time-traveller, a seemingly immortal presence. He presents a single voice, carried forward across the mysteries of time and space, or space-time, from the 'big bang' of 'In the Beginning' (dated 20 billion BC) right through to a future space expedition 'On the Way to Barnard's Star (2300 AD)'. He reveals himself to his audience as pre-existing the origins of the universe, 'swinging in my spacetime hammock / nibbling a moon or two, watching you' (p. 23). The human presence of readers or listeners is thus signalled from the start, within an eternal perspective without boundaries.

The 'eternal' is beyond our concepts of measurement and to be distinguished from the 'sempiternal', an endless sequence of days. But for clarity in performance, the sequence is chronological, moving with the time-traveller past dinosaurs, the Flood, the construction of pyramids by the Nile, a band of Vikings enacting funeral rites for their leader at the river Volga, and so on. The sequence is given unity not by history, however, but by the varying imagery of waves, in different forms in each of the twenty sections (waves of grass, of water, of applause, etc.) and also, in performance, by waves of sound from the jazz orchestra's polyrhythmic, improvised phrasing. One might even sense a glance here at the wave-particle duality that drove explorations in quantum physics, as poetic particles of historical events emerge within the pulsing wave of time. The humanities and sciences are not contradictory in this perspective.

Morgan's enduring distaste for traditional worship means that science always trumps religion in this sequence. This is evident in the section 'The Lisbon Earthquake (1755 AD)', which describes the tens of thousands killed in city churches packed for All Saints Day, and the thousands more in the following tsunami. 'It tore the Enlightenment to tatters', the speaker says. 'It made philosophers of men in stumps'.[20] In its wake Voltaire challenged Leibnitz's theodicy of the divine will as having a benign, if inscrutable, purpose – satirising the idea in *Candide* as 'All is for the best in the best of all possible worlds'. But if this earthquake shook the foundations of contemporary philosophy, it was also the first to be studied scientifically, giving rise eventually to seismology and earthquake engineering. The poem's speaker foresees this:

> Throw away your candles, I said. It's a new age.
> Study the earth. Listen to its plates grinding.
> Power is yours, not up there – I pointed –
> (ll. 28–30)

Yet progress is not only linear or scientific. In 'The Sputnik's Tale (1957 AD)', the time traveller meets an early Russian space satellite and they travel together in earth orbit (in Russian, *sputnik* means 'travelling companion'). It emerges that the satellite has not always been bound in metal. Its 'spirit' or intellectual energy has survived from other ages:

> I was a bard in the barbarous times,
> Widsith, the far-traveller. The world was my mead hall.
> Goths gave me gold. I blossomed in Burgundy.
> (p. 40, ll. 27–29)

The shift into Old English alliterative metre here returns us to 'Widsith', probably composed in the seventh century (with later additions) and one of the oldest poems in English, a bardic repertoire of stories.[21] *Widsith* means 'far-traveller'; the modern technological traveller and the ancient bardic traveller are one and speak with one voice. This intersection of ancient poetry with 1950s space technology suggests a possible co-existence of spirit, voice, movement, and memory that may offer a glimpse of the afterlife. For Morgan, it appears, it is not that after death there is nothing there at all – but, very possibly, everything.

The final prophetic voice in *A Book of Lives* is that of Jesus in 'Conversation in Palestine'. He asserts his own human ordinariness, the simplicity of his questions, a dislike of hierarchy. He foresees and extols Ludwig Wittgenstein (1889–1951):

> Ferociously honest, a life pared to the bone.
> If you want processions, hierarchies,
> he's not your man. Swish vestments
> are anathema to my father [...]
> (p. 105, ll. 27–30)

Wittgenstein would give away a fortune; he was possibly bisexual; and although a Jew he was baptised and buried a Catholic. Identity is complex, then, and moral judgement should take place under the broad perspective of a starry sky. There is, though, an ambiguity about the cosmic perspective of the final lines. The person talking with Jesus says, 'The stars will soon be out', and Jesus answers: 'I think so: the beam, the blinter, and the blaze.' Are these stars appearing ('out in the night sky') or disappearing ('out like a light')? Or are some still present shining brightly, and others failing or already dead, but so distant from the earth that their light still reaches us millennia later? Jesus from provincial Galilee uses a Scots word here, *blinter*, meaning 'to shine with a feeble or glimmering light'. In a vast universe, all kinds of light are possible.

The final *Dreams and Other Nightmares*

After Death in *Cathures*, Judgement in *A Book of Lives*, and a re-visioning of hellishness in 'Demon', glimpses of Heaven and Hell appear in Morgan's final collection, *Dreams and Other Nightmares: New and Uncollected Poems 1954–2009* (2010). It was published just three months before he died. There is the haiku heaven of 'A Definition of Six' (p. 20):

> Heaven is a wet
> pavement with streetlights painting
> people like ikons.

It is an urban heaven: Glasgow blended perhaps with Moscow or other Russian cities that Morgan had visited on a study tour in 1955. Hell is also a social occasion:

> Hell is a cocktail
> party where the hostess sweeps
> new soul mates apart.

These mates, presumably male, are separated by pressure from a female guardian of conventionality. The soul seems linked with touch here, as in 'Love and a Life'. At greater length, 'Heaven' is seen as a dark mansion with many extensions, and rings of keys at the gate ready for each person arriving, but 'no instructions to find your own place' (p. 23). We follow a winding drive with dark rhododendrons overhanging it – the place seems derelict, and yet:

> We tiptoe up the stair
> to the last room
> with the last key
> and get it to growl
> round in its hole
> and let us push into
> paradise, paradise
> please, if we may.
> (ll. 19–26)

So, there is a tentative approach to heaven, and perhaps a somewhat anxious desire to enter. That 'growl' is disconcerting, however, and may suggest an ironic agnosticism.

In 'Testament' (p. 31) the figure of Jesus is described by an evangelist who had witnessed him walk on water. It is dramatically written, all the more so because intercut with unreferenced words from Chapter 20 of Jack London's early adventure novel, *The Cruise of the Dazzler* (1902). The description of a sailor, Red Nelson, is first quoted directly within the storm scene on Lake Galilee and later transferred with an altered enjambment to Christ on shore:

> his sou'wester gone
> and his fair hair plastered in wet, wind-blown
> ringlets about his face. His whole attitude breathed
> indomitability, courage, strength. It seemed
> almost as though the divine were blazing forth from him.
> (ll. 18–22)

This bold homoerotic vision is as memorable as the final testament of the marks of Christ's footprints on the water, 'soldered to it in characters of fire': the human and the divine are fused in a blending of opposing elements.

'Testament' and 'Heaven' were originally in *Grafts/Takes* (1983) but omitted from *Collected Poems*.[22] They were co-written in the early 1970s with his publisher Michael Schmidt, using fragments from the latter's unfinished poems. More recent is 'From a Nursing Home' (p. 15), where the poet still takes pleasure in small details of his more constrained life, in '[b]ed and book case and good book-booty' (he lists some titles in alliterative style), and in the raucous gulls, or a shrubbery wren, and even the fearsome roar of jets overhead on a training flight: 'haecceitas is all,' he decides, watching 'the new design' of the day 'emerge and shine' (l. 32). *Haecceitas* means 'Thisness', of course, taking the reader back to Gerard Manley Hopkins's discovery of Duns Scotus, whose focus on the individual thing as being immediately knowable by the intellect in union with the senses ran counter to the standard theology of Aquinas, that the 'individual' is really unknowable, with only the 'immortal' or the ideal being truly known.[23] This stress on the senses and individual particularity was liberating for Hopkins, validating his sensitivity, technical brio, and fascination with language.

Jesuit interests also figured (mistakenly, it transpired) in Morgan's extended philosophical discussions from 1994 onwards with a Spanish priest and member of Opus Dei, Father Gonzalo Gonzales.[24] His intense gaze, ascetic demeanour, and neo-scholastic line of argument led the poet to assume that he must be a Jesuit of a traditionalist cast of mind. Morgan's intellectual combat with someone whom he ironically called his 'father confessor' is of a piece with his oppositional stance towards a religious order which had failed to recognise and foster Hopkins's gifts.

In what follows, therefore, I am not suggesting that Morgan underwent any easing into acquiescence with traditional religion. It is the fissures and contradictions within the poet's anti-religious stance that are of interest, and his eschewal of reconciliation. To gain a wider perspective, it may be best to look back from Morgan's last decade towards his remarkable 1960s expansion of aesthetic form and international publication. And here it appears that the Catholic obverse to his Protestant schooling within a sectarian Scotland was a riddle that he had long been puzzling over.

The persistent and subtle poetic presence of Hopkins in his life had clearly opposed the mistrusted anti-Reformation Jesuit order. Gonzales, whom Morgan had mistaken for a Jesuit, had only confirmed his dislike of Catholic theology of an unreconstructed type. But what of Hopkins's genuine Jesuit successors during that 1960s decade of liberation, and to what extent would Morgan have been aware of them? Had he kept in touch through newspapers, book reviews and radio programmes, or indeed *The Month*, with the ongoing work of reform in Catholic theology through the Second Vatican Council of 1962–65? Morgan was in professional contact with Sister Marie Vianney of the teaching order of Sisters of Notre Dame in Glasgow in the early 1960s, helping to reshape the English Literature curriculum in their training college for Catholic primary teachers near Glasgow University.[25] His friendship later in the decade with Dom Sylvester Houédard (1924–1992), Benedictine priest and experimental poet, altered his view of what visual and sonic poetry could achieve, and both men were recognised as leading British exponents of concrete poetry. Houédard was also a notable translator and was literary editor of the new *Jerusalem Bible*, which would reshape the lectionary for Catholic worship in much of the English-speaking world.

Some of Morgan's intellectual ties made in this period were also to men of a Catholic background. The poet Tom Leonard (1944–2018) and Bob Tait (1943–2017), Morgan's future co-editor on the *Scottish International* journal, were among the increasing number of working-class Catholic students entering Scottish universities. The Dominican priest and scholar Anthony Ross O. P. (1917–1993) was on the Board of that journal and provided editorial accommodation in Blackfriars, Edinburgh. He was an activist in social issues, including support for prisoners and for gay people at a period when homosexual activity was still illegal. Given this range of Catholic acquaintance, it would be surprising indeed if Morgan had not been aware of significant theological changes taking place in a religion he had been brought up to regard with suspicion.

But where would Morgan have encountered the theology underpinning these changes? *The Times Literary Supplement* (*TLS*) seems a likely starting point. In the 1960s, Morgan began to appear in the journal as a reviewer and translator. Earlier, he had had only two letters published, on Russian transliteration (2 August 1947) and on the final phrase of Hopkins's 'The Windhover' (27 May 1949).[26] Nothing appeared in the 1950s. In the 1960s, by contrast, he had two articles on concrete poetry, eleven reviews (mainly on contemporary Russian poetry and avant-garde writing), one poem 'Message Clear' (and subsequent correspondence over three weeks), and translations of the poetry of Brazilian and German concrete poets. In the same decade, fourteen books by Karl Rahner S. J. were reviewed, together with a biography of this prodigious theologian by Herbert Grimler: *Karl Rahner. His Life, Thought and Works* (reviewed 12 May 1966: p. 410).[27]

It seems not unlikely that Morgan's critical eye would have been drawn in the *TLS* to this German Jesuit, as influential in Catholic matters now as Hopkins must have seemed almost irrelevant in his own time. And yet Rahner too had met with incomprehension. His doctoral thesis had been refused in the 1930s as insufficiently neo-scholastic, and by 1962 his creative and radical theology had been censored by the Vatican, so that he was forbidden to publish or lecture without prior permission. His *On the Theology of Death* (1961) was typically disturbing of the status quo. Yet the range and depth of his thought ensured that when the Second Vatican Council opened later in that same year of 1962 he was appointed 'peritus' or expert advisor to the German Cardinals and became highly influential in reshaping Catholic thought and practice. Most intriguing, possibly, was his concept of 'Anonymous Christianity', the conviction that all human beings have a latent experience of a transcendent ultimate reality, and that they may in their fundamental orientation be open to God's salvation through Christ, even though they have never heard the Gospel. Less influential, although just as intriguing, was his openness to the prospect of extra-terrestrial intelligence and cosmic evolution, and he argued against the prohibition of this idea.

It is of course impossible to tell which reviews of Rahner might have caught Morgan's attention. There was no coincidence of both men's work appearing within a single issue; and yet it is clear from Morgan's early Scrapbooks and concrete poetry that he was everywhere alert to patterns in print, and also that the abbreviation S. J. for the Society of Jesus had long held for him powerful associations of both attraction and suspicion. He could scarcely have failed to notice. If there were a key work that stimulated interest, it could well have been in the *TLS* of 3 May 1967 (p. 382), where Volume IV of Rahner's *Theological Investigations* was reviewed. Volume III would be reviewed on 23 November 1967 (p. 1108). Volume IV not only contains 'The Hermeneutics of Eschatological Assertions' (pp. 323–46) and 'The Life of the Dead' (pp. 347–54), but also 'Poetry and the Christian' (pp. 357–67).[28] In that same busy summer and autumn of 1967, Morgan reviewed (rather negatively under the headline 'Good Man, Good Poet?') *Edwin Muir: Man and Poet*, by Peter Butter, then Regius Professor of English Literature at Glasgow University (6 July 1967); poetry collections by Joseph Brodsky, Yevtushenko and Voznesensky (20 July and 2 November); and Mikhail Bulgakov's experimental novel *The Master and Margarita* (7 December). So, he was clearly focused on the journal, and his creative and scholarly interests were not confined to literature or criticism but interdisciplinary and wide-ranging.

The Bulgakov review is particularly interesting. The Master, a devil with a darkly satirical sense of the absurd, seems a precursor of Morgan's Trickster Demon. The unorthodox world of *A.D.* is also hinted at, as the plot focuses partly on a forty-year-old polyglot novelist writing about the relationship of Pilate and Jesus (Yeshua). Morgan's review, headlined 'Diabolical Experiment', is enthusiastic:

> This is an utterly non-canonical and virtually non-Christian refocusing of the story, in which Pilate is studied in depth as a man greatly sympathetic to Yeshua but unable to save him, in which the only disciple is a ragged hysterical Matthew who hectically records his garbled parchmentful of Yeshua's sayings [...], in which Judas does not kill himself but is murdered in a marvellously subtle scene by Pilate's orders [...]? It is hard to explain how extraordinarily gripping and moving these scenes are [...].[29]

It is clear that Morgan was alert in these months to the intersection of Christianity and literature, in Bulgakov as in Edwin Muir; Rahner might well have impinged in this context. What would have been of particular interest was his theological argument that on death the soul did not necessarily separate from the body, as traditional eschatology taught. Instead, the soul might enter a cosmic relationship with the world. No longer bound by the body, it could assume a deeper linkage with the universe, and Rahner argues that it is permissible to assume that the 'the human spiritual soul' can, in some sense, maintain a relationship with the world.[30] Such a view of death as a transformation of the human being into free spirit is difficult to reconcile with traditional ideas of death as the penalty for human sinfulness. Christ's death and descent into hell or limbo signals a connection with the deepest level of the world, intrinsic to its transformation. Death therefore makes possible an integration of the human spirit with world, expanding the destiny of the universe. Such a sense of cosmic identity, capable of alteration but still engaged with the world and time, is a key theme of 'Planet Wave', as noted above.

And yet it seems unlikely that Morgan would have had the time or inclination to engage with the subtleties of Rahner's syntax or the complexity of his theological reasoning. There was another Jesuit, however, who had been Rahner's doctoral student and had the added attraction of Hungarian nationality, in a decade in which Morgan was beginning to read and translate more widely in Hungarian poetry.[31]

Ladislaus Boros was of Morgan's generation. His *Mysterium Mortis: Der Mensch in der letzen Entscheidigung* (1962) was translated as *The Moment of Truth: Mysterium Mortis* by the Benedictine Gregory Bainbridge and reviewed in the *TLS* on 23 September 1965. The book is much briefer than Rahner, but clearly based upon his thinking. This review appeared at a time when Morgan's father was grievously ill with cancer: he would die on 25 November 1965. The idea for Morgan's poem 'Message Clear' came to him on the bus returning from a hospital visit during that autumn.[32]

For Boros, the moment of death is a waking of consciousness, a moment of decision for or against God. The restless alienation and lack of fulfilment of daily life falls away, and the limited human intellect is suddenly faced with an absolute expanse of being, the infinite reality which is God. Boros sees the human soul (or identity) not as escaping from the world at death, or freed from the body in a dualistic sense, but as being brought into closer proximity to the natural world. Christ's death and descent into the lower reaches of the world established a new relationship with humanity, so that it becomes possible to meet him everywhere – reminiscent of the way that Hopkins 'caught' Christ in the dawn flight of the windhover, or of his realisation that

> Christ plays in ten thousand faces,
> Lovely in limbs, and lovely in eyes not his
> To the Father through the features of men's faces
> ('As Kingfishers Catch Fire')

For Boros, the soul needs the body, and resurrection must occur at the moment of death when, wholly ourselves, we enter into a pan-cosmic relationship with the universe.

This is heady reasoning, and buttressed by readings in French philosophy and in the poetry of Heinrich Heine; Morgan had translated Heine into Scots in the 1950s.[33] We cannot know with certainty whether Morgan read Boros, but the Latin and English titles of his book are interestingly conflated in 'The Moment of Death' (*CP*, p. 555), a concrete poem written on 30 September 1968.[34] Winding down over a full page where the words 'unite' and 'untie' part and coalesce and part again, as if uncertain where the truth of that moment might lie, it invites comparison with the 'emergent' 'Message Clear' – which might more properly be called a convergent poem since its variations home in on the completed final line, 'i am the resurrection and the life'. In 'The Moment of Death', conversely, the movement is dispersant, the final line stretching as far as the margins reach with an elongated and variable spacing between the single letters of 'untie' that conveys the impression of reaching out in each direction. With a white sheet of paper large enough, we feel, this poem could stretch 'equally unbounded in every direction', like the universe of Lucretius, or of Rahner. The very last letter flying wide and free in its final line is – 'e' – the initial of the poet's first name, or his Christian name as he and his generation would have termed it.

Endnotes

1. Edwin Morgan, *Collected Poems* (Manchester: Carcanet Press, 1996), p. 26. Hereafter *CP*.
2. See James McGonigal, *Beyond the Last Dragon: A Life of Edwin Morgan* (Dingwall: Sandstone Press, 2012), pp. 96-97. Hereafter *A Life*.
3. Edwin Morgan Papers, University of Glasgow Library, MS Morgan B/2/3.
4. *CP*, p. 445, ll. 4-5. Further citation given in the text.
5. See letter of 16 April 1967, *Edwin Morgan: The Midnight Letterbox. Selected Correspondence 1950-2010*, ed. James McGonigal and John Coyle (Manchester: Carcanet Press, 2015), pp. 189-90. Hereafter *Selected Correspondence*.
6. See *A Life*, pp. 377-85.
7. *A.D.*, p. 223. These are the trilogy's final lines.
8. Possibly derived from 'gallows humour'. 'Gallus' (p. 53) describes one such character.
9. James McGonigal and Sarah Hepworth, 'Ana, Morgana, Morganiana: A Poet's Scrapbooks as Emblems of Identity', *Scottish Literary Review* 4.2 (2012), pp. 1-23 (p. 17).
10. *Cathures*, p. 93, ll. 1-2.
11. Morgan owned six copies of Lucretius (1921, 1922, 1951, 1976 and 1992), all now in the Mitchell Library, Glasgow. This is typical of his scholarly approach even in creative work.
12. Walt Whitman, *Leaves of Grass* (New York: The New American Library of World Literature, 1958), p. 144.
13. Edwin Morgan, *Essays* (Cheadle: Carcanet Press, 1974), p. 5.
14. Letter to Robert Bridges, 18 October 1882, quoted in Hopkins lecture, MS Morgan B/2/3.
15. University of Glasgow Library, MS Morgan B/2/3.
16. Chris Jones, 'While Crowding Memories Came: Edwin Morgan, Old English and Nostalgia', *Scottish Literary Review* 4.2 (2012), pp. 124-25.
17. Recounted in ll. 553-69 of *Beowulf* (Carcanet Press, 2002), p. 15.
18. University of Glasgow Library, MS Morgan B/2/2.
19. 'Cathurian Lyrics', *Cathures*, pp. 81-89.
20. *A Book of Lives*, p. 36, ll. 25-26.
21. Jones, p. 143, note 49.
22. See *A Life*, pp. 231-32.
23. See, for example, Timothy McDermott, *Summa Theologiae: A Concise Translation* (London: Eyre and Spottiswoode, 1989) pp. 14-15, 3.3: 'Essence or nature includes only what defines the species of a thing: *human nature* means what defines man, what makes man man, and that does not include *this* flesh and *these* bones and *this* colour or anything particular to *this* man. [...] In contrast, the individuality of things not composed of matter and form does not derive from this or that individual matter: the forms of such things are intrinsically individual and stand on their own as things.'
24. *A Life*, pp. 343-44, 449.
25. Ibid., pp. 138-39.
26. See Hamish Whyte, 'Edwin Morgan: A Checklist', *About Edwin Morgan*, ed. Robert Crawford and Hamish Whyte (Edinburgh: Edinburgh University Press, 1990), p. 187.
27. *The Times Literary Supplement Index 1940-1980* (Reading: Research Publications, 1982), 3 P-Z.
28. Karl Rahner, *Theological Investigations*, trans. Kevin Smith, 23 vols (London: Darton, Longman & Todd, 1966), IV.

29 Reprinted as 'What the Devil?' in the *TLS* of 15 March 2017, available at www.the-tls.co.uk/articles/public/what-the-devil-bulgakov/.
30 Rahner's eschatology is outlined in William J. La Due, *The Trinity Guide to Eschatology* (London: Continuum, 2004). More detailed is Morwenna Ludlow, *Universal Salvation: Eschatology in the Thought of Gregory of Nyssa and Karl Rahner* (Oxford: Oxford University Press, 2000).
31 James McGonigal, 'Edwin Morgan: A Translator's Notebook 10. From Budapest to Glasgow', *PN Review* 244 (2018), pp. 64–68.
32 *A Life*, pp. 156–58.
33 *An Anthology of German Poetry from Hölderlin to Rilke in English Translation*, ed. Angel Flores (Garden City NY: Doubleday, 1960); Hamish Whyte, 'A Checklist', p. 164.
34 University of Glasgow Library, MS Morgan P/1/415 (a).

15. God, War, and the Faeries: Mentoring and Carrying Stream in Writing *Poacher's Pilgrimage*

ALASTAIR McINTOSH

> Yes, about the fairies and all that. They say they are here for a century and away for another century. This is their century away.
> —*Nan MacKinnon of Vatersay, 1981.*[1]

Those words, having been spoken in the twentieth century, significantly so, serve both to introduce and culturally to legitimise my purpose here. It took me twelve meandering days in 2009 to walk from the most southerly tip of the Isle of Harris to the Butt of Lewis in Scotland's Outer Hebrides. As the spiritual gravity gradually became apparent, it took a further seven years to see the publication of *Poacher's Pilgrimage: An Island Journey* and, in the course of writing as a more specialised theological spin-off, *Island Spirituality: Spiritual Values of Lewis and Harris*.[2] While *Soil and Soul* is my most influential book judging by its sales for a book of its kind and citations linked to public awareness of Scotland's land reform debate,[3] I consider *Poacher's* to be my most beautiful: a paean to and of the island where I was not born but grew up on from the age of four in 1960. I was thrilled for it to be launched at the 2016 conference of the Association for Scottish Literary Studies, the theme of which was *Literature and Religion in Scotland*.

I want in this chapter to look at the role that mentoring and its cultural grounding played in the writing of it. The word *mentor* is cognate with words like 'mental', 'mantic', and 'mantra'. Their shared Latin, Greek, Sanskrit and ultimately proto-Indo-European root, *men-, has produced a modern semantic range that is far wider than the merely cognitive application. It also points towards a sense of spirit.[4] On that basis I will use the term to suggest, ultimately, to lead out qualities of the soul.

Normally, we think of mentoring as taking place in a one-to-one or a person-to-person capacity, as in an eldership relationship. But I also want to look at mentoring in visionary states of waking consciousness, and in the dreams of sleep. Through these three modes – personal, visionary, and dream – I want to look at mentoring's role in writing. I will focus on its legitimising role when working with the creative unconscious as the cultural 'carrying stream'. Why the concern with legitimacy? Because to go beyond ego requires the assurance of being held in transpersonal structures of the community.

An ecology of the imagination

I set out on the pilgrimage with a fishing rod. The poaching teaser both held gastronomic hopes and functioned as a foil. In Lewis and Harris, pilgrimage was stamped out by the clergy after the Reformation of 1560. Even into my 1960s childhood, we had at least one primary schoolteacher who would speak of 'Papist superstitions'. But armed with a fly rod, if anybody local asked what I was doing, I could (and did) just say that I was on a poaching pilgrimage: peregrinating from loch to loch out on the moors and 'having a wee cast'. Given the nature of landlordism, it used to be, back in the days, that islanders who would take 'just one for the pot' had something of a Robin Hood persona. That is changing now with community land reform and local angling trusts. But it still made for a fun conversational gambit, as well giving theological metaphors and a bit of derring-do *en route*.

The book is framed around both an outer and an inner set of three 'carrier themes'. Those whose backgrounds are the arts, unlike mine in the sciences, may have another term for this. To me, it was just my way of organising the threads to weave a single narrative. The outer carriers were physical historical features in the landscape. These served as my pilgrim stopping stations on the way:

- The teampaill: ruined chapels or pre-Reformation 'temples'
- The tobraichean: holy or, in post-Reformation parlance, healing wells
- The bothan: beehive shieling huts once used in summer when the cattle were out on remote moors

So much for the outer. The inner carrier themes relate to how the book emerged as what I came to think of as an ecology of the imagination. My work has been influenced by deep ecological philosophy, eastern mystical thought, and the Ayrshire poet Kenneth White's writings: his 'poetry, geography – and a higher unity: geopoetics'.[5] Such a sense of higher unity and poetry in the widest sense invites the question: Do we merely have imaginations, or do we also move within a greater imagination? Could consciousness be a quality that permeates, and even gives rise to, ecology itself? Is the world an ongoing process – the 'Creation' as the creative product of divine imagination – in which we find ourselves located in space-time? My context during the pilgrimage was specific, but the thought itself is ancient. As the *Upanishads* of Vedic metaphysics have it: 'We should consider that in the inner world Brahman [God] is consciousness [...] and in the outer world Braham is space.'[6]

My carrier themes for inner exploration emerged as *God*, *war*, and the *faeries*. As one book reviewer wrote: 'It could sound jokey, but it isn't.'[7] *God*, because I wanted to reflect on both island organised religion and its underlying spirituality. Theologically, to press beyond the prevalent doctrine of penal substitutionary atonement that is predicated on God, as Calvin put it, 'armed for vengeance', and to deepen to a nonviolent theology. This, as a third-millennium Christianity whereby 'the cross absorbs the violence of the world'.[8] *War*, because the island's landscape and its social history slips back in time to apply a powerful focus on the political theology of our recent international conflicts. This, effected by reflecting, as I walked, on some of the first-hand accounts of conflict told to me by serving soldiers while guest-lecturing (on nonviolence) at military staff colleges, especially the UK Defence Academy, over the past couple of decades. *The faeries* – or rather, 'faerie' as a realm of consciousness – the lore of which permeates the island and remains in remnant, but still-just-present experience. On the walk, this found powerful geographical focus through the playwright J. M. Barrie's otherworldly study of war trauma, *Mary Rose* (1920), key scenes of which were situated at Loch Voshimid (Bhoisimid) on the Isle of Harris.

Imagination, faerie, and the carrying stream

The depth psychology of faerie may help provide context for my examples of mentoring. In Scottish Gaelic and wider Celtic settings, as well as in many other indigenous cultures (including fragments from an older England), the realm of faerie or its equivalents serves as shorthand for the 'Otherworld'. Such is the inner psychological world of myth, legend, the psychic, the spiritual, and ultimately – where it touches on the divine – the mystical.[9] Carl Jung called it the collective unconscious, while the Italian post-Jungian, Roberto Assagioli, observed it also has characteristics that might be described as the 'superconscious' of 'higher intuitions and inspirations – artistic, philosophical', and similar.[10] Given this, I would suggest that T. S. Eliot appears to work spiritually with faerie in *Four Quartets* (1943), especially in the rose garden of 'Burnt Norton' with its 'unheard music hidden in the shrubbery' and 'leaves were full of children', as well as in 'East Coker', keeping rhythm of the seasons with 'weak pipe and little drum / [...] dancing around the bonfire', ending when 'The dancers are all gone under the hill'.[11] Perhaps, also, there is an echo of faerie in 'Little Gidding':

> the children in the apple-tree
> Not known, because not looked for
> But heard, half-heard, in the stillness
> Between two waves of the sea.[12]

From such 'Mirth of those long since under earth / Nourishing the corn'[13] flows what the ethnographer Hamish Henderson described as the 'carrying stream'. In his last poem before his passing, he showed it as the ground of cultural renewal:

> Change elegy into hymn, remake it –
> Don't fail again.
> [...]
> Tomorrow, songs
> Will flow free again, and new voices
> Be borne on the carrying stream[14]

Timothy Neat, Henderson's biographer, says that the carrying stream is 'an old folk phrase' that Henderson used 'as a metaphor for the folklore process itself', folklore being in Henderson's words 'the proper study of mankind'.[15] Henderson's drift is far from isolated. Recently, a gathering of eleven 'rurally syndicated' women from the Highlands and Islands produced a remarkable collaborative essay on the human ecology of contemporary creativity, heritage, and community regeneration. Acknowledging Henderson's carrying stream, they state:

> This carrying is the continuum of Highlands and Islands traditions and practices nurtured, through times, as particular responses in specific environments. These practices express the critical and creative adaptivity of those who have been able and/or have chosen to stay here.[16]

In looking at Gaelic oral narrative, Michael Newton observes that 'speaking about the Otherworld may be a way of speaking about the creative process'.[17] Karen Ralls-MacLeod points to numerous examples in the literature where 'the overall impression is that of an unbroken line of musical performers [...] from the purely supernatural to the most mundane, with the originating and most powerful influences coming from the Otherworld'.[18] The medievalist John Carey, looking mainly at early Irish literature, connects Otherworld faerie narratives to scripture, finding there a remarkable 'imaginative reconciliation' in which the Otherworld inhabitants become 'guardian angels, the messengers of God'; this, as one of the texts has it, because 'they were faithful to the truth of nature'.[19] As the late John MacInnes summed up the Scottish Hebridean tradition:

> We could take the fairy knoll as *a metaphor of the imagination*, perhaps an equivalent of the modern concept of the Unconscious. From this shadowy realm comes the creative power of mankind. An old friend of mine use to say when he produced songs or legends that I did not realise he knew: 'Bha mi 's a' Chnoc o chunnaic mi thu' ('I was in the [fairy] Hill since I saw you'). And others had similar

vivid expressions. None of them was to be taken literally but there was a system of belief behind the expression.[20]

Here, 'metaphor' is spoken of from within a culture where the metaphorical can be perceived as more real than the literal. Nor are such worldviews only fossil remnants of the past. It is still just possible to have a conversation on the streets of Stornoway where biblical allusions bounce off one another. They linger at the fringes, a half-living tradition, that can comprise the sometimes-late-night conversations of poets and musicians. Expressed in literature, these views nod towards G. Gregory Smith's much-dissected quality of the 'Scottish Muse' that holds together, in bottled polar tension, 'a strange union of opposites': an 'antisyzygy' that generates potential difference (which is the physicists' formal name for voltage) and issues forth in knotwork braiding of 'the real and fantastic' and lands us 'in the fun of things thrown topsy-turvy, in the horns of elfland and the voices of the mountains'.[21]

By way of illustration: in 2021 I worked with SEALL (the rural performing arts promotor, whose Gaelic title means 'look') and Atlas Arts in the Isle of Skye to bring about the first full English bilingual publication of *Agus mar sin Car a' Mhuiltein / And So Somersault* by the Staffin poet Maoilios Caimbeul (Myles Campbell, b. 1944).[22] The reader here is tumbled into antisyzygy. In expressing a wild and haunting beauty, punctuated with humour and the occasional biblical allusion, the poet tells of William's night away in the *sithean*, the faerie hill. Having fallen from a horse on his way home from a wedding, he goes somersaulting through the torments and the ecstasies of the Otherworld until the faerie queen declares: 'You will accept it—accept the flood—accept the calmness—accept the otherworld people—and accept human beings.' And so somersault, and we land back in the glen where William's nonplussed wife is telling him to come on back home because the sheep are needing fed.

So it was that I sat in our house in Glasgow late one evening shortly before embarking on the pilgrimage. My journey book lay open on my knee. On page four: some mileages, map grid references (Saint Bridgit's Shieling, the Last Battle), and the times for the rising and the setting of the sun. On page three: a to-do list of such supplies as oatcakes, salt and pepper, and fishing flies (Stoat's Tail, Blue Charm, and Hairy Mary). But on pages one and two... In the wee small hours I had lain awake the night before, mind drifting through the in-between states the way minds do. Somebody had sent me pages from an Adam Nicolson book about the Shiants. A passage where a force had spooked him as he slept alone one night in the islands' solitary cottage. I thought too of the time that George MacLeod rose to pray early in the morning in Iona Abbey. He came running back out, or so it was said, overwhelmed by some dread presence. The deeper recesses of the psyche are not just all things bright and beautiful. And so, inscribed on pages one and two, like whistling in the dark, I laid out my intentions:

> I am going on this pilgrimage into the heart of the island, disguised as a poacher's pilgrimage: but really, it is a journey into the Otherworld, into the Hill, a seeking to be in the presence of the Devil, the Faeries, the dead and God .... Why the Devil? Because the Devil symbolises fear, and that is our greatest blockage to entering into the creative spiritual .... I have been reading Michael Newton's paper on creativity in Scottish Gaelic tradition. It is mind-blowing, and it is what I am about and request to deepen into [through] the come-what-may of the come-to-pass of facing it.

Mentoring in person: Catherine MacKinven

Ben Okri wrote: 'All true artists suspect that if the world really knew what they were doing they would be punished.'[23] Taking 'artists' in the widest sense, and especially when working in challenging ways within our own culture, we may indeed at times require to overcome a sense of transgression. It can help to have another person to guide us and affirm the legitimacy of what we are attempting. Indeed, this goes deeper than mere affirmation. A stronger word than 'affirmation' is 'blessing'. Specifically, blessing that legitimises the opening or widening of channels from the collective carrying stream. This takes us beyond mentoring as more ordinary forms of training and instruction, such as tips on where to cross a river or stylistic points in writing. I think of it as meta-mentoring: that which helps lead out another's soul and does so, in a legitimising way that gives expression to the spiritual. By 'the spiritual' in this context, I mean the inner meaning, as Rabbi Abraham Heschel said: 'God is the meaning beyond all mystery.'[24]

Several mentors make an appearance in *Poacher's Pilgrimage*. Here I will confine my focus to one whose role was major in the writing. There is an intimacy here that I find a little embarrassing to share, but I do so, thinking: 'How else do we share the meaning of mentoring?' In 2006, I received a lovely card and letter from an elderly woman, Catherine MacKinven, who lived laterally in Kinlochiel. A native Gaelic speaker, a Knapdale MacKinven of Argyll, she had been a lady of the manse earlier in life. She had heard me speak on *Soil and Soul* in the *Aos Dana* book festival at Sabhal Mòr Ostaig in the Isle of Skye that year and took thereafter to corresponding regularly by post or email. As our friendship developed, she would often read what I had just drafted. She would send back sheafs of photocopied material from Gaelic tradition along with her remarks, commentaries, and sometimes her own translations. I do not have the Gaelic, but she wanted to affirm and support me in deepening my feeling for the culture's attitude of mind. Over the seven years to October 2014, she sent me 503 emails and sufficient letters and papers to fill a couple of lever-arch box files. I see from my computer files that I wrote about the same number of emails in reply. Not for nothing is she named in *Poacher's* dedication as 'tradition bearer, dear mentor'. She also features in the acknowledgements where I describe how 'at times, what will come through as my voice is really hers behind me'. Not just the 'me' but the 'we'.

On 1 June 2011, she took it on herself to bus down from Fort William. She would spend a night at our place in Glasgow, and we would talk through the first draft of *Poacher's*. The following extracts from our emails from around that date will give a feeling for the nature of the mentoring relationship.

26 May (six days before she arrived, and we were confirming travel) I ended with an aside:

> Was very tired and went and slept. Woke up dreaming that you were explaining some point of Gaelic poetry to me.

Her reply the next day:

> Angus Patrick's column in the WHFP [West Highland Free Press] is dynamite this week—real and serious concerns about the exploitation and colonisation of Gaelic. Dreaming about Gaelic is good —remember the Hugh MacNeilage quote: 'There were things he would say in Gaelic that he would never think to say in English … as though he had a secret knowledge that only existed in Gaelic and which he could only reveal to those whom he trusted and knew the language … the language was a key to something beyond the language.' See you on Wed. Please don't slave over a hot stove—I like simple food!

Me, same day:

> Last night I went back to Martin Martin on N. Rona. Quite remarkable stuff. I will need to weave some of it in … the way he talks of the 'sincere love' of those people, and their huge generosity.

She, 30 May:

> Have booked on the 11:00 from here on Wed, arrives Glasgow 2:04 … Lorries are rumbling up and down the road, unloading stones into Mallaig harbour—marina for the leisure boat market. The fishermen's mission is closing, and local folk with wee boats won't be able to afford the harbour dues for the marina. See you Wed. Cath.

Me, same day:

> I was re-reading [the manuscript] last night and can see I'm going to have to lose most of the early parts. Too much foreshadowing what emerges later. Also, need to work lightness into the text. Be good to discuss with you.

Cath insisted she would only stay one night in Glasgow and then hurry back, saying that she could not leave her cat alone for more than two days with no-one in the house. I quipped, 'It's just a cat!' She quietly let it pass, but I sensed her disappointment.

At a peak point in our discussions after her arrival on 1 June, Cath took me viscerally to task. I vividly recall the moment. She told me that I was not to be inhibited in what I was trying to write about. She fixed me with her eyes and said *'You are a bard, Alastair'* and repeated it. She said that I should not hold back from stepping into what was being called for. I was not to let myself be inhibited by self-doubt or a 'what-might-people-think?' reserve if I let go into the depth of register sometimes required. It felt like an initiation, the touch of blessing.

Me, 3 June:

> I am very grateful [for your visit] ... we were able to get into some deep space that I found helpful both in the specifics and the generality of what you were saying. It was a reassurance that I am on the right tracks, not overstepping with the bardic voice and as such, can relax the academic voice a little ... I am wrestling with whether or not there is real substance in the faerie material, or whether the wind passes and it all turns to dust ... but I must set to work!

She, 6 June:

> I really, really enjoyed my visit to Govan. What a wonderful atmosphere there is in the Galgael ... Did you get a chance to talk to Finlay

> [Dr MacLeod of Shawbost] about the faeries? I've posted you the School of Scottish Studies version of Uamh an Oir [Cave of Gold]. I did quite a lot of research on this—and am still puzzled, and intrigued. Alan Bruford wrote an article about where the story is found (that's all over), but didn't, like so many of his generation, venture into meanings, analysis, *imagination*. Also put in note on Gaelic bible. It's raining again in FW—cold rain. All the best, Cath.

She, later the same morning, perhaps meant to embolden:

> Bardic immunity—v. useful. Rev Roddy Macleod told me a story about a case in Lochmaddy—poaching or something not too serious. The sheriff did the your-name bit: 'You are Donald Iain MacDonald' ... 3 times, no response—till he got cross and snapped 'Och, Sheonaidh, a' Bhaird, won't you answer?' Well, that was it—case dismissed. Apparently if you are proclaimed as a bard or recognised as a bard, you have bardic immunity! Know any lawyers who can confirm this? Cath.

In the autumn of 2013, Cath assisted me in running a week themed *The Pilgrimage of Life* at Iona Abbey. I taught in the mornings, and she offered an optional beginners' class in Gaelic some afternoons. It had been a joyous double act, and we had been invited to repeat it again in September 2014. Cath was excited at the prospect. Early that summer, she went back to the island, and emailed on returning. The message, sent 11 July 2014, ended cheerily enough: 'My retreat to Iona was great. Have acquired CD of Vatersay Boys to blooter out traffic noise! all the best, Cath.'

Those are her last words in my files. Email number 503, and I ran *The Pilgrimage of Life* alone with just the regular abbey staff support. She had walked on faster than our pace. She loved and used the old Highland expression – 'If we're spared' – but this time, time had run its course.

Before her passing on 12 October, I visited her in the Fort William hospital. The cancer was invasively incisive. We knew that that was that, and this was it. She told me of her heartbreak: that just a week before she had been taken in for palliative care, her cat had died. It may have been a mercy under the circumstances, but frankly, I had never got it with the cat. Truth was, I did not 'know' cats at the time. Some eight months later, a stray turned up outside our house. It howled and howled and howled for several weeks out in the garden. It slept on the kitchen window ledge, tail hanging down over the edge and dampening in the rain. One day, we had left the back door open and came in to find it sitting in the armchair. We knew then we had to let her in to stay.

Cath's ashes now lie scatted on Iona. Through dear Mabelle, our much-loved cat, I humbly make my posthumous amends. And from somewhere out beyond Columba's Bay, Cath cackles through the ether at such feline servitude. No more by email but with a twinkling eye.

Mentoring in vision: the Reverend Kenneth Macleod

Notice what's just happened there. If I have succeeded in the telling, the cat has helped to lead us into a greater mode of seeing. It is no longer just Cath and her pet, but their ground of being that has edged open. In Gaelic ontology, there is a word, 'cùram'. Normally it just means 'care', but it also has a double meaning for a depth of faith that reveals the world and life transfigured. Here we glimpse the 'meta' as that which is 'behind' or 'beyond' the 'physical': the metaphysical as the spiritual realm.

Often when I go back to Leurbost and thereabouts in Lewis, I'll hear that old so-and-so has died. Friends in the village will say sorrowfully: 'There'll soon be no more left of them.' I've started to catch and bounce that back. There will be no more left, I will say, unless *we* pick up their baton. *Pace* Hamish, 'and new voices / be borne on the carrying stream.' This requires both depth of care and a kind of vision of cultural continuity: 'dualchas' as it's called in Gaelic.

By 'vision', I do not mean 'visions' in the sense of hallucinations. I mean a transiently increased depth of the field of consciousness. A visionary 'seeing' from immersion in an expanded flow of inner life, typically at times of high emotional intensity or when enraptured in the Muse. I touch on vision at several points in *Poacher's*. In the second chapter, I weave into my walking narrative reflection on an incident that took place some years earlier. My wife Vérène and I had been visiting the Isle of Gigha. We were standing inside the little Church of Scotland at a magnificent stained-glass window dedicated to the island's onetime minister, the tradition-bearer Kenneth Macleod of Eigg. Macleod died in 1955, the year that I was born; and the church stands on Cnocan a' Chiuil, the Hill of Music: in other words, a faerie hill. It lauds him with the triptych epitaph – 'preacher, pastor, poet' – and a Gaelic proverb: 'Thig crìoch air an t-saoghal / Ach mairidh gaol is ceòl' (*'The world will come to an end / But love and music will endure'*).[25] Saint Patrick confers blessing. Saint Columba's on his *immram* (or pilgrim sea voyage) to Iona. And tenderly, Brìghde, Saint Bride, the Shepherdess of the Flocks and foster mother of Christ, cherishes a lamb.

As we gazed, a sudden burst of sunshine quickened the window into life. I do not cry easily, but I inexplicably burst into tears. Tears equally of tragedy and joy. Tears of brokenheartedness at all that has been lost. Yet tears of joy at the wellspring that is still present. Vérène was alarmed. She thought that something was happening to me; and for a few fleeting moments, I wrestled in embarrassment to regain composure. Later, I would write that it was as if 'a silver pool had spilled and overwhelmed my disconsolation, lifting it to rapture'.[26] I had similar experiences before, notably when launching the original Isle of Eigg Trust and, later, during an opening ritual led by an Irish nun at a groundbreaking International Transpersonal Association conference in Ireland, 1994, on the theme: 'Toward Earth Community: Ecology, Native Wisdom and Spirituality'.[27] In both those instances, long before I had heard of 'the carrying stream', the silver stream was made up of the voices of the old people. Importantly, and this is where the mentoring comes in, the vision at the window in Gigha affirmed me in a sense of calling to as-yet unspecified work ahead. With hindsight, I would see *Poacher's* as a fulfilment – an experience that felt as if a touch of blessing from the realm of saints. Not least amongst them, the dear Reverend Kenneth, whose mother taught him on her knee the meaning of the lark's song: 'Often, often, often, / Goes Christ in the stranger's guise.'[28]

Mentoring in dream: J. M. Barrie

Whereas visionary states of transiently heightened consciousness take place in the waking state, a dream comes from the depths of the unconscious during sleep. I find that when I write a book, the prolonged intensity of immersion often irrupts into my dream life. Reading the motifs can function as a form of mentoring from within.[29] Several such dreams helped to spur on and shape *Poacher's Pilgrimage*. One of these, involving a traditionalist Hebridean church congregation and the blue mountain hare, is recounted in the book. But being of the writing, not the walk, I have hidden it away in the 'acknowledgements' at the back for the eyes of only the most persevering of readers.[30] The dream that I will share here involved the playwright J. M. Barrie (1860–1937). Not least with *Peter Pan* (1904, 1911), Barrie did more than any other writer to rehabilitate the faeries – or a version thereof – back into the early twentieth-century British psyche.

My walk had led me to a remote beehive dwelling at an evocative spot called Clàr Beag on the Harris-Lewis boundary. From there, I had walked down to the coast, picking up the river that flows out of a North Harris loch, called Voshimid. Only while writing *Poacher's* did I come fully to realise Voshimid's significance. It had been the location for key scenes in Barrie's 1920 psychodrama *Mary Rose,* a play that (in my view) explores childhood trauma in the immediate aftermath of the First World War when he and so many of his audience had lost loved ones.[31] Barrie knew the Isle of Harris because he had leased Amhuinnsuidh Castle for a fishing holiday with his friends over the summer of 1912. Today, the rocky outcrop in the loch, just sixty feet across and with a few scrubby trees, is known as Mary Rose Island.

Mary Rose is a little English girl whose family went to Harris for a holiday. Her father, Mr Morland, is a gentleman of the upright and uptight manners of his era. While fishing for sea trout, he drops her off on 'the Island that Likes to be Visited' and goes off in the boat. As Mary Rose sits and sketches by a rowan tree, an old legend reactivates. Carried away in a faerie wind, she reappears twenty days later but with no conscious memory of the lapse in time. Back home, she grows up and marries Simon 'Sobersides' Blake, a young naval officer, but her psychological development remains arrested in a childlike state. She begs Simon to take her back to Harris for their honeymoon. There they set out fishing on Loch Voshimid with Cameron, the ghillie. Simon is so engrossed in his distinguished naval career that when they picnic on the island, he has even forgotten how to make love. While he and Cameron ready to depart after the picnic, the faerie wind comes back and Mary Rose is off again. From here, the play glides to and fro between the worlds. Mary Rose drifts as a lonely ghost until, in the final act, her runaway son comes back to their now-abandoned home after the War, a demobbed ANZAC soldier. His love sets free her troubled soul. The faerie call returns, the music this time rises to a pitch, celestial, and she journeys on to heaven.

God, war, and the faeries! It could almost be mistaken for kailyard. But in a 1938 lecture, Sir Walter Langdon-Brown, the Regius Professor of Medicine at Cambridge, described the play as 'one of the completest expositions of the working of the unconscious mind to be found in contemporary literature'.[32] Alfred Hitchcock grumbled that his backers never let him make the movie. In my view, a more likely explanation is that the screenplay he commissioned underwhelmed them.[33] He attributed the alleged veto to their fancying that audiences were not yet ready for such 'irrational' and 'twilight-zone' material.[34] *Mary Rose* remains a movie waiting to be made – perhaps not as an Americanised ghost story, as in Vincent Agazzi-Morrone's 2016 production,[35] but about a battle-weary soldier from a modern war, wandering off into the Hebridean moors armed only with her fishing rod.

In a curious way, the legend that Barrie created (or was captivated by) in *Mary Rose* became entwined with the real people who lived, and still live, in Harris. Cameron, the younger ghillie in the play, is described in the stage directions as 'not specially impressive until you question him about the universe'.[36] After reading my discussion of the play in *Poacher's Pilgrimage*, David Cameron, the proprietor of the Harris Garage and a leading figure in the island's land reform, sent me an undated note typed by his late father, who had acquired a typewriter in his nineties.[37] It concerns David's paternal uncle, the physician Dr David Rose Cameron (1896–1995), and either copies what looks like a local newspaper snippet, or authors such a piece as if written by a third-party observer. It would be typical of the kind of local news item that the *Stornoway Gazette* would have run from local contributors in the past:

> Recently Harris had a visit from an interesting family. Dr Cameron, York (brother of Tom Cameron, the Harris hotel) enjoyed a week in Harris.
>
> Dr Cameron was in Sir E. Scott [School], Tarbert before going on to Dollar Academy and St Andrews University. During the 1913 [*sic*] holiday Dr Cameron acted as engineer on a launch chartered by J. M. Barrie who had the let of Amhuinnsuidh Castle. At the end of the season, Sir James told Dr Cameron he would portray him in a book or play. Hence the Ghillie in the well-known play *Mary Rose*.
>
> 1914 war started and Dr Cameron like so many went into the army. He was sent to Salonika but R.F.C. called and the Doctor was sent to Egypt to train then to France where he was shot down by a German plane ending up in the notorious prison camp of Holamindon [Holzminden].
>
> The year ending [the First World War], Barrie was made rector of St Andrews University where Dr Cameron was back doing medicine. The summer at Amhuinnsuidh was recalled by both. Sir James scratched his initials on a pane of glass in the Hotel dining room window which is still there.

Corroboration of the Barrie-Cameron connection is in Angus Duncan's history of Scarp.[38] Duncan recounts that Amhuinnsuidh Castle was then served by the proprietor's yacht, a small steamer used for daily shopping trips, and 'a small steam launch which looked odd with its short funnel'. Barrie's six weeks in the summer of 1912 included the company of authors Anthony Hope (Hawkins), E. V. Lucas, and A. E. W. Mason. Duncan also cites a letter he received in 1966 from the youngest of the five Llewelyn Davies boys whom Barrie adopted, Nicholas. This vividly recalls the moment when the lad and Barrie had gone up to Loch Voshimid – probably the playwright's only visit – and as they looked across to what is now Mary Rose Island, Barrie recalled 'the old [Scandinavian] legend' of the time-warp-vanishing Father Anselm, told to him by Nansen, the Norwegian explorer.[39]

It may seem odd that David Rose Cameron might have been the boat's 'engineer' (operator) when he would have been only around sixteen at the time, but I had my first summer job as a ghillie in school holidays at the age of fourteen, and in those days, boys were taught such skills young. Indeed, a medical obituary tells that David Rose Cameron's father was himself an engineer turned hotelier (at the Harris Hotel, where Barrie's signature is now framed in the lobby), and his mother, a sea captain's daughter.[40]

This acquaintance formed on Barrie's visit to Harris, and the enfolding of real people into the play, even had a curious influence on my own family's connection to the island. In *Poacher's Pilgrimage*, I tell how my mother, who was English, was deeply moved by 'the island that likes to be visited' when she saw *Mary Rose* in the Birmingham Rep as a student nurse, probably in the 1950 season.[41] When my Scottish father saw a vacancy for the North Lochs medical practice advertised in the British Medical Journal, she felt moved with an irrational degree of emotion to persuade him to apply. Perhaps it was befitting, as I worked through my notes in the weeks following the pilgrimage, that my thoughts emerging into consciousness would turn toward *Mary Rose* and her author. Here, then, is a lightly edited version of what I set down of the dream while writing *Poacher's Pilgrimage*:

> The third big dream came on the eve of summer's solstice. I'd sat up late into the evening. It was a month after I'd got back home, and I was now reading *Mary Rose*. I was re-living the walk as I did so, reflecting on war trauma and what soldiers have said about the realities of conflict. The last of the summer's long daylight was squeezing through our sitting room window. I was finding Barrie's play incredibly moving and a thought came to me about its meaning: 'The dead need to be freed to be dead; the living, too, need to be freed from beyond death.'
>
> Writing it down, I then looked at it [and] thought how cryptic it was. I felt embarrassed by my own abstruseness, and added in my

notebook: 'Not sure what I am saying.' What does it mean that the dead might free the living? How could that happen?

I went to bed, and in the small hours of the morning ... there I am ... back at the Clàr Beag double beehive dwelling on that little island of ground between the braiding river's strands ... and I am with Barrie. We're the closest of friends, and I'm desperately helping him to build *the Supergun*. Everything depends upon the Supergun. That alone will decide the war.

Barrie is exactly as he is in the biographical descriptions I've been reading ... the photographs inside the books ... Johnny Depp's performance in *Finding Neverland* ... in fact, he's more real than all of these, because this is *the real* J. M. Barrie; and his gun is huge, mounted on a bed of gravel in the stream, right there beside the Clàr Beag beehive bothan. It's a Nelson's column of black cast iron, pitched at a forty-five-degree trajectory, ready to fire up over the looming mountains of Harris and to land somewhere far down to the sou'-sou'-east.

For this is the decisive bullet. This will stop the war. All war. And he's dashing about around the corbelled stone hut. He's getting this and that, adjusting the gun's range-finding wheels and ratchets, readying it for firing.

He's quite a pixie of a man. In real life, as a teenager his growth had stopped when he was only five feet tall. As he rushes here and there, he's flashing me the occasional smile, making sure I'm staying with him in the all-important project, anxious at the enormity of what must succeed. And his face is burning with intelligence. It's the compassion in his eyes that I most notice. An imploring love, beseeching me to help him in the task he had at hand.

I know that he knows that he's tuned in with a process that runs so much deeper than himself. There, for all his peccadilloes, is the prophetic depth of J. M. Barrie's mission to the world. And we? We, of a world so suave, urbane, and superior to his supposed Crimes of Kailyard in his writing? We thought it just about the faeries. We didn't know what faerie really meant. We didn't know in his tradition, in our tradition—a man from Kirriemuir for goodness' sake—the meaning of the carrying stream.

Barrie's Supergun is like a cross between a medieval cannon and Saddam Hussein's 'doomsday gun' 'Big Babylon' of Project Babylon. Work came to an end on this latter-day Tower of Babel, as it were, at Teesport Docks in April 1990. British customs officials intercepted the barrel and its confiscated parts – two huge steel pipes bolted together and disguised as high-pressure components for the petrochemicals industry – now form part of the Royal Armouries' permanent collection at Fort Nelson, Hampshire.[42] In my dream:

> Barrie grows increasingly frantic. To fire the gun, he needs to get some nitric acid. That's what you mix with glycerine for making nitroglycerine. I know the island. That's why he's pleading that I help him. It's down to me. I'm surging with anxiety and dredging through my knowledge banks.
>
> 'Maybe from the school labs?' I suggest. 'Or a quarry, where they mix their own explosives?' I can't come up with anything more substantial. But I'm determined not to let him down. And then I wake up.

In Sigmund Freud's view, 'The interpretation of dreams is the royal road to a knowledge of the unconscious activities of the mind'.[43] But this one calls out less for Freud than Jung. Here was what I think of as a 'big dream' – one that, on awakening, leaves a sense of being meant for more than me alone. With such, I will look at what its motifs symbolise to me. I will dwell back into it, a kind of 'scrying' of my own and, perhaps, collective currents in the unconscious. Over several hours and even days, a meaning usually starts to crystallise.

Several themes stood out here. The gun's range and direction of trajectory. Its situation in a border zone, a place so redolent in social history. There was that pixie quality in Barrie's mood that came straight from out the faerie hill. And most of all the backdrop of war trauma. Not just in *Mary*

Rose, but also at the University of St Andrews, in May 1922, when Barrie warned the students in his Rectorial Address to learn the lessons of the Great War, otherwise they would soon again be 'doddering down some brimstone path'.[44]

Then there was the nitroglycerine. What were my associations there? In 1979 in Papua New Guinea, I documented a village sorcerer whose list of ways to harm included nitric acid taken from the school science lab.[45] My father knew a boy at school who had blown the bathroom window out experimenting. And when I was a student in the summer of 1974, I had a labouring job with the renowned Stornoway builder, Willie 'Bucach'. One day, as we all packed into the back of the Land Rover when putting in the Breasclete water main, several boxes of gelignite for blasting lay at our feet. The sticks were out of date. 'Sweaty jelly' they called it, a glistening dew of extruded nitroglycerine. 'Slow down! Slow down!' shouted the gaffer, as we bounced over a bump, 'or you'll have us blown to kingdom come'. Alfred Nobel stabilised nitroglycerine, first inventing Dynamite then gelignite, but was so upset to be associated with his explosives' use in war that he left most of his fortune for the Nobel Peace and other prizes. And in another healing twist by way of shifting war to peace: nitroglycerine dilates the arteries. It is given as a medicine to help the blood to reach the heart.

As I woke up in this swirl of loose associations, the meaning of the dream spread out before me. It came like a voice in my head with the phrase: 'The bullet in the Supergun is for the gun of love'. The image has a precedent. In his great poem 'Hallaig', Sorley MacLean (1911–1996) portrays the ghosts of his ancestors who were evicted on Raasay off Skye in the 1850s Highland Clearances. The enigmatic ending has time itself – its trials and tribulations – depicted as a deer that grazes round the ruins. It falls before the marksman's bullet, fired 'from the Gun of Love'.[46] And so, in fulness of *apocatastasis* – 'the times of restitution of all things'[47] – we sense that everything returns at last into the arms of love.

The Isle of Skye scholar Iain MacKinnon has drawn my attention to an earlier precedent for MacLean's imagery. In *The Men of Skye*, a 1902 study of the island's evangelical lay preachers, Roderick MacCowan tells of Norman MacLeod (Tormad Saighdear) of Bracadale. As a soldier back from Egypt where he had been fighting in the Napoleonic wars, he heard a sermon 'that was blessed to him' from the fabled Dr MacDonald of Ferintosh:

> He was walking one day on the street in Edinburgh, when a word came to him, 'Ceannich Biobull' (Buy a Bible). He obeyed the voice, and from this dates the commencement of his awakening to a sense that he was a lost sinner. [...] Afterwards, in telling freely his experiences to some of the Lord's people in Skye, he would say: 'It was in Edinburgh I was struck with the bullet of love.'[48]

And so, the cross absorbs the violence of the world. Barrie's dream helped me constellate what *Poacher's Pilgrimage* came to be about. It condensed many of the main elements: war, trauma, and the gun's trajectory to the far sou'-sou'-east. Perhaps to London and its empire. Perhaps a Babylon beyond. Perhaps the shadow in us all. Long after I ceased walking, the pilgrimage voyaged on into a deepening spirituality – not, I hope, just individually, but if I might so put it, as a cultural psychotherapy.[49]

For J. M. Barrie's spirit is not dead. The greater part of what a person is, is never born. Barrie remains present in my *Haus Tumbuna,* as they would say in Papua New Guinea. The Spirit House, that is tended up the back of my mind. There, with Cath, the Reverend Kenneth, and all the other mentor ancestors. Surrounded, not by reliquary bones or ceremonial masks, but with a bullet: fired by medicine for the healing of the human heart.

Honey of the carrying stream

What binds together our three modes of mentoring – the personal, the visionary, and the dream – is my suggestion of a common inner source: the carrying stream as the wellspring of creative process in the unconscious. This carries us beyond our small selves into something greater, from the personal into the transpersonal. True poetry is of the 'thine' and not 'that's mine'. Celtic cultures are not alone in this. Plato, for example, said the poets tell us, '[t]hat the melodies they bring are gathered from rills that run with honey, out of glens and gardens of the Muses, and they bring them as the bees do honey'. Furthermore – and Cath would have loved this – he has

Socrates after waxing so lyrical pull the flyting makars down a peg, adding: 'And to prove this the deity on purpose sang the loveliest of all lyrics through the most miserable poet.'[50]

As the cultural critic Lewis Hyde has written, 'The gift must always move'.[51] If stopped, the flow stagnates and turns to toxin. The Apache philosopher Viola Cordova tells of being a student in a class about the philosophy of time. The professor insisted she should answer questions in the 'I' and not the 'we'. 'Who is this "we"?' she petulantly demanded, pointing out that there was only one Viola sitting in the chair. Cordova said that she says 'we' to honour the shared notions in her thinking. 'I believe,' she answered, 'that there are no self-made persons. There are only those who cannot (or refuse to) acknowledge their debts.'[52]

Gratitude completes the cycles of grace. Only then can the gift keep giving life. When we write, or paint, or play music, writes Brenda Ueland, we express 'the purpose of existence [...] to discover truth and beauty and [...] share it with others'.[53] Whilst writing is a solitary act, this turns it into more than just solipsism. It is through such relationality that mentoring can find a way in. As the adage has it: 'When the student is ready the teacher arrives.'[54] People sometimes ask me where and how. I might suggest that they look out receptive contexts. Perhaps join a writing or faith group, go on a guided retreat, give service in community, and get involved with nature. Processes like counselling and therapy, journalling and recording dreams, and work with music or crafts can also give the settings for a mind that is set receptively. But more than that, I will maybe pose an age-old question: 'What seek ye?'[55] What do you desire? And why? And to serve what?

Jung had a special name for self-realisation, the process of becoming progressively more real to life and to oneself. He said, 'I use the term *individuation* to denote the process by which a person becomes "in-dividual", that is a separate, indivisible unity or "whole".'[56] Separate, that is, from being drawn along unconsciously in the consensus trance of familial and cultural norms. Such individuation is not to be confused with egocentric individualism. Rather it means, he said, 'the better and more complete fulfilment of collective qualities'. As the ego becomes grounded in the greater self, atman, or soul, we become less and less the subject of blind unconscious forces, and more and more equipped to see and serve that which gives life.[57]

This calls us into knowing not just the 'me', nor even just the 'we', but to edging ever closer towards Rabbi Heschel's 'meaning beyond all mystery'. Neither is it only individuals that can individuate, but whole communities and even those writ large, as nations. For such is where the carrying stream flows on to.[58] In the biblical imagery, it flows out from underneath the threshold of the temple, watering the Tree of Life on both sides of its banks. Its leaves are for 'the healing of the nations' – those, as were scattered in the hubris of the world's first warrior, Nimrod at the Tower of Babel.[59]

The healing that is held out here is for the nations, plural, in their richness of diversity, in their Pentecostal mutuality. Such nationalism is internationalism. 'Thy kingdom come' for a' that, even in the face of apocalyptic wars, novel coronavirus, and relentless climate change. And it is Barrie's eyes that linger with me. Their intelligence. Their beseeching. Their compassion, as he sets the sights and readies to fire the supergun of love.

Endnotes

1. Nan MacKinnon, qtd in Barbara McDermitt, 'Nan MacKinnon (1903–1982)', *Tocher*, 6.38 (1983), pp. 2–11 (pp. 9–10).
2. Alastair McIntosh, *Poacher's Pilgrimage: An Island Journey* (Edinburgh: Birlinn, 2016); *Island Spirituality: Spiritual Values of Lewis and Harris* (Kershader: The Islands Book Trust, 2013). The Feb. 2023 new edition of *Poacher's* is now subtitled: *A Journey into Land and Soul*. www.alastairmcintosh.com/articles/2013-Island-Spirituality-by-Alastair-McIntosh.pdf
3. Alastair McIntosh, *Soil and Soul: People versus Corporate Power* (London: Aurum, 2001).
4. Calvert Watkins (ed.), *The American Heritage Dictionary of Indo-European Roots*, 3rd edn (San Diego: Harcourt, 2011), p. 56; see also Douglas Harper (ed.), 'Etymology of *men-', *Online Etymology Dictionary* www.etymonline.com/word/*men-
5. Kenneth White, 'Elements of Geopoetics', *Edinburgh Review* 88 (1992), pp. 163–81.
6. Juan Mascaró (trans.), 'Chandogya Upanishad', in *The Upanishads* (London: Penguin Classics, 1965), p. 115.
7. Sue Weaver, 'Book Review: Poacher's Pilgrimage', *Voice for Arran* 73 (April 2017) voiceforarran.com/old_issues/index2017_04mag73.shtml
8. John Calvin, *Institutes of the Christian Religion*, trans. Henry Beveridge (Edinburgh: Calvin Translation Society, 1845–1846; repr. Grand Rapids: Christian Classics Ethereal Library, n.d.), 2:16:1 and *Poacher's*, pp. 331–33. The line about the cross was an addition to the 2018 paperback edition, p. 333. Only later did what I was trying to describe crystallise so crisply.
9. Ronald Black (ed.), *The Gaelic Otherworld* (Edinburgh: Birlinn, 2005).
10. Roberto Assagioli, *Psychosynthesis* (Lonon: Turnstone, 1975), p. 17.
11. T. S. Eliot, *Four Quartets* (London: Faber, 1959), 'Burnt Norton', ll. 27, 40; 'East Coker', ll. 27–28, 100.
12. Eliot, 'Little Gidding', ll. 248–51.
13. Eliot, 'East Coker', ll. 38–39.
14. Hamish Henderson, 'Under the Earth I Go', qtd in Timothy Neat, 'Hamish Henderson – the Art and Politics of a Folklorist', in *The Carrying Stream Flows On*, ed. Bob Chambers (Kershader: The Islands Book Trust, 2013), p. 53.
15. Neat, *op. cit.*, p. 46.
16. 'The Carrying Stream: Towards A Plurality of Possibilities', *Enough*, 3 June 2021 www.enough.scot/2021/06/03/the-carrying-stream-towards-a-plurality-of-possibilities/
17. Michael Newton, '*Bha mi 's a' chnoc*: Creativity in Scottish Gaelic Tradition', *Proceedings of the Harvard Celtic Colloquium* 18/19 (1998, 1999), pp. 312–39.
18. Karen Ralls-MacLeod, *Music and the Celtic Otherworld* (Edinburgh: Polygon, 2000), p. 47.
19. John Carey, *A Single Ray of the Sun: Religious Speculation in Early Ireland* (Andover and Aberystwyth: Celtic Studies Publications, 1999), pp. 12, 38.
20. John MacInnes, 'Looking at Legends of the Supernatural', in Michael Newton (ed.), *Dùthchas Nan Gàidheal: Selected Essays of John MacInnes* (Edinburgh: Birlinn, 2006), pp. 459–76, my italics on the English but both styles of parentheses are his.
21. G. Gregory Smith (on the Caledonian antisyzygy), *Scottish Literature: Character & Influence* (London: Macmillan, 1919), pp. 19–20.
22. Maoilios Caimbeul, *Agus mar sin Car a' Mhuiltein / And So Somersault* (Portree: Atlas Arts, 2021), a limited edition of 100 poetry pamphlets in Gaelic about a night in the

faerie hill, with the author's own parallel English translation and an introduction by Alastair McIntosh, Catherine MacPhee and Iain MacKinnon, launched at the Isle of Skye SEALL Festival 2021, curated by Sara Bain. Podcast of the reading and panel discussion: www.seall.co.uk/feasgar-am-measg-nan-sithichean-a-night-among-the-faeries/ and PDF of pamphlet: www.alastairmcintosh.com/articles/2021-And-So-Somersault-Caimbeul.pdf

23 Ben Okri, *A Way of Being Free* (London: Phoenix, 1998), p. 63.
24 Susannah Heschel (ed.), *Abraham Joshua Heschel: Essential Writings* (Maryknoll: Orbis, 2011), p. 164.
25 'Gigha and Cara Parish Church', *Isle of Gigha* www.gigha.org.uk/Church. For a photograph of the window, see: The Carlisle Kid, 'NR6448: Gigha & Cara Parish Church – Windows – (4)', *Geograph* www.geograph.org.uk/photo/2995043
26 *Poacher's*, pp. 39–40.
27 For which, see respectively, *Soil and Soul*, pp. 185–86, and 'Community, Spirit, Place: a Reviving Celtic Shamanism', *The Trumpeter: Journal of Ecosophy* 13.3 (1996), pp. 111–20: trumpeter.athabascau.ca/index.php/trumpet/article/view/250/365. The *Ecosophy* (deep ecology) paper was drafted two years before I started writing *Soil and Soul* and served as a template.
28 Kenneth Macleod, 'Rune of Hospitality', in *The Road to the Isles* (London: Adam & Charles Black, 1927), p. 25. His maternal source is specified in his 'Two Celtic Runes', *The Celtic Review* 7.25 (1911), pp. 50–51.
29 See examples in *Soil and Soul* with the dream of the returning salmon (pp. 224–25), and in *Riders on the Storm* with dreams both of an activist being assassinated and of helping people to cross a flooded river (pp. 126–27).
30 *Poacher's*, pp. 361–62.
31 J. M. Barrie, *Mary Rose* (London: Hodder & Stoughton, 1925). For further analysis of *Mary Rose* in relation to Barrie's other writings, see Andrew Birkin, *J. M. Barrie and the Lost Boys: The Real Story Behind Peter Pan* New Haven and London: Yale University Press, 2010); R. D. S. Jack, *The Road to Neverland: A Reassessment of J M Barrie's Dramatic Art*, 2nd edn (Glasgow: humming earth, 2010); Valentina Bold and Andrew Nash (eds), *Gateway to the Modern: Resituating J. M. Barrie*, Occasional Papers 18 (Glasgow: Scottish Literature International, 2014). For spiritual analysis, see John Patrick Pazdziora, 'The Absence of God in J. M. Barrie's Post-War Writings: Mary Rose (1920) and Courage (1922)', *Religions* 2022, 13(8), 706 doi.org/10.3390/rel13080706
32 Walter Langdon-Brown, 'Myth, Phantasy, and Mary Rose', in *Thus We Are Men* (London: Kegan Paul, 1938), pp. 123–51.
33 Jay Presson Allen, *Mary Rose: Screenplay* (1964), WritingWithHitchcock.com www.stevenderosa.com/writingwithhitchcock/scripts/mary_rose.pdf
34 Francois Truffaut, *Hitchcock: A Definitive Study of Alfred Hitchcock* (New York: Simon and Schuster, 1985), pp. 307–09; Tony Lee Moral, 'Mary Rose', in *Hitchcock and the Making of Marnie*, rev edn (Scarecrow Press, Lanham, 2013). Chapter 'Mary Rose', pp. 197–221 (this chapter is not in the earlier edition).
35 *Mary Rose*, dir. Vincent Agazzi-Morrone (Castle Hill Productions, 2016); '"Mary Rose … A Ghost Story" Feature Film', www.youtube.com/watch?v=jJ8x0mQy_Ak [accessed 23 May 2022].
36 Barrie, p. 66.

37 David Cameron, pers. comm. 28 Nov 2016, and subsequent emails.
38 Angus Duncan (ed.), *Hebridean Island: Memories of Scarp* (East Linton: Tuckwell Press, 1995), pp. 150–53, 155, 200–01.
39 Cf. *Poacher's*, pp. 216–17.
40 'David Rose Cameron', *Royal College of Physicians* history.rcplondon.ac.uk/inspiring-physicians/david-rose-cameron.
41 *Poacher's*, p. 102.
42 William Park, 'The tragic tale of Saddam Hussein's "supergun"', BBC Future, 18 March 2016 bbc.in/34qylQq. Babel is the Hebrew name for Babylon.
43 Sigmund Freud, *The Interpretation of Dreams*, trans. James Strachey (New York: Basic Books, 2010), p. 604.
44 For which see *Poacher's*, pp. 215–17.
45 Alastair McIntosh, 'Sorcery and its Social Effects Amongst the Elema of Papua New Guinea', *Oceania* 53.3 (1983), pp. 224–32.
46 Sorley MacLean, 'Hallaig', *Scottish Poetry Library* (2011) www.scottishpoetrylibrary.org.uk/poem/hallaig/ (bottom tab for English translation).
47 Acts 3. 21.
48 Email from Iain MacKinnon to me, 8 September 2010, passage quoted from Roderick MacCowan, *The Men of Skye* (Portree: John MacLaine, 1902; repr. Edinburgh: Scottish Reformation Society, 2013), pp. 74, 75.
49 See Alastair McIntosh, *Hell and High Water: Climate Change, Hope and the Human Condition*, (Edinburgh: Birlinn, 2008), pp. 210–44; *Rekindling Community: Connecting People, Environment and Spirituality* (Totnes: Green Books, 2008); *Soil and Soul*, pp. 4, 168, 202.
50 Plato, 'Ion', in Edith Hamilton and Huntington Cairns, *The Collected Dialogues of Plato* (Princeton: Princeton University Press, 1961), 220–221 (534a–e).
51 Lewis Hyde, *The Gift: Imagination and the Erotic Life of Property* (New York: Vintage, 1983), p. 4.
52 Viola Cordova, *How It Is: The Native American Philosophy of V. F. Cordova* (Tuscon: University of Arizona Press, 2007), p. 158. Her parentheses. As I have split the quote, I have added in the question mark.
53 Brenda Ueland, *If You Want to Write* (Saint Paul: Graywolf Press, 1987), p. 179.
54 Sometimes attributed to the Buddha, this seems to have originated from Mabel Collins, a disciple of Madame Blavatsky. See Bodhipaksa, 'Fake Buddha Quotes' blog, 16 March 2013 fakebuddhaquotes.com/when-the-student-is-ready-the-teacher-will-appear/
55 John 1. 38.
56 Carl Jung, *Archetypes and the Collective Unconscious*, trans. R. F. C. Hull, 2nd edn, *Collected Works*, IX (London: Routledge, 1968; repr. 1991), p. 275 (par. 490).
57 Andrew Samuels, Bani Shorter, and Fred Plaut, 'individuation', in *A Critical Dictionary of Jungian Analysis* (London: Routledge, 1986), pp. 76–79. See also, 'participation mystique', pp. 105–06, though Jung's borrowing of Lévy-Brühl's term is problematic as it conflates with mysticism.
58 For example, in Hamish Henderson's alternative anthem, 'The Freedom Come All Ye' (1960), *Scots Language Centre* www.scotslanguage.com/articles/node/id/442.
59 Ezekiel 47. 1–12; Revelation 22. 2.

Notes on Contributors

J. H. Alexander taught in the Department of English at the University of Aberdeen from 1968 until 2001. He published several studies of Walter Scott and Wordsworth and was a general editor with the Edinburgh Edition of the Waverley Novels from 1984 until its completion in 2012. He is currently engaged in textual and annotatory research for the Oxford Edition of the works of Charles Dickens.

Barbara Bell has researched and published widely on the nineteenth-century Scottish theatre, Victorian medievalism, Fannish Making and contemporary Scottish playwriting, alongside pedagogical studies around e-learning and the Performing Arts student.

Linden Bicket is Lecturer in Literature and Religion in the School of Divinity, University of Edinburgh. Author of *George Mackay Brown and the Scottish Catholic Imagination* (2017) and (with Douglas Gifford) co-editor of *The Fiction of Robin Jenkins: Some Kind of Grace* (2017), she co-edited (with Kirsteen McCue) a new edition of George Mackay Brown's *An Orkney Tapestry* (2021). Her research focuses on patterns of faith and scepticism in twentieth-century fiction and poetry.

Ian Brown, FRSE FRHistS, Honorary Senior Research Fellow (Scottish Literature, Glasgow University) and Professor Emeritus (Drama, Kingston University, London), is widely published on theatre, literature, and cultural policy, editing a wide range of volumes. A playwright and poet, his most recent monograph is *Performing Scottishness: Enactment and National Identities* (2020).

Dominique Delmaire is a Senior Lecturer at the University of Lyon. He is the author of a book on George Mackay Brown – *L'Ascèse de l'écriture dans la poésie de George Mackay Brown* (1999) – and essays and book chapters on Scottish poetry and literature (Burns, Stevenson, MacCaig, and Brown) as well as on Caribbean poetry (Brathwaite and Walcott).

Claire Harrill studied at the universities of Oxford and York before completing a Ph.D. at the University of Birmingham, where she worked as a lecturer for several years. She now works for the charity The Brilliant Club, helping students of all backgrounds access university.

Mike Kugler teaches Modern European History at Northwestern College in Orange City, Iowa (USA). He works primarily on the Scottish Enlightenment, but also writes on historical narrative in film and comic books. His first book, *Into the Jungle! An Adolescent's Comic Strip History of World War II*, will appear in 2023 with the University Press of Mississippi.

David Jasper is Emeritus Professor of the University of Glasgow where he was Professor of Literature and Theology. He has served as Changjiang Chair Professor at Renmin University of China, Beijing. He has been an Anglican priest for forty-five years and is Canon Theologian at St Mary's Cathedral, Glasgow.

J. Walter McGinty is an ordained minister, having trained for the Ministry of the Church of Scotland at the University of Glasgow and Trinity College Glasgow. He is the author of three books on Robert Burns and a biography of John Witherspoon.

James McGonigal is Emeritus Professor of English in Education at the University of Glasgow, a poet and editor. He is Edwin Morgan's biographer and literary executor and co-edited Morgan's *In Touch With Language: A New Prose Collection 1950–2005* (2020) and *The Midnight Letterbox: Selected Correspondence 1950–2010* (2015).

Alastair McIntosh is Honorary Senior Research Fellow in the School of Education of the College of Social Sciences at the University of Glasgow, a founding trustee of the GalGael Trust and former director of the Centre for Human Ecology.

Rebecca McLean is an independent researcher based in the East Neuk of Fife. Her research interests include Scottish Victorian Literature, and the Gothic. Under the name of Langworthy, her recent publications include work on George MacDonald and on Michel Faber.

Silvia Mergenthal has been professor of English and Literary Theory at the University of Konstanz since 1997. Published extensively on eighteenth- and nineteenth-century British poetry and prose, she is also interested in contemporary literature, with a particular focus on constructions of identity at the interface of gender and nation, in crime fiction across the centuries, and in the spatial turn in literary and cultural studies.

John Patrick Pazdziora is project assistant professor at the College of Arts and Sciences of The University of Tokyo. He researches Scottish literature in the long nineteenth century and children's cultures, with emphasis on the interplay between literature and religion. He is the author of *Haunted Childhoods in George MacDonald* (2020).

Duncan Sneddon is Lecturer in Celtic at the University of Edinburgh. He has previously taught at the University of Aberdeen and Sabhal Mòr Ostaig and was a research assistant at the University of Edinburgh for the Harvard University-based Fionn Folklore Database project. He gained a PhD in Scottish History from the University of Edinburgh in 2018 for a thesis on Adomnán's *Vita Sancti Columbae*.

Index

Aberdeen, 37, 47, 57, 60–61, 65, 107, 115, 129
Adam (first man), 76–77, 135, 254
Adam (monk), 23
Adaman, 48
Addison, Joseph, 90
Adomnán, 1–8, 10–12, 14 (notes 7, 11)
afterlife, xxix, 147, 151–62, 169, 171–72, 254–55, 258
Agatha (mother of Margaret), 17
Aikenhead, Thomas, 71
Alighieri, Dante, 157, 159
Anderson, Alan Orr, 7
Anderson, Marjorie Ogilvie, 7
Andrew, Saint, 10, 28
Anne (queen), 58
Anselm (priest), 285
Antonioni, Michelangelo, 228
Apollyon, *see* devil, the
Aquinas, Thomas, 250, 260
Aristotle, 123
Arminianism, 135
Arnot, Hugo, 53, 64, 67
Arthur (king), 249
Assagioli, Roberto, 272
Aston, Anthony, 61
Athanasius, Saint, 74
Auden, W. H., 194
Augustine, Saint, 77, 242, 250

Baglow, John, 186
Bainbridge, Gregory, 265
baptism, 12, 80, 168, 258
Barnabas, Saint, 48
Barrie, Alexander, 91
Barrie, J. M., 271, 282–89, 291
Barthes, Roland, 129
Bartlett, Robert, 12, 24
Baudelaire, Charles, 179
Begg, James, 66
Bennet, William, 92, 98
Bentley, Walter (Begg, William), 66
Bernard of Clairvaux, Saint, 21, 44
Beveridge, A. H., 180
Bible, The, ix, 1–2, 20–21, 25, 45, 48, 56, 72, 90, 113, 119, 133, 169, 172, 210, 262, 274, 289, 291
  see also scripture
Blair, Hugh, 63–64
Blair, Kirstie, 92
blasphemy, xv, xxvii, 54, 71, 73, 180, 206, 209, 230

'Blind' Harry (poet), 36
Bold, Alan, 180
Bonhoeffer, Dietrich, 242
Book of Common Order, 37, 42, 46–47
Book of Common Prayer, 38, 43, 45–46, 49
Boros, Ladislaus, 246, 265–66
Boston, Thomas, 90–91, 113
Bothwell, Adam, 207
Bouok, William, 60
Brighde, Saint, 281
Broadie, Alexander, 250–51
Brodsky, Joseph, 263
Broichan, 8–10
Brooke, Rupert, 173
Brontë, Emily, xvii
Brown, Callum, ix
Brown, George Mackay, xxix, 181–82, 199 (n. 30), 202–22
Brown, Ian, 92
Brown, Jordana, 226–27
Brown, Stewart J., 49
Bruce, George, 179, 183, 187–91, 193, 195–97
Bruce, Robert, xxi
Brude, 8, 11
Bruford, Alan, 279
'Bucach', Willie, 288
Buchan, John, 166, 171–72, 175–76
Buchanan, George, 56, 60
Bulgakov, Mikhail, 263–64
Burnet, George, 47
Burns, Robert, ix, 76, 91, 211
Butter, Peter, 263
Bynum, Caroline Walker, 16
Byron *see* Gordon, George

Caimbeul, Maoilios, 274
Calvary, ix, 44, 216, 238
Calvin, John, 204, 216, 271
Calvinism, xxiv, 53–55, 62, 71, 79, 124–25, 130, 134–36, 139, 145 (n. 29), 151, 159, 179–80, 182–83, 191, 195, 214–15, 217, 251
Cameron, Alasdair, 65
Cameron, David, 283
Cameron, David Rose, 283–85
Cameron, Tom, 284
Campbell, Donald, 217
Campbell, John (Lord Glenorchy), 64
Camus, Albert, 241
Capobianco, Richard, 193

299

INDEX

Carey, John, 273
Carlyle, Alexander 'Jupiter', 63–64
Caraman, Philip, 245
Carmichael, Alexander, 227
Carpenter, John 229
Catholicism, xiv, xxix, 43, 46, 54–56, 58, 71, 73, 79, 94, 111, 176, 181, 203–05, 207, 210, 213–15, 217–19, 222, 229–30, 236, 239, 245, 258, 261–63
Charles I, 46
Charles II, 58
Charles V, 256
Chaucer, Geoffrey, 39, 41–43, 129, 131–32
Christ, Jesus, ix, xiii, xv, xxii–xxv, xxx, 2, 14 (n. 6), 20–21, 40, 43–44, 49, 54, 58, 74, 79, 96, 109–10, 114, 124–26, 129, 130–31, 133, 139, 141, 153, 168–69, 171–73, 189, 191, 202, 205, 209–12, 216–17, 220–21, 227, 229–32, 234–35, 237, 240, 242, 245–47, 258, 260, 263–65, 281
Christina (aunt of Matilda of Scotland), 19
Christianity, ix–xi, xiii, xv–xvii, xix–xx, xxii, xxiv–xxv, xxvii–xxxi, xxxiii (n. 24), 5, 11, 29–30, 38, 71–72, 75, 79, 82, 85, 90, 96, 103, 110, 114, 117, 123–24, 126, 130–31, 140, 148, 151, 156, 165–67, 169–73, 178 (n. 16), 180, 207, 218, 227, 229–31, 234, 237, 239–42, 255, 263–64, 266, 271
Christmas, 41, 48, 56, 230–31, 236
Church, ix, xvi, xxix, 16, 35–36, 38, 41–43, 45, 49, 71–74, 110, 117, 123, 126, 129, 131, 170, 207, 209, 212, 245
    see also Kirk, the
Church, James, 89
Church of Scotland, ix, xiii, 53, 71, 74, 85–86, 124, 166–68, 179, 281
Clancy, Thomas Owen, 1
Clark, William, 58
Clifford, Ellen, 152
Cnut, 17
Cocozza, Enrico, 249–50
Coghill, Annie Louisa (Walker), 148, 150, 152
Cogitosus, 11
Colburn, Henry, 107
Colcu (son of Cellach), 2–3
Coleridge, Henry, 245
Columba, Saint, 1–12, 14 (n. 7), 28, 48, 180, 191, 281
Columban *familia*, 1, 6
Conrad, Joseph, 240
Constantine, 29, 73–74
Cordova, Viola, 290

Covenanters, xviii, 58–59, 73, 86, 91, 97, 100, 118
Cranmer, Thomas, 36–39, 43, 46, 49
Crawford, Robert, x, xxxi
Craven, Wes, 229, 236
creeds, ix, 38, 46, 74,
Crichton Smith, Iain, 179, 182–84, 188–91, 193, 195–96, 199 (n. 30)
Cromwell, Thomas, 55, 58, 72, 73, 119
crucifixion, xxiv, xxix, 29, 133, 205, 236–37, 246–47
Culbertson, Robert, 91
Cuming, Geoffrey, 47
Cuthbert, Saint, 12
Cynewulf, 29

Daiches, David, xxxi
Daly, MacDonald, 176
David I, 19
Davidson, John, xxv–xxvi
Davidson, Robert, xxviii, 85–93, 95–103, 104–05 (n. 17)
Davis, Miles, 231
Dawson, William, 89
de Graef, Ortwin, 226
de Groot, H. B., 92
de Wall, Esther, 197
Deodatus of Nevers, 4
Depp, Johnny, 286
Derrida, Jacques, 197
devil, the, xviii–xix, 23, 26, 45, 53, 76–77, 135, 175, 211, 275
Dobosiewicz, Ilona, 147
Donaldson, Gordon, 38, 47,
Douglas, Gavin, 41, 49, 54
Drostane, Saint, 48
Dryden, John, 90, 129, 131–32
Duffy, Eamon, 48, 214
Dunbar, William, 35, 37–46, 49
Dundee, 54, 60, 61, 65, 228
Dunfermline, 16, 18–19, 21, 26, 30, 43
Dunn, Douglas, 180, 197
Duns Scotus, 189–90, 246, 251, 260
Dunstan of Canterbury, 10

Eadmer of Canterbury, 10
Edgar the Ætheling, 17
Edinburgh, xi–xiv, xxi, xxxi, 40–41, 47, 53–55, 57–58, 60–66, 71, 75, 183, 228, 262, 289
Edward I, 36
Edward VI, 46
Edward the Confessor, 17

INDEX

Edward the Exile, 17
Edwards, Jonathan, 135, 145 (n. 29)
Edwards, Michael, 184
Edwards, Miss Christian, 90
Einstein, Albert, 252
Eliot, T. S., 179, 252, 272,
Elisha (prophet), 1
Elizabeth I, 37,
Ellington, Duke, 231
Elliot, Mark W., x, xxvii,
Endō, Shusakū, 242
Enlightenment (Scottish), xxvii–xxviii, 63–64, 85, 95, 97, 99, 203, 209, 251, 257
Episcopalians, xiii, 39, 43, 49, 58, 62
Erskine, John, 108
Erskine, Ralph, 90–91
Este, Thomas, 63
Eucharist, xvi, xxiii–xxiv, 205, 209, 212, 215–16, 229–30, 237
Eure, William, 55
Eusebius, 74
Eutichius (abbot), 5
Evangelicalism, xiv, 62–64, 108, 206, 240, 260, 288
Eve, *see* Adam (first man)

fairies, 269, 273
Farquhar, George, 62
Ferguson, Adam, 64
Fergusson, David, xxvii, 9, 216
Ferrara, Abel, 229, 236
Findlay, Bill, 53, 56
Findlugán, 6
First World War, xxix, 165–72, 282,
Flint, Valerie, 4, 12
Flodden, Battle of, 28, 31, 95
Foltz, Bruce V., 194,
Fox, George, 249–50
Fraser, G. S., 179, 186,
Freud, Sigmund, 287, 186
Fussell, Paul, 170

Gabelman, Daniel, 128–29
Gaelic language, xxix–xxxi, 227, 233, 273–74, 276–77, 279–80, 281
Gàidhealtachd, xxx, 57
Gabaldon, Diana, 228
Galt, John, 65
Garrick, David, 64
Geddes, Jane, 37
Geddes, Jenny, 47

Gibson, William, 126–27, 129, 136
Giles, Saint, 43
Gish, Nancy, 184
Glasgow, xvi, xxxii (n. 2), 37, 56, 59–60, 65, 71, 228, 245, 248–52, 259, 261, 274, 276–78
God, xiii, xvi, xix–xxii, xxvi, xxx, 4, 7, 10–11, 20–21, 23–24, 26, 28–31, 42, 45, 72–74, 77–78, 120 (n. 15), 125–26, 130–33, 135–36, 141–42, 145 (n. 29), 147, 149–51, 153, 155–56, 158–61, 165, 168, 171, 173–76, 179–83, 188, 191, 197, 198 (n. 5), 202, 204–05, 208–10, 212, 215–16, 219, 222, 227–28, 234, 237, 241, 263, 265, 271, 273, 275–76, 283
Goldie, John, 77–78
Gonzales, Gonzalo, 261,
Gordon, David W., 96,
Gordon, George (Lord Byron), 113, 249
Gordon, George Huntly, 106–07, 109, 113, 115–17
Gower, John, 42
Graham, W. S., 249
Grassic Gibbon, Lewis, 226
Gray, A. Herbert, 166, 168–69
Gray, Margaret, 160
Greene, Graham, 208, 245
Gregory the Great, Saint, 4, 5
Grey, Thomas, 91
Grimler, Herbert, 262

Heidegger, Martin, 179–184, 186–87, 189, 191–97
Heine, Heinrich, 266
Helena, Saint, 17, 26–30
Henderson, Hamish, 272–73
Henry I, 19
Henry VIII, 55
Henryson, Robert, 41, 43–46
Hervey, James, 90
Heschel, Abraham, 276, 291
Hewitt, William, 82
Hildulph, 4
Hill, Peter, 76
Hirohito, 256
Hitchcock, Alfred, 283
Hogg, James, xvii, 90–92, 135, 211
Home, John, 63–64
Hope (Hawkins), Anthony, 284
Hopkins, Gerard Manley, 188–89, 191, 195, 245–46, 252, 260–62, 265
Houédard, Sylvester, 261–62
Hoy, John, Jr, 90
Huber, Marie, 71
Hughes, Thomas, 169

INDEX

Hume, David, 64, 251
Hunter, John, 249
Hussein, Saddam, 287
Hyde, Edward, xv–xvii
  see also Jekyll, Henry
Hyde, Lewis, 290

Inglis, James, 41
Iógenán, 6
Iona, xxviii, 1, 5, 6, 10, 12, 14 (n. 11), 191, 275, 279–81
Ireland, 6–7, 14 (notes 8, 11, 14), 218, 281
Ironside, Edmund, 17
Irving, Henry, 113

Jackson, John, 57
James I, 41
James IV, 35, 39–40, 256
James V, 45, 55
James VI/I, xxi, 47
James VII/II, 58–60
James, M. R., 147
James, Saint, xxi, 2
Jasper, David, xvi
Jay, Elisabeth, 153
Jekyll, Henry, xiv–xvii, xxiii
  see also Hyde, Edward
Jenkins, Philip, 166
Jesuits, 181, 245, 261–62, 265
Jesus, see Christ, Jesus
Jerusalem, xii, 21, 29, 133
Jews, xxx–xxxi, 29, 71, 110, 248, 258
John of the Cross, Saint, 255
John of Wemyss, 27
Johnson, Samuel, 182
Jones, Christopher, 90
Joyce, James, 191
Judaism, 71, 110
Jung, Carl, 272, 287, 290

Keene, Catherine, 27
Keitel, Harvey, 229
Keitt, Andrew, 204
Kelman, James, 226
Kennedy, Walter, 35, 37
Kentigern, Saint, 37
Kerrigan, Catherine, 180
Kirk, The, xiii–xiv, xxvii–xxviii, 47, 53–54, 56–67, 99, 102, 124, 214–17
Kleiberg, Ståle, 248
Knapp, Lewis M., 81

Knox, John, xii, 35, 37, 46, 54, 182, 184, 197, 203, 205, 219
Kyllour, John, 54–55

Langdon-Brown, Walter, 283
Langland, William, 37
Largs, Battle of, 28–30
Latin, 24, 35–36, 39, 41–42, 45–46, 56, 58, 190, 247, 249, 266, 269
Laud, William, 38, 47
LeBlanc, John, 227
Lee, Joseph, 173–74
Lee, Nathaniel, 58
Leibnitz, Gottfried Wilhelm, 257
Leighton, Angela, 194
Leonard, Tom, 262
Leslie, John, 62
Levi, Primo, 234
Lewis and Harris, 183, 269–71, 280, 282–86
Lewis, C. S., 35, 40, 242
Liddell, Eric, 228
literature (Scottish), ix–xi, xvi–xvii, xxi, xxiv–xxv, xxvii–xxxi, 31, 35–36, 38, 42, 44, 53–57, 67, 85, 91–92, 103, 124, 171, 173, 176, 179, 180–81, 183, 185, 203–04, 225–28, 236, 264, 269, 273–75
liturgy, ix, xvi–xviii, xx–xxi, xxiii, xxviii, xxx, 4, 35–49, 126–27, 141, 205, 214, 229, 237–38, 240
Livingstone, David, 169
Llewelyn Davies, Nicholas, 284
Locke, John, 71
Lockhart, J. G., 106–07, 109, 115–16
Loíguire, 11
London, 47, 59, 64, 107, 123, 132, 230, 289
London, Jack, 260
Lovelace, Ada (née Byron), 249
Lucas, E. V., 284
Lucretius, 251, 266
Lugaid Lathir, 7
Lunardi, Vincent, 249–50
Lutheranism, 215
Lyall, Scott, 180
Lydgate, John, 37, 39, 41
Lyndsay, David, 45–46, 55, 60

Mabelle (cat), 280
MacCaig, Norman, 179–80, 186–87, 189–95
McCarthy, Cormac, 240
MacCowan, Roderick, 288
MacDiarmid, Hugh, ix, xxv–xxvi, 179–80, 182–86, 188–91, 196

INDEX

MacDonald, John (of Ferintosh)
MacDonald, George, xxviii, 123–25, 128–31, 133–136, 139, 141–42
MacDonald, George, Sr, 131
MacDonald, Greville, 131
MacDonald, Louisa, 123
McDonnell, Viki, 66
MacDougall Hay, John, 171
McGavin, John, 54–57, 67
MacGill, Patrick, 171–72
Machar, Saint, 37
MacInnes, John, 273
McIntosh, Alastair, xxxii
McKenzie, Jack, 58
MacKinnon, Iain, 288
MacKinnon, Nan, 269
Mackintosh, E. A., 174
MacKinven, Catherine, 275–80
McLean, Duncan, 226
MacLean, Norman, 170
MacLean, Sorley, xxx, 288
MacLeod, Finlay, 279
MacLeod, George, 275
Macleod, Kenneth, 280–81
MacLeod, Norman (Tormad Saighdear), 288
MacLeod, Roddy, 279
McNeil, Kenneth, 102
MacNeilage, Hugh, 277
Maddrell, Avril, 157
Magnus, Saint, 204, 207, 217
Malcolm III, 16, 18
Mann, Hamish, 174
March, Christie L., 227
Margaret of Scotland, Saint, xxviii, 16–32, 37, 48
Marion, Jean-Luc, 197
Márkus, Gilbert, 1
Marrow-men, 86
Marsland, Elisabeth, 170
Martin, Martin, 277
Martin of Tours, Saint, 14 (n. 14)
Mary (mother of God), 14 (n. 14), 16, 21, 24, 26–31, 40, 229, 231–32, 239, 241
Mary of Guise, 55
Mason, A. E. W., 284
Matilda of Scotland, 19
Maugin, 6–7, 15 (n. 19)
Maurice, Frederick Denison, 151
Melville, Elizabeth (Lady Culross), xxi–xxiv
Merleau-Ponty, Maurice, 186
Merlin, 249
Merton, Thomas, 245

Mill, Anna Jean, 53, 67
Milton, John, 90, 111
miracles, xxiii, 1–2, 4–6, 8, 10–12, 14 (notes 7 and 14), 19–27, 30, 32, 73, 182, 197, 202, 210–11, 219
missionaries, 73, 124–25, 136
monasticism, xxviii, 1, 5–6, 10, 39, 205
monks, xxviii, 6–7, 12, 16–17, 19, 21, 23–26, 30, 37, 202
Moody, D. L., xiv–xv
Morgan, Edwin, xxix, 179, 245–59, 261–66
Morgan le Fay, 249
Morison, Walter, 91
Moses, 110, 113
Muir, Edwin, ix, 43, 194, 204, 206–07, 210, 221, 263–64
Muir, John, 167
Muirchú, 11–12
Mungo, Saint, 48, 249
Murray, Patrick (Lord Elibank), 63

Nansen, Fridtjof, 285
Neat, Timothy, 273
Newton, Michael, 57, 273, 275
Nicolas, Vérène, 281
Nicolson, Adam, 275
Ninian, Saint, 48
Nub of Bowmont, 100

Oban, 227, 230, 235, 239
Okri, Ben, 275
Oliphant, Cyril, 149–50, 152–54, 157, 160–61
Oliphant, Francis, 147, 149–50, 152–54, 161
Oliphant, Frank, 148
Oliphant, Maggie, 147, 149–55, 157, 160
Oliphant, Margaret, xxix, 127–28, 147–62
Orkney, xxix, 202–10, 212–18, 222
Owen, Wilfred, 90, 170

Parliament (Scottish), 35, 47, 55, 256
Pascal, Blaise, 242
Patrick, Angus, 277
Patrick, Saint, 11–12, 281
Pattison, George, 181, 194–95
Paul, Saint, xxi, 2, 46, 48
Pelagius, 249–51
Peter, Saint, 133, 207, 210–11, 213
Petrie, Duncan, 225, 227
Picts, 6, 8, 10–11
Pilate, Marcus Pontius, 247, 264
Pitcairne, Archibald, 59–60

INDEX

Plassmann, Benno, 253
Plato, 182, 184, 289
Pope, Alexander, 91
Pound, Ezra, 252
prayer, ix, xvi, xix–xxi, xxiii, xxviii, 7, 15 (n. 19), 22, 35, 36, 38–39, 42, 45, 47–48, 77, 81, 86, 91, 108, 110–11, 125, 133, 153, 155–56, 161, 169, 174, 176, 206, 208, 214–15, 227, 230, 241, 275
Presbyterianism, xiii, xxi, 39, 48, 53–62, 64, 86, 90, 103, 106, 118–19, 166–67, 176, 177 (n. 5), 183, 207, 210, 218, 227
Protestantism, ix, 35, 41–43, 55, 57, 82, 111, 126, 144 (n. 15), 145 (n. 29), 203–210, 214–15, 223 (n. 2), 245, 261
Puritans, 35, 48, 58, 62, 72, 118, 183, 218

Rahner, Karl, 246, 262–66
Ralls-MacLeod, Karen, 273
Ramsay, Allan, 61–63, 67
Ramsay, Lynn, 225
Reformation, the, xxi, 35–36, 38, 39, 42, 46–47, 53–58, 67, 180, 182, 202–219, 226, 251, 261, 270
relics, 1–2, 4, 6, 11–13, 13 (n. 3), 14 (notes 11, 12, 14)
Rendall, Jocelyn, 206–08, 214
repentance, xiv, 22, 70, 86, 110, 133, 137–38, 151, 167–68
Robertson, William, 63–64, 108
Roderick (king), 249
Rokele, William, 41
Roman Catholicism, *see* Catholicism
Rosenberg, Isaac, 170
Ross, Anthony, 262
Rowe, Nicholas, 60
Rubenstein, Mary-Jane, 182, 192, 194
Rutherford, James, 85

Sabbath, xiii–xiv
sacrament, xxiii, 49, 80, 180, 197, 203, 206, 208–09, 211–12, 216, 219–222, 227, 241–42
saints, 1–2, 4, 10, 12, 17, 19, 26, 28–29, 31, 37, 48, 170, 202–03, 281
see also specific saints
Salmond, J. B., 173
Sankey, Ira D., xiv
Sarum Rite, 36–37, 43
Sassoon, Siegfried, 170
Schmidt, Michael, 260
Schor, Esther, 155
Scots language, xxiv, xxx, 35, 43, 54, 61, 175–76, 226, 258, 266

Scots people, ix–xi, xxx–xxxi, 17, 26–28, 30, 36, 47–48, 53, 59, 167, 226, 228, 233
Scott, Walter, xvii–xxi, xxviii, 102, 106–19, 131, 236
Scottish Episcopal Church, 35–36, 39, 48–49
Scottish Prayer Book, xxviii, 35–36, 38, 44, 46, 48–49
Scribner, Robert, 209, 215–16,
scripture, xvi, xix, xx–xxii, 29, 46, 72, 76–77, 108, 111, 118, 123, 126–27, 129, 130, 132, 153, 216, 233, 273
see also Bible, The
Scullion, Adrienne, 61
Sergios I, 29
Serres, Michel, 182
sexuality, xiii, 215, 245
Shakespeare, William, 66, 90
Shaver, Gilbert J., 181
Sidaway, James D., 157
Silnán, 6
Simpson, Leslie, 149
Sitwell, Edith, 245
Smith, G. Gregory, 185, 274
Smith, Tommy, 256
Smollett, Tobias, xxviii, 70–71, 73–76, 78–83
Snape, Michael, 169
Socrates, 172, 184, 195, 290
Sorley, Charles Hamilton, 171–73
Sowerby, Rick, 14 (n. 11)
Spark, Muriel, xi–xiii, 226, 245
Spinoza, Baruch, 71
Stephens, Edward, 49
Sterne, Laurence, 74
Stevenson, Robert Louis, xv
Story, Janet, 149
Stravinsky, Igor, 234
Stuart Restoration, 58, 65

Tait, Bob, 262
Talbot, Neville, 169
Taylor (minster at Coldstream), 102
Taylor, Jeremy, 142
Tennant, John, 249–50
theology, x–xi, xx, xxiii, xv, xxvii, 41, 44–45, 49, 54, 56, 71, 75–77, 85, 91, 98, 109, 116, 123, 125, 130, 134–36, 139, 148, 150–51, 156–57, 159–160, 162, 169, 181–82, 184, 227, 229, 237, 240, 242, 246, 260–65, 269, 270–71
Thennoch, Saint (mother of St Mungo), 240
Theresa of Avila, Saint, 255
Thomas, Dylan, 230

Thomson, Andrew, 91
Thomson, James, 90
Tillich, Paul, xxvi–xxvii
Tírechán, 11
Tobin, Terence, 53
Todd, Margo, 56
Tolkien, J. R. R., 219, 222
Trollope, Anthony, 139
Tudor, Mary, 37
Tulloch, John, 151
Turgot, 18, 31

Ueland, Brenda, 290

Vatersay Boys, The, 279
Vianney, Marie, 261
Victoria (queen), 66
Violante (Italian singer), 61
Virgin Mary, *see* Mary (mother of God)
Voltaire, 257
Voznesensky, 263
Vulgate, the, 45

Walker, Patrick, 119
Walsham, Alexandra, 203, 210
war, xxiii, xxix, 89, 165–68, 170–74, 176, 219, 245–47, 253, 271, 282–91
Warden, Henry, 111, 115, 119

Warner, Alan, xxix, 225–30, 232–33, 235–36, 240–42, 243 (n. 9)
Watson Kerr, Roderick, 171, 173
Watson, Thomas, 76–77
Watts, Isaac, 91
Waugh, Evelyn, 245
Weber, Max, 203–05, 208, 212, 216, 221
Wedderburn, James, 40, 46, 54–55
Wedderburn, John, 40
Wedderburn, Robert, 40
Welsh, David, 87
Wesley, John, 75
White, Kenneth, 271
Whitehouse, J. C., 208
Whitman, Walt, 252–53
Whyte, Iain, 85
Wickman, Matthew, 225
Wilde, Oscar, 256
Winter, J. M., 165
Witherspoon, John, 91
Wittgenstein, Ludwig, 258
Wolfe, Tom, 226
Wordsworth, William, 205
Wynkyn de Worde, 26

Yarrow, Simon, 2
Yeats, W. B., 194, 252
Yevtushenko, 263

Biblical References

Genesis
1. 2, 234
2. 23, 235

Leviticus
26. 19-20, 5

II Kings
13. 20-21, 1

Job
3. 11, 141 (n. 36)
10. 18, 146 (n. 36)

Psalm
23 (22). 4, 20 (n. 13)
34 (33)., 14 (n. 16)
37 (36)., 112
51 (50). 10, 45
119 (118). 105, xix

Ecclesiastes
7. 6, 115

Song of Songs
6. 3, 21 (n. 14)
8. 7, 44

Isaiah
9. 6, 41
45. 8, 41

Ezekiel
47. 1-12, 291 (n. 59)

Daniel
5. 27, xv

Matthew
4. 8, 175
5. 17, 109
5. 30, 229
8. 23-27, xxiii (n. 46)
9. 20-22, 2 (n. 6)
12. 45, 139
13. 13-14, 129 (n. 19)
13. 34-35, 129 (n. 19)
14. 22-34, xxiii (n. 47)
14. 34-36, 14 (n. 6)
23., 111
23. 27, 131 (n. 23)
26. 34, 133 (n. 26)
26. 74-75, 133 (n. 26)

Mark
4. 33-34, 129 (n. 19)
4. 35-41, xxiii (n. 46)
6. 45-53, xxiii (n. 47)

Mark (cont.)
6. 53-56, 14 (n. 6)
9. 43, 229
14. 30, 133 (n. 26)
14. 72, 133 (n. 26)
16. 1, 234

Luke
8. 10, 129 (n. 19)
8. 22-25, xxiii (n. 46)
8. 42b-48, 2 (n. 6)
10. 42, xv
18., 111, 133 (n. 25)
22. 34, 133 (n. 26)
22. 61, 133 (n. 26)

John
1. 1-3, 234
1. 38, 290 (n. 55)
2. 1-11, 210
3. 4, 141 (n. 36)
3. 7, 141 (n. 37)
5. 8-9, 20
6. 15-21, xxiii (n. 47)
6. 48-70, 230
7. 11, 232
10. 6, 129 (n. 19)
11. 25, 247
13. 28, 133 (n. 26)
14. 13-14, 153
18. 27, 133 (n. 26)

Acts
8. 9-24, 140 (n. 35)
19. 11-12, 2

Romans
3. 8, xix
6. 4, xxxiii (n. 24)
7. 15, xxi

I Corinthians
12. 12-14, 212

Hebrews
6. 18-19, xxii
11., xxi

James
1. 6, xxi

Revelation
2. 17, 15 (n. 20)
22. 2, 291 (n. 59)
22. 15, 33 (n. 21)

www.ingramcontent.com/pod-product-compliance
Lightning Source LLC
Chambersburg PA
CBHW052051230426
43671CB00011B/1865